PREFACE.

Being in the Royal Regiment of Foot of Ireland, which was one of the Twelve that our late Sovereign Lord King William, of ever glorious Memory, sent with the Honourable Brigadier General Richard Ingoldsby, *in the Fleet from* Britain *and* Ireland *over into* Holland, *as Imperialists, in* 1701; *Curiosity induced me to take a Journal of our Voyage thither, and afterwards, in like manner, of our Army's Proceedings in the War; and being from thence, by the great Goodness of God, safely preserv'd with the said Regiment during the War, an Eye-Witness of most of the imminent Dangers and sore Fatigues of the twelve Campaigns thereof, ended in* 1712, *I continued my Journal during the same, of all Things that happen'd most note-worthy therein; and then having seriously perused my several Fragments, Curiosity again induced me, and the Persua-*

sions

PREFACE.

fions of some others, curious Gentlemen, not to let my Journal or Memorial die, or lie quite hid in Oblivion; but to form and compose thereof, somewhat more compendiously, a small Treatise for my own, and their Satisfaction, and others, the Curious, whose Hands it may afterwards happen to greet.

All which I have therefore truly and punctually done in brief, according to the very best of my Knowledge; neither intending, or pretending thereby to be a Setter out of any Book, but leaving that for the Employment and Gain of the more Ingenious and Eloquent, being myself neither covetous of Gain nor Applause thereby; but freely embracing my Labour for my Pains, it having been the Employment of many of my vacant Hours, both in Camp and Garrison, the which might have been much better employ'd; nevertheless, I'll wind up my Excuse for the same with the old vulgar proverbial Saying, Better so than Worse.

A COMPENDIOUS

JOURNAL

Of all the

MARCHES,

Famous BATTLES, SIEGES,

And other moſt note-worthy, heroical, and ever memorable ACTIONS of the

Triumphant ARMIES,

Of the ever-glorious

CONFEDERATE HIGH ALLIES,

In their late and victorious WAR

Againſt the

Powerful ARMIES of proud and lofty *FRANCE,*

In and on the CONFINES of

HOLLAND, GERMANY, and FLANDERS,

So far as our ſucceſsful BRITISH TROOPS extended in *Conjunction* therein.

Digeſted into

TWELVE CAMPAIGNS, begun *A.D.* 1701, and ended in 1712.

All, but the firſt and laſt, the *Grand Confederate Armies* were under the Conduct and Command of our Honourable and much Honour-worthy, ever-renown'd, graceful, and excellent war-like HERO

JOHN DUKE of *MARLBOROUGH,* PRINCE of the HOLY EMPIRE, &c.

Truly and punctually collected, form'd, compos'd, and written in the Time of the ſaid WAR,

By *JOHN MILLNER,*

Serjeant in the Honourable Royal Regiment of Foot of *Ireland*; Having been therewith during the War an Eye-witneſs of the moſt of the following Marches and Actions of the ſaid War.

Compleated at *Ghent* on the 31ſt Day of *December* 1712.

The Naval & Military Press Ltd

Reproduced by kind permission of the Central Library, Royal Military Academy, Sandhurst

Published by
The Naval & Military Press Ltd
Unit 10, Ridgewood Industrial Park,
Uckfield, East Sussex,
TN22 5QE England
Tel: +44 (0) 1825 749494
Fax: +44 (0) 1825 765701
www.naval-military-press.com
© The Naval & Military Press Ltd 2004

In reprinting in facsimile from the original, any imperfections are inevitably reproduced and the quality may fall short of modern type and cartographic standards.

INTRODUCTION.

HAVE briefly set down in the following Sheets, a compleat Journal of all the Marches, famous Battles and Sieges, and other most note-worthy, heroical and victorious, memorable Actions of the triumphant Army of the ever-glorious, grand, confederate, high Allies, and of their Conquests in their late and victorious War, over and against the proud and lofty *French* powerful Armies, in and on the Confines of *Holland*, *Germany*, and *Flanders*, so far as our *British* Corps extended, in Conjunction with our other Allies therein, under the Command of his Grace the Duke of *Marlebro'*; digested into Twelve Campaigns, begun *Anno Dom.* 1701, and ended in 1712; shewing exactly the Times of each particular Day's March of our grand Army, and Number of Leagues march'd from one Incampment to another, according to the Turnings and Windings thereof; and for each Movement or Time when our grand Army extended, open'd or clos'd Camp, either to Right, Left, or Center, to make Place for other Troops as they came, to fall into their

INTRODUCTION.

Posts in Camp, or to fill up the Places of those which at any Time went from thence, as Occasion required Troops to come and go, as it often happen'd in the Time of the War. I have accounted for each Day's March, and set down the Number of Leagues; and in all my Reckonings of Time made use of the Old Style. Every thing is regularly set down as it happen'd, on each March and in each Camp; and when and where ours and the Enemies grand Army consisted of most Strength of Battalions and Squadrons, what Ordnance and other Utensils of War conform at each first general Rendezvous after taking the Field, or otherwise afterwards. I have set down, in the Place of Names and Lines of Battle, the Number of Battalions and Squadrons only in Figures, the Names of Battalions, Regiments of Horse and Dragoons being omitted, as superfluous and too tedious for this brief Journal, both Armies commonly increasing and decreasing in each Campaign, as Occasion required Troops to come and go therein; and besides, in the most of the Lines of Battle, as given out, there were inserted the Names of several Regiments that were then in Garrison, and not in Camp, but daily expected up thither, the which sometimes came up to Camp, and sometimes not; so that I seldom or ever could find, that when view'd and number'd, they answer'd the Names and Numbers as given out in the Lists or Lines of Battle, which made our Numbers commonly near equivalent to the Enemy's effective Number of Battalions and Squadrons then in their Camp; and therefore they were often far superior to their Allies in their Number of Men, but much more inferior in Courage and Valour. Moreover, I could not properly set down the Number of the Regiments of Horse and Dragoons, but only the Number of Squadrons, being some Regiments consisted

but

INTRODUCTION.

but of two, others of three Squadrons. The Length of each Campaign, Number of Days and Leagues march'd therein, and in each Day thereof, and in all by our grand Army, is computed from the Time of our Ordnance or Train of Artillery's setting out of Winter-Quarters, to the Time of its Return thither again, it being the Metropolitan Enfign in Time of War.

The Times when and where each Battle was fought, and Skirmifh happen'd; by whom and againſt whom, and by what Number of Troops and Artillery, and what Loſs fuſtain'd thereat on either Side, both of the Offendant and Defendant, in Tables of the feveral Stations of killed, wounded, taken and deferted, with alfo the Number of Ordnance and other Utenſils of War taken thereat.

The Times when, how and where, and by whom, and by what Number of Troops and Artillery each Siege was begun, carried on, and ended, againſt either Towns, Cities, Caſtles, or Forts, and how defended, *viz.* the Times after inveſting each befieged Place, when the Befiegers made their Circumvallation and Contravallation Lines, and of their making and bringing of Faſcines, Gabions, Pick-Axes, Mauls, Hurdles, or fuch like Neceſſaries, for the expeditious carrying on of a Siege, &c.

The Times when, and by whom, and by what Number of Men, with or without Arms, the Befiegers firſt open'd their Trenches or Approaches againſt each befieged Place, and by what Stratagem and Loſs; when, and of what Number of Cannon, Mortars, Howitzers, their feveral Batteries confiſted at moſt; when they firſt began to play, and alfo what Number of Ordnance their Batteries confiſted of when each were taken or forced to furrender.

INTRODUCTION.

The several Times when, and by whom, and with what Number of Men, the Besiegers carried on each particular Storm or Attack; on their several Attacks against each besieged Place, *viz.* against either Breaches of Walls, Counterscarps, Counterguards, Bastions, Ravelins, Half-Moons, Horn-Works, Flanks, Glacis, Covert-Ways, Sconces, Redoubts, Fleches, or the like, &c. the springing of Mines and Countermines, the laying of Bridges, of Fascines and Hurdles, over grand and small Fosses to Breaches; the opening of Saps, Zigzags, and otherwise of the like manner, as Occasion required; the Times of the Besieged's several Sorti's or Sallies on the Besiegers Approaches; by whom, and by what Number, and what Loss on each Side, both of the Assaulters and Repulsers, in and on each Action thereof; the several Times also when and where the *French* grand Army made several Attempts to reinforce the Besieged, or to raise the Besiegers from thence; and how couragiously maintain'd by the good Conduct of our heroical Generals, and undaunted, victorious, triumphant Armies, never foil'd during the War.

The several Times of the several Besieged's beating of Parleys or Chamades, of their Surrenderings, and by what Conditions or Capitulations, and how, and to what Place, and what Number of Men they march'd out; and at the End of each Siege I have set down the Length or whole Duration thereof, with nigh Computations of each Side's general or particular Loss, in Tables of the several Numbers of kill'd, wounded, taken, and deserted thereat; and also what necessary Utensils of War and other Stores were taken or found in, and at each besieged Place, as taken throughout the whole War, wheresoever our Corps were employ'd or concern'd in the Siege or Cover thereof, with our other Allies; collected as nigh as possible

by

INTRODUCTION.

by the best occurrent Accounts that I could find: And note, that in the several following Accounts, wheresoever the Word is often used at Battles, Sieges, or otherwise, *about* such and such a Number kill'd, wounded, taken or deserted, and not *positively* such and such a certain Number, it is when and where the true Particulars were kept obscure, and were not, nor could not, be readily and exactly found, as it often happen'd. — *Note*, that our Horse and Dragoons at Sieges sustain'd little or no Loss throughout the whole War, the greatest Burden lay always in every respect on the Foot.

In the Beginning of my Journal of the War, I took the Names of each Regiment of Horse and Foot, and General Officers at Battles and Sieges, and otherwise as on Actions, and also the Names, as nigh as could be found, of each particular Officer as killed or wounded on our Side, and of the Enemies as taken, in and on each thereof; but that proving too tedious, I waved them; and in this last Correction only retain'd the Names of some of the most noted general Persons, at some of the most noted certain Places; and also waved several other Things of little Consequence, which I before had retain'd, as superfluous to give any Reader, which never knew any thing thereof; and at any Time after, that any Troops went off from our grand Army to Sea, as often as Occasion required, I meddled no more with their Proceedings, or any thing else out of my Reach, farther than an Eye-Witness: But, for the punctual compleating of my Journal, I could not avoid hinting a little at some certain Passages which were done on our Side, in the Seat of the said War, where our Troops were not fully concern'd; yet being in maintaining the Field on that Side, upholding a great Part thereof, tho' at a Distance, I thought

it

INTRODUCTION.

it proper to note somewhat of the most note-worthy, as nigh as possible I could collect somewhat of the Particulars thereof, for Brevity and Curiosity Sake, for the better compleating of my Intention in this Work. All the following prescribed memorable, glorious, and heroical ever-renowned Victories, obtain'd by the grand confederate high Allies, couragious and victorious, triumphant, conquering Armies, over and against the proud and lofty *French*, powerful Armies, may, by the Assistance and Goodness of the All-sufficient Being, be justly attributed to the judicious Care, good Conduct, and undaunted Courage of our excellent prudent General and warlike Hero, the Duke of *Marlborough*; who therewith, and thereby, every where, wheresoever he went and came, foil'd, beat, defeated and subdu'd, and totally routed the Enemies Troops before he left them; each and every Soldier, in their several Stations or Rank of the whole Army under his Grace's Command, being animated by his graceful Presence, and inviting Example, did in like manner, with heroical Spirits, and undaunted Courage, unanimously fully imitate the Steps of the same Leader, in the full Pursuit of all thereof; making their proud, haughty, and lofty Enemies fly every where before them; and also at the Report of his and their awful terrifying Approach toward several eminent Places of great Note and Strength, the Enemies thereat and therein instantly abandon'd, forsook, quite retired, and fled from thence before his and their Arrival, they mightily fearing and dreading thereof, being often totally foil'd thereby, as it evidently appear'd throughout the whole War. All which, in short, did greatly redound to the Honour of Queen *Anne*, her Majesty's Kingdoms and Troops, and to the Duke's, and also Prince *Eugene*'s, and all our grand Allies in general, and

on

INTRODUCTION.

on famous Record of glorious Memory to succeeding Generations, and to the Enemies great Dishonour and Abasement; being that they, in and on all thereof, by their own common Computations and Accounts, exceeded the Allies Army both in the Number of Strength and Loss in all Battles and Skirmishes, Sieges excepted, in which their Loss also in every respect whatsoever thereof, was always accounted equivalent with the Besiegers, considering their mighty strong Empostments, Number of Strength, and Cover of the Fortifications thereof. And during the whole War, I all along noted, that after General *Ginkle*'s Retreat with our small Army from *Cranenburg*, from the *French* grand Army in the Duke of *Burgundy* and General *Boufflers* Command, in the Time of the Siege of *Kieserswaert*, before the Duke of *Marlborough*'s Arval at our Army, and before its joining at *Nimeguen*; but more especially after that the Duke with our Army defeated the *French* and *Bavarians* on the Attack at *Schellenburg-Hill* near *Donawert*, and of their grand Army at the fatal Battle of *Hochstat*, on the *Danube* in the Year 1704, to the Time of our *British* Troops withdrawing under the Command of the Duke of *Ormond*, from the *Holland* and *Germans* Army from *Cambresis*, with a Cessation of Arms or Entrance of our odd Peace with *France* and *Spain* in 1712; the *French* Armies former fiery Courage daily abated, and they were quite dishearten'd, and still retain'd a Fear of being beat by our worthy Hero and couragious and victorious Army, wherever they met therewith; the which all along every where accordingly happen'd, and ours were fully satisfied and transported with the Hopes thereof: That wheresoever they met them, they were able to beat them; so that in short, during our Abode in the War, the grand Allies Armies remain'd the Conquerors, and the

French

INTRODUCTION.

French the conquered; ours the Honour, and theirs the Dishonour; so that ours, wheresoever they had but the Word to fall on, and beat the Enemy, it was accordingly done in a Trice, and that with the greatest Dexterity, Vigour and undaunted Courage imaginable: But here I must stop the Carreer of my Pen, lest I should either extol the one, or debase the other too much thereby; the one proving often a chastening Rod to the other; the Battle being not given to the strong, nor the Race to the swift; nor Riches to Men of Understanding, but to whosoever it pleaseth God to give either unto.

But before I can proceed in tracing the aforesaid Particulars, I must, the better to work upon, hint and touch a little by way of Information, at the first and chief publick Scope of the War, and wave the rest, being wholly unacquainted with State-Affairs, and the private Resentments of Princes; but, without all doubt, as no House can be built without a Foundation, neither can any War be begun without some mental Causes, of which, *viz.* on the 21*st* of *October* in 1700, *Charles* II, King of *Spain* dies, and, by a supposed Will dated *October* 2, 1700, he was immediately succeeded by *Philip* V, formerly Duke of *Anjou*, and Grandson to the King of *France Lewis* XIV, who immediately aided him therein; and on the 26*th* of *January* following, the Duke of *Bavaria*, then Viceroy of *Flanders*, connived privately with, consented to, and admitted the *French* Troops to repossess most of the Garrisons, Cities and Towns in and about the Confines thereof; and after the same, they instantly began to encroach openly on the Territories of *Holland* and *Germany*: After which the Emperor *Leopold* declared War against *France* and *Spain*, and that on the 7*th* of *June* 1701, in order to redress the same, and dispossess the said *Philip*, and to possess his own Son of *Spain*, as his lawful

INTRODUCTION. xiii

lawful Succeffion, *Charles* III, the then Duke of *Auftria*, but was not declared therein till the 12*th* of *September* 1703: That he was aided by a competent Number of the *Britifh* and *Holland*'s Fleet, with a confiderable Body of their Troops, which then went from thence over with him into *Spain*; and foon after that thofe Difputes, Differences, and Broils, in the Spring of 1701, the Emperor and States of *Holland* having courteoufly defired Aid and Affiftance from *England* againft *France*, King *William* accordingly inftantly granted and fent over Admiral *Fairbourn*, with a Fleet of Eighteen Sail of War-Ships, and Brigadier General *Ingoldfby* with Twelve Battalions of Foot into *Holland*, as Imperialifts for their Affiftance on that Side againft *France* (from which I begin my General Journal); and therefore in the next Spring, after the Death of King *William*, March 8, 1701-2, Princefs *Anne* of *Denmark* being proclaim'd Queen of *Great Britain*, the ufurping King of *France*, Infufer of Broils and Mifchief, declared the pretended Prince of *Wales* King of *Great Britain*, in the Place of the abdicated King, *James* II, who died at *St. Germains* in *France*, on the 5*th* of *September* in 1701; and alfo, further to augment the Quarrel, the *French* Men of War, by Order, ftopt and took fome *Englifh* and *Holland* Merchant Shipping; fo that thereby, and feveral other Aggravations given, which I muft wave as aforefaid, they both alfo, in Conjunction with the Emperor of *Germany*, declared War againft *France* and *Spain*, in their own Behalf, in order to redrefs the aforefaid Abufes, and that on the 4*th* of *May* 1702; into which War all continued in Conjunction on that Side triumphant and victorious to the 6*th* of *July* 1712, that our Sovereign Lady Queen *Anne* having obtain'd her Demands of the *French* King, and otherwife for *Great Britain*, order'd off her glorious and

victo-

INTRODUCTION.

victorious Troops; the which then instantly withdrew, under the Duke of *Ormand*'s Command, from the *Germans* and *Holland*'s Troops, from their Camp at *Cambresis*, with a Cessation of Arms or Entrance of our odd Peace: Which was not fully accomplish'd before the 31*st* of *May* 1713, that the *Hollanders* having first likewise obtained their Demand, withdrew also from the *Germans*, and that Winter came to a Composition also with *France* and *Spain*; but the *Germans* continued apart till the Spring, that the Emperor *Charles* having also in like manner obtain'd his Demand of his two Adversaries, came to a Composition; whose punctual Particulars I must wave, and proceed with what I know best of the Marches and Actions of the War on our Side.

Note, That according to the old proverbial Saying, it often happens, and that truly, by woful and expensive Experience, *That the Parter of a Quarrel becomes commonly Sharer in the Blows.*

I may safely and truly say, in a few Words, that the whole War on our Side run away in a glorious Current of daily Conquests, but not without a considerable Flood of Blood, the like not to be gain'd without it, &c.

Note, That of all the Cities and Towns taken throughout the whole War on our Side thereof, none stood a Storm, but at the last Extream surrender'd on reasonable Conditions; but several Castles, Citadels, and Forts, &c. were taken by Storm, as herein inserted.

A JOURNAL

A

JOURNAL

Of the Late

WAR, &c.

THE FIRST CAMPAIGN,

Begun the 7th of June, 1701.

WHEREAS in my Title-Page I have computed the late War, on our Side, to confist of Twelve Campaigns; therefore, to make out the fame, and this one, and the firft thereof, I have begun it on the *7th* of *June*, for two very remarkable Reafons, *viz.* It being the Day that the Emperor *Leopoldus* of *Germany* declared War againft *France* and *Spain*; and

also

Campaign I. also the self-same Day that the first of our Troops
Anno 1701. embark'd from *Ireland*, with Brigadier *Ingoldsby*, for *Holland*, for the Emperor's and States of *Holland*'s Assistance on that Side of the War, then ensuing; and I have ended the Twelfth and last Campaign with the 1*st* Day of *October* 1712, it being the Day that the last of our Troops dispers'd to Winter-Quarters from *Ghent*, after our withdrawing with the Duke of *Ormond* from the *Germans* and *Holland*'s Troops, with a Cessation of Arms with *France*, declared at *Wansack*, when march'd off from *Cambresis* Camp *July* 6, 1712.

The said War then ensuing about the Beginning of *June* 1701, our gracious Sovereign Lord King *William* III, of ever glorious Memory, sent Admiral *Fairbourn* with a Fleet of Eighteen War-Ships over into *Ireland*, in order to transport the said Brigadier and Twelve Battalions over into *Holland*, for their Assistance as aforesaid, to act as Imperialists on that Side, as Occasion should or might require them, till otherwise determinated; and in order thereunto, the said Brigadier, having received his Orders from the King, instantly assembled with his own and Earl *Stanly*'s Battalions at *Carrickfergus*, where, therewith, on *Sunday* the 7*th* of *June*, he embark'd in two War-Ships, in order for *Holland* as aforesaid.

And from thence I begin and proceed with my Journal of the War; shewing first the Voyage and Journal of the Honourable Brigadier-General *Richard Ingoldsby*, with Twelve Battalions of *Britons*, from *Ireland* and *Britain* to *Holland*, as Imperialists, in the Beginning of the said Emperor of *Germany*, our and the *Holland*'s late War against *France* and *Spain*, in this our first but short Campaign, commenc'd the 7*th* of *June* 1701, and ended the 22*d* of *September* following, in the fourteenth and last Year of our Sovereign Lord King *William*.

June

June the 7*th*, the Honourable Brigadier em- Campaign I. *Anno* 1701.
bark'd with the Two Battalions at *Carrickfergus*,
as aforesaid ; the 15*th*, they set Sail from thence
towards *Holland*, where they arrived on the 30*th*,
and landed safe at their appointed Garrisons of
Worcum and *Heusden* ; a Round from *Carrickfergus*
of very near 200 Leagues.

15, The Ten Battalions following, *viz.* Two of
Royal Britons, Princess *Anne*'s, Lieutenant-General
Stewart's, Sir *Bevil Greenville*'s, Sir *John Jacob*'s,
Colonel *How*'s, Sir *Matthew Bridges*'s, Colonel
Frederick Hamilton's, and Marquis *Puizar*'s, assembled at the Cove of *Cork*, from several Parts of
Ireland, and embark'd in sixteen Ships of War in
Admiral *Fairbourn*'s Command, in order for *Holland*, as aforesaid.

24, The said Fleet weigh'd Anchor at the Cove
of *Cork*, and set Sail from thence the same Day
towards *Holland*.

29, All our Fleet arrived in Company near unto *Beachy-Head* ; where, the next Day, General
Stewart's Regiment left us, and landed at *Portsmouth*.

July 4, Our Fleet continuing their Voyage,
sailed past *Deal* and *Dover* with a very slow and
calm Wind.

6, Our Fleet, all in Company, sailed past *Margate* ; from which that Morning King *William*, with
the First Battalion of *English* Guards, set off towards the *Hague* in *Holland*, where they the next
Day arrived safe and landed ; from which, soon
after, the King sent the Guards to their appointed
Garrison at *Breda*.

7, All our Fleet, in Company, about Noon set
quite off the Coast of *England* towards *Helvoetsluice* in *Holland*.

8, About Nooon all our Fleet, in Company, arrived safe, and cast Anchor at *Helvoetsluice*.

B 9, About

Campaign I.
Anno 1701.

9, About Noon, the aforesaid Battalions disembark'd out of the War-Ships, and embark'd in *Holland* Ships, and sailed from thence up the River *Maes*, a little past *Williamstat*, and there anchor'd, and lay by most Part of that Night.

10, By Break of Day all weigh'd Anchor, and sailed from thence up the River towards *Dort*, where, about Sun-rising, we arrived and cast Anchor, and there abode that Day.

11, By Break of Day all weigh'd Anchor, and sailed from *Dort* up the River towards their several respective appointed Garrisons, at which, about Sun-setting, all arrived safe, and landed therein, viz. *Breda*, *Gorcum*, *Worcum*, *Geertruydenberg*, *Heusden*, and the *Borsch*; a Round in all, from the Cove of *Cork*, of near 170 Leagues.

Sept. 15, Brigadier-General *Ingoldsby*, with the aforesaid Troops in his Command, being order'd by King *William* from their respective Garrisons, in order to be review'd by him on *Breda-Heath*, assembled thitherward; and the said Day the Brigadier, with his own and the Royal Regiment of *Ireland*, set out of their Garrison of *Heusden*, and also all the others out of their respective Garrisons, *Breda* excepted; and that Night the most of all thereof canton'd in and about the Villages of *Sprange* and *Langestraet*, four Leagues.

16, All thereof removed from their several Cantonments, and march'd to, and join'd, pitch'd and encamp'd at *Osterhout*, with the Garrison of *Breda*, on the Plain a little to the East of the City, somewhat apart from a small Camp of *Holland*'s Troops in General *Ginckle*'s Command, four Leagues.

21, King *William* review'd all the Troops a little to the Front of their Encampment; and that Day he immediately after dismiss'd them from thence to their aforesaid Garrison; all which, as aforesaid, remarch'd from thence to, and canton'd

that

that Night, as before, in and about the Villages of *Sprange* and *Langestraet*, four Leagues.

Campaign I.
Anno 1701.

22, Each Battalion of our Corps removed from their several Cantonments, and remarch'd from thence into their aforesaid respective Garrisons; and soon after the same, King *William* went from *Breda* to the *Hague*, four Leagues; and from thence to *London*, where he died on the 8th of *March* 1701-2; and at that Juncture of Time, Princess *Anne* of *Denmark* was proclaim'd Queen of *Great Britain*, and Lord *Marlborough* appointed and declared Captain-General of all her Majesty's own and Auxiliary Troops, then in; and design'd for the Low Countries or Netherlands of *Spain*; and continued very victorious therewith during the Ten Campaigns next following.

Commenced the Day of his first Arrival at our Army at *Nimeguen* on the 16th of *June* 1702, and ended the Day of his Departure from our Army, after his Dispersement thereof from the Siege of *Bouchain*, which was on the 24th of *October* in 1711.

To the making up the Number of Twelve Campaigns as aforesaid, I have computed this to be one, and the first thereof, altho' but very short and pleasant, commenc'd the 7th of *June*, and ended the 22d of *September*, accounting it in Length, by Land and Sea, of which we march'd and sail'd twenty-four Days, and therein about 216 Leagues, or 648 Miles *English*; and of that Time on Land both of going to, in, and returning from Camp; commenced the 15th, and ended the 22d of *September*, of which we march'd four Days, and therein 16 Leagues or 48 Miles *English*.

The End of the first and short Campaign, A.D. 1701.

THE
Second CAMPAIGN,

Begun on the 9th Day of March, 1702.

March 9. ALL Preparations being made for the expeditious carrying on of this Campaign on all Sides, and for the early opening thereof, the Honourable Brigadier-General *Ingoldsby*, then commanding our *British* Troops in Chief, on that Side as aforesaid, having before received in general his Orders for taking the Field as Imperialists, he set out therewith, from their respective Garrisons or Winter-Quarters, in order for Camp; and that Night most thereof canton'd in and about the Villages of *Sprange, Langestraet,* and *Venlo opt Zand,* five Leagues.

10, All removed from their several Cantonments by Break of Day, and about Noon pass'd over the River *Merk,* and march'd through *Breda,* and join'd its Garrison; and about Ten o'Clock at Night past through *Rosendal,* eight Leagues, and over the River *Demer,* and join'd, pitch'd and encamp'd on the West-Side thereof, somewhat apart from a small Camp of *Holland*'s Troops, under the Generals *Cochorn* and *Spar*'s Command, who then lay near unto *Bergen-op-Zome* in *Holland*'s *Brabant,* where they soon after consisted of Thirty Battalions

of

of Foot, and Thirty-two Squadrons of Horse and Dragoons, with Ordnance conformable, waiting very alertly the Motion of an equivalent Number of *French* Troops, which had then assembled on that Side of their *Brabant*'s Line, near unto *Antwerp*, in order for a General Rendezvous of their Troops thereabouts: They also daily expecting the Allies General Rendezvous to be thereabout, we having taken Field so near unto them; of which Expectations they were suddenly frustrated soon after, by Monsieur *Overquerque*'s good Conduct in assembling far contrary with a great Body of the *Holland*'s own and auxiliary Troops as Imperialists, and several Imperial Troops, *viz.* of *Prussians, Hanovers, Hessians, Palatines* or *Lunenburghers,* and also some *Danes,* who join'd and pitch'd Camp on the East-Side or Brink of the River *Wael* and *Rhine* near unto *Emrich,* in a Part of the Dukedom of *Cleves,* or Kingdom now of *Prussia,* in the Lower Part of *Germany,* in full Order and Design to lay close Siege to *Keiserswaert*; being that some time before, the Duke of *Bavaria* had revolted from the Emperor, and deliver'd up to the *French* all the fortified Places he had in *Flanders,* (who made all the Troops of the States-General, then therein, Prisoners of War) in Hopes of the Empire to himself. The Bishop and Prince of *Liege* and *Cologne* had revolted from the Emperor of *Germany* to the *French* King, who had then thereby taken into his Possession *Keiserswaert, Bonne, Rhineburg* and *Liege,* and several other Places of the said Prince's Dominions; and began farther tyrannical Encroachings on several other Parts of the *German* Empire.

24, King *William*'s Death was made publickly known to our *British* Troops in our Camp at *Rozendal,* and Princess *Anne* of *Denmark* declared Queen

<small>Campaig. II.</small>
<small>Anno 1702.</small>
<small>Siege of Keiserſwaert</small>

Queen of *Great Britain*, to whom, in a few Days, all our Troops took the Oath of Fidelity.

April 5, It was firſt block'd up by Prince *Naſſau Saarbruck*, with a Body of Thirteen Battalions of Foot, and a few Squadrons of Horſe and Dragoons of the ſeveral aforeſaid Corps's, in which there was then a Garriſon conſiſting of Five Battallions of Foot, in Town and Caſtle, commanded by one Major-General *Blanville*; and ſoon after the Prince being reinforced, he cloſely inveſted the Town and Caſtle, and his Army then conſiſted of Thirty Battalions and Thirty-one Squadrons, with Fifty-two Cannon and Thirty-four Mortars and Howitzers, with alſo all other neceſſary Utenſils of War conform, for the expeditious carrying on of the ſaid Siege. The Beſieged being ſome time before reinforced by Six Battalions, they then conſiſted of in all Eleven Battalions, with upwards of Thirty Cannon and Ten Mortars and Howitzers, mounted on the Town and Caſtle, with alſo all other neceſſary Utenſils of War, for the ſtanding of a Siege as then laid; and, ſoon after that, it was laid as cloſe as the Ground and the *Rhine* would permit. The Beſiegers begun making and bringing Faſcines and Gabions, Hurdles, Pickets and Mauls, and all other Neceſſaries for the expeditious carrying on of the Siege, and open'd their Trenches againſt the Town and Caſtle, rais'd and erected competent Numbers of Batteries, and ſmartly play'd the ſame; and from thence proceeded as gradually as could be expected, but with a great deal of Difficulty, being that the Weſt-Side of the Town and *Rhine* lay in a manner quite open to the Enemies grand Camp; which, ſoon after that the Allies had form'd a regular Siege, had from ſeveral Parts aſſembled and join'd a puiſſant Army at *Sancton*, on the Weſt-Side of the *Rhine*, within about one League of the Siege;

which

which made the Siege prove very tedious to the Besiegers, but very easy to the Besieged in many Respects; being thereby, from that Side of the River, often assisted in desperate Sorti's or Sallies against the Besiegers, the most of whose Particulars I must wave, none of our *British* Troops being employ'd at the Siege: but being in the Field, and apart in the Cover thereof, I could not well quite omit inserting the most of the most noted Actions thereof, as received by the best Information of an Eye-witness of all thereof; and we also lying very near thereunto, having, soon after that it was form'd, assembled from *Rosendal* to *Cranenburg*, in the Dukedom of *Cleves* or Kingdom of *Prussia*, a little to the West-Side of the River *Wael*, or Part of the *Rhine*, within about four Leagues of the said Siege, the better on that Side to preserve and secure the Besiegers Communication with *Nimeguen* and *Holland*; and in order thereunto, we assembled from *Rosendal* to *Cranenburg*, in the manner following, *viz*.

13, At Break of Day, Brigadier-General *Ingoldsby*, with our *British* Troops, decamp'd at *Rosendal*, and march'd from thence with some *Holland* Artillery toward *Cranenburg* past the River *Demer*, a little above *Rosendal*, and about Noon pitch'd Camp on the Heath at *Kalfsdonck*, four Leagues; and that same Morning, before we begun our March, our Quarter-Master-General and Quarter-Colours advanced near to *Bergen-op-Zome*, with a Feint or Blind, as designing to pitch Camp there, and take up Ground for a General Rendezvous of our Army; the which Feint so blinded the Enemies Troops on that Side, of our real Design, that we thereby got the full Start thereof: so that after reconnoitring a little, our Quarter-Colours and Quarter-Master-General in a Trice withdrew, and fell into the Front of our Troops as we begun our

March

Campaig. II. March from *Rosendal*, and continued the said Start
Anno 1702. to *Cranenburg*.

14, Our Troops decamp'd at *Kalfsdonck*, and march'd from thence over the *Merk*, a little above *Breda*, to, and pitch'd Camp at *Osterhout*, four Leagues distance, with Twenty four Cannon, Eight Mortars and Howitzers, with Twelve Pontons of *Holland*'s Artillery, which join'd us from *Breda*, as said before.

15, Decamp'd at *Osterhout*, and march'd from thence to, and pitch'd Camp at *Tilborg*, six Leagues.

16, Decamp'd at *Tilborg*, and march'd from thence to, and pitch'd Camp at *Nerhost*, four Leagues.

18, Decamp'd at *Nerhost*, and march'd from thence to; and pitch'd Camp at *Evrock*, a little to the West-Side of the *Grave* and River *Maes*, seven Leagues.

19, Decamp'd at *Evrock*, and march'd from thence to, and pitch'd Camp at *Mookherheyde* near *Nimeguen*, on the West-Brink of the River *Wael*; and that Day past thro' the *Grave* and over the River *Maes* thereat, four Leagues.

21, Decamp'd at *Mookerheyde*, and march'd from thence to, and pitch'd Camp between *Cranenburg* and *Cleves*, seated as aforesaid; and having join'd a small Camp of *Holland*'s Troops, three Leagues, under the Earl of *Athlone*'s, Duke *Wirtemburg*, and Count *Tilly*'s (having before join'd their Body) Command. We then consisted of in all Twenty-five Battalions of Foot, and Forty Squadrons of Horse and Dragoons, accounted Sixteen Thousand Men, with Thirty-two Cannon, Eight Mortars, and Sixteen Pontons; and soon after amounted to about Twenty-five Thousand Men. Monsieur *Overquerque*, with the Grand Body of *Holland*'s and other Allies Troops, lay firm near *Emmerick*, as aforesaid, and cover'd the Communication

nication on that Side of the Siege with *Nimeguen* and *Holland* both, and all Sides very alert: And also General *Coehorn* and *Spar* were very vigilant on that Side, with the Troops under their Command, in *Brabant*; whose small Particulars I have waved, and return'd to the Particulars in and about the said Siege. Our Armies being posted, by this Time, as aforesaid, three great Bodies of the *French* being join'd in one at *Santen*, in the Duke of *Burgundy*'s, Monsieur *Bouffler*'s, and Count *Tallard*'s Command; they were computed to consist of about Ninety-four Battalions of Foot, and One Hundred Ninety-two Squadrons of Horse and Dragoons, accounted to amount to between Sixty and Seventy Thousand Men, with Eighty-eight Cannon, Twenty-two Mortars and Howitzers, and Thirty-two Pontons, with all other necessary Utensils of War conform, within about one League of the Siege, as aforesaid; the which, from *Tallard*'s Camp of Thirteen Thousand Men at *Dusseldorp*, fourteen Days before, being the 1*st* Day of *May*, was reinforced by Six Battalions; after which, the said Hero made several Attempts to raise the Siege, with their huge Army, but all proved in vain, being judiciously maintain'd by the good Conduct of our Generals and undaunted couragious Armies. They were forced to lie by indifferent quiet, during the most Part thereof, only their Nighness as aforesaid made it difficult to the Besiegers, and easy to the Besieged; *Tallard*, with his Flying-Camp, having erected and play'd several Batteries against the Besiegers, and succour'd the Besieged often with Men and Ammunition.

May 1, The same Day which *Tallard* join'd General *Boufflers* about Sun-rising, our Camp at *Cranenburg* was alarm'd, by the Information that the Enemies Grand Army had decamp'd, and was advancing thither, with Design to fall thereon; whereupon

Campaig. II.
Anno 1702.
Ten Thousand Men.

<small>Campaig. II.
Anno 1702.</small> upon we immediately ſtruck Tents, and ſtood to Arms, in order to retire to *Nimeguen*, to prevent their Communication from thence, and of joining the reſt of our Army thereat, where our General Rendezvous was intended, as ſoon as poſſible, at the End of the ſaid Siege; for, as aforeſaid, our Army lay then very wide in covering and maintaining the ſame, in four diſpers'd Bodies, and could not inſtantly join and ſuſtain one another. But the ſame Day, about Noon, after we had ſtood upwards of ſix Hours to our Arms, our Generals had freſh Intelligence that, as aforeſaid, their Armies had but only join'd and regulated into one, taking in more Ground; whereupon our Army was order'd to pitch Camp on their former Ground, and ſtrong advanced Guards poſted a conſiderable Way in our Front, to be very alert to prevent Surprizals; after which we lay indifferent quiet till the latter End of *May*, that the Enemy took a freſh Project in Hand.

10, Lord *Cutts* arrived in our Camp at *Cranenburg*, with a Declaration of the late War againſt *France* and *Spain* on our Side, in Conjunction with the *Germans* and *Hollanders*, with full Powers to put the Martial Law in Force; where, ſoon after, the Severity thereof was put in Execution upon ſeveral Deſerters, becauſe at that Time many had, and were daily deſerting to the Enemy, and otherwiſe, notwithſtanding that ſome time before each Regiment, and particular Man, had taken the Oath of Fidelity to our Sovereign Lady Queen *Anne*.

27, A Body of Four Battalions and One Thouſand Grenadiers of the ſaid Beſiegers vigorouſly attack'd a great Part of the Out-works in the Front of their Approaches; the which, after ſeveral ſharp Aſſaults and Repulſes, with great Loſs on both Sides, they took and fully poſſeſs'd themſelves thereof.

28, Another

28, Another competent Body of the Besiegers in like manner attack'd some high Works of the Town, adjoining to the Castle, from which they were thrice very sharply repuls'd, and obliged to retire therefrom with very great Loss.

Campaig. II. Anno 1702.

The same Day a great Body of the said Besiegers couragiously attack'd some more of the remaining Part of the Out-works in the Front of their Approaches; but by the Strength of the Place, and the Superiority of the Besieged's firing, they were obliged to retire therefrom, in like manner as they had done on the second Attack *May* 28. The Duke of *Burgundy*, after the ill Success of his first Enterprize, sent Count *Tallard* with Ten Thousand Men to *Rhineburg*, to cover it from being reduced; and in a few Days after posted another Detachment at *Santen*, &c.

Attack at Keiserswaert

29, Another great Body of the aforesaid Besiegers, at Eight at Night, attack'd the aforesaid unfortunate * Outworks and Castle, and that with a great deal of more undaunted Courage and Vigour than at any Time before; but being desperately flank'd, and repuls'd by the Castle and others, they were again likewise obliged to retire from thence; yet at last gain'd it, and that with a great deal of Loss; nevertheless the Desperateness and Courage thereof so terrified the Besiegers, that they in a very few Days beat a Parly or Chamade, capitulated, and surrender'd up the Garrison, on Conditions to march out thereof with the usual Marks of Honour to their Grand Camp. Our Generals (being not willing to slip any Opportunity in forwarding the farther Progress of our Campaign as then in hand) granted their Demands, according to the full Tenour thereof; whose several Particulars I have waved in this and all Sieges following. The *6th* of *June*, the Besieged accordingly

June 4, the Town surrender'd.

---
* Counterscarp and Ravelin.

Campaig. II. dingly march'd out to their Grand Camp, and the
Anno 1702. Besiegers took full Possession of *Keiserswaert*.

During the eight Weeks and five Days Siege against *Keiserswaert* (commenced the 5th Day of *April* and ended the 4th of *June*) the Besieged's Loss was computed at about a Thousand Men, killed and wounded, besides a great many deserted (as commonly did at each Siege following on both Sides). The Besiegers Two Thousand Nine Hundred kill'd and wounded, all Stations included, according to their several Particulars thereof in the Table following.

STATIONS.	Killed.	Wounded.
Centinels	687	2000
Colonels	1	3
Lieutenant-Colonels	4	0
Majors	2	1
Captains	6	10
Subalterns	14	21
Serjeants	20	31
Of the Artillery kill'd and wounded		100
Total kill'd and wounded		2900

Note, That in some Copies the Serjeants were cast in amongst the Men, and in some apart; and also Commission'd Officers, whose Particulars I could not readily find.

Earl of Ath- 30, About Noon, the Duke of *Burgundy*, then
lone's Retreat commanding the *French* Army in Chief as Gene-
to *Nimeguen*. ralissimo, finding no Opportunity of raising the said Siege, he therefore with a Stratagem decamp'd his Army at *Santen*, and advanced from thence, by Way of the Forest of *Cleves*, towards our small Army, in full Design to slip in between it and the *Grave* and *Nimeguen*, in order to prevent our General Rendezvous thereat; which was design'd soon, as aforesaid, and mainly to take Possession of *Nimeguen*.

guen. And the aforesaid Day, a little before Night, the Earl of *Athlone* having some Intelligence of their Designs, he, about Taptoo, decamp'd our small Army at *Cranenburg*, and immediately march'd off from thence in two Lines of Battle, on great Expedition, towards *Nimeguen*, in four Bodies, *viz*. 1*st*, Major-General *Rowe*, with Two Regiments of Horse, and Six Squadrons of Dragoons; 2*d*, Duke *Wirtemberg*, with Twelve Squadrons to support him in possessing the Eminencies of *Mooker* near *Nimeguen*, before the Enemies Arrival thereat; and Count *Athlone* follow'd him with all the rest of the Cavalry, and Count *Tilley*, with all our Infantry, follow'd close in his Rear, the straitest Way to *Nimeguen*; and continued our tedious March all that Night with great Expedition; and the next Morning, about Eight o'Clock, as we all arrived in Sight of the Town, the Enemies Grand Army appear'd in a manner round us, marching in great Bodies on our Right, Left, and Rear, with great Expedition to surround us, and to get between us and the Town, and take Possession thereof as aforesaid; of all which they were suddenly frustrated, by the Assistance of God, and the good Conduct and undaunted Courage of our valiant Generals, by, in a Trice, joining their Bodies in one, ranging our Cavalry in Order of Battle, and falling back our Left Wing of Infantry to range with the Right, and making thereby a proper Front to the Enemy, which made the Town to be exactly in the Rear of the Center of our Army: A Feint as if fully design'd to give them Battle; the which Feint put the Enemy to somewhat of a Hurry and Stand for a small Time, conjecturing the same; after which they instantly began forming apace in order thereunto; so that in the Time thereof, our small Army was not idle, and by often Facings, Haltings, and slow Retreatings,

we

Campaig. II.
Anno 1702.

we arrived about Noon indifferent safe within the Out-works of the Town; and in the Time and Covering thereof, and as Duke *Wirtemberg* by Order abandon'd *Mooker* before rejoin'd *Athlone*, I must needs say, and that truly, that he, with the *Holland*'s Carabineers, and a few other Squadrons, behaved themselves with the greatest Vigour, Valour, and undaunted Courage imaginable against the *French Gens d'Arms*, and treble their Number of other Squadrons, and had several smart Skirmishes, till the Time that upwards of One Hundred and Fifty Pieces of Cannon (which had been before drawn off to the Arsenal) were again remounted on the Walls and Out-works of the Town, by some of our Men and the Burghers, in a Trice after, and play'd smartly, and made the Enemies whole Army retire out of the Reach thereof, with the Loss of upwards of a Thousand Men, kill'd and wounded, besides upwards of as many deserted; and had also a great many of their Horse kill'd and disabled; and the Allies had not above Two Hundred Men kill'd, wounded, taken, or deserted, Officers included, and including a Captain of Lord *Barrymore*'s Regiment, with a Detachment of One Hundred Men, posted in our Front in the Wood a Night before, for a Rear-guard to discover the Enemies Approach, whose Van-guard, as their Front enter'd the Wood, sorely attack'd them, and kill'd the Captain and most of his Command. All that Night after, the Enemy retiring out of the Reach of our Cannon as aforesaid, our whole small Army kept under Arms, in a moving Posture, on the Inside of the Palisadoes of the Out-works of the Town, facing and marching sometimes to the Right, sometimes to the Left, and all our Haltings betwixt were with our Arms levelled over the Palisadoes, and, as it behoved us, very alert in every Respect whatsoever; waiting the

the Enemies wandering Motion alſo, till the next Morning, *June* 1, about Five o'Clock, that the Enemy finding no Advantage to be made of the Project, they withdrew from thence, and march'd Rearward to, and pitch'd Camp on our old Ground at *Cranenburg* and *Cleves*, five Leagues. At the ſame time our Army, under the Earl of *Athlone*'s Command, encamp'd in and about the Out-works of *Nimeguen*, till ſome time after the End of the Siege of *Keiſerſwaert*.

June 8, The Earl of *Athlone*'s Camp being reinforced by Ten Battalions, and ſeveral Regiments of Horſe and Dragoons, came down the Eaſt-Side of the *Rhine* and *Wael* from the aforeſaid Siege: He removed his Camp from out of the Works of *Nimeguen*, and rang'd them thus, *viz.* the Foot on the Weſt-Brink of the *Wael*, and the Horſe and Dragoons on the other Side with himſelf, towards *Schenkenfort*, moſt advantageouſly poſted againſt all Enterprizes of the Enemy, and for a General Rendezvous, waiting Lord *Marlborough*'s Arrival, which was long'd for, and expected every Day.

13, The Earl of *Athlone* fell ſomewhat back with his Army to *Nimeguen*, being ſtill doubtful of ſudden Surprizals before our General Rendezvous; being often alarm'd by great Parties of the Enemy reconnoitring and gaſconading, being ſtill ſuperior, they Seventy Thouſand, and we after all not above Thirty Thouſand Men. The Enemy never had a better Opportunity of defeating our Army in the whole War, than they had at that Time at *Nimeguen*; of which more afterwards.

Before I could proceed any farther, our ever renowned warlike Hero arrived here.

He being ſo famous and excellent above what I am able or capable to expreſs of him, according to his good Demerits, I could not avoid ſpeaking ſomewhat thereof by the Way, *viz.* firſt of that
Honour

Campaig.II. Honour confer'd upon him before and after the
Anno 1702. Death of King *William*, and when he left *England*
about the Beginning of the said late War ; and
when, and after what manner, he arrived at our
Army then in *Holland*, with which, by the Blef-
sing and Goodness of God vouchsafed unto him, he
continued very prosperous from thence for the Space
of the Ten Campaigns following, commenced in
1702 and ended 1711.

King *William*, of ever glorious Memory, some
time before his Death foreseeing a War ready to
blaze Abroad, and Broils arising at Home, having
a thorough Knowledge of the Earl of *Marlborough*'s
great Parts and Ability, and for his former good
Services done Abroad and at Home, constituted
him Plenipotentiary and Commander in Chief of
the *English* and their auxiliary Troops then in and
design'd for *Holland*, the Low Countries or Netherlands of *Spain*. After which, the King being dead,
and the War then ensuing, and our Sovereign Lady
Queen *Anne*'s Majesty being ascended to the Throne
of her Ancestors, she confirm'd the same Honour
on him as attributed to him by the late King, and
further constituted him, and sent him instantly Am-
bassador-Extraordinary and Plenipotentiary over to
the *Hague* in *Holland*, to congratulate the High and
Mighty Lords thereof, in her Name, and to make
known to them her Affliction for the Death of the
late King her Brother, and to renew and confirm
the former Union of Alliance between her Prede-
cessor and them ; where he arrived on the 17th of
March, and soon after having Audience, and several Conferences with them of the same, and all o-
ther necessary Matters, for the better Preservation
of both Countries against all Opposers, and of the
Grand Confederacy, for the expeditious carrying
on of the said War, as then begun against *France*
and *Spain*. He soon after return'd to *England* with
their

their loving and friendly Answer, with great Acclamations of Joy, to the Queen his and our Mistress; from whence, on the 1st of *May* following, he again set out for the *Hague*, to settle Matters relating to this Campaign, where he arrived the 4th Instant, and made but a very short Stay till he return'd to *England*; from whence he again went back to the *Hague*, and then the States-General created him Generalissimo of all their Forces; which Addition of Honour bestow'd by them on him, highly endear'd the Queen's Love to them; and at the same time they sent to all their General Officers and others to obey him as such; and soon after he had had some more Conferences with them, of several important Matters herein waved. *June* the 19th he set out from the *Hague*, in order to Head the Army, and bring the same to a General Rendezvous as soon as possible. *June* 21, he arrived at *Nimeguen* Captain-General as aforesaid; at which Time the Earl of *Athlone*, General *Dopff*, and all the other principal Officers of our Army met, and paid him the usual Compliments due to such; and at the same Interview he gave all necessary Orders for the instant assembling of the Army from their several Quarters together; all which was accordingly done, and first the Princes of *Hesse* and *Lunenburg*, with Nineteen Battalions from the aforesaid Siege of *Keiserswaert*; Lieutenant-General *Lumley*, with the rest of our *British* Troops, Five Regiments of Horse, and some Artillery from *Breda*; and General *Coehorn* from *Brabant*, and those in his Command; and several others from the several Places assembled towards *Nimeguen*, with all Expedition imaginable, in order for a General Rendezvous at *Duckenburg*.

26, Lord *Marlborough*, then commanding the Army in Chief, advanced therewith from *Nimeguen* to, and regularly pitch'd Camp at *Duckenburg*

Campaig. II. and *Budweik*; and there, in a few Days, all the
Anno 1702. aforesaid Bodies join'd from their several Quarters; and then our Army, under Lord *Marlborough* and Monsieur *Ouverquerque*'s Command, amounted to in all Seventy-six Battalions of Foot, and One Hundred and Twenty Squadrons of Horse and Dragoons, with Sixty-two Cannon, Eight Mortars and Howitzers, and Twenty-four Pontons, with also all other necessary Utensils of War conform; then in Number nigh equal to the Enemy, who by that Time had retired from *Cranenburg*, and begun daily to draw nearer towards their own Borders, which they for some time had overshot, and then lay between *Goch* and *Gennep*, on the West-Side of that small River near the River *Maes*, and then, as I had an Account, computed to consist of about Eighty Battalions of Foot, One Hundred and Fifty Squadrons, Ninety-two Cannons, Twenty-one Mortars and Howitzers, and Thirty-two Pontons, with all necessary Utensils of War conform. Here his Grace held a Council of War, consisting of all the General Officers, to concert the further Operations of the Campaign; and here Dame *Fortune*'s Wheel turn'd contrary to the *French* Expectations, and continued so till the End of the whole War, that the *British* Troops drew off from the *Germans* and *Hollanders*, and then she smiled on them a little in the latter End thereof.

July. Now we, who a little time before had retired within Cover of *Nimeguen*, before Lord *Marlborough*'s Arrival, had the Honour and Pleasure to see the Enemy fly before us in their Turn, after his Arrival. — Note, That in the Time of the Siege against *Keiserswaert*, General *Coehorn* being sent with a Body of Ten Thousand Men into *Flanders*, to demolish the Lines between Fort *St. Donant* and *Isabella*, he was very successful: He took *Middleburg*, a small Town in the *Spanish* Territories, which

which the *French* had begun to fortify, and made himself Master of *St. Donant* Fort, and levelled those Lines which the Enemy for many Months had been making with great Labour and Expence, and put the greatest Part of the *Chatellany* of *Bruges* under Contribution to the Confederates.

Campaig. II. Anno 1702.

3, Lord *Marlborough* and Monsieur *Overquerque* review'd the whole Army standing, and marching at the Head of their Encampments.

5, They decamp'd the Army at *Duckenburg*, and march'd from thence to, and encamp'd at *Sutterburg-Cloister*, on the East-Side of the *Maes*, with a Third Part on the other Side *Over-Assclen* near the *Grave*, three Leagues; with Bridges of Boats over the same, the better to preserve our Communication one with the other, and to prevent sudden Surprizals, if Occasion should require; and also the lesser Part, the better to secure their Flanks and the Pass, entrench'd and erected Batteries thereon, ready and in order to repulse, if attack'd by the Enemy, which lay within about two Leagues of our Camp, at their aforesaid Ground at *Goch*.

15, We decamp'd at *Sutterburg* our main Body, cross'd the *Maes* by, and a little below the *Grave*, and join'd the lesser; and march'd from thence to, and pitch'd Camp at *Bruegel*, in the Dukedom of *Brabant*, five Leagues.

17, Decamp'd at *Bruegel*, and march'd from thence to, and pitch'd Camp between *Geldorp* and *Achel*, on that Heath, four Leagues; where, in the Night, there happen'd great Thunder, Lightning, and Rain; which, it is said, often happens when there is an Army thereon: The which Motion of ours obliged the Enemy to pass the same River at *Venlo*, the readier to prevent our cutting them off from their *Brabant* Lines.

19, We decamp'd at *Geldorp*, and march'd to, and encamp'd between *Grevenbrouck* and *Hospital-Chateau*,

Campaig. II. *Chateau*, four Leagues; in which there was a Gar-
Anno 1702. rifon of *French*, confifting of a Captain and One
Hundred Men, which, next Morning betimes,
Lord *Cutts* in Perfon, with a fmall Detachment of
our Army, with the Affiftance of Four Cannon and
Two Howitzers, attack'd and took in a Trice, and
the faid fmall Garrifon Prifoners at Difcretion,
with only two Men wounded, and the Enemy no
Lofs, having inftantly furrender'd. Here, the fame
Day, our *Britifh* Artillery arrived in Camp from
Holland, under a Convoy of Two Regiments of
our Horfe, and Two Regiments of Foot, which
had left *England* in the Beginning of *June*; and
then our Corps confifted of Seven Regiments of
Horfe, and Fourteen Battalions of Foot, Thirty-
four Pieces of Field-Cannon, Four Howitzers or
fmall Mortars, and Eighteen Tin-Boats or Pontons
for Bridges, with all other neceffary Utenfils of
War conform thereunto.

22, We decamp'd at *Grevenbrouck*, and march'd
to, pitch'd and encamp'd between *Little Bruegel*
and *Navare*, two Leagues; where the next Morning, by Break of Day, all ftood to Arms in very
good Order, and full Defign to advance on, attack
and force the *French* Grand Army to Battle (between *Bruegel*, *Hamont*, and *Peer*) with great Advantage; they, by the firft Report, being then
not above half up, having the two Days and Nights
before had a very tedious March, and retreat from
Gennep over the *Maes*, with great Expedition retiring towards their *Brabant* Line and Garrifon of
Huy, upwards on the *Maes*, for Succour therefrom,
quite leaving *Spanifh Guelderland*; of which Defign
and fair Opportunity our Generals were deceitfully
fruftrated, by the falfe Information of our other
Roguifh Spies, by reporting that the Enemies whole
Army was up in very good Order, and ready,
ftrongly and advantageoufly pofted for Battle; the
which,

which, by other Spies, was soon after found to be false; for which false Report they were immediately hang'd, and our Army fell back to, and re-pitch'd on their former Ground. The Deputies of the States-General also being not willing to force the Enemy to a Battle, but rather to wear them out of *Spanish Guelderland* by besieging their Towns, the Navigation of the *Maes* being then interrupted, and the important *Maestricht* in a manner block'd up to their Advantage; but afterwards the Duke had always full Power to act as he thought fit, especially after this Campaign, without any Controul.

25, Our Army decamp'd at *Navare*, and march'd to, pitch'd and encamp'd at *Peer* (in the Bishoprick of *Liege*) five Leagues; which, in two Days after, our Army dismantled, in order to prevent its being any Refuge to the Enemy.

August 1, Decamp'd at *Peer*, and march'd to, pitch'd and encamp'd between *Grevenbrouck* and *Everbeck*, five Leagues; which was a two Days March before, now one. The *French* being then reinforced by Count *Tallard*, and upwards of Twenty Thousand Men, attempted to enter the Marsh of *Bois-le-Duc* near *Eyndhoven*, for Plenty of Forage, thinking then to hazard a Battle; in which Courage fail'd them, the Duke of *Burgundy* having no Order from Court for it, and only reinforced those Garrisons Duke *Marlborough* had an Eye to besiege, the first of which was *Venlo*, since he could in no respect drive them to Battle; and before the Siege he used a Stratagem to win them to Battle, by detaching our Army, to make a Feint to lay the Siege, to try if they would attempt to attack the same, that he might make one with them: And therefore, as on another Design, he detach'd General *Opdam* and Lord *Cutts*, with Ten Battalions of Foot, and Twenty Squadrons

Campaig. II. of Horse and Dragoons, as only to meet and con-
Anno 1702. voy Lord *Albemarle* from the *Bosch*, with Bread and
Money to our Grand Camp; for which he had
been gone from thence fourteen Days before; and
that Night *Opdam* pitch'd at *Lind*, about four
Leagues Eastward from our Grand Camp; towards
which, next Morning, as he began his March, with
the Troops from thence, upwards of Ninety Squadrons of the Enemy appear'd in Order and full Design, advancing to attack him; of which the Duke
of *Marlborough* being aware, having present Intelligence thereof, the Enemy were suddenly frustrated,
and that by the expeditious appearing of an equal
Number sent by the Duke from our Grand Camp
to General *Opdam*'s Assistance: Whereupon the Enemy immediately retired to their Grand Camp, and
ours withdrew; and, about Two o' Clock in the
Afternoon, the Heath being found clear of any
Ambush, he proceeded on his March, and about
Ten at Night pitch'd his Camp at *Helmont*, where
the next Day struck Tents, in order to march to
Hamont; but having Intelligence that Lord *Albemarle* would not be there that Night, and that the
Enemy were gasconading, he repitch'd Camp on
his former Ground: And that same Day, *August* 5,
General *Schults*, with a small Detachment from our
Grand Camp, with Six Cannon and Two Howitzers, advanced to, and took the Town and Castle
of *Weert*, with little Resistance and Loss, having
instantly surrender'd, after their Batteries (being
before erected) had play'd four Rounds. *Helmont*
is distant four Leagues East of *Leenden*.

6, General *Opdam* decamp'd with his Troops at
Helmont, and march'd to and encamp'd at *Hamont*;
where, the next Morning, Lord *Albemarle* arrived
from *Bosch*, as aforesaid. *Hamont* is four Leagues
North-East of *Helmont*.

8, About

8, About Three o' Clock in the Afternoon, he *Campaig. II.*
decamp'd from *Hamont*, and remarch'd from thence *Anno 1702.*
with all his Grenadiers in his Rear, the former two
Days March in lefs than one, nearer than by the
Way of *Helmont*; and about Ten o' Clock that
Night repitch'd his Camp on his former Ground
at *Lind*, eight Leagues.

9, He decamp'd at *Lind*, and remarch'd to, and
pitch'd a little in the Rear of our Grand Camp at
Grevenbrouck, where they had before left them,
four Leagues.

11, Our Grand and Flying Army decamp'd at
Grevenbrouck, and pitch'd Camp between *Navare*
and *Bruegel*, fomewhat apart as before; the Flying
Army at *Helchteren*, in the Rear of the Grand Army.

12, Both Armies decamp'd at their feveral A-
partments, and march'd from thence to, and pitch'd
Camp at *Everbeck*. General *Opdam*, with our Flying Army, pitch'd in the Rear of our Grand Army,
again intending to force the Enemy to Battle.

The Scheme being laid, in order to force Battle *Action at*
as aforefaid, on the 13*th* Day of *Auguft*, by Break *Peer.*
of Day, our warlike Hero decamp'd at *Everbeck*
with our Grand Army, and march'd from thence,
and about Noon pitch'd and encamp'd at *Helchteren*, on the far Side of that Heath, a little Southward from *Peer*, in order to force the Enemy to
quit their Camp at *Bergheick*, to give us Battle, or
to cut off their Convoys and Communication with
their Garrifons on that Side; but General *Opdam*,
with our Flying Army, begun not his March from
Everbeck till Eight next Morning; which Delay
gave much Way and Encouragement to the Duke
of *Burgundy* with the *French* Army to advance,
and fall thereon, and cut off his Communication
with our Grand Army, then lying nearer thereto;
for as he was on his March after the Grand Army
in Order, and very near about to join it, as en-
C 4 camp'd,

(26)

Campaig. II.
Anno 1702. camp'd, the Enemy, who had but a little before appear'd in Battle Array, behind several Morasses and Defiles, as our Grand Army came to their Ground, begun now to appear plainly, expeditiously, and boldly advancing furiously in a full Career; and had almost accomplish'd the same, had not my Lord *Marlborough* and Monsieur *Overquerque*, by being very alert, put a sudden Stop thereto, by immediately putting the Troops under Arms, and advancing couragiously therewith, in two Lines in very good Order for Battle, for General *Opdam*'s Assistance: At which Appearance, the *French* lofty Army immediately withdrew from their Attempt, and fell backward behind that Marsh, on that Side of the Heath Southward from *Peer*; and there strongly and advantageously posted themselves, with a Wood and Scrub in their Rear, and Hedges and Ditches on their Right and Left; in which Time General *Opdam*, with his Flying Army, got safely up, and fell in and join'd in Line of Battle on the Right of our Grand Army, all ready and in good Order for Action, and immediately expecting Battle, which was about Three o'Clock in the Afternoon, and then our Army begun Cannonading the Enemy, and they us, which continued very smart on both Sides till past Six at Night, that the Enemies whole Army fell intirely into the Wood, to consult on some fresh Projects for a Retreat: After which our Army inclin'd a little towards the Right, and lay on their Arms the remaining Part of the Night, expecting that the *French* Army would give us Battle the next Morning; but they, not being desirous thereof, joyfully embraced the Canopy of the Night; the Duke of *Burgundy* retired with their main Body quite thro' the Wood and Scrub, in their Rear towards *Huy* as aforesaid; when they pass'd the *Maes* at *Venlo*, leaving only next to us, where their main

Front

Front had been, a few Battalions and Squadrons for a Rear-Guard, or Cover to the Retreat of their main Body till it got clear out of the Wood; which Detachment in the Morning wonderfully falsified and gasconaded next to us, as if their whole Army had been instantly posting to give us Battle, as we for some time at the first expected, which we soon after found to be the least of their real Design. But in the interim thereof my Lord *Marlborough*, with a few Squadrons, had been reconnoitring their Proceedings, he penetrating thereinto, fully discover'd their real Design; whereupon, the better to discover the same, and to see if he could recal them to Battle, to which they the Day before had been, to Appearance, preparing to receive us, he sent Brigadier *Ross*, with a few Squadrons in their Rear, to reconnoitre, who found the Gasconaders making off after their main Body with all Haste imaginable, in some Disorder and Confusion; the which he mightily improv'd and increas'd, falling in therewith, and charging the Rear thereof, with much Courage and Bravery, for upwards of a League, from their former Post; which did much redound to his Honour, and the Enemies great Dishonour. That being done, he instantly after return'd back to our Army, which immediately form'd, pitch'd, and encamp'd on the same Ground where we had stood to Arms the Night before. In which Action I cannot safely say that either Side lost above One Hundred Men in all, kill'd, wounded, and taken; but a great many deserted from the Enemy, whose certain Number could never be truly found. Here our Army amounted to the greatest Strength of that Campaign in Field, and consisted then of in all Eighty-four Battalions of Foot, One Hundred and Fifty Squadrons of Horse and Dragoons, Ninety-two Cannon, Twenty-one Mortars and

Howitzers,

(28)

Campaig.II. Howitzers, with Forty Pontons, and all other ne-
Anno 1702. cessary Utensils of War conform for the Army.

The *French* Army at that Time was much superior to ours in Number, but much inferior in Courage, Valour and Bravery, and computed to consist of in all Ninety-four Battalions, One Hundred and Ninety-two Squadrons, Eighty-eight Cannon, Sixteen Mortars and Howitzers, and Thirty-two Pontons, with all other necessary Utensils of War conform.

Duke *Marlborough* finding no Means to draw the Duke of *Burgundy* to run the Risque or Hazard of a Battle, resolved to make what other Conquests he could, in taking of Towns, &c. and the Siege of *Venlo* was first undertaken.

The Siege of *Venlo*. On the 15th Day of *August*, Duke *Marlborough* detach'd and sent off thereunto, General in Chief, Prince *Nassau Saarburg*, General *Opdam*, and Lord *Cutts*, with Twenty Battalions of Foot, and Sixteen Squadrons of Horse and Dragoons, and some of our Artillery, who on the third Day after arrived there; of which more afterwards.

18, Duke *Marlborough* decamp'd the Grand Army at *Helchteren*, and march'd therewith from thence, and pitch'd between *Ghenck* and *Asch*, in order the better to cover the said Siege; which that Day was begun thus, viz. Prince *Nassau Saarburg*, with the aforesaid Troops, invested the Town on the North and West-Side thereof, and River *Maes*, as also Fort *St. Michael*; the Margrave of *Branderburgh* and Prince *Anhault*, with Twelve Battalions, and Twenty Squadrons of *Prussian* and *Munster* Troops, invested the Town on the East and South-Side thereof, and the River *Maes*; and then the Siege being regularly form'd, the Besieging Army on both Sides consisted of Thirty-two Battalions, and Thirty-six Squadrons, with Sixty-four Cannon, and Twenty-four Mortars and Howitzers,

besides

besides a great Number of little Hand-Mortars, with Eighteen Pontons, and all other necessary Utensils of War conform for the expeditious carrying on of the Siege. The Besieged in Town and Fort consisted in all of *French* Troops, Six Battalions of Foot, and Two Squadrons of Horse, with Thirty-eight mounted Cannon, and Twelve Mortars, with great Stores of Ammunition, commanded by Count *D'Van*, Major-General *L'Abade*, and Two Brigadiers, who made but an ordinary Defence after the Arrival of General *Coehorn*, Director of the Attacks, with our battering Train.

Soon after this Siege was laid, the Duke of *Burgundy*, to avoid Reproach, and not to be an Eye-witness of any more Misfortunes of that Campaign, return'd to *Paris* [*], leaving the sole Command to General *Boufflers*.

This Siege was carried on by two Attacks, *viz.* Lord *Cutts*, on the Right, carried on his against Fort *St. Michael* and the Town, on the West-Side of both, and River *Maes*, smartly; Prince *Anhault*, on the Left, carried on his on the North-East-Side thereof, close by the Brink of the River.

20, The Besiegers against Fort *St. Michael* begun making and bringing of Fascines, Gabions, Piquets, Mauls, and all other such Necessaries for the expeditious carrying on the Siege thereof; and on the second Day after they begun their Contravallation-Line.

24, In the Night, the besieging Army on both Sides stood to Arms, being somewhat alarm'd by Two Battalions of *French* from *Roermonds*, who attempted to reinforce *Venlo* on the Margrave's Side of the Siege; but being instantly discover'd thereby, they were forced to withdraw, and retire back to *Roermond* in great Disorder and Confusion, and considerable Loss on their Part.

[*] Instead of coming to learn to fight, learn'd to avoid it.

27, Lord

Campaig. II.
Anno 1702.

27, Lord *Cutts*, under the Cover of Four Battalions, and a competent Number of Workmen, without Arms, about Eight at Night, open'd his Trenches against Fort *St. Michael*, on its West-Side, and that with very little Loss, by getting into good Cover before discover'd by the Enemy; and the same Night Prince *Anhault*, with a competent Number of Men, with and without Arms, open'd the Trenches on his Attack against the Town, on the North-Side thereof, by the Brink of the River *Maes*, and that also with very little Loss, by getting somewhat into Cover before discover'd by the Enemy; and afterwards both Attacks proceeded gradually; and that same Day the Left Attack was reinforced by some *Munster* Troops, and then accounted in Number near equal to those on Lord *Cutts*'s Attack, both commanded in Chief by Prince *Nassau Saarbrugh* and General *Opdam*.

Sept. 2, Our Grand Army decamp'd at *Asch*, and march'd from thence to, and pitch'd at *Suttendael*, within two Leagues of *Maestricht* on the *Maes*, the better to cover the Siege, and preserve both Armies Communication therewith.

3, A great Quantity of our heavy Train, and great Stores of other Ammunition and Provision, arrived safe at the Besiegers Camp, from *Holland*, up the *Maes*; but Prince *Nassau Saarbrugh* doubting that there was not sufficient thereof for the quick Dispatch of the Siege, the next Morning sent from thence a Major-General, with a Detachment of Four Thousand Foot, and some Horse, towards *Wesel* on the *Rhine*, in order to bring from thence to the Siege an Addition of heavy Artillery, who continued his March two Days thitherwards in Lower *Germany*; but on the third, the Prince finding what he had sufficient, by the two Days before vigorous Proceeding of the Batteries on both Attacks, he countermanded them.

5, At

5, At Six in the Morning, the several Batteries on Lord *Cutts* Attack being erected, consisting of Thirty-six Cannon, and Sixteen Mortars and Howitzers, besides Hand-Mortars, or *Coehorn*'s Grenadiers, (so called, being invented by him for throwing of Granades in a great Number) begun to play, and play'd very smartly and furiously against and into the Fort and Out-works of *St. Michael* three Days running.

6, About Six in the Morning, the several small Batteries on Prince *Anhault*'s Attack, consisting but of Fourteen Cannon and Four Mortars, began to play, and play'd indifferent smartly against the Bastion on the North-Side of the Town, and Corner of the main Hill thereof, seven Days following, to the 12*th* at Night; but was far short of the Attack on the Right, in their vigorous Proceedings. The same Day some more heavy Artillery arrived from *Holland* up the *Maes*; and the Day following the aforesaid General and Detachment, which had been gone for Artillery four Days, return'd to the Siege somewhat before the Attack was made on Fort *St. Michael*, which was in the following manner:

7, About Six at Night, the Prince having given Orders to Lord *Cutts* and Brigadier *Hamilton*, with his own and General *Hukelom*'s Regiments and a Lieutenant-Colonel, with Two Hundred Grenadiers and One Hundred and Fifty Fusiliers, with Officers conform, and a competent Number of Engineers, with Three Hundred and Twenty Workmen, under Colonel *Blood*, to attack and make an Lodgement between the Bastion which is next the Plain, and the Ravelin that is on the North thereof: The Signal was the blowing up of a Tun of Powder, for both Attacks, and the Discharge of all the Batteries in general of Cannon and Mortars; and first of ours against Fort *St. Michael*.

At

(32)

Campaig. II.
Anno 1702.

At the aforesaid Time, and that very vigorously, with a great deal of Bravery and undaunted Courage, the said Grenadiers and Fusiliers in the Van, attack'd and first clear'd the Covert-Way; and finding it practicable, enter'd the Ravelin with Sword in Hand, being immediately sustain'd by the other Troops, having first clear'd the Counterscarp with their furious Fire, and avoiding the Mine, were soon Masters of the Ravelin, the Enemy confusedly retiring to the Rampart of the Fort, from which they made a great Fire on the Assaulters; but, in the interim, they so closely pursued the Enemy, before they could cut and break down the Bridge, that they in a Trice enter'd the Fort itself, amongst the very Middle of them, and also possess'd the same, with Sword in Hand slaughtering all before them, till Lord *Cutts*, of his compassionate Clemency, stop'd the Soldiers: The which being done, the Governor of the Fort was taken, with Two Brigadiers, Thirty other Officers, and Two Hundred and Twenty-five Centinels, Prisoners at Discretion; being all that were left of Eight Hundred Men that were posted therein when attack'd, but what were either kill'd in the Heat of the Action, or drowned in their retiring from thence over the *Maes* in Boats to the Town, as the Besiegers enter'd the Fort, and that surpriz'd them much sooner, and contrary to their Expectations. After which, all the Troops (but the necessary Guards that were posted) were drawn up on the Rampart of the Fort facing the Town, turn'd the Cannon and discharg'd them against it; thereby letting our Camp know that all was well, and continued under Arms all Night; and our Drummers beat our several Beatings quite round the Rampart of the Fort, all the Magazines being seiz'd in the Fort first; in which there was found, and about the Rampart, Thirty fine Cannon of Brass, Six Mortars,

Mortars, and a very great Quantity of Powder and Ball, and large Stores of Corn, Meal, and Brandy, and all other neceſſary Proviſions. The Prince of *Hanover*, Uncle to our preſent Sovereign, a Voluntier, behaved with a great deal of Gallantry at this Siege; that Night before the Attack, he was in the Trenches with Lord *Cutts*, and the Night after in the Fort. On this Action, Attack or Siege againſt Fort St. *Michael*, the *Engliſh* had in particular killed and wounded in all Two Hundred and Ninety-ſeven, according to the following Table.

Their ſeveral STATIONS.	Killed.	Wounded.
Captains	1	2
Subalterns	3	5
Serjeants	2	4
Centinels	130	150
Total —	136	161

Total kill'd and wounded — 297

The other Allies Loſs thereat was computed equal to the *Engliſh*, amongſt which ſome few loſt againſt the Town on our Side are included.

Note, That on this famous Action on Lord *Cutts*'s Attack, there went on Voluntiers Lord *Cutts*'s Aid de Camp, Captain *Bollas*, and one Enſign *Eley*, who were killed; Prince *D'Auvergne*, Lord *Lorn* now Duke of *Argyll*, Earl *Huntington*, Lord *Mark Kerr*, Sir *Richard Temple*, Colonel *Webb*, and Mr. *Dalrymple*; General *Coehorn* and Colonel *Blood* Engineers.

At the ſame Time, and with the ſame Signal, Prince *Anhault*, with the ſame Number of Men, attack'd on the North-Side between the Baſtion and Ravelin, with a great deal of Bravery, and alſo with Sword in Hand, carrying the Ravelin on their Side; but the *French* having broke down that
Bridge

Campaig. II. Bridge between it and the Fort, it was impossible
Anno 1702. for the *Prussian* Troops to pass: Nevertheless, they
took a Ravelin and a Glacis, and several other
Places in the Front of their Approaches on that
Side, with considerable Loss, and made it good at
the same time.

9, About Eight in the Morning, the Batteries
erected and compleated on Fort *St. Michael*, to the
Number of Forty Cannon, and Twenty Mortars
and Howitzers, &c. began to play, and play'd
furiously cross the *Maes* against the Walls of the
Town, flanking and widening the Breaches of
Prince *Anhault*'s Attacks; they also play'd vigorously with great Expedition for a general grand
Assault or Storm on the Town, and that very smart
for three Days following, very dreadful to the Besieged and Inhabitants.

10, Our Grand Army had a Thanksgiving at
Suttendael, for the Victory obtain'd by Prince *Eugene*, in the taking of *Landau*; and at Night had
a *Feu de Joye* for the same, with a triple Discharge
of all their Cannon and small Arms; which Siege
had proved very tedious to him and the *German*
Troops, from the 16th of *June* to about that
Time.

Surrender of 12, About Sun-setting, as the besieging Army
Venlo. at *Venlo* were expressing their Joy in like manner
for the same News, those in the Camp by their Circumvallation Line, fired a third Round of small
Arms quite round the Town, so far as the Camp
reach'd; and all the Batteries from their Approaches
having furiously fired the same Number into the
Town, it so much terrified and amazed the Besieged, taking it for the Signal of a grand Storm
thereon, (as the Signal against *St. Michael* was) that
with a great Fear and Dread thereof, they immediately beat a Parly, and the next Day capitulated
to surrender, on Condition to be admitted to march

out

out with Baggage and small Arms only, and to be conducted to *Antwerp*. Prince *Nassau Saarbrugh* would not grant them any other Conditions. Pursuant to their Capitulations, they surrender'd the Town the 14*th*, and were immediately conducted by a few of our Guards from thence to *Antwerp*.

During the Siege against *Venlo*, which lasted four Weeks, commencing *August* 18, and ending *September* 14, against Town and Fort, on both Attacks, the Besieged's Loss was computed to be Thirty-nine Commission'd Officers killed and wounded, and upwards of Eight Hundred Men of all Stations, whose Particulars are obscure. The Besiegers Loss on both Attacks exceeded not Six Hundred and Eighty-four kill'd and wounded, Officers included, and Sixty of the Artillery; the Particulars varied. Our Batteries on both Attacks consisted of at most Fifty-four Cannon, Twenty-four Mortars and Howitzers, and Hand-Mortars in great Number. This Siege being over, and Prince *Nassau Saarbrugh* placed a Garrison sufficient in *Venlo*, the Duke of *Marlborough* resolved to push on the rest of the Campaign in Conquests of Towns, the Prince not being willing to venture a Battle; and therefore order'd the said Prince, with the same Troops, to remove from *Venlo*, and to lay close Siege to *Roermonde*.

18, By Break of Day, Prince *Nassau Saarbrugh* detach'd and sent before Count *Tilly* with Twelve Hundred Horse, in order that Night to block up *Roermonde*, in which there was a Garrison of *French* consisting of Four Battalions of Foot, with Twenty-four Cannon and Six Mortars mounted, commanded by Prince *de Horne*; and that Day, about Ten, the Prince with the Remainder of the aforesaid Besiegers decamp'd at *Venlo*, and cross'd the *Maes* a little above the Town, and march'd from thence with Prince *Anhault*'s Attack from that Side in
their

Campaig. II. Anno 1702. their Rear, and at Night join'd and pitch'd Camp behind the small Hills and in the Bottoms, about a League and half Eastward from *Roermonde*, then block'd up.

20, They decamp'd from thence, and march'd to, and pitch'd Camp at *Hartem*, as regular as the Ground about the Rivers *Roer* and *Maes*, on the South and West-Side of the Town, within Cannon-Shot thereof, would allow; and the Margrave and Prince *Anhault*, with the *Prussians*, and other Corps in their Command and former Attack, pitch'd on the East-Side of the Town, with their Left extended to the Brink of the *Maes*: And thus *Roermonde* was invested round by two Attacks by the same Troops, as was *Venlo*, and had the same Number of Artillery; but there being a great Marsh on the North-Side of the Town, they were oblig'd to let it lie open thereto, without any great Danger, our Army being fully Masters of the Field.

Stevenswaert invested, And the same Day General *Schults*, with a competent Detachment from our Grand Army, invested *Stevenswaert*, a little Fort seated in a small Island in the Middle of the River *Maes*, two Leagues South-West of *Roermonde*; in which there then was Four Hundred *French*, commanded by a Colonel, with Two Iron Cannon.

and taken. 21, The Besiegers erected two smart Batteries against the Fort, the one of Six Cannon, the other of Two Mortars; the which began to play against it on the 22d, at Seven o'Clock in the Morning, and play'd very smartly against it all that Day, in order for a sudden Breach and general Grand Storm thereon; for which the next Morning, by Break of Day, the Ladders were laid to the Walls, and the Attempt made to storm the same; but the Dread thereof so terrified the Besieged, that about Seven that Morning they beat a Parly, and immediately

diately capitulated and furrender'd the Fort to the Allies, and themfelves Prifoners of War.

During this fmall Siege of four Days, begun the 20*th* and ended the 23*d* of *September*, neither Side loft above Twenty Men, killed and wounded. Thefe laft two Days the Befiegers againft *Roermonde* were bufily employ'd in making and bringing Fafcines, *&c.* and all other Neceffaries of the like Kind, for the expeditious carrying on of the Siege, made moft by the Horfe and Dragoons on the 20*th*, 21*ft*, and 22*d* Ditto.

23, At Night, the aforefaid Leaders as at *Venlo*, with a competent Number of Men, with and without Arms, on both Attacks open'd their Trenches againft *Roermonde*, and that with very little Lofs, by getting into good Cover before difcover'd by the Befieged; having rais'd and erected fome Batteries the Day before, all which the very next Day was fully compleated, *viz.* Lord *Cutts*'s Attack two, the one of Twenty-eight Cannon, and the other of Twelve Mortars and Howitzers; on Prince *Anhault*'s two, the one of Sixteen Cannon, and the other of Six Mortars, *&c.* The firft againft the South-Broad Side of the Town very regularly; the fecond againft the Eaft-Corner of the main Wall of the Town, by the Brink of the *Maes.*

25, At Seven in the Morning, all the Batteries on both Attacks begun to play, and play'd all that Day very fmartly, vigoroufly, and furioufly without any Stop, for a fudden grand Breach on the thin Brick Walls of the Town, (and for a general Grand Storm thereon) till about Eight at Night; in which Time they beat down fo much thereof, that it was ready, fit, and in order for the fame: And firft of all the Out-works thereof, the which was expected to be made in the Morning following; of which the Befieged being very doubtful, they therefore, through Fear and Dread of the fame,

Campaig. II.
Anno 1702.

Roermonde befieged,

and furrender'd.

Campaig. II. fame, immediately, as we were about the relieving
Anno 1702. of our Trenches, cry'd out aloud from off the
Walls of the Town to our Batteries to forbear firing any more againſt them, the Drums at the ſame Time beating a Parly; the which at firſt could not be heard for the Fury and Violence of our Batteries. But at length being heard, our Batteries ceaſed, and the Beſieged capitulated, and ſurrender'd the Town according to the Conditions of *Venlo*; which being granted, they the next Morning deliver'd up to the Allies the South-Gate of the Town, and the Day following, being the 27*th* Ditto, they march'd out of *Roermonde*, and was conducted by a Party of our Horſe from thence to *Louvain*.

During this ſmall Siege againſt *Roermonde* of nine Days, commenc'd the 18*th* and ended the 26*th* of *September*, the Beſieged had about Forty or Fifty Men killed or wounded, but they had a great many fell ſick in the Time thereof; the Beſiegers in both Attacks had not above Sixty Men killed and wounded, Officers included: For ſome time in the End of this Siege, and that at *Venlo*, the Beſiegers lay in Huts, a Fence againſt Cold, expecting neither to end ſo ſoon. — *Note*, That General *Schults* in his return to our grand Camp after the taking of *Stevenſwaert* on the 24*th* of *September*, took the ſmall Town and Caſtle of *Wert*, and therein a Captain and Fifty *French*. It's ſeated on the Weſt Brink of the *Maes*, half Way between *Maeſeyck* and *Maeſtricht Erklins*, a little ſmall Town belonging thereunto the *French* abandon'd. In the Time of theſe Conqueſts the *French* Army, then under Monſieur *Boufflers* Command, lay moſtly entrench'd near *Tongres*, where they had come on the 31*ſt* of *Auguſt*, and was then reinforced with Prince *Tſerſclas* and Six Thouſand Men; and expecting that the Duke of *Marlborough* had a Deſign to compleat

his

his Campaign, with the taking in of the famous City of *Liege*, went thither with the Duke of *Maine*, and some Engineers, to view the Fortifications of that Citadel, and of the most advantageous Ground between it and *Maestricht*, as if he intended to remove his Army thither for its Security; but Courage fail'd him, fearing that the Duke of *Marlborough* would attack him there, and force him to Battle contrary to his Inclination; and therefore withdrew his Project, and also with great Precipitation (at the first Motion of our Army towards *Liege*) he made a Motion, and retired with his Army from *Tongres* (where our Army from *Asch* attempted to attack them, but finding it impossible without great Risque forbore) towards *Brabant*, behind the *Main*, to those Places that were not then design'd to be attack'd. But the Duke of *Marlborough* finding no Means to bring them to a Battle, was fully bent to strengthen and secure what he had already conquer'd, and to add Honour and Reputation to the Allies, design'd to assemble with his whole Army at *Liege*, and as aforesaid compleat the Glory of this Campaign, with the subduing thereof, as soon as possible; and therefore he sent express Orders to Prince *Nassau Saarbrugh* to assemble with the Flying-Army thitherward with all Expedition.

Sept. 29, The said Prince having settled the Affairs of *Roermonde*, and left a sufficient Garrison therein, decamp'd and remov'd from thence, cross'd the *Maes* a little below *Stevenswaert*, and pitch'd Camp at *Maeseyck*, about five Leagues Westward of *Roermonde*; having left the Margrave with the *Prussians* and *Munster* Troops, which had belong'd to the former two Attacks as aforesaid on that Side of the *Maes* and Country, who join'd us no more that Campaign.

(40)

Campaig. II.
Anno 1702.

Sept. 30, Prince *Naſſau Saarbrugh*'s Flying Army decamp'd at *Maeſeyck*, and march'd from thence to, and pitch'd Camp at *Haut Chateau*, in the Rear of our Grand Army at *Suttendael*, which had remain'd very alert during the Time, and covering the two aforeſaid Sieges, &c. four Leagues Weſt of *Maeſeyck*.

Liege beſieged.

October 1, About One o'Clock in the Morning, the Duke of *Marlborough* decamp'd the Grand Army at *Suttendael*, and march'd from thence in two Columns towards *Liege*, and croſs'd the *Jecker*, a little above *Maeſtricht*, leaving the *Maes* to their Left; and at Eight the Flying Army ſtruck Tents and march'd after from *Haut*, in the Rear of our Grand Army; and about Four in the Afternoon our Front advanced, and arrived within Cannon-ſhot of the High Citadel, and about Sun-ſetting both Armies join'd, form'd and pitch'd Camp along the Hill near thereto, and on the North-Side thereof; and thus block'd up the Citadel, City and Low Fort, of all which was Governor and Commander in Chief Lieutenant-General *Violaine*, with Twelve Battalions of *French* Foot, and on the Walls of the Citadel and Chartreuſe, or Low Fort, were mounted upwards of Forty-eight Cannon and Mortars, and great Stores of all manner of Ammunition and other neceſſary Utenſils of War, fit for the Garriſon, and to ſtand a ſtrong Siege; with alſo great Proviſions for their Grand Army.

The City given up.

2, Our whole Army decamp'd, and removed a little nearer to the City, one League, and pitch'd ſomewhat more regular; and at the ſame time the *French* Garriſon ſet the Suburb of *St. Walburgh* on Fire, and Eight Battalions with the Governor went into the Citadel, and Four into the Low Fort; and that Evening the Chapter and Magiſtracy treated with the Duke on reaſonable Terms, as they neither could nor would ſtand a Siege of the City;

City; whereupon, at Ten that Night, one of the Gates was deliver'd up to the Allies, where Lord *Cutts* with Ten Battalions of the aforesaid Besiegers was posted that Night, and the next Morning took full Possession of the City, the Key thereof being given up to the Duke in a very humble manner.

3, Our Grand Army in general encamp'd a little nearer to the City, one League, and immediately form'd a regular Siege against the Citadel; the Duke himself in Person commanding the Siege, carried on in general by one grand Attack of the whole Army on the East-Side thereof, with all Expedition and Vigour imaginable, as the Weather then would permit, directed by General *Coehorn*, Head Engineer, and Colonel *Blood* under him.

4, The Grand Army in general were employ'd in making and bringing Fascines, &c. for the quick Dispatch of the Siege.

7, At Night, Lieutenant-General *Somerfelt* with Four Battalions of *English*, and Lieutenant-General *Fagel* with Four Battalions of *Dutch*, (besides Four of Reserve) and a competent Number detach'd of the Army, with and without Arms for Work, open'd their Trenches against the Citadel, and at the same time attack'd and took a high Entrenchment from the Enemy, with much Vigour and Bravery; which the Governor and most of his Garrison instantly attempted to retake, but were soon sharply repuls'd, with considerable Loss on their Side, besides the High Entrenchment, Redout and Cover'd Way thereof.

9, At Sun-rising, all our several Batteries being erected, and compleated ready, consisting of Forty-four Cannon and Twelve Mortars, began to play against the Citadel very vigorously and furiously, and thereby fired and blew up a Magazine of the Enemies, with upwards of One Thousand loaded Bombs and Granades, and several Barrels of Powder;

Campaig. II. Anno 1702.

der; and in like manner, on the 10*th*, they fired and blew up a Magazine of Six Thousand loaded Granades, and a great Quantity of Powder, which made a very terrible Noise; and on the 11*th*, our Batteries being enlarged, their Bombs in like manner fired and blew up two other great Magazines; each made a hideous Noise.

Our Batteries having for four Days play'd in as much Order, Dispatch and Success as ever before was seen, had made a sufficient Breach on the Counterscarp and main Wall of the Citadel, and blown up four of the Enemies Magazines; and the Enemy being beat out of most of their Out-Lodgments, a Consult was made to attack the Counterscarp, which also carried the Citadel, *viz.*

The Citadel taken by Storm.

October 12, At Four in the Afternoon, the Signal being made by a general Discharge of all our Batteries, to begin the Attack on the Counterscarp, Lieutenant-General *Somerfelt* on the Right, with Four entire Battalions, and a Detachment of Five Hundred Grenadiers, and Lieutenant-General *Fagell* on the Left, with the like Number, (with a competent Number of Workmen on Occasion) advanced on with undaunted Courage, Vigour and Fury, attack'd the Counterscarp, and instantly beat the Enemy out thereof, got into the Cover'd Way, pushing the Enemy before them, pass'd the Ditch, and mounted the Breach of the Citadel with incomparable Bravery; so that after one Hour's very hot and sharp Dispute, they beat the Enemy from off the Breach, and enter'd the Fort amongst them with Sword in Hand, killing all before them; and had killed all therein, had not the *French* instantly thrown down their Arms, and earnestly beg'd for Quarters, which our People soon after granted them, being always prone to give Mercy, where Need most requires; which being done, we possess'd the Place, and took therein the Governor

Lieutenant-

Lieutenant-General *Violaine*, the Duke *de Charost*, and the remaining Part of the Eight broken Battalions, Prisoners at Discretion.

Much of the Honour of this Action may be attributed to Lord *Cutts*'s good Conduct, in sending up speedily an Assistance of Twelve Hundred Men from the Ten Battallions in the Town, which suddenly rush'd in on the Side of the Citadel next to the City, in the very greatest Heat of the Action, before the Enemy was aware thereof, contrary to their Expectation; the which did very much surprize and daunt the Enemy, and made them quit the Breach much sooner than could have otherwise been expected: In all which the Duke's Presence, good Conduct, and necessary Orders was very aiding. But in the End of this glorious Victory a small Accident happen'd amongst us, *viz.* some of our own Men employing their small Arms after possess'd of the Place, gave Occasion to our Batteries to believe, that the Enemy had rallied again on the far Side of the Citadel; whereupon they throw'd in a whole Shower of Bombs at Random amongst us, which did very much surprize us, and the Prisoners; that we were hastily gathering together, till the Matter and Mistake was discover'd, and then they ceased. There was found in the Citadel Thirty-eight Cannon, and Nine fine Mortars of Brass, and great Store of Corn, Meal, Brandy, Wine, and all manner of necessary Provisions for their Army, and a great Quantity of Ammunition; besides a great Booty of Money in the Treasury, Thirty Thousand Florins of Gold and Silver, and Notes for One Million Two Hundred Thousand Florins on substantial Merchants at *Liege*, as good as Money, accounted above Two Months pay to their Army.

<small>Campaig.II.
Anno 1702.</small> In the gaining of this Victory, the *English* in particular had killed and wounded in all on the Attack, according to the following Table.

Their several STATIONS.	Killed.	Wounded.
Colonels	1	0
Lieutenant-Colonels	0	0
Majors	1	0
Captains	3	6
Subalterns	6	14
Centinels	143	360
Total —	154	380

Total kill'd and wounded — 534

The other Allies Loss on this Attack was computed equal to the *English*.

The Prince of *Hesse Cassel* went on Voluntier, and received no Hurt; Mr. *Wentworth*, Brother to Lord *Raby*, formerly Page to King *William*, was killed. The Enemies Loss in this Action was computed to double our Number.

<small>The Fort of the Chartreuse surrender'd.</small> *October* 18, About Eight in the Morning, General *Somerfelt*, with a great Detachment of the Army, with and without Arms, pass'd the *Maes*, and presently erected two small Batteries against the Low Fort, of Twelve Cannon and Eight Mortars. About Ten that Morning the Mortars began first to play against the Fort, and play'd very vigorously; so that in about two Hours after they set most of the Buildings thereof in Flames of Fire, and then the Cannon began smartly also to batter the Walls thereof for a grand Storm; so that the Dread thereof, and the Fate of the other, so terrified the Besieged, that they immediately beat a Parly to capitulate; whereupon Hostages were exchanged and Conditions were made, and the next Morning

Morning deliver'd up one of the Gates to the Allies.

20, In the Evening, according to their Conditions, they march'd out thereof with their small Arms, Colours flying, Drums beating, and two small Pieces of Cannon; and were conducted from thence by a Party of our Horse, by the Way of *Tongres*, *Vogelsank*, and *Herentals*, to *Antwerp*.

During this Siege against the Citadel and Low Fort of *Liege*, from the 1*st* to the 18*th* of *October*, the Besieged had upward of Twelve Hundred Men killed and wounded, and the remaining Part of Eight Battalions taken. The Besiegers in every respect, Officers included, about Twelve Hundred Sixty-eight killed and wounded.

23, The Duke of *Marlborough* having settled the Affairs of *Liege*, and a sufficient Garrison therein, dispers'd the Confederate Army from thence to their Winter-Quarters. The Lieutenant-Generals *Lumley* and *Churchill*, with our *British* Troops and Artillery, having march'd off apart, pitch'd and encamp'd near *Tongres*; and that Day the Duke and one of the States Deputies, Monsieur *Geldermalsel*, embark'd at *Liege* for *Holland*, and General *Obdam* with a small Convoy of a Lieutenant and Twenty-five Men aboard with them; besides, Monsieur *Coehorn* had Sixty Men in the Boat with him, for their better Security; who, the next Night about Twelve, their Boats being scatter'd, was surpriz'd, half Way between *Venlo* and *Grave*, by a skulking Party of Thirty-five *Frenchmen*, from their Garrison of *Gelder*, who seizing the Rope by which the Boat was drawn in which their Excellencies were, drew it ashore, and discharged their small Arms therein, and threw in also several Granades, by which some were wounded; and after having enter'd the Boat, examin'd several Passports, with-

out

out knowing the Duke, fearch'd the Trunks, and took what Plate they could find, and took his fmall Guard of Foot, and by Five in the Morning retired with their Booty; and the Duke proceeded from thence on his Voyage to the *Hague*, where he arrived on the 7*th* in the Evening, and had fome Conference with the States for the proceeding of the next Campaign; and from thence, on the 15*th* of *November*, he went for *England*, and on the 17*th* arrived at *Whitehall*. Each Place received him with a great deal of Joy.

Oct. 25, General *Lumley*, with our other Troops, decamp'd at *Tongres*, and march'd from thence and pitch'd Camp at *Suttendael*, three Leagues.

26, Decamp'd at *Suttendael*, and march'd from thence and encamp'd at *Peer*, fix Leagues.

27, Decamp'd at *Peer*, and march'd from thence and encamp'd at *Werchem-Weert*, feven Leagues; where we halted the next Day, having received the bad News that the Duke of *Marlborough* and two of the States were taken, but efcaped as aforefaid, which at firft furpriz'd us; and that Morning, by Break of Day, the Governor of *Venlo* march'd out with his whole Garrifon to inveft *Gelder*, &c.

29, Our Troops difpers'd from *Werchem-Weert* to their refpective Winter-Garrifons; and that Day the Generals *Lumley* and *Churchill*, with the Garrifon of *Breda* and Artillery, march'd off apart, and canton'd in *Oirfcot*, four Leagues.

30, Removed from *Oirfcot*, and canton'd in *Venlo opt Zandt*, four Leagues.

31, Removed from *Venlo opt Zandt*, and march'd into their Winter-Quarters in *Breda*, four Leagues.

The Campaign in 1702 began on the 9*th* of *March*, and ended on the 31*st* of *October*. It was in Length Thirty-one Weeks and Five Days; of which our Corps with the Grand Army, and apart,

march'd

march'd in all Forty Days, and therein One Hun- Campaig II. dred and Thirty-eight Leagues, or Four Hundred *Anno* 1702. and Fourteen Miles *English*. All other Marches of the Flying-Army's, or Besiegers, and other Parties, are not included in these Totals, nor in any of the like in the following Journals.

The End of the Second Campaign, A. D. 1702.

THE

THE
Third CAMPAIGN,

Begun on the 19th Day of April, 1703.

BUT before I can proceed with my Journal of this Campaign, I must speak a little of some Passages that happen'd before it begun, *viz.*

Rhineberg, which for some time before had been block'd up by Count *Lottum*, with a considerable Body of the *Prussian* Troops, the Governor thereof, Count *de Gramont*, surrender'd it up, on reasonable Terms, to Count *Lottum January* 29; and afterwards he block'd up *Gelder*, which also in a considerable Time after surrender'd.

His Grace the Duke of *Marlborough*'s necessary Presence being much wanted, and desired at the *Hague*, to concert Measures for the early opening of the Campaign on the Lower *Rhine* and *Maes*, by her Majesty Queen *Anne*'s Order he set out from *London* to the *Hague* on the 3d of *March*, and on the 6th he arrived there, and was met and complimented by Monsieur *Overquerque*, Generals *Dopf* and *Coeborn*, Lord *Paget*, and several Foreign Ministers; and the next Day all the General Officers dined with him: And on the 16th he set out from thence, in order to review the *English* Forces in their respective Garrisons; and from thence order'd

the

the Troops near *Liege* to be immediately in a Readi- Campaign
ness to take the Field, and also dispatch'd General III.
Coehorn to make all Preparations for the Siege of Anno 1703.
Bonne, which was first intended ; and *March* 22,
he return'd to the *Hague* ; and after some further
weighty Conferences with the Deputies of the State,
he went from thence on the 29*th* of *March* to *Nimeguen*, and there met General *Coehorn* ; and on the
31*st* Ditto set out for *Venlo*, and the next Day pass'd
through *Roermonde*, *Stevenswaert*, *Maeseyck*, and so
to *Maestricht*. He was received in all those Places
with great Respect, the Garrisons being drawn out
and Cannon discharged ; and on the 3*d* of *April* he
visited *Liege*, and had several Conferences with the
Governor Count *Zinzendorf* ; and return'd at Night
to *Maestricht*, having given his necessary Orders
every where how to act offensive and defensive, as
Occasion might require ; being fully resolved and
bent to open this Campaign with the Siege of
Bonne.

April 13, All necessary Preparations being made The Siege
for the expeditious carrying on of the Siege, Lieu- of *Bonne*.
tenant-General *Bulow*, with a considerable Body of
Prussian and *Lunenburg* Horse, block'd up *Bonne*
by the Duke's Orders, who himself commanded in
Chief at the Siege : The next Day he went to *Cologn*, whilst Lieutenant-General *Fagel*, with the
Foot for the Siege, were on their March thither,
and with General *Opdam* arrived that Night, and
encamp'd at *Kratsburg* ; where, on the 15*th*, Lieutenant-General *Coehorn* arrived with the heavy Train
and the Pontons by Water, and presently laid a
Bridge thereof over the *Rhine* at *Rhinsdorf*, from
the Besiegers Camp, ranged and extended as far
as *Kruitsburg* ; and the next Day the Siege was regularly form'd, and then the Besiegers consisted of
in all Forty Battalions of Foot, and Sixty Squadrons of Horse and Dragoons, and upwards of
One

Campaign III. Anno 1703. One Hundred large Cannon, and Thirty-six Mortars, with sufficient Pontons, and all other necessary Utensils of War conform, for the expeditious carrying on of the Siege. The Garrison in Town and Fort consisted of Eight Battalions of *French*, with Thirty-two Cannon and Eight Mortars mounted, with also all other Necessaries conform for the Defence of the Place; commanded in Chief by Marquis *D'Alegre*, a Lieutenant-General.

The Siege was carried on by three Attacks, and on each thereof Twelve Battalions: The first was commanded by Lieutenant-General *Coehorn*, and under him Major-General *Freisheim* and *Erbervelt*, with Monsieur *La Rocque* for Chief Engineer; the second by the Hereditary Prince of *Hesse-Cassel* and Major-General *Tettau*, with Monsieur *Hazard* as Chief Engineer; and the third by Lieutenant-General *Fagel*, and with him Major-General *Dedem* and *St. Paul*, with Colonel *Reinchard* for Chief Engineer.

The Siege being thus regulated, the besieging Army instantly begun making and bringing of Fascines, &c. for the expeditious carrying on of the Siege; after which, they gradually proceeded with all imaginable undaunted Courage, Vigour, Valour and Bravery; from which I will pass a little, and begin with the setting out of our Corps, and set down every thing most note-worthy as happen'd in our Journal, regularly, both here and elsewhere, according to the Tenour of my Introduction.

On the 19*th* Day of *April*, Lieutenant-General *Lumley* and *Churchill*, with the *British* Troops and Artillery, set out of their respective Garrisons; and that Day, at Night, they of the Garrison of *Breda*, with our Artillery, canton'd in and about *Longstraet*, four Leagues; and the rest about the same Distance from their respective Garrisons.

20, All removed from their several Cantonments, and march'd to and canton'd in and about *Oirfcct*, four Leagues.

21, All removed from their several Cantonments, and march'd from thence to, join'd, pitch'd, and encamp'd at *Hamont*, four Leagues; and then our *English* Corps consisted of Seven Regiments of Horse and Dragoons, and Fourteen Battalions of Foot, with Thirty-two Field Cannon, and Eight Mortars and Howitzers, with Twenty Pontons, &c.

22, At Night, the aforesaid Generals on the three Attacks, with a competent Number of Men, with and without Arms, open'd their Trenches against *Bonne* Town and Fort, with very good Success, and but little Loss, thro' the good Care and Conduct of their Generals and Engineers.

24, General *Lumley*, with our *British* Corps, decamp'd at *Hamont*, and march'd from thence to, and pitch'd Camp at *Ladner-Heath*, five Leagues.

25, Decamp'd at *Ladner*, and march'd to, and encamp'd at *Chateau D'Horn* near *Roermond*, five Leagues.

26, Decamp'd at *D'Horn*, and march'd to, and pitch'd Camp at *Maeseyck*, five Leagues; and there the Grey Dragoons rescued the Money that was taken coming up to the Army, from a Party of the Enemy that had surprized *Lumley*'s Horse, (thro' their great Negligence) to which they had been the Convoy.

27, At Break of Day, all the Batteries on the several Attacks against *Bonne* and the Fort being erected, and fully compleat, of upwards of Sixty-four Cannon and Twenty-four Mortars, begun to play, and play'd against them with a great deal of Vigour and Fury; so that thereby that Day they broke the Chain of the Flying Bridge, by which they cut off the Communication of the Fort from

Campaign III.
Anno 1703.

the Town; and the Bridge being ſtaved to pieces, was carried away by the Stream: And the next Day, the Battery which play'd againſt the Fort, made ſuch a Breach thereon, that the General deſign'd inſtantly to ſtorm it; but the *French* thinking themſelves not ſafe therein, fired the Cazerns, and retired into the Ravelin, in order to get into the Town; of which they were ſuddenly fruſtrated by the Beſiegers Diligence and Valour, who took the Governor of the Fort and Thirty of his Men Priſoners; being all that was left thereof, but what was either kill'd or drown'd. A little before the gaining of the Fort an Accident happen'd on *Dedem*'s or *Fagel*'s Attack; One Hundred and Fifty Bombs and a Hundred and Fifty Granades unfortunately took Fire, and were blown up, with a Lieutenant and five Bombardiers; nevertheleſs, it hinder'd not the Progreſs of the Beſiegers Attack, in making themſelves Maſters of the Fort and Ravelin, which afterwards was very ſerviceable. Now our Forces in *Brabant* being about to make a General Rendezvous at *Maeſtricht* under Monſieur *Overquerque*, till the Duke had made an End of the ſaid Siege, and the *French* Army in *Brabant* under Marſhal *Villeroy*, already in the Field, I muſt wave the Siege a little, and take each in their Turn.

April 27, At Taptoo, the Generals *Lumley* and *Churchill* having Intelligence that *Villeroy*, with the *French* Army, was in Motion to get between our Corps and *Maeſtricht*; we thereupon immediately decamp'd, and march'd off from *Maeſeyck*, on great Expedition, towards *Maeſtricht*; where, the next Day about Noon, we arrived ſafe, and pitch'd Camp in the Cover thereof, in and about the Outworks, with ſome *Holland*'s Troops in Monſieur *Overquerque* and General *Dopf*'s Command; and then we conſiſted of in all Thirty-two Battalions and Fifty-two Squadrons, with Ordnance conform;

and

and so put a Stop to *Villeroy*'s Enterprize, whose Army was then computed to consist of Sixty-four Battalions of Foot, and One Huudred and Twenty Squadrons of Horse and Dragoons, with Ordnance and all other necessary Utensils of War conform: But Forty Thousand Men, who the next Day (the 28*th*) advanced upon *Tongres*, where Two Battalions lay, *viz. Hepburn*'s and *Elst*; and to vent their Fury, fell thereon; and, after about twenty-four Hours brave Resistance, they forced them to yield at Discretion; it being in a manner open and of little Strength.

<small>Campaign III. Anno 1703. Two Battalions taken at *Tongres*.</small>

29, *Villeroy*'s Project being thus stifled, and his Courage cool'd, to tempt him farther, Marshal *Overquerque* advanced his small Army a little from the Out-works of the Town, and regularly ranged and pitch'd his Camp across the rising Ground between the Citadel on our Left, and *Haut Chateau* on our Right, facing outwards under Cover of the City and Citadel.

30, The aforesaid Besiegers of *Bonne* erected and compleated on the aforesaid Fort, against the main Counterscarp and Town-Walls, two great Batteries, the one of Seventy Cannon, and the other of Eighteen Mortars; in order to make two grand Breaches, for a sudden and general Grand Storm thereon, from the Prince of *Hesse*'s and *Dedem*'s Attack; which on *May* 1, by Break of Day, begun to play, and play'd very furiously all Day; which so terrified the Besieged, that next Day about Noon One Thousand of their Foot, and all their Horse and Dragoons, boldly sally'd out on *Dedem*'s Attack, who at first put the Cover of the Trenches in some Disorder; but soon recovering themselves, they furiously beat the Enemy, and repuls'd them back to their former Lodgements, with the Loss of about One Hundred Men killed on each Side, and some Prisoners taken on both Sides:

<small>The Siege of *Bonne* continued.</small>

<small>Campaign III.
Anno 1703.</small>

And that same Day, about Eight at Night, the Prince of *Hesse* with a competent Number, with Major-General *Tettau* and Brigadier *Palandt*, vigorously attack'd the Counterscarp, seconded by a continued Fire, from the Cannon and Mortars of their several Attacks, drove the Enemy from their Works, and lodged themselves thereon.

In this Action General *Tettau* was wounded, with about Ten other Officers, and One Hundred and Fifty Soldiers killed and wounded, with the Engineer that commanded in the Works. This so much Bravery of the Besiegers, and amazing Tempest of artificial Thunder and Lightning, astonish'd and terrified the Besieged to that Degree, that, fearing another Assault, they next Day beat a Par- *Bonne* sur- ly, and on honourable Conditions surrender'd the render'd. Place on the 3d of *May*, sign'd by the Duke of *Marlborough* and Marquis *D'Alegre*; the Duke being very earnest to put his Projects in Effect in *Brabant*.

May 5, The Besieged march'd out, and was conducted to their upward Garrisons.

During this Siege against *Bonne*, of three Weeks, begun on the 13th of *April*, and ended the 3d of *May*, the Besieged had upwards of Eight Hundred and Sixty killed and wounded, &c. the Besiegers not Six Hundred, Officers included.

4, At Break of Day, *Villeroy* with the *French* Grand Army advanced from *Tongres*; and about Seven, their Front appear'd in Battle-Array on *Duysburg-Hill*, in full Design to attack the small Army under Monsieur *Overquerque* at *Maestricht*, before the Duke's Arrival thereat from *Bonne* and elsewhere, with some more Troops, that Siege being then over; of which Monsieur *Overquerque* being somewhat aware, immediately put the Troops under Arms, and advanced out therewith a little in the Front of our Encampment, and in a Trice form'd form'd in Two Lines, in order for Battle: Our Foot in the First or Front Line, and our Horse and Dragoons in the Second or Rear Line, with most thereof on the Right Wing of our Foot, extended to *Lonaken*, in which a Brigade of *English* Foot was posted, to secure that Flank, in the Wood, Hedges, and Scrub; and a Regiment of Dragoons near that Church, to sustain One Hundred and Fifty Foot posted in the Church-yard to defend the Pass from the Heath of *Beesemer*, with our Left Wing extended cross that Rising-Ground near unto the Citadel, on the same Ground where the Enemy thought to have first posted themselves; and at the same time, when form'd, a running Trench was cast up in our Front, by One Hundred and Twenty Men of each Battalion, with some Field Cannon, before the Enemies entire Arrival; which put *Villeroy* and *Boufflers* with their Army to such a sudden Stand and Consternation, that they knew not well what to do; for indeed wheresoever they bent their Strength, our Generals with great Care doubled their Opposition. About Ten they made a general Motion to attack us; whereupon several of their Brigades of Foot advanced down a little in two Columns, between *Duysburg-Hill* and *Veltwesel* Village: but when come within Reach of our Cannon, they and their main Body made a Halt, the Brigades stretching their Right towards *Duysburg* and behind *Veltwesel*, receiving the Salutation of four Pieces of Cannon from our Trenches, and of several others from the Citadel on their Right Wing, which made them fall back out of the Reach thereof: And thus both Armies stood gazing at each other till about Three or Four o'Clock in the Afternoon; and then the Two Marshals finding all their Projects and Motions to no Effect, but only gasconading for their Pains, they retired with their Army the Way they came from

Campaign III. Anno 1703. to *Tongres*, leaving us the Honour of the Day; who immediately after fell back from our Entrenchment to our former Camp Ground, leaving some small Guards in the Line to be very alert, and wait the Enemies Motion, in case they should have made a second Attempt. On this Action or Gasconade, there was no Mention of any Loss on either Side.

This great Piece of Prudence, Experience and Valour of Monsieur *Overquerque*'s contributed much to the Preservation of the Confederate Army from total Ruin, being then weak and much scatter'd, &c.

May 6, The Duke of *Marlborough* having settled the Affairs and a sufficient Garrison in *Bonne*, arrived with several of the besieging Troops in our Camp between *Haut* and *Maestricht*, and also several other Troops join'd us; and then our Army consisted of Sixty-six Battalions and One Hundred and Thirty-six Squadrons, (including Seven Battalions and Six Squadrons of *Dutch* that soon after join'd) with Eighty-eight Cannon, Twenty Mortars and Howitzers, and Forty-four Pontons, with also all other necessary Utensils of War conform; then nigh equal to the Enemy, who lay at *Tongres*, and was computed to consist of Seventy Battalions and One Hundred and Forty Squadrons, with upwards of Eighty Cannon, Twenty Mortars, and Thirty-two Pontons, &c. who then begun to look about them, more for retreating and acting the defensive Part, than for advancing and acting the offensive Part in battling; all their early Projects that Year being quite blasted, and vanish'd as a Dream; having projected to open the Campaign with the Siege of *Liege* on the 29th of *April*, for which they had provided Fifteen Thousand Pioneers, and Three Thousand Waggons, &c.

8, Our

8, Our Army had a *Feu-de-joye* for the taking of *Bonne*.

11, The Duke of *Marlborough* and Monsieur *Overquerque* review'd the whole Army; and in this Campaign used all the Stratagems and visible Means imaginable to draw *Villeroy* and *Boufflers*, with the *French* Army, to Battle; but could not prevail, they still keeping within Reach and Cover of their *Brabant*'s Line, but made several Gasconades to give us Battle, Courage failing them when it came to the Push; of which more afterwards in its Turn.

13, The Duke of *Marlborough*, at Taptoo, sent our Quarter-Master-General with all our Colours, under the Cover of the Picquet of our Army, Leftward towards *Liege*, in order to take up new Ground for a fresh Camp at *Hautin*, where they arrived the next Morning by Break of Day, and pitch'd our Camp, and prevented the Enemy of the Intention of foraging there that Morning.

14, The Duke with the whole Army decamp'd between *Haut* and *Maestricht* about Sun-rising, and march'd after our Quarter-Colours and Picquet over the *Jecker*, and about Noon pitch'd Camp at *Hautin*, two Leagues; at which Advance the Enemy removed somewhat backward, and continued under Arms all Night, being apprehensive of our Armies forcing them to Battle.

15, We decamp'd at *Hautin*, and march'd to, and pitch'd Camp at *New Dorp*, one League; and the Enemy with great Precipitation march'd to *Borchworm*, not daring to hazard a Battle; they also quitted *Tongres*.

19, We decamp'd at *New Dorp*, and march'd to, and pitch'd Camp between *Lamin* and *Thys*, two Leagues; at which Time we advanced thitherward, the *French* drew up in order of Battle, and sent away their Baggage on that Intent; but Courage fail'd them once more, and so retired within their Lines at *Hanuye*; and that Day they quitted *Tongres* they first blew up the Walls and Tower. The Duke advanced after them within half a League of their Camp, but the *Jecker* parted the two Armies, and the Enemy secured all the Bridges and Passes thereof; nevertheless, thinking themselves not secure there, they retired from *Hanuye*, as aforesaid, and pitch'd between *Latremenge* and *Hiers*.

May 25, Our Army decamp'd at *Thys*, and march'd to, and pitch'd Camp at *Hanuye*, two Leagues, on the East-Side of the little River *Eury*; over which, soon after, our Army made several Bridges, and a Feint to advance over the same that nighest Way, to attack the Enemies Entrenchment, with great Batteries thereon, at *Opher*, where they then lay, near *Huy*, for its Security, about two Leagues in the Front of our Camp, where our Generals full Design then lay to besiege; whereas they, who before our Army join'd, were much projecting the gaining of Ground, now begun to lose it apace.

June 11, The Duke and Monsieur *Overqverque* review'd the Rear-Line of our Army.

15, Review'd the Front-Line, and held a Consultation either to remove the Enemy from *Huy*, by marching round that Way, or else to get beween them and *Antwerp*, or draw them to Battle; the Allies and also the *French* having then on that Side each two Flying-Armies, by which some great Feats were done to Admiration.

First, Generals *Coehorn* and *Spaar* lay in the Country of *Waes*, with a Body of Seven Battalions and Twenty Squadrons, with Ordnance conform, besides *Coehorn*'s Detachment of Two Thousand Five Hundred, in Opposition of General *La Motte*, with Fourteen Battalions, and Four Regiments of Horse and Dragoons, and Six Thousand Militia, &c.

Second,

Second, Generals *Obdam* and *Slangenberg* lay between Eckeren and *Outeren*, with a Body of Thirteen Battalions and Twenty-six Squadrons, with Ordnance conform, in Opposition to the Marquis of *Bedmar*, with Thirty-three Battalions and Thirty-two Squadrons, &c. These separate Bodies of the Enemy on that Side lay very alert for the Defence of their Line, in order to be succoured by their Grand Army. Those of the Allies, as aforesaid, although much inferior, made several Motions for an Inlet for themselves and our Grand Army, which was on their March with great Expedition to sustain them.

16, About Two in the Morning, our Grand Army decamp'd at *Hanuye*, and repass'd the *Jecker*, (where *Hamilton*'s Brigade had cover'd the laying over our Tin-Boats the Night before). At Taptoo our Right Wing march'd and pitch'd Camp at *Borckloen*, on the little River *Herck*. About this Time Generals *Coehorn* and *Spaar* had very good Success in *Waes*: First *Coehorn*, with a Detachment of but Two Thousand Five Hundred Men, pass'd the *Scheld*, made an Attack on a Place called the Fort *Van Callo*, and with little Resistance took the Redout called *St. Antonio*, and the *Pearl* Fort, on the Enemies Entrenchments; but General *Spaar*, with but Seven Battalions, on the second Attack near *Steken* Village, met with much greater Opposition from Count *La Motte*, with Eight Regular Battalions and Six Thousand Militia, who made a much more vigorous Defence than the disciplin'd Troops, by firing from the Houses of the Village after they had enter'd the Line, which much annoy'd and destroy'd many of *Spaar*'s Men; whereupon he order'd that no Quarters should be given them.

In this glorious Action, of General *Spaar*'s Detachment Twelve Hundred Men were killed and wounded, among whom there were several Officers

Campaign III.
Anno 1703.

of Note, particularly Monsieur *De Vaſſey*, Governor of *Saſ-van-Ghent* killed, two Brigadiers wounded, one Colonel killed and one wounded, two Lieutenant-Colonels, two Majors, and twelve Captains killed and wounded, and several other Officers, &c. The Enemies Loss was great, besides eighty Men made Prisoners.

June 19, About Three o'Clock in the Afternoon, our other separate Body in General *Obdam*'s and *Slangenburg*'s Command, between *Eckeren* and *Outeren* was vigorously attack'd by Marquis *Bedmar* with Thirty-three Battalions, Thirty-two Squadrons, and Forty-seven Companies of Grenadiers, being assisted by General *Bouffler* and Prince *Tſerclas*, with Thirty Squadrons and Thirty Companies of Grenadiers from *Villeroy*'s Grand Camp, in several Places at once, on each Side of their Camp. The Dispute in short continued very smart of sharp Assaults and Repulses from Three till dark Night, too tedious for me fully to relate, and then oblig'd the Enemy to retire; and the next Morning, at Break of Day, General *Slangenburg*, then with the Confederate Troops in Command, march'd from *Outeren* to *Lillo*, General *Obdam* being missing, who in the beginning of the Action fled with only Thirty Horse to *Breda*. General *Hompesch* commanded the Horse on the Right Wing, and General *Fagel* on the Left; and all in general behaved with all the undaunted Bravery imaginable. The Enemy at first took Four of the Allies Cannon, but soon forced to quit them. The Night before the Action the Allies sent all their heavy Baggage to *Bergen-op-Zoom*.

In this glorious and praise-worthy Action of the Allies, General *Fagel* received two Wounds, one Colonel was killed, and two wounded; several other Officers of Distinction, and upwards of Two Thousand killed and wounded. But the *French* report,

port, that the Allies had Four Thousand killed on the Spot, and abandon'd the Field and wounded; and that they took Five Hundred Prisoners, Six Cannon, Forty-four Mortars, and One Hundred and Fifty Waggons of Ammunition and Provision, and many Colours and Drums.

Campaign III. Anno 1703.

Of the *French* One Thousand were killed, and Eight Hundred wounded, whose just Number was not given. Took of them one Colonel, one Lieutenant-Colonel, many other Officers, and about one Hundred Centinels, one Cannon, and some Ammunition; several Pair of Kettle-Drums, two Standards of their *Gens d'Arms*, and some Colours. By the *French* Account they consisted of Thirty Thousand effective Men, and the Allies but Ten Thousand, yet maintain'd the Field, and had a Reinforcement that Night of several Battalions from *Coehorn*'s Camp.

Those Actions happen'd some few Days before our Grand Armies Arrival on that Side; otherwise, I do believe that we should have made a grand Entrance into *Flanders* much sooner than we did.

19, Our Grand Army decamp'd at *Borchloen* by Break of Day, and march'd from thence a tedious Road, most but in one Line, towards *Haffel*, on the Little River *Demmer*, near unto which our Army arrived about Twelve o'Clock at Night, and thereby halted in the Road on our Arms till the next Day (the 20th) about Noon, four Leagues; and then our Army removed from thence, and cross'd over the *Demmer* at *Haffel in the Marsh*; and about the Sun-setting of that Day pitch'd and encamp'd between *Outhalen* and *Zonoven*, two Leagues.

22, Decamp'd at *Outhalen*, and march'd to, and pitch'd Camp between *Balen* and *Moll*, five Leagues.

June

Campaign III.
Anno 1703.

June 23, Decamp'd at *Balen*, and march'd to, and pitch'd Camp between *Kaſtierle* and *Thielen*, four Leagues.

26, Our Army decamp'd at *Kaſtierle*, and march'd to, and pitch'd Camp at *Bavin* near *Turnhout*, two Leagues.

July 10, At Taptoo, the Duke and Monſieur *Overquerque* detach'd the Quarter-Maſter-General and Quarter-Colours, under the Cover of the Picquet of our Army, and advanced Rightward towards *Hoogſtraeten*, in order to pitch out Ground for a freſh Camp, but firſt, and moſt to ſee if the *French* Army would advance thereon, and thereby to draw them from their *Brabant* Line to give us Battle, which they had promiſed the Duke ſome few Days before; and therefore the next Morning, about Three of the Clock, the Duke decamp'd with our Army at *Bavin*, and advanced after our Picquet thitherward, in very good Order for Battle, in ſeveral Columns, to *Hoogſtraeten*, to ſee if *Villeroy* would be as good as his Word, within about half a League of their Camp, to which they had advanced from their Line the Day before, and was in a Motion in good Earneſt, preparing to give us Battle, as we expected; for which we alſo made ready and formed; but we could not prevail that Day, the Enemy being more ready to retreat than to fight, yet kept their Ground; and our Army pitch'd Camp on theirs, on the Plain between *Hoogſtraeten* and *Emitt*, two Leagues.

12, By Break of Day, our Army again formed in Lines of Battle, and advanced nearer to the Enemy, in order thereunto, or to ſlip in between them and *Antwerp*; and at the ſame time General *Slangenburg*, with Eight Battalions and Twelve Squadrons of the aforeſaid Troops from *Lillo*; who early that Morning, after marching all Night, having poſted himſelf betweeen *Eckeren* and *Capelle*,
had

had the Signal of Four Pieces of Cannon fired by the Duke's Order, to begin the first Onset or Attack on the Enemy; and he himself at the same Time, with the main Body of our Army, on the Plain over-against the main Body of the Enemy, was also ready and fully bent to attack them; but all in vain: for at the very full Appearance of our Design to attack, *Villeroy* having no Orders from Court to fight, nor willing to risque the Hazard of a Battle, set Fire to his Camp, and fell back; and with great Precipitation retired within their Lines and Entrenchments, and covering the City of *Antwerp*, and throwing it exactly in their Rear, and so baulk'd the Duke of his Design and Expectation; who himself, with several other General Officers, and a Detachment of Four Thousand Horse, closed after to view their Lines and Entrenchments; and at the same time a Lieutenant and Thirty of our Royal Dragoons attack'd a Party of an Out-Guard of Forty Horse of the Enemy, who at the first Charge retired to the Barrier of their Entrenchment; by which the Duke and other Generals had an Opportunity to view their Lines within Musket-shot thereof: And from that Time the Duke laid a Scheme to force them, but the Execution of that Project from Time to Time was industriously put off by the Deputies of the States-General. The Duke seeing it impossible to draw *Villeroy* to a Battle, or to get between them and *Antwerp*, fell our Army a little backward, and rang'd and pitch'd Camp on the Plain between *Vlimmeren* and *Vorselar*, three Leagues; and since no Battle could be had, he concerted fresh Projects to end this Campaign with besieging *Huy* and *Limburg*. About this Time *Guelders* was bombarded, capitulated, and surrender'd to Count *Lottum*, with the *Prussian* Troops (many Men becoming Victims to their Imprudence, &c.)

July

Campaign III. *Anno* 1703.

July 15, The Duke and Monsieur *Overquerque* again review'd the Army at the Head of their Encampment.

21, General *Slangenburg*, with the aforesaid Troops, fell into their Post in the Army.

23, The Duke, in order to invest *Huy*, decamp'd with our Army at *Vlimmeren*, and march'd backward, or Leftward from thence, our two former (as next followeth) Days March thither in one, and repitch'd Camp between *Balen* and *Moll*, five Leagues; and thereby getting the Start of *Villeroy*, put them off from *Huy*, and soon after accomplish'd his Design thereon.

24, Our Army decamp'd from *Balen*, and march'd from thence, also the other two former Days March, in one; and again repitch'd Camp between *Outbalen* and *Zonoven*, six Leagues.

25, Decamp'd at *Outbalen*, march'd from thence, recross'd the River *Demmer* at *Hassel*, and pitch'd Camp between *Borckloen* and *Aelst*; the one on the River *Herck*, and the other on the *Jaez*, six Leagues.

August 2, Decamp'd at *Borckloen*, and march'd to, and pitch'd Camp at *Oerle*, three Leagues, and demolish'd all the Entrenchments thereabouts which the *French* Army had made, for fear of being attack'd by our Army, in the Time we lay at *Hanuye*, when we made Bridges over the little *Urroy*, in the Front of our Army; a Feint, as if design'd to attack them, but our main Design was to draw them to Battle, otherwise as aforesaid.

3, Decamp'd at *Oerle*, and march'd from thence to, and pitch'd Camp at *Tourine*, three Leagues; and the same Day Count *Noyelles*, with Thirty Squadrons of Horse and Dragoons from our Grand Army, block'd up *Huy* Town and Castle, and two Forts, *St. Joseph* and *Picard*; in which there was in all Two Battalions of *French*, accounted Nine
Hundred

Hundred Men, with Twenty mounted Cannon and Four Mortars, commanded by Major-General *Melun* and two Brigadiers; who, at the firſt of Count *Noyelles* Appearance thitherward, broke down the Bridge between the two Towns, and wholly retired with his Garriſon into the Caſtle and two Forts, and another little one called the *Rouge*, or Red Fort, and left the North-Side of the Town to the Allies.

Campaign III. Anno 1703.

4, The Duke decamp'd with our Grand Army at *Tourine*, and march'd to, and pitch'd Camp at *Valnotredame* near *Huy*, three Leagues, and cover'd the Siege to the End of it; the which next Day was begun by Prince *Anhault* and Brigadier *Hamilton*, with Twenty-four Battalions and Forty-two Squadrons, including the Thirty Squadrons which *Noyelles* was detach'd with thereto *Auguſt* 2, aſſiſted by our whole Army; at which all the reſt of our Army-Artillery were made uſe of, and all for the quick Diſpatch of the Siege, begun by two Attacks and ended in one, *viz.* Prince *Anhault* againſt *Joſeph*'s Fort, and Brigadier *Hamilton* againſt *Picard* Fort, and both ended againſt the Caſtle.

The Siege of Huy.

5 and 6, The Beſiegers, and alſo our Grand Army, were buſily employ'd in making and bringing of Faſcines, *&c.* of the like Kind, for the expeditious carrying on of the ſaid Siege, that the ſooner *Limburg* might alſo be beſieged, or elſe ſome more renowned Victory obtain'd.

6, At Night, Prince *Anhault* and Brigadier *Hamilton*, with a competent Number of the Beſiegers, with and without Arms, open'd the Trenches on both the aforeſaid Attacks; that againſt Fort *Joſeph* was carried on about Two Hundred Paces very regular; but the Engineer againſt Fort *Picard*, by reaſon of the Darkneſs of the Night, fell into a hollow Way, which carried them off from the ſaid Fort; ſo that it was defer'd on that Side till the next

Campaign III. Anno 1703.

next Night, the 7*th*; and afterward both went on very regular and conformable, with little Loss.

August 9, The heavy battering Train arrived at the Siege from *Maestricht*.

10, About Eight in the Morning, the Besiegers several Batteries on both Attacks being all erected and full compleated, in order to play against the Castle and three Forts, some thereof began, and threw several Bombs into the Enemies Works; and the next Morning, all thereof consisting of Forty Cannon and Sixteen Mortars, began about Seven, and fired very smart against these four several Places till past Three in the Afternoon; which so terrified those in the three Forts, consisting of Two Hundred Men, that they beat a Parly; 1*st*, Fort *Joseph*; 2*d*, Fort *Picard*; and 3*d*, the *Redout*, or Red Fort; all seated very high on the South and South-West of the *Maes*, Town and Castle; and at Seven that Evening desired to be admitted to retire to *Namur*, with their Arms and Baggage; but the Duke would not grant nor allow them any other Terms, than to be Prisoners at Discretion, or to retire into the Castle, and to take their Fate with the rest; and at the last the continued Fire of our Batteries obliged them to abandon the Forts, and that after the third Round thereof; of which the Besiegers immediately took Possession, and they retired to the Castle for Succour, into which the Governor thereof, Monsieur *Melun*, would not admit them to come, and therefore made into the Town, where they were immediately seiz'd, disarm'd, and made Prisoners at Discretion. The Besiegers, after first opening of their Trenches, made themselves Masters, and had taken full Possession, of the Town; it not being able to stand a Siege, being mostly open; after which, the remaining Part of the Siege went on very regularly and smartly wholly against the Castle; all the Batteries

teries that had been raised against the Forts were removed, and the two Attacks made into one Grand Attack against the Castle; all which, for the three Days following, play'd very furiously against it, in order for a general Grand Storm thereon as soon as possible.

Campaign III. Anno 1703.

14, All the Forenoon, and most Part of the Afternoon, the Besiegers several Batteries play'd more furiously and vigorously against the Castle than at any Time before; and thereby swept from the Castle upwards of One Hundred of the Enemy, and wounded the Governor; and several other of their Officers were besides killed and wounded, by the violent firing of our Batteries without Intermission. In the Afternoon, the Disposition being made for a Grand Attack, the Besiegers advanced, and laid several Ladders at the Foot of the Castle, which was only design'd for a Feint; nevertheless, the Fear and Dread of all thereof so terrified the Governor and his Besieged, that they beat a Parly about Six that Afternoon to surrender, on Conditions to march out to *Namur*, with the usual Marks of Honour; but the Duke would only allow the Officers and Soldiers to keep all that belong'd to them, and to lay down their Arms, and to be exchanged for the like Number of Men, when *Villeroy* should desire it, and to be allow'd till Three the next Morning to send a positive Answer. But upon the Governor's Refusal of these Terms, by the Duke's Orders the Besiegers again renewed their Assaults, and that very vigorously; whereupon, the Garrison refusing to defend the Place any longer, the Governor freely embraced the Duke's Proffer, and submitted, with himself and the two Brigadiers, and Nine Hundred Men, including those that had left the Forts, to remain Prisoners of War, till the two Regiments taken by their Army at *Tongres*

Tongres in the beginning of that Campaign were released, Man for Man.

Aug. 16, In the Morning, the Garrison march'd out of the Castle, and were all disarm'd, except the Officers, whom the Duke, out of a generous Compliment, allow'd to keep their Swords; and from thence they were conducted, by a Convoy of our Horse, to *Namur*.

During this Fourteen Days Siege against *Huy*, commenced the 2d and ended the 15th of *August*, the Besieged had upwards of Two Hundred Men killed and wounded, Officers included; and the Besiegers in all, Officers included, not above Sixty killed and wounded.

The Day before this Siege was over, the Duke's brave, heroical, warlike Spirit, (being ever fully bent for the Honour of his Country, and to the Grand Allies Honour and Gain) was still very eagerly desirous to force or draw the *French* Army to Battle; whereby he hoped, (with the Help of God) with the Allies Army under his Command, to gain more Honour and Ground by one Battle (and that with less Loss) than could be expected to be gain'd by besieging in a whole Year. A grand Council of War was held at *Val-notre-dame* Camp, to decide the Question in Debate, what should next be undertaken after *Huy*; wherein were present the Duke, the Deputies of the States-General, Monsieur *de Overquerque*, Monsieur *de Slangenburg*, the Lieutenant-Generals, and several Major-Generals. The Siege of *Limbourg* being proposed, these Generals here mention'd gave the following Opinion, rather for attacking the Enemies Line between *Mahaigne* and *Leuwe*, as an Enterprize that would contribute much more to the Glory and Advantage of the Armies of the High Allies; and that *Limbourg* might be attack'd by a Detachment when the Season was more advanced, *viz.*

I. " The

I. "The Enemy having great Magazines at
" *Namur*, for the Subſiſtance of their Army, and
" we being, by our Superiority in Number, in a
" Condition to give them Umbrage on that Side,
" they will be obliged, after that we are poſſeſs'd
" of *Huy*, to put a Garriſon into that Place for
" the Security of their Magazines; our Superiority
" then being ſo much the greater, and they will
" be the leſs able to oppoſe our Efforts."

II. "We having here a level Ground before us,
" of above two Leagues and a half in Extent,
" where the Enemies Lines are weakeſt, it ſeems
" to be the only Place where we ſhould chuſe to
" attack them; and ſeeing our whole Army may
" act, it is to be believed, if the Enemy ſhould
" ſtand us, it would be impoſſible for them to de-
" fend ſuch an Extent."

III. "In caſe they ſhould venture an Engage-
" ment with us, ſeeing it is what we have been
" ſeeking all this Campaign, we are of Opinion,
" we ought gladly to embrace the Occaſion, be-
" cauſe we have a greater Superiority at this Time
" than ever."

IV. "If we do not attack the Enemy in this
" Place, with the fineſt Troops that can be ſeen,
" and ſuch a Superiority as we cannot expect to
" have next Year, it will be evident not only to
" the Allies (to their great Diſcouragement), but
" the Enemy with Reaſon boaſt that theſe Lines,
" which they will make ſtronger every Day, are
" an invincible Barrier againſt the Troops of the
" Allies."

V. "In caſe we do not attack the Lines, there
" is no other Courſe to be taken, than either to
" retire to the other Side of the *Maes*, or to march
" away to the Right, to be near to the Mayory of
" *Bois-le-Duc*, there being no Forage left in theſe
" Parts: The firſt would be diſhonourable to the
" Army

Campaign III. Anno 1703.

"Army of the Allies, for the getting the River between them and the Enemy would look as if they durst not stand them; and the latter might be very dangerous to the State: And besides, the Enemy, by Means of their Magazines, would be in a Condition to undertake any thing; whereas, if we attempted their Lines, should they pretend to defend them, we may, with the Assistance of the Almighty, hope to gain a compleat Victory, the Consequence of which may be of more Importance than can be foreseen; and should they think best to retire, there is Ground to hope we might push forward very successfully, and draw mighty Advantages from it."

VI. "We consider likewise the Enemy being more superior in *Italy* and in the Empire, and being out-number'd no where but here; the Eyes of all the Allies are fixed upon us, and they will have Cause justly to blame our Conduct, if we do not do all that is possible to relieve them, by obliging the Enemy to call back Succours into these Parts, which is not to be done, but by pushing boldly."

Sign'd by his GRACE.

Generals of the ENGLISH, { *Cha. Churchill, Cutts,* and *H. Lumley.*

DANES, { *Cha. Rudolph,* Duke of *Wirtenberg,* and *J. Scholten.*

LUNENBERGHERS, { *C. Somerfelt, M. Bulow, Ernest August,* Duke of *Brunswick,* and Count *Noyelles.*

HESSIANS, { *Frederick* Prince of *Hesse, Spiegel de Liesenberg,* and *A. Van Tettau.*

These Reasons were opposed by the Deputies of the States and the *Dutch* Generals, who would not consent content to hazard their Troops in Action, which they say at best was very dubious, and which, if attended with Success, would yield no farther Advantage, than to find the Enemy retired into their fortified Towns; whereas, on the contrary, should the *French* get the Victory, the United Provinces would remain exposed to their Incursions: Thereupon the Project of attacking their Lines was laid aside, and the Resolution taken to besiege *Limbourg*. Notwithstanding the Vogue on the Deputies of the States-Generals Side carried their Opinion, it was agreed upon by all, that first a faint Attempt should be made on the Lines, and afterwards to proceed to the said Siege as soon and regularly as possible.

Aug. 25, By Break of Day, the Duke and *Overquerque* having settled the Affairs of *Huy*, and given their necessary Directions for repairing all the Breaches thereof, they decamp'd at *Val-noire-dame*, with the Grand Army and the Besiegers, and march'd from thence to, and pitch'd Camp at *Hanuye*, within about two Leagues of the *French* Grand Camp, where they then lay in their Entrenchments, on the Inside of that Part of their *Brabant* Line near *Arschot*, between *Mahaigne* and *Leuwe*, consisting of Seventy-four Battalions and One Hundred and Forty Squadrons, with upwards of One Hundred and Twenty Pieces of Cannon and Twenty-four Mortars mounted on their Entrenchment and Line in the Front; the Allies Army then consisting of Eighty Battalions and One Hundred Forty-two Squadrons, with Ordnance conform: And the same Day, as we enter'd our Camp, all our Horse and Dragoons were immediately employ'd in making and bringing Fascines, &c. as if fully design'd to attack the Enemy in their Entrenchments; and at the same time the Duke, and several other Generals under the Cover

(72)

Campaign III. Anno 1703. of Forty Squadrons, advanced a little out in the Front of our Encampment, within almost Cannon-shot of the Enemies Line, reconnoitring and viewing their strong Situation; which put the Enemy in so great a Hurry, that they immediately mann'd their Line, expecting nothing less than to be attack'd in good Earnest, to which the Duke could see no visible Possibility of Success, without running too great Risque; whereupon in the Evening he return'd to Camp, in order to put his other Projects in Execution; which was first to post the Army at *St. Tron*, and then proceed to the Siege of *Limbourg*, and to finish the Campaign therewith; for there could no Means be used, more than was used, to force or draw the Enemy to Battle in this Campaign, but could not, as before prescribed.

Aug. 26, Our whole Army decamp'd at *Hanuye* by Break of Day, and a little after march'd from thence Rearward, and pitch'd Camp at *St. Tron*, where lay and cover'd the Motions of the *French* Grand Army, during the said Siege after laid.

28, The Duke detach'd and sent off before, towards *Limbourg*, General *Bulau*, with Twenty-four Squadrons; and on the 30*th* he arrived thereat, and block'd it up, in which there was a Garrison in Town and Castle of Four Battalions, Twelve Cannon, and Four Mortars, mounted, and commanded by a *French* General.

The Siege of Limbourg. *Sept.* 1, The Duke with the Hereditary Prince of *Hesse Cassel*, and Fifteen Squadrons and Twenty-four Battalions of Foot, march'd off from our Camp at *St. Tron* after General *Boulau*, to the said Siege, in order to command the Siege himself, where he arrived two Days after, and then the besieging Army consisted of Twenty-four Battalions of Foot, and Thirty-nine Squadrons of Horse and Dragoons, with Ordnance conform, where it arrived

rived from *Liege* the 9th Inſtant, with alſo all other Neceſſaries for the expeditious Progreſs of the Siege, which was carried on indifferent regular, conſidering the Badneſs of the Weather, which made it ſomewhat the more difficult and tedious to the Beſiegers; who, the 10th, begun making and bringing what Faſcines, &c. they could, and us'd all poſſible Means for the quick Diſpatch of the Siege.

Campaign III. Anno 1703.

12, In the Morning, the Beſieged ſurrender'd up the Town to the Duke, and march'd into the Caſtle, in order to ſtand a Siege therein, and that ſame Night General *Boulau*, with a competent Number of the Beſiegers, with and without Arms, open'd their Trenches by one Attack againſt the Caſtle, with very little Loſs.

14, By Break of Day, their ſeveral Batteries being erected and compleated, conſiſting of Twenty-four Cannon and Eight Mortars, begun to play, and play'd very ſmart and vigorous, Day and Night, againſt the Caſtle, for a ſudden Grand Breach and general Grand Storm thereon, to the 16th, and made a large Breach for an Aſſault, for which the Beſiegers were then preparing that Morning; ſo that the Fear and Dread thereof ſo terrified the Beſieged, that they beat a Parly, and ſurrender'd Priſoners of War, in one Hour after the Parly, and deliver'd up the Gates in the Duſk, no more Time being allow'd them; and the Officers and Soldiers had their Baggage, and Twelve Waggons to carry it, being ſo agreed upon; and having laid down their Arms, they march'd out, and were conducted to *Namur* the next Day, conſiſting of Sixteen Hundred Men.

Limbourg ſurrender'd.

During this Siege againſt *Limbourg*, of Three Weeks, begun on the 28th of *Auguſt*, and ended the 16th of *September*, the Beſieged had but about Sixty killed and wounded, and Beſiegers not above One Hundred.

F 4

Campaign III. Anno 1703.

In a few Days after that the Duke had settled the Affairs of *Limbourg*, he return'd to our Grand Camp, which in his Absence was under Monsieur *Overquerque*'s Command, and had entrench'd on the Left, which lay open before, to prevent Surprize.

Sept. 24, General *Bulau*, with most of the aforesaid Besiegers, removed from thence towards our Grand Camp at *St. Tron*, where they soon after arrived; from which, soon after, each Corps of the Allies sent off an equal Number of Horse, Dragoons and Foot, in order to go over to *Spain* with King *Charles* III. for his Assistance on that Side: Those of the *English* were the Carabineers and *Raby*'s Dragoons, Sir *Matthew Bridges*'s, Lord *Barrymore*'s, who were afterwards join'd at *Comstat* and *Helversluyse* by *Portmore*'s, *Stewart*'s, &c. where they embark'd, the 20*th* of *November* following, One Regiment of Horse, Two of Dragoons, and Eleven of Foot, under General *Schomberg*'s Command, in Six War-Ships under Sir *Cloudesly Shovell*'s. About *Christmas* they came to Anchor at *Spithead*, and were join'd by some more Troops and Artillery; and in eight Days after set Sail from thence for *Spain*, and on the 9*th* of *March* following they disembark'd at *Lisbon*. (This tho' is superfluous to my Intention.)

30, About Two in the Morning, our Grand Army decamp'd and march'd off from *St. Tron* to, and about Twelve at Night pitch'd between *Tongres* and *Althoesfelt*, where at the same time some of the aforesaid Besiegers join'd, and took their Post in Camp; and the next Day all began Hutting to defend us from the Cold, which had then approached. But before we left *St. Tron*, the Duke went off from thence to *Dusseldorp*, to congratulate the King of *Spain*, *Charles* III, in our Queen's Name, who presented the Duke with a fine Sword, provided for him

him on purpose; from thence the Duke accompanied him to the *Hague*, where, with the States, he settled some important Affairs, and sent Orders to distribute the Forces into Winter-Quarters; and on the 19*th* of *October* he arrived in *England*.

October 12, Monsieur *Overquerque* sent off several of the Troops of the Allies from our Camp at *Althoesfelt*, to their Winter-Quarters, who had the farthest to go upwards on the *Rhine*; but the Body of our Army abode there eight Days longer, that they might enter their Winter-Quarters much about one and the same time.

20, Monsieur *Overquerque* dispers'd the rest of our Grand Army from our Camp between *Althoesfelt* and *Tongres* to their Winter-Quarters; and the same Day Generals *Lumley* and *Churchill*, with our *British* Troops and Artillery, march'd off by themselves from the other Corps's from thence to, and pitch'd Camp at *Suttendael*, four Leagues.

21, Decamp'd at *Suttendael*, and march'd to, and pitch'd Camp at *Peer*, six Leagues.

22, Decamp'd at *Peer*, march'd to, and pitch'd Camp at *Leende*, four Leagues.

23, Decamp'd at *Leende*, march'd to, and pitch'd Camp at *Falkenswaert* or *Wercumsweert*, four Leagues.

25, Our *British* Troops dispers'd from *Falkenswaert* to their respective Garrisons; and the same Day General *Lumley*, with the Garrison of *Breda* and Artillery, march'd off by themselves to, and canton'd that Night at *Oirscot*, four Leagues.

26, Remov'd from *Oirscot* to, and canton'd in *Venlo-op-Zandt*, four Leagues.

27, Remov'd from *Venlo-op-Zandt*, and march'd to their Winter-Quarters, or Garrison of *Breda*, four Leagues; and the same Day the last, or farthest to go, of our Corps enter'd also their respective Winter-Quarters or Garrisons.

The

Campaign III. Anno 1703. The Campaign in 1703 began on the 19*th* Day of *April*, and ended on the 27*th* Day of *October*. It was in Length Thirty Weeks and Three Days; in which our Corps, with the Grand Army, and apart, march'd in all Thirty-seven Days, and therein One Hundred and Thirty-four Leagues, or Four Hundred and Two Miles *English*.

The End of the Third Campaign, A. D. 1703.

THE
Fourth CAMPAIGN,

Begun on the 24*th Day of* April, 1704.

BEFORE I could proceed in the Journal of this Campaign, somewhat having intervened, I could not avoid speaking a little by the bye, *viz.* In brief, the Duke of *Marlborough* seeing and understanding what a deplorable State and Condition the Empire lay then in, by the Revolt of the Duke of *Bavaria* and Usurpation of *France*, who made daily great Havock thereof, projected its speedy Relief. At this Juncture his Presence was much wanted and requested at the *Hague*, for concerting those necessary important Matters, and others then in hand, for the common Cause and Good of *Europe*; and in order thereunto, he, on the 4*th* of *January*, embark'd for the *Hague*, where on the 7*th* he arrived, and was complimented by the publick Ministers and Persons of Quality, and had several Conferences with the Deputies of the States-General, of some very important but secret Affairs. He return'd from the *Hague* on the 31*st* of *January*, and arrived in *London* the 3*d* of *February*. This Project of his for relieving the Necessities of the Empire, by advancing with our Troops, and others sufficient thereunto, into the Heart of the Empire, was for a considerable Time kept secret

from

<small>Campaign IV.
Anno 1704.</small> from many, and disclosed but to very few, in whom he could most confide, till ready to put in Execution; and till then none of the Imperial Court knew what he had projected for their speedy Relief, altho' suing for it: And in order thereunto, he embark'd at *Harwich* about the Middle of *April*, with several other General Officers; and in two Days after he arrived at the *Hague*, and was again complimented, and had Conferences, as aforesaid, *April* the 12th, about what Measures he thought most proper for the ensuing Campaign; and sent Orders to the Troops in *Maestricht*, *Liege*, and the Neighbourhood thereof, to assemble and pitch Camp on the Rising-Ground at *Deloine* and *Hacour* Village, on the West-Side of *Maestricht*.

April 21, He had another Conference with the Deputies of the States-General, and publickly declared to them his Project, long before concerted, which he had only hinted at to some when before at the *Hague*, that his marching into *Germany* would most be conducive to the Advantage of the Grand Confederacy. They spent a whole Day in Consultation upon his Proposals; and the next Day he had a Conference with the States-Generals themselves, and Council of State, representing the Danger that threaten'd the whole Empire, and indeed all *Europe*, if a speedy Resistance were not given to the furious Career and Progress of the *French* and *Bavarians* in *Germany*; and being Masters of the *Maes* and *Spanish Guelderland*, a small Number of Forces were sufficient to secure their Frontiers; whereupon all other Operations of this Campaign was in this Conference happily adjusted. After which, on the 24th of *April*, he set out from the *Hague*; 27th arrived at *Roermonde*, giving Orders to the *English* Troops, and others posted thereabouts, to join and march towards *Coblentz*; and in two Days after he went to *Maestricht* and review'd
the

the *Dutch* Army, where they had affembled fome time before; of which more afterwards. From which Digreffion I pafs to my Journal, with each in their Courfe. This Journey and Campaign being intended to be in *Germany*, as aforefaid, and the Duke being defirous, before he fet out, to view the *Holland*'s Army that was to ftay behind for the Security of the Netherlands in his Abfence: therefore, to keep their Garrifons till they fet out, a fufficient Detachment of the *Englifh*, under Brigadier *Ferguson*'s Command, was order'd from their refpective Garrifons in *Holland*, confifting of Four Thoufand Men out of the Thirteen Battalions therein, the Guards excepted; with which Particular I muft begin before I can proceed with my general Journal, *viz.*

March 8, The faid Detachment being commanded from their feveral refpective Garrifons, (in order for *Roermonde* and *Maeftricht*, as aforefaid, that the *Holland*'s Troops might rendezvous at *Maeftricht*, for an early Campaign in thofe Parts, a farther Progrefs as aforefaid being in Agitation in *Germany*, &c.) that Night thofe of the Garrifon of *Breda* canton'd at *Waalveick*; and the next Day all the Detachments from their feveral Garrifons join'd at the *Bofch*, (three Leagues) under the Honourable Brigadier *Ferguson*'s Command.

10, The Brigadier, with the faid Command, march'd from the *Bofch* to, and canton'd in *Ofch*, four Leagues.

11, March'd from *Ofch* Village to, and canton'd in the Village of *Wanray*, five Leagues.

12, March'd from *Wanray* to, and canton'd in *Grounock* Village, four Leagues.

14, March'd from *Grounock* to, and canton'd in *Griffenfwaert*, on the Weft-Side of the *Maes*, near unto *Venlo*; and the next Day crofs'd the *Maes*, early in the Morning, and march'd thence thro'
Roermonde

Roermonde to, and canton'd in and about the Village of *Harten*, (five Leagues) a little Southward from *Roermonde*; where the Brigadier left Major *Cornwallis* with a Reinforcement of Nine Hundred Men, being the Detachment of Three Battalions.

March 16, The Brigadier with the rest march'd from *Hart* to, and canton'd in *Spaubeck*, six Leagues.

17, March'd from *Spaubeck* into, and reinforced *Maestricht*, as aforesaid, three Leagues.

This Journey contains about thirty-nine Leagues.

21, The *Holland*'s Garrison march'd out of *Maestricht*, and left the keeping thereof to Brigadier *Ferguson*, with the *English* Detachment, and join'd a great Body of their own and auxiliary Troops on *Peter's Hill*, on the West-Side of the Town, for a general Rendezvous, having assembled there some Days before for that purpose, and other important Matters then in hand, secret to me; and then consisted of Forty-four Battalions and Sixty-two Squadrons, with some Ordnance conform.

24, Monsieur *Overquerque* review'd all thereof at the Head of their Encampment.

26, He dispers'd them from thence again to the nighest of the neighbouring Garrisons and Villages, with Orders to be ready to draw out thither again, or elsewhere, as Occasion might require, when call'd for.

April 12, Monsieur *Overquerque* recall'd thither again, and they rejoin'd and assembled thereat, the Number of Sixty Battalions and One Hundred Squadrons, Sixty-two Cannon, Twenty-four Mortars, and Thirty Pontons, &c. and there and thereabouts they abode, and spent the most Part of that Campaign; whilst on the other Side in *Germany* we totally routed and quite defeated the *French* and *Bavarian* Army under *Tallard* and *Bavaria*'s Command, &c.

Here

Here our *British* Troops, &c. began their March into *Germany*, in the following manner.

Campaign IV.
Anno 1704.

April 24, All necessary Preparations being made for the same, the Generals *Lumley* and *Churchill*, with the remaining Part of our Troops and Artillery, set out of their respective Garrisons, in order for *Germany*; and that Day, at Night, the Garrison of *Breda* and Artillery canton'd in and about the Village of *Waalweick*, five Leagues.

25, All our Corps march'd from their Cantonments, join'd, and pitch'd Camp at the *Bosch*; where, the next Day, the Duke of *Marlborough* review'd them all; and from thence he went before with a Guard of Horse, and several other General Officers, towards *Maestricht*, three Leagues, in order to review the *Holland*'s Troops then there assembled as aforesaid, and to give his necessary Directions for the better Security of all the Netherlands in his and our Absence from thence; where, on the 29*th*, he review'd all those Troops, and went from thence on the 5*th* of *May* to the Bath of *Aix-la-Chapelle*, in order from thence to meet our Troops, when all join'd, at *Bedburgh*, &c.

28, General *Churchill*, with the *British* Troops and Artillery then under his Command, decamp'd at, and march'd from the *Bosch* to, and pitch'd Camp at *Carnock*, five Leagues.

30, Decamp'd at *Carnock*, and march'd to, and pitch'd Camp at *Boxmeer*, five Leagues.

May 1, Decamp'd at *Boxmeer*, march'd to, and pitch'd Camp at *Bleerhack*, four Leagues.

2, Decamp'd at, and march'd from *Bleerhack* to, and pitch'd Camp at *Griffenswaert* near *Venlo*, four Leagues.

4, Decamp'd at *Griffenswaert*, and march'd to, and pitch'd Camp at *Chateau de Horne* near *Roermonde*, four Leagues; where, the same Day, Major *Cornwallis*, with the Reinforcement of Nine Hundred

<small>Campaign IV.
Anno 1704.</small> Hundred Men, rejoin'd their respective Regiments: And also the same Day Brigadier *Ferguson*, with the aforesaid Detachment under his Command, set out of *Maestricht*, in order to join their respective Regiments at *Bedburgh*, who that Night lay on their Arms at *Herstal*, four Leagues Southward of *Maestricht*; and the next Day march'd from thence to *Linneg*, a little Town in the Principality of *Newburg*, four Leagues.

May 6, General *Churchill* with the Troops decamp'd at *Chateau de Horne*, pass'd the *Maes* at *Roermonde*, and march'd from thence to, and pitch'd Camp at *Duber*, four Leagues; (but the Detachment halted.)

7, Decamp'd at *Duber*, march'd to, and pitch'd Camp at *Bedburgh*, four Leagues; and at the same time Brigadier *Ferguson*, with the Detachment who had that Day march'd from *Linneg*, fell in and join'd their respective Regiments; and also the Duke at the same time arrived in our Camp, as form'd, from *Aix-la-Chapelle*.

8, The Duke of *Marlborough* review'd our Corps, which being then join'd, consisted of Fourteen Battalions of Foot, Five Regiments of Horse and Two of Dragoons, with Thirty-four Field Cannon, Four Howitzers, and Twenty-one Pontons; but after our Arrival into *Germany*, there were added to our Corps, of *Holland*'s own and auxiliary Troops, Seven Battalions of *Danes*, One of *Hessian*, Sixteen Squadrons of Horse, Five of Dragoons, of *Hollanders*, all under Duke *Wirtemburg*.

9, The Duke with our Troops decamp'd at, and march'd from *Bedburgh* to, and pitch'd Camp at *Kerpen*, three Leagues.

10, Decamp'd at, and march'd from *Kerpen* to, and pitch'd Camp at *Kalsechen*; where he received an Express from Prince *Lewis*, that the *French* were instantly intended to pass the *Black Forest*, and join

the

the Duke of *Bavaria* with an Addition before his Arrival, &c. Hereupon, for the greater Expedition, he advanced before with his Horse towards Prince *Lewis*, where he then lay, between *Lanſheim* and *Upring*, with the *German* Forces, and daily threaten'd to be attack'd; leaving our Foot and Artillery under General *Churchill*'s Command, to follow after with all the Expedition imaginable; and I muſt needs ſay he perform'd that March with very good Conduct, by beginning every Day's March by Break of Day or Sun-riſing: ſo that every Day, before it was extream hot or Noon, we were fully encamp'd in our new Camp: ſo that the remaining Part of the Day's Reſt, was nigh as good as a Day's Halt.

11, Our Troops decamp'd at, and march'd from *Kalſechen* to, and pitch'd Camp at *Meckenheim*, four Leagues; but the Duke with our Horſe and Dragoons advanced on before to the *Germans*, in the Circle of *Suabia*, and view'd ſeveral Garriſons in his March.

12, General *Churchill* with our Foot and Artillery decamp'd at, and march'd from *Meckenheim* to, and pitch'd Camp at *Zinzich*, on the Weſt-Side of the River *Rhine*, four Leagues. — There we had firſt Plenty of Wine and *Spaw* Water.

14, Decamp'd at, and march'd from *Zinzich* up the Weſt Brink of the *Rhine* to, and pitch'd Camp at *Andernach*, three Leagues; and that Day took a Party of Forty Men of *French*, which had been lurking on the Road-Side in a Scrub from the Garriſon of *Traerback*, in order to catch ſome of our Stragglers or feeble; and that ſame Day the Duke with our Horſe arrived, and pitch'd Camp at *Newdorff* near *Coblentz*, not above three Leagues ſtart of us; the Duke willing to bring all up cloſe and near together, having ſomewhat ſlacken'd his March thereto, and having Intelligence that Count *Tallard*,

Campaign IV. *Tallard*, with the Nine Thousand Men, which be-
Anno 1704. fore had reinforced the Duke of *Bavaria*, was marching back again with the rest of his Army. There met and complimented the Duke, the Queen's Agent from *Franckfort*, and Monsieur *De Amelot*, Envoy-Extraordinary for the States-General, and Count *Wratislaw*, late Envoy from the Emperor to the Queen, for settling all Things for his farther March and Conjunction with the Imperial Army.

May 15, General *Churchill*, with the Troops under his Command, decamp'd at, and march'd from *Andernach* to, and pitch'd Camp between *St. Thomas* and *Newdorff*, three Leagues; from which, that Forenoon, our Horse and Dragoons, with the Duke, pass'd the *Rhine* and *Moselle* at *Coblentz*; and in the Time thereof, he visited the Elector of *Triers* at his Castle of *Hermanstein*, where he was saluted with a triple Discharge of all the Cannon round the Place, and after dined with the Elector. He march'd with his Troops to *Braubach*.

16, General *Churchill*, &c. decamp'd at *Newdorff*, pass'd over the *Rhine* at *Coblentz*, and march'd from thence, pass'd a little River at, and near *Lohnstein*, three Leagues, and pass'd *Upper Lohnstein* to, and pitch'd Camp at *Broubach*, or *Braubach*, and halted two Days, making Way for our Train, then ascending a higher Region; and the same Day the Duke march'd with his Troops to *Nastedin*; and the same Day the Landgrave or Prince of *Hesse de Armstadt* made a Visit to the Duke.

17, Our Artillery was sent two Leagues before the Army, under the Convoy of Two Battalions, up a very narrow and steep Road, that the Army might the better pass that Way; because in those Parts the Army could march as much in one Day, as the Artillery could in two: And the same Day with our Horse march'd to, and pitch'd at *Schwalbach*; there Lieutenant-General *Bulow*, Commander

der in Chief of the *Lunenburgh* Troops, came and paid his Respects to the Duke; and the same Day received Letters from the Hereditary Prince of *Hesse* and General *Hompesch*, that they were come to *Mayence*, waiting his Orders; and also from the States-General, that a Reinforcement of Eight Battalions and Twenty-one Squadrons were order'd with all Speed to follow and join him, as aforesaid; and on the 18*th* the Duke removed with his Troops to *Cassel* Village on the *Rhine*, over-against *Mayence*, where he immediately paid a Visit to the Elector of the City, and was saluted by a Discharge of all the Cannon round the City; dined with the Elector, and had some Conferences with the Generals for the further Motions of the Confederate Army in *Germany*, and visited the Fortifications.

19, General *Churchill* with the Troops decamp'd at, and march'd from *Braubach* up the aforesaid steep Way, pass'd the Artillery to, and pitch'd Camp at *Millen*, five Leagues, in a Bottom, in the Princedom of *Hesse*; and the Artillery press'd forward in the Rear, in a very tedious Road; where, the same Day, there fell a great Shower of Hail, each thereof as large as a Musket-Ball: And the same Day the Duke pass'd the *Maine* with our Horse, and pitch'd at *Grootgohout*.

20, General *Churchill* with the Troops decamp'd at, and march'd from *Millen*, in a very tedious Road and through a Wood and Scrub, to, and pitch'd Camp at *Kemel*, four Leagues, with the Artillery a little in our Rear: In the same Wood several of the Artillery Waggons and others went astray for some Hours, before that they could get up to join the Army at *Kemel*; and the same Day the Duke with the Horse march'd to, and pitch'd Camp at *Zwingenberg*.

22, General *Churchill* with our Troops and Artillery decamp'd at, and march'd from *Kemel* over

Campaign IV.
Anno 1704.

a very steep Hill and tedious Road to, and pitch'd Camp at *Caſſel*, four Leagues, in a more level Country, on a Point between the River *Rhine* and *Maine*; the *Maine* that comes down from *Franckfort* runs on its North-Side, and the *Rhine* on its West-Side, opposite to the famous City of *Mayence*: And the same Day the Duke with our Horse march'd to, and pitch'd Camp at *Weinheim*; and the next Day our Troops at *Caſſel* were review'd by the Bishop of *Mayence*; and that Day the Duke removed to *Ladenbourg*, but his Horse pass'd the *Necker* on Bridges of Boats, and pitch'd Camp on the other Side against the Town, where he halted two Days, that ours and the auxiliary Troops, who were to serve in those Parts under his Command, might not be too far behind him.

May 23, Duke *Wirtemberg*, with the aforesaid Reinforcement of Eight Battalions and Twenty-one Squadrons, set out from *Holland*'s Camp at *Maeſtricht*, in order with all Expedition to join us before we should engage in any Action in those Parts, whither we were then all posting apace, which they accordingly did at *Gingen* in *Suabia*.

This bending of the Duke's March to the *Danube* was a very great Surprize to the *French*, who conjectured by his March to *Mayence*, that he design'd to act on the *Moſelle*, or to advance up to the *Upper Rhine*, or lay Siege to *Landau*, by the Governor of *Philipſburg*'s making a Bridge over the *Rhine*. Upon this Suspicion, *Tallard* repass'd the *Rhine* at *Ottenheim*, in order either to join *Villeroy*, or to oppose the Duke's Passage of the said River, where our real Design was not then intended.

24, General *Churchill* with our Foot and Artillery decamp'd at, and march'd from *Caſſel* over the *Maine* to, and pitch'd Camp at *Croſſegart*, four Leagues.

25, Decamp'd

25, Decamp'd at *Croſſegart*, and march'd from thence to, and pitch'd Camp at *Zwingenberg*, four Leagues.

26, Decamp'd and march'd from *Zwingenberg* to, and pitch'd at *Wenheim*, four Leagues; and the ſame Day the Duke march'd with the Horſe from *Ladenbourg* to *Wiſloch*.

28, General *Churchill*, &c. decamp'd at *Wenheim*, four Leagues, march'd from thence, croſs'd the *Necker* on Boats a little below *Heidelburg*, where he pitch'd Camp: The Day before the Duke removed with our Horſe from *Wiſloch* to *Eppingen*, and the ſaid 28*th* to *Great Gartach*; during which ſeveral auxiliary Troops join'd him; and from thence General *Churchill* received the Duke's Orders to meet him with all Speed at the Rendezvous at *Gilengen*; as alſo the reſt. Here Baron *Staffterol*, Lieutenant-General Marſhal to Duke *Wirtenberg*, complimented the Duke in his Maſter's Name, aſſuring the Duke that all poſſible Aſſiſtance ſhould be given our Troops in their March through his Territory.

29, The Duke with our Horſe removed from *Great Gartach* to *Mondelſcheim*; where, the next Day, Prince *Eugene* of *Savoy* met and dined with the Duke, where they ſpent the Remainder of that Day in weighty Conferences, with mutual Eſteem for each other; who were equal in Fame; Courage and Conduct in Military Exploits; Prudence, Counſel, Dexterity, and Addreſs in Management of Affairs; Politeneſs, Temper, and Affability in Converſation; the two greateſt Men in the Age, with great Friendſhip and Confidence in each other.

30, General *Churchill* with our Infantry and Artillery decamp'd at, and march'd from *Heidelburg*, four Leagues, to, and pitch'd Camp at *Wiſloch*, on the little River *Vezatz*; there we paſs'd ſome of

Campaign IV.
Anno 1704.

the demolish'd Entrenchments, where the *French* Army, the Year before, had defeated the *German* Army under Prince *Lewis*'s Command.

May 31, Decamp'd at, and march'd from *Wisloch* to, and pitch'd Camp at *Stamford*, five Leagues; and the same Day the Duke with our Horse, accompanied by Prince *Eugene*, march'd from *Mondelsheim* to *Great Heppach*, where the Troops drawn up in Battle-Array were review'd by the Prince, who was surpriz'd to see them in such good Order after so long a tedious and quick March, and much praised the goodly Appearance of the Men's Cloathing, Accoutrements, and Horse; which highly pleased the Duke, who complimented him accordingly, telling him, that the brave Spirit which he said he saw in his Men, was inspired by his Presence.

June 1, General *Churchill*, &c. decamp'd at, and march'd from *Stamford* to, and pitch'd at *Setten*, four Leagues, a little Town in the Dukedom of *Wirtenburg*, most inhabited by *Jews*; there we had first Scarcity of Beer, but Plenty of Wine; there were we obliged to halt two Days by the Badness of the Weather, which stopt our Train. The 2d Ditto, Prince *Lewis* came Post to *Great Heppach*, and complimented the Duke that he was come to save the Empire, that in a manner was at the last Stake. After their mutual Compliments, the Generals held a Conference, wherein it was resolved, that the auxiliary Troops in the Neighbourhood should join the Army on the *Danube* for some Days; and that Prince *Lewis* and the Duke should have each a Day of Command alternatively while they continued together; and Prince *Eugene*, with a separate Body, to repair towards *Philipsburg*, to defend the Passage of the *Rhine*, the Lines of *Stolhoffen*, and Country of *Wirtenburg*, or to act otherwise according to the Motions of the *French*. After which

which, the next Day after Dinner, Prince *Lewis* return'd to his Army on the *Danube*, and Prince *Eugene* went Post to *Philipsburg* to his Army on the *Rhine*, and his Grace the Duke of *Marlborough* went to his Troops at *Eberpach*, to which they had come that Morning before the three Heroes parted. And for the better compleating of my General Journal, and that nothing should be omitted therein that I thought note-worthy of inserting, I have here hinted and transcribed by the bye, as transmitted to me by a Friend, two of the most noteworthy Actions of the *Holland* Army, in Monsieur *Overquerque*'s Command, in this Campaign in *Brabant*; which are, viz.

2, O. S. General *Dopff*, with a great Body of *Holland* Troops, advanced from their Camp between *Maestricht* and *Liege*, and pass'd over a part of the *French Brabant* Lines, near *Marsereigne* on the River *Mehaigne*, properly between *Holland* and *Flanders Brabant*, and raised Contribution in the Country round *Namur*, and they retired to their Grand Camp as aforesaid: From which, soon after, Monsieur *Overquerque* advanced with the most Part of his Army over another Part of their Line towards *Namur*; from which, for fear of being overpower'd, he was soon obliged to retire the nearest Way, between *Haller* and *Marsereigne*, back to his former Ground near to *Maestricht*: And this is all I could note or find to say most worthy of their whole Campaign; they on that Side acting more the defensive, than the offensive Part; from which I pass to the greater Glory and prosperous Proceedings of our Army to and in *Germany*.

4, General *Churchill* with our Foot and Artillery decamp'd at, and march'd from *Stetten*, pass'd *Brackenhaim* and *Penake*, to, and pitch'd Camp at *Erlickham*; but that Day all our Artillery could not get up, the Way being very heavy, deep and tedious,

Campaign IV.
Anno 1704.

tedious, which then and several other Times detain'd us from expeditious marching. There we saw the first cut Corn of that Year.

June 5, General *Churchill* decamp'd at, and march'd from *Erlickham*, cross'd the *Necker* at *Pinikheim*, where there is very fine Water-Works, to, and pitch'd Camp at *Hesberge* Fort, four Leagues, very remarkable, being seated high on a little round Mount, void of all others, to be seen at a great Distance, in a level plain Country, for about six or seven Miles round it every way. The same Day the Duke with our Horse march'd from *Eyberspach* to *Grossaxenhaim*, the auxiliary Troops being then in the Neighbourhood, under the Prince of *Hesse* and Monsieur *Bulau*, marching also in two Bodies, encamp'd at some Distance from the Duke, but all in such a manner, as they could join Prince *Lewis* in one Day, as soon as he should make a Motion towards his Grace. At this Time *Villeroy* having join'd *Tallard* with Twenty Thousand Men at *Landau*, had several Conferences, but as yet undertook nothing; and Prince *Eugene* was join'd by the *Prussian* Troops, and then his Army on the *Rhine* consisted of near Thirty Thousand Men.

6, General *Churchill* decamp'd at, and march'd from *Hesberge*, pass'd *Hanckstrat*, four Leagues, to, and pitch'd Camp between the *Necker* and *Stutgart*, a famous City, the Metropolitan of *Wirtenburg*; where, in the Prince's Garden, there are very fine Inventions of Water-Works, spoke of in another Place; and on the East Side of the *Necker*, opposite to *Stutgart*, there stands an ancient Castle, seated high, from whence that Duke's Title derives; and farther on the North-Side of the City, in a Hollow between two Hills, it is said that there Dr. *Faustus* (so much spoken of) began his early devilish Pranks.

8, Decamp'd

8, Decamp'd at, and march'd from *Stutgart* towards the West-Side of the *Necker*, five Leagues, cross'd it at that ancient City of *Eszling* to, and pitch'd Camp at a little above the City, on a Point between the *Necker* and little River *Wils*, where they join. There the People appear'd more swarthy than in any other Part of the Country.

Campaign IV. Anno 1704.

10, Decamp'd at, and march'd from *Eszling* to, and pitch'd Camp at *Wang* near *Gipping*, three Leagues on the River *Wils*; and the same Day the Duke with our Horse march'd from *Grossaxenham* to, and pitch'd Camp between *Launsheim* and *Urspringen*; and that Day on his March he was join'd with the auxiliary Troops of *Lunenburgh*, *Hanover*, and *Hesse*; and the next Day made a Motion to join Prince *Lewis* at *Westerstetten*, where the Right of his Camp then lay. Prince *Eugene* having desired a farther Reinforcement of Troops from the Duke, for the Security of the *Rhine* and Lines of *Stolhoffen*, he order'd Lieutenant-General *Scholten*, with the Seven Battalions of *Danes*, to join the Prince, and take his Orders, who was come from the *Maes*, and advanced as far as *Franckfort*. At the same time the Elector of *Bavaria* sent a great Detachment to possess themselves of *Laugingen* and *Dilengen*, that at the Advance of the Confederate-Army towards the *Danube*, his whole Forces might possess themselves of that Camp with the *Danube* in their Rear.

12, General *Churchill* decamp'd at *Wang*, cross'd the River *Wils* at *Gipping*, and march'd from thence to, and pitch'd Camp at *Scessen* near unto *Urswanglach-Fort* and *Stapping-Chateau*, three Leagues, both seated very high on two round Hills. The same Day Prince *Lewis* and the Duke continued in the Camp at *Launsheim*, to form the Line of Battle; and the Duke that same Day review'd the Twelve Regiments of Foot that came into those Parts with General

Campaign IV.
Anno 1704.

General *Goor* the preceding Year, with the Four Battalions of Duke *Wirtenberg*'s in the State's Pay, all compleat, and in good Order; and the next Day, which was the 13*th*, the Army under Prince *Lewis* and Duke of *Marlborough* being join'd, decamp'd at, and march'd from *Launsheim* and *Westerstetten*, and pitch'd and encamp'd with their Right at *Elchingen* near to the *Danube*, and the Left at *Languenaw*, where they halted three Days till *Churchill*'s Arrival.

June 13, Decamp'd at *Sieffen*, and march'd from thence that Day over *Wils* three Times, to, and pitch'd Camp at *Efzling*, a ſtrong Paſs in *Swabia*, and Entrance of a higher Region, inviron'd with very high Hills and Mountains; remarkable on the Top of one, on the Weſt-Side of the Town, there ſtands a high round Watch-houſe; and on the Top of one Eaſtward from the Town, near to the Road Side, there ſtands a little Fort.

14, General *Churchill*, with our Foot and Artillery, decamp'd at, and march'd from *Eyſling* ſlantingly up that ſteep Hill and narrow Road, where there could not go above Two in a Breaſt, or Three at the moſt, and in ſome Places not above One at a Time, till we arrived at the Top of the Hill, and then we enter'd a ſomewhat more leveller Country, although ſeated much higher than the former, and we pitch'd Camp at *Lonzee* in *Suabia*, four Leagues; but our Artillery could not be taken that Way; therefore it march'd off a little to our Right, up through a hollow Way or Cliff between two Hills, very ſteep alſo, but not altogether ſo ſteep as the Way the Army march'd.

15, Decamp'd from *Lonzee*, and march'd from thence to, and pitch'd Camp at *Alta* near *Languenow*, four Leagues; from which that Day Prince *Lewis* and the Duke of *Marlborough*, with the Confederate Grand Army, decamp'd and march'd to, and

and pitch'd Camp with their Right at *Herbreting*, and the Left at *Giengien* on the River *Brentz*, within two Leagues of the Elector of *Bavaria*'s Army, which then lay between the Town of *Dillingen* and *Lavingen*, with the River *Brentz* between the two Armies.

Campaign IV. Anno 1704.

16, General *Churchill*, with our *British* Foot and Artillery, decamp'd at *Alta*, and march'd from thence (with One *Prussian* Battalion, which had join'd us on our March) to, and took our Post in the Line, where an Interval had been left for us the Day before, and join'd with, and pitch'd Camp upon the Left Wing of the *Germans* or Confederate's Grand Army, where they then lay, as before described, in the Dukedom of *Wirtenburg* in *Suabia*. Having join'd our Army under Prince *Lewis Van Baden* and the Duke of *Marlborough*'s Command, it consisted of then in all Ninety-six Battalions of Foot, Two Hundred and Two Squadrons of Horse and Dragoons, Forty-four Field Cannon, Four Howitzers, and Twenty-four Pontons, with all other necessary Utensils of War conform. As for the Duke of *Bavaria* and his Army, who then lay as aforesaid, I was inform'd that they consisted of in all (including those posted at *Donawert*) Eighty-eight Battalions of Foot and One Hundred and Sixty Squadrons of Horse and Dragoons, Ninety Cannon, Forty Mortars and Howitzers, and Thirty Pontons, with also all other necessary Utensils of War conform. The same Day that General *Churchill* join'd, our Generals held a Council of War, wherein it was resolved and determined to draw our Army near to *Donawert*, in order to attack that Pass; whereupon, on the 19*th* of *June*, our Generals decamp'd with our Army at *Giengien*, cross'd the *Brentz*, and pitch'd Camp between *Lanthausen* and *Baltmershofen*, two Leagues; the first on our Right, and second on our Left.

June

(94)

Campaign IV. Anno 1704.

June 20, Decamp'd at *Lanthausen*, and march'd in Sight of the *Bavarians* Camp on our Right at *Dillingen*, to, and pitch'd Camp with our Right at *Amerdingen*, and Left at *Onderingen*, three Leagues. By this March the Elector of *Bavaria* judged right, that the Prince and Duke were fully intended to attack *Donawert* the next Day; whereupon, that Night, he sent to Count *De Arco* a strong Detachment of the very best of his Troops to reinforce the said Count on *Schellenbergh*, where he had already made very strong Entrenchments by some Thousands of Pioneers, employ'd thereon for several Days before to perfect those Works which cover *Donawert*, on that Point between the River *Brentz* and *Danube*, in order to prevent our Army crossing the same, and our entering the Country of *Bavaria*; on both which our Generals full Designs were wholly bent. There was strongly posted upon it, commanded by Lieutenant-General *De Arco*, Field-Marshal to the Elector, Lieutenant-General *Luxemberge*, Count *Maffey*, and two *French* Lieutenant-Generals, Two Battalions of the Electors of Life-Guards, One of Grenadiers, Thirteen other *Bavarian* Battalions, Five of *French*, Four Regiments of *Curassiers*, each Eight Hundred Men strong, and Three Squadrons of Dragoons, making in all about Eighteen Thousand Men, all choice Troops. The same Day, as our Army enter'd their Camp at *Amerdingen*, our General, with a Guard of Sixty Squadrons, advanced a little, reconnoitring the Enemies strong Post and Encampment; and in a Trice after return'd, in order to prepare all Things that Night to put their Project in Execution the next Day.

Attack of Schellenberg.

21, At Three that Morning, the Duke of *Marlborough* advanced towards *Donawert*, with a Detachment of Six Thousand Foot, and Thirty Squadrons of *English* and *Dutch* Horse, and Three

Batta-

Battalions of Imperial Grenadiers, with Lieutenant-General *Gore*, Major-General *Nemore*, and Brigadier *Ferguson*, and several other General Officers, conform, went on in the Van of our Army; with which, about Eight, Prince *Lewis* decamp'd, and march'd after him from *Amerdingen* with all Expedition; but the Way being very bad, long and tedious, it was Noon before the Duke could get up with the Detachment to the River *Wernitz* at *Donawert*; and it was Three in the Afternoon before they could get over that River with the Artillery: After which the Duke, having pass'd the same at the Head of the Horse, view'd the Entrenchments, and made the necessary Dispositions for the attacking thereof; at which Time the *English* and *Dutch* Artillery being got ready, began to play, and that very brisk and furious, against the Enemy, who answer'd the same from their Batteries as briskly; which made us to judge, by their Dispositions, that the Action would prove very hot: Whereupon a Reinforcement of Twenty-six Squadrons and Five Battalions of *English* were added to the aforesaid Detachment: So that before all Things were ready to make the Attack it was near Five of the Clock in the Afternoon; and then Lieutenant-General *Goor*, Major-General *Nemore*, and Brigadier *Ferguson*, with the aforesaid *English* and *Dutch* Troops, began the Attack, and advanced on therewith, and that with the greatest and undaunted Vigour, Courage, and unparallel'd Valour imaginable, before the Imperialists came up; and met with such vigorous Defence, that they were twice sharply repuls'd: But at last, after an Engagement of near One Hour and Three Quarters of very hot Dispute, with several sore and sharp Repulses to their several vigorous Assaults, the Imperialists being by that Time come up, forced and beat the Enemy out from their strong Entrenchments, and from

the

Campaign IV. Anno 1704. the Pass, with a terrible Slaughter, and pursued them to the *Danube* in their great Disorder and Confusion; where *De Arco* and several other Officers saved themselves by swimming over the River, but a great many others were drown'd in their Hurry retiring over the River, to their Loss of the Pass, and upwards of Five Thousand Men killed, wounded, drowned, or deserted in the Action, and confused or precipitate Retreat over the *Danube*; but by their own common Computation given out, they had only Five Hundred and Four killed, and One Thousand Four Hundred and Ninety-six wounded, besides Four Thousand taken Prisoners at Discretion. In this glorious Action we took Fifteen Pieces of Cannon, Thirteen Colours, with all their Ammunition, Tents, and Baggage, and a great Quantity of other War Utensils; besides all *De Arco*'s Plate, and other rich Booty, which was distributed amongst our victorious Soldiers. Besides, the next Morning, after our Troops had enter'd the Town of *Donawert*, without any Opposition, there was found therein Two Thousand Sacks of Meal, great Store of Oats, and other Corn, and of all other Sorts of Provisions and Ammunition, which the Enemy had not Time to destroy; all which, at that Time, did very much assist our Army, Provision then, and for some time after, being very scarce, and hard to be got for Money. The Elector finding those Troops quite defeated, sent Orders the same Night to the Garrison of *Donawert* to set Fire to the Town, to burn the Bridges and Magazines, and then retire to him, who at the dismal News quitted his advantageous Post between *Dillingen* and *Lauingen*, and posted himself on the other Side of the *Danube*, over-against *Donawert*, in his March to the *Lech*, to prevent our cutting off his Retreat to his own Country; who made but little Stop till he got on the other Side of of the *Lech*, and entrench'd under the Cover of the Cannon of *Augsburgh*. And as for the Garrison of *Donawert*, our Troops the same Night being advanced into the Suburbs thereof, and laid their Bridges to pass into the Town, they fearing their Retreat to be cut off, and regarding their own Safety more than the Elector's Orders, after having put Straw into every House, they only burnt the Bridges and some Magazines, and retired early the next Morning after him in great Disorder from the Town (whereby the Inhabitants saved their Houses); and our Troops at the same time took Possession thereof, and found therein as aforesaid. In another Account they had but Seven Hundred killed, and One Thousand wounded. In the gaining of this glorious Victory, whereby we got a free Entrance into the *Bavarian* Country, and forcing the Elector to retire as aforesaid, the Allies in general had Five Thousand Three Hundred and Four Men killed and wounded, Officers included, as in the following Table of each Corps's Particulars doth appear.

CORPS

Campaign IV. Anno 1704.

CORPS LOSS.	Colonels		Lieut. Cols.		Majors		Captains		Subalterns		Centinels		Total		Tot. each Kd. Wd.
	Killed	Woun.	Killed	Woun.	Kd.	Wd.	Kd.	Wd.	Killed	Woun.	Killed	Wounded	Killed	Wound.	
German Horse and Foot	1	2		1		3	4	10	9	36	268	1130	284	1182	1466
Hollanders	2	1	2			4	5	19	8	53	361	856	378	953	1311
Hanover	1			2	1	2	2	10	10	20	189	417	204	451	655
Hessians		2				1	2	11	3	14	91	195	97	223	320
Britains		2	2	6	1	5	13	12	16	58	420	1001	452	1084	1536
Total	4	7	7	9	3	15	26	62	46	181	1329	3599	1415	3893	5308

Note, Of the above Corps there were of the Lieutenant-Generals killed 6, wounded 5; Major-Generals killed 2, wounded 2; Brigadiers wounded 1.

Prince

Prince *Lewis* being up with the Army before the Attack could begin, the Detachment was sustained by Fifteen Battalions of our Right, and Fifteen of the Left Wing.

I have here as followeth specified the Names of the General Officers of the Allies that were killed and wounded on the said Attack, by Reason there were more of them lost here, than in any other Action elsewhere throughout the whole War.

KILLED.

Lieutenant General *Goor*.
Prince *Homburge*.
Prince *Beveren*.
Count *Erback*.
Count *Schuylemberge*.
Major General *Benheim*.
Count *Stirum*.
  Nemere.

WOUNDED.

Captain General Prince *Lewis Van Baden*.
Lieutenant General *Thungen*.
Prince *Hesse Cassel*.
Prince *Alexander* of *Wirtemberg*.
Prince of *Saxony*.
Count *Horn*.
Major General *Pallandt*.
Brigadier *Bodmer*.
Major General *Wood*.
The Corps to which they belonged I am obliged to omit.

Although the Duke of *Marlborough* commanded the Attack, Prince *Lewis* was not wanting in performing the Part of a brave and great General. The Forlorn Hope, or Van of this Action, was led on by Lord *Mordant*, with Fifty Granadiers of the *English* Guards, of which, only came off himself and ten of his Men. I had an Account by several that this Pass had been attacked Fifteen Times before by the *Germans* and others, but never was taken till then by the Duke of *Marlborough*.

In and during the Time of the Action, our Army being all up, stood to Arms, ready, and in very good Order to assist the Attackers, and to repulse otherwise if opposed by the *Bavarian* Army intire; but they lay firm till over, and then retired as aforesaid. And all that Night after our grand Army lay on their Arms, as on their Line of March, and the Detachment that had attacked, fell back to their respective Regiments, and the others of intire Regiments halted also on their Arms all Night.

June 22, Or Day after the Attack, our whole Army was formed, and pitch'd Camp regularly cross the rising Ground at *Uber-Margen* on the West and North Side of the *Danube*, *Wernitz*, and *Donawert*, and buried our Dead, and sent away our Sick and Wounded to *Amerling*.

24, Our whole Army decamped at *Uber-Morgen*, crossed the *Danube* on several Bridges of Pontons near *Donawert* and River *Wernitz*, and pitch'd Camp between *Hyzel* Cloister and *Merdingen*, in the Dukedom of *Bavaria*.

25, Was a Day of Thanksgiving throughout the Army for the late Success, and Prince *Lewis* caused *Te Deum* to be sung in his Camp, and all the Towns adjoining. And the same Day Duke *Wirtenberge*, with the *Danish* Horse from *Schellenburg*, where they had come the Day before, passed the *Dannbe*, and fell into the Ground appointed for them, in the Camp Line.

27, The Duke willing to lose no Time, nor Advantage, detach'd Count *Frize* with Four Thousand

Thousand Men, and Twelve Pieces of Cannon, in Order to prepare Bridges for the whole Army to pass over the *Lech* near *Gendrichn*, the which they finished that Evening, without any Opposition of *Velde*, which they then abandoned, and march'd over and took Post in *Bavaria*.

28, The Right of our Camp removed a little forward to *Hamler*, and our Left extended to the Brink of the *Lech* at *Genrichn*, or opposite thereto; and that same Afternoon a Reinforcement of Six Thousand Men were sent over to Count *De Frize*, who had then block'd up *Rain* for a Siege, the which *De Arco* with his scattered Troops had left three Days before, leaving therein one Brigadier *Mercy*, with a small Garrison of between Four and Five Hundred Foot; and the same Day at the first Intelligence of those Troops passing the *Lech*, the Enemies Garrison of *Newberg* abandoned it, and retired to *Ingoldstat*, whereupon the Duke sent a Detachment there, and took Possession thereof; and Prince *Lewis* ordered General *Herberville*, with his separate Body of Four Thousand Men, on the other Side of the *Danube*, to remain there for the Security of the Place, being of great Importance, for the bringing of Provisions out of *Franconia*, for the Subsistence of our Army whilst in *Bavaria*.

29, Our Army decamp'd at *Gendrichn*, and there crossed the *Lech* and pitch'd Camp, with our Left at *Burchaim*, and Right at *Staudbaim*, near to the *Lech* and *Rain*, with the *Danube* a little in our Rear; and the same Day Count *de Frize*, with the aforesaid Detachment of Ten Thousand Men, fell into their respective Regiments, they being relieved by Nine Battalions and Fifteen Squadrons, with which the said Count was to carry on the Siege against *Rain*.

July

Campaign IV. Anno 1704. Rain besieged.

July 1, The said Count and Troops formed the Siege, and at the same Time to favour the Enterprize, the Right of our grand Army was moved a little forward, and the Left a little backward; and Prince *Lewis* of *Baden* set Fire to the Conntry in *Bavaria*, and began first at his own Quarters at *Staudhaim*, and destroyed upwards of Three Hundred Towns, Villages, and Castles, including one with another, little and big, open and walled; and the same Day the Duke had Advice by Count *Vehlen* from Prince *Eugene*, that Marshal *Villeroy* and *Tallard*, with Forty Five Thousand Men, otherwise computed but Fifty Battalions and Sixty Six Squadrons, had passed the *Rhine* by *Fort-Kehl*, in Order to succour the Elector of *Bavaria*, before farther Action, *&c.* Whereupon at Prince *Eugene*'s Desire, that he might be the better able to observe the Enemies Motion, the Duke the next Day sent Prince *Maximilian* of *Hanover* with a Reinforcement to him of Thirteen Battalions and Thirty Squadrons of Imperial Horse over the *Danube*, to join him as soon as possible, who was then also on his March towards *Dillengen*, some Days March behind *Tallard*; Prince *Eugene* then consisting of but Eighteen Battalions and Nineteen Squadrons, including the Reinforcement; for although we had gained the Pass, we could not be too secure, powerful Armies being then on Foot against us.

2, At Night a competent Number with and without Arms opened the Trenches against *Rain*, and the next Day the Besiegers erected and compleated their Batteries of eighteen Cannons and six Mortars.

4, At Seven in the Morning the said Batteries began to play, and played all that Day very vigorous and smart against the Town, for a sudden Storm thereon, so that the Fear and Dread thereof of so terrified the besieged, that they the next Morning about the same Time beat a Parley, capitulated, and surrendered the Town and themselves Prisoners of War, yet were allowed their small Arms and Baggage; and the next Day being the 6th Instant, they marched out thereof, and were conducted by a Party of our Horse to their grand Camp at *Augsburg*, and a Detachment of Four Hundred of the Besiegers took Possession of the Town, in which there was found Twenty Four Brass Cannon, some Ammunition, a great Quantity of Corn, and other Provisions, which did much assist our Army: During this nine Days Siege, began on the 27th of *June*, and ended on the 5th of *July*, neither Side had above Twenty killed and wounded; after which Count *de Frize* with another Detachment was sent off to, and took the Castle of *Dillengen*, and a small Garrison therein Prisoners of War, and levelled the Entrenchments which the *Bavarian* Army had made there some Time before, upon our joining the Imperial Army at *Gingen*.

6, The Duke and Prince *Lewis*, after having given Orders for the providing all necessary Magazines at *Newburg* and *Rain*, for the better subsisting of our Army, they decamp'd therewith and marched from *Burcheim* and *Staudhaim*, three Leagues, to and pitch'd Camp with our Right at *Holtz*, and Left at *Osterhausen*.

7, Decamp'd and march'd from *Holtz*, and pitch'd Camp with our Right at *Kuepach*, and Left extended to *Aicha*, which the Enemy that Morning abandoned at the first Appearance of our Army's approaching, and retired with great Expedition to their grand Camp at *Augsburg*, three Leagues; but Nine Hundred Boors after a small Attack were made Prisoners of War, but what were killed thereof, which refused to submit;

Campaign IV. Anno 1704. and thereupon the Town was suffer'd to be plunder'd, and nothing to be seen for a great Way round but an universal Desolation of Sixty Villages in Flames, burning to Ashes, and nothing omitted that the Laws of War would allow: After which, the same Day, the Duke sent in a sufficient Detachment of our Army to Garrison the Town, and there erected Magazines of all necessary Provisions, which did very much assist our Army during the Time of our Abode on that Side of *Bavaria*, till we withdrew out thereof, and gain'd a fresh and entire Conquest over the *French* and *Bavarians*.

July 10, Our Army decamp'd, and march'd from *Aicha* to, and pitch'd Camp at *Metta Chetave*, three Leagues.

11, The Duke, with a Guard of Sixty Squadrons, advanced in the Front of our Camp near to *Fridberge*, within about one League of the *Bavarian* Camp, viewing the Country for a fresh Camp, and the Enemies strong Encampment at *Augsburg*, where they then lay within the Cover of the Cannon thereof, and strongly entrench'd with the *Lech* in their Front, and a little River in their Rear; with also a great Marsh on their Right and Left Wing: And the same Day a Party of the Enemy, after a smart Brush, at the Duke's Appearance towards *Fridberg*, retired from thence to their Grand Camp at *Augsburg*; after which the Duke return'd to our Camp at *Metta*, with a Design to remove it from thence to *Fridberg*.

12, The Duke and Prince *Lewis* decamp'd with our Army at *Metta*, and advanced to, and pitch'd Camp at *Fridberg*, three Leagues, along the Rising-Ground opposite to, and within one League of the *Bavarian* Camp at *Augsburg*, as aforesaid. It is seated in a Bottom, in a very pleasant Valley by the *Lech*, about eight Leagues Northwards from the high Mountains of *Tyrol*, or Lower Part of

the

the *Alps*, a Ridge of Mountains which parts *Ger-*   Campaign
many and *Italy*, accounted the highest Hills in IV.
Christendom. This was the farthest of our *British* Anno 1704.
Troops and Artillery's Extent from *Holland* into
Germany, after forty eight Days March or Remo-
vals, upwards from *Breda*; and according thereunto, *Augsburg* is distant about one Hundred and
seventy Leagues Southward. There we abode on
that Side twelve Days, in View of the Enemies
strong fortified Camp; on which no Attack could
be made without infinite Disadvantage, nor no moving the Elector from thence, till join'd by *Tallard*
with a great Body of *French* Troops, who were
then advancing thitherward. The Duke and Prince
Lewis therefore thought it proper to reduce the
strongest Places in *Bavaria* by besieging, or otherwise as it might happen; and so to remove from
Fridberg, and to begin first with *Ingoldstat*; the
which Prince *Lewis* undertook with the Imperial
Troops and the Duke to cover the Siege with the
auxiliary Forces; and, if Need required, to be
joined by Prince *Eugene*, who by that Time was
advanced to *Dillengen* with the aforesaid Troops,
all ready to assist each other, either in besieging or
battling, as Occasion might require, or offer first,
and best. All which, soon after, was accordingly
effected, and that very gloriously, and for ever memorable.

24, Our whole Army decamp'd at *Fridberg*, and
remarch'd over the River *Par* to, and pitch'd at
Kitbach, six Leagues, with our Left at *Aicha*, and
Right Wing beyond *Vinden* Castle, burning all the
Villages between those two Towns that before had
been spared.

25, Decamp'd at *Kitbach*, and again pass'd the
River *Par* near *Schrobenhausen* on our Right, three
Leagues, and pitch'd Camp with our Left Wing
at *Klosterberg* near *Hochenwart*, and the Right behind

<small>Campaign IV. Anno 1704.</small> hind *Schrobenhausen*; and the same Day Prince *Lewis* review'd the Artillery and our Preparations at *Newberg*, for the Siege at *Ingoldstat*, and return'd the 29*th*.

July 28, Decamp'd at *Klosterberg*, and march'd to, and pitch'd Camp at *Zantditzall* near *Newberg*, three Leagues; and the aforesaid Day, after Prince *Lewis*'s Return, Prince *Eugene* having left his Troops at *Hochstat* the 26*th*, came to the Army at *Hochenwart*, to confer with the Duke and Prince *Lewis*; where they held a Council of War, and it was agreed to continue in their late Resolution, of Prince *Lewis*'s besieging *Ingoldstat*, and the other two to observe the Elector of *Bavaria*, who, the 26*th*, had removed out of his Entrenchments, and encamp'd by *Tuerhaupten*, on the other Side of the *Lech* near *Ribrach*, (where, every Day, he expected Count *Tallard* with a Reinforcement of Twenty-two Thousand Horse and Foot, leaving Monsieur *de Chamaran* with Eight Battalions and Four Squadrons in *Augsburg*; and on the 28*th* Ditto they join'd *Tallard* and *Bavaria*) intending, when join'd, to pass the *Lech*, and attack our Army: But this Feint was only to cover his real Design, which was to pass the *Danube* at *Lavingen*, and to fall on that separate Army with Prince *Eugene* at *Hochstat*, which he had brought from the Lines of *Bioul*, before he could be reinforced. But the said 26*th*, at Night, Prince *Eugene*'s Army, by his Order, removed to a more advantagious Post from *Hochstat*, and pitch'd on a Height, which reach'd from *Munster* Villages and *Erlinghoven* to the Wood near *Apershoven*, with a Rivulet before it, which he maintained till the Duke's Arrival with our Army thither, two Nights before the Battle of *Hochstat*.

<small>*Ingoldstat* besieged, and surrehder'd.</small> 29, The Duke, with our Army under his Command, decamp'd at *Zantditzall*, three Leagues, march'd to, and pitch'd Camp with his Left at *Enheim*,

Enheim, and Right at *Tillengen*, within two Miles of *Rain*; and Prince *Lewis*, who the 28*th* at Night encamp'd with the Emperor's Troops, somewhat apart from those which the Duke at *Potmes* march'd from thence another Way, with Twenty-two Battalions and Seventeen Squadrons, and bent his March to *Newburg*, to repair from thence to *Ingoldstat*; which Place he invested the 31*st* Ditto, in which there was a Garrison of Four Thousand Men, commanded by a Lieutenant-General, who in ten Days after surrender'd, with little Opposition, to Prince *Lewis* with little Loss, finding their Army quite defeated at *Hochstat*; whose Particulars I must wave, and speak of which I know most: And the said 29*th*, the Enemy removed from *Bibrach* to *Lavingen*, in order to pass the *Danube* there; and Prince *Eugene*, who had left the Duke the same Day, came back in two Hours after, and acquainted him therewith, and returned to his Army.

30, About Three in the Morning, the Duke of *Marlborough* sent the Duke Regent of *Wirtenberg* before, with the Twenty-eight Squadrons of Imperialists that Prince *Lewis* had left behind, in order to pass the *Danube*, and to reinforce Prince *Eugene* with all imaginable Expedition at *Munster:* The Enemy that Morning betimes having also pass'd the *Danube* and *Lavingen*, and advanced from their former Camp between it and *Dillingen*, and pitch'd with their Right extended as far as *Steinheim*, and Left to *Lavingen*, with a Design to attack the Prince before the Duke of *Marlborough*'s Arrival; who also, by Six that Morning, sent General *Churchill* with Twenty Battalions, in order to reinforce the Prince, who, that Afternoon, pass'd the *Danube* at *Marxhaim* below *Gendrichn*, and pitch'd on the West Brink of the River, between *Morksea* and *Morksain*; and also a little after that General *Churchill* began his March. The Duke

Campaign of *Marlborough*, with our grand Body, decamp'd
IV.
Anno 1704. at *Enheim*, and also march'd after with all Expedition, and about the going down of the Sun pitch'd Camp with his Right at *Mitleſtet*, four Leagues, and Left at *Pluckingen*, with the Town of *Rain* in his Front, and the Quarter-Master-General at *Nidſchonefeld*, where Bridges had been already laid croſs the *Danube*, where the Horſe Dragoons, Foot and Artillery, with *Wirtenberg* and *Churchill*, had paſs'd at *Marxhaim*. Prince *Eugene* coming early from the Duke that Morning to his Camp, found it ſtruck, in order to poſſeſs themſelves of the Entrenchments of *Schellenberg*; he that commanded in his Abſence not thinking Eighteen Thouſand to be able to withſtand the Enemies great Power at *Munſter*; but the Prince cauſed the Army to pitch there again, and ſent all his Baggage to *Donawert*, conjecturing that the Enemy, who had paſs'd the *Danube* that Day at *Lavingen*, could not conveniently come near him that Evening: But being thoroughly inform'd, by Five Squadrons, that the Enemy were advanced as aforeſaid, who were well acquainted with his Weakneſs, and fully bent to attack him the next Day. He diſpatch'd an Expreſs to the Duke thereof, and cauſed all his Foot and part of his Horſe to march to *Schellenberg*, keeping only Twenty-two Squadrons of his Dragoons with him, with the Twenty-eight which came with *Wirtenberg*; and with thoſe few he paſs'd the Night at *Munſter*, with the Horſes ſaddled ready, in order to preſerve that Poſt if poſſible, though without coming to any Engagement, till joined by the Duke, towards whom all were a poſting with great Haſte. All the Four ſeveral Bodies, at moſt within two Leagues of each other, ready and in very good Order for mutual Aſſiſtance, upon the firſt Occaſion, more eſpecially

cially Prince *Eugene*, whom the Enemy then threaten'd most.

July 31, By Two in the Morning, the Duke with our main Body decamp'd at *Mitlstet*, and General *Churchill* at *Marxhaim*, who by Noon joined and reinforced those of Prince *Engene*'s at *Donawert*, where they had lain on their Arms all that Night very alert, waiting the Enemies Motion, and our Armies Assistance. That Morning betimes the Duke sent an Express to Prince *Eugene*, and assured him, that he would join him that Evening at *Munster*, and added, that by that Time General *Churchill* was very near: Whereupon Prince *Eugene* also being informed that the Enemy had made no Motion that Day towards him, caused all his Troops, which he had the Day before sent to *Schelenberge*, to return to his Camp at *Munster*. That Morning the Duke's first Line past the *Lech* at *Rain*, and the *Danube* and *Wernitz* near *Donawert*: And the Second Line passed the *Danube* at *Nidschonefeld*, and the *Wernitz* at *Oppermorgen*, and by Four in the Afternoon the Rear of all was up at *Donawert*, and from thence all continued their March and advanced to, and about Ten at Night arrived and joined Prince *Eugene* at *Munster*; and then all the aforesaid Bodies being joined, we pitch'd and form'd Camp regularly between the Villages of *Munster* and *Erlinghoven*, and that of upper *Hoven*, about five Leagues Westward of *Donawert*, and two Eastward from *Hochstat*, where the *French* and *Bavarian* Army then lay strongly encamped as aforesaid: And threatning that in one or two Days after they would advance, and attack our Army, who in the said Time saved them the Trouble, and victoriously advanced, attacked and quite defeated them, as afterwards will appear

August

August 1, At Break of Day, our Generals with all the Picquet, confisting of Twenty-eight Squadrons, advanced out to view the Enemies strong Encampment, designing to advance the Army as far as *Laaken*, and *Volperstete*; but perceiving upwards of Twenty Squadrons of the Enemy in the Plain of *Overklaw*, and also by their Prospective-Glasses from a Height, that their whole Army was in a Motion, and their Horse marching forward, and from off the Top of *Thiffengen*, the Duke and Prince took Notice that their advanced Squadrons stopp'd short, after that they had perceived our Squadrons. About One in the Afternoon we saw their Quarter-Master General set up their Camp Standard, and mark out the Camp from *Blenheim* to *Lutzing*. Our General being returned, ordered necessary Passages to be made, and sent out Pioneers to *Thiffengen* to make Bridges of Communication on a Rivulet, which was narrow, but had high Banks; they were hardly got to work till the Enemies advanced Guard came as far as between *Schiveining* and *Thiffengen*, and their Hussars obliged the Pioneers to retire to our advanced Guard, which alarmed our Camp; whereupon about Two, the Duke with all the Picquet, and Seven Squadrons of Dragoons which were encamped before our Quarter-Master General, with the Battalions of *English* Guards, and Five Battalions of *Row*'s Brigade, which were followed by a Brigade of *Hesse*, and a great Part of our Army advanced to the Rivulet, where the Pioneers had been repulsed; and being come thither, they not only found the Enemy retired from thence, but also on full Gallop to their grand Army. Our advance Guard was reinforced, and left under the Command of a Major General, with also the Two Brigadiers of Foot, that were in *Thiffengen*, under another Major General, who carefully posted them

in

in the Hedges and Ditches thereabouts. About
Four in the Afternoon, from off the Top of
Thiffengen, our Generals saw that the Enemies
Camp was pitch'd advantageously on a Hill, and
that their Right Flank was covered by the *Danube*, and *Blenheim* Village, and their Left by the
Village of *Lutzing*; and before them a Rivulet
with high Banks, and the Bottom Marshey,
thought unpassable, as it afterwards was found in
several Places. And in those Circumstances it
was thought a very hazardous Enterprize to attack
such a numerous Army, as they then were so advantageously posted, to which we could not approach, but by filing off and passing in View of
the Enemy a marshy Rivulet, which could not be
done in good Order: But then it seemed to be an
indispensible Necessity of immediately falling upon
them, before they could have Time to fortifie
themselves in that Part; and besides, our Army
would much want Forage before *Ingolstat* could be
taken. And farther, *Villeroy* having left Monsieur *de Coyney* at *Offenburg* with a sufficient Body
of Troops to keep within the Lines of *Biehl*, the
Forces that they had there were ready to make an
Eruption into *Wirtemburg*, which might have acted
in Concert with the Elector of *Bavaria*, and be reinforced by Detachments from him to fall afterwards on the Rear of the Lines of *Biehl*; so that
thereby the *French* Armies would have established
a free Communication from the *Rhine* to the *Danube*, and forced all to submit as far as the *Main*;
whilst the Elector from *Hochstat* might have ruined a great Part of the Circle of *Franconia*, and
brought Things to that Pass, that the Auxiliaries
under the Duke should not have been able to find
either Subsistence or Winter Quarters on the *Danube*, and in *Upper-Germany*; though on the other
Hand, that great and seasonable Supply could not
have

Campaign IV.
Anno 1704.

have left the Empire in the Winter, without exposing it to the Brink of Ruin, and leaving an entire Superiority to the Enemy: These prevailing Reasons made the Duke of *Marlborough* and Prince *Eugene* resolve to fight, and to force the Enemy to Battle the next Day, without farther Delay, which the Enemy little expected, having threatened much to attack us; so that after the Generals had spent that Day, and Afternoon, in viewing the Enemies strong Encampments, and that it was too late in the Day to begin such a glorious Action, and gain the Victory that we then hoped to obtain over our lofty and proud Enemy, after having posted our advanced Guard as aforesaid, to wait the Enemies Motion, remarched the rest of our Army that Evening back to *Munster* to their Camp, which had stood unmoved in our Absence, under the Cover of several Squadrons of *Hussars*, and some others: Where that Night all necessary Dispositions were made for the Attack to begin the next Morning betimes, as soon as possible. And all that Night the most of our Army kept in a moving Posture, making ready, posting and putting themselves in good Order, Horse, Foot and Artillery, for the Battle, which was regularly done accordingly in several Attacks, *viz.* Our Right Wing in Prince *Eugene*'s Command, consisted of Ninety-two Squadrons of Imperialists Horse and Dragoons, and Eighteen Battalions of Foot, Seven *Danes*, and Eleven *Prussians*. And our Left Wing in the Duke of *Marlborough*'s Command, consisted of Ninety-six Squadrons of Horse and Dragoons, and Forty Eight Battalions of Foot, made up of *Britains*, Fourteen Battalions and Eighteen Squadrons; of *Hollanders*, Fourteen Battalions and Nineteen Squadrons; of *Lunenberghers*, Thirteen Battalions and Twenty-five Squadrons of *Wirtenburgers*,

Seven

Seven Battalions and Five Squadrons of *Hessians*, Seven Squadrons of *Danes*, Twenty-two Squadrons. Total on both Attacks, One Hundred Eighty Eight Squadrons and Sixty Six Battalions, besides otherwise Ten Battalions of *Hessians*, and Eight Squadrons of *Wirtenburgers*, with Fifty-two Cannon, Four Howitzers, Twenty-four Pontons, and all other necessary Utensils of War conform, in Order for Battle, computed Fifty-two Thousand Men. The *French* and *Bavarian* Army, which lay as aforesaid under Count *Tallard*'s and the Duke of *Bavaria*'s Command, consisted of Eighty-seven Battalions of Foot, and One Hundred and Sixty Squadrons, computed Sixty Thousand Men, with One Hundred and Twenty Cannon, Fifty small Mortars and Howitzers, and Twenty-four Pontons, with also all other necessary Utensils of War, conform for Battle, regulated thus. Their Right in Count *Tallard*'s Command, consisted of Forty Battalions and Sixty Squadrons, of the best of the *French* Troops. Their Left in the Elector of *Bavaria*'s with his *Bavarians*, and Marshal *de Marsin*'s, with some *French* Troops in his Command, consisted of Forty Seven Battalions, and one Hundred Squadrons.

About Three that Morning, our heroick General decamp'd with our Confederate Army at *Munster*, and advanced from thence Frontward over *Kessel* Rivulet, on several Bridges, and filed off in Eight Columns; of which Two of Imperial Foot march'd quite to the Right of all, towards the Height along the Wood, with Two Columns of Imperial Horse on their Left. The Left Wing, composed of Auxiliaries, march'd also in Four Columns, *viz*. Two of Foot on the Left off the Imperial Horse, and Two of Horse on the Left of all. And thus our whole Army advanced to the

the Rivulet near *Thiffengen*, where the advanced Guards fell into their respective Bodies: But Major-General *Wilks*, with the Two Brigadiers of *Hessians* and Fifteen Squadrons, was ordered, and formed a Ninth Column on the Left of all; and so we advanced to *Schiveining*; and as soon as our Nine Columns were arrived between that Village and the Wood, we made a Halt to observe the Enemy, whom we did not perceive to make any Motion. About Six the Duke and Prince *Eugene* called to them on a Rising-Ground all the Generals, and gave them the necessary Directions to attack the Enemy; and then our Army advanced into the Plain, and were drawn up in Order of Battle at about Seven. The Enemy, at the Approach of our Van-Guard, gave a Signal, by the firing of two Pieces of Cannon, to call in all their Foragers, and set the Villages of *Onderklaw*, *Volperstet*, *Viller*, *Oufhausen*, and *Sweinebach* on Fire; and then we saw all their Camp in a Motion; their Generals and their Aid de Camps galloping to and fro, to put all Things in Order; and at the same time Lord *Cutts*, Lieutenant-General and Major-Generals *St. Paul* and *Wilks*, with Brigadiers *Row* and *Ferguson*, with two Brigadiers of Foot, to be supported by Major-General *Wood*, with Fifteen Squadrons, were order'd on our Left, to possess themselves of the two Water-Mills near *Blenheim*, which the Enemy immediately set on Fire. In the mean time, our Army advanced as far as the *Morass*; which being found very marshy and unpassable for our Army, we quickly made five Bridges with the Planks of our Pontons, and repaired the Bridge on the High Road, which the Enemy had destroy'd; and at the same time Prince *Eugene* caused the Right Wing to march along the Wood, to fall on the Flank of the Elector, who extended his Left proportionably, to prevent

Prince

Prince *Eugene*'s gaining his Flank. The Enemy fearing also that we should gain the Flank of their Right Wing, by possessing ourselves of the Village of *Blenheim*, sent that Way several Detachments of Foot, and posted therein Twenty-eight Battalions, and Twelve Squadrons of Dragoons: They also posted some Infantry in the Villages of *Overklaw* and *Lutzingen*, which extreamly weaken'd their main Battalia, and was one of the principal Causes of their Defeat. To favour the Passage of our Left Wing, Lord *Cutts*, with the Two aforesaid Brigadiers, was order'd to pass the Rivulet first; which done, they posted themselves in a Bottom, near the Village of *Blenheim*; and for several Hours, with wonderful Resolution, they stood the Fire of six Pieces of Cannon, planted on the Height near that Village; and at the same time the Enemy fired very smart and brisk on the Bridges that were laid for the Passage of our Foot; but they were quickly answer'd by Two of our Batteries, the one of *English*, and the other of *Dutch*; which cannonading did considerable Execution on both Sides. About Noon all Things were ready on our Left Wing for the Attack; but in some Places Fascines being wanted for the Horse to pass the *Morass*, each Squadron in our Second Line was order'd to provide for themselves Twenty; and by this Time a good Part of the Infantry of our main Battalia had posted themselves in and about the Village of *Overklaw*; and the Prince of *Holsteinback* posted himself in that of *Weilerorschenback*, and caused a Counter-Battery to be erected there. Both Armies cannonaded each other very smartly and vigorously with several Batteries, from Eight in the Morning till past Twelve at Noon, with great Loss. A little before One o'Clock in the Afternoon, all being ready to begin the Attack, the Duke order'd the Left to begin; and immediately Major-General

Campaign IV.
Anno 1704.

I ral

ral *Wilks*, with Brigadier *Row* and his Brigade of Five Battalions of *English*, made the first Onset or Attack, with Four Battalions of *Hessians*, supported by Lord *Cutts* and Major-General *St. Paul*, with Eleven other Battalions, and Major-General *Wood* with Fifteen Squadrons. Those Five Battalions led on by Brigadier *Row* advanced on with undaunted Courage, and with unparallel'd Intrepidity attack'd the Village of *Blenheim* on the Muzzles of the Enemy, and some of the Officers exchanged Thrusts of Swords with the *French* through their Pallisades; but being exposed to a Fire much superior than theirs, they were soon forced to retire with a Loss of near a Third Part of their Men either killed or wounded, and the Brigadier mortally wounded, of which he died in a few Days after; and being pursued by Thirteen Squadrons of the *French Gens d'Arms* and Carabineers, they would have entirely cut 'em to pieces, had not the *Hessian* Foot by a great Fire put a sudden Stop to their Career; and by that Time Five Squadrons of *English* having pass'd the Rivulet chased, and made the Enemy fly in their Turn: But whilst they rally'd, some fresh Brigades of the Enemy, superior in Number, charged our Horse with great Vigour, and obliged them to repass the Rivulet with Precipitation; and here again the *Hessian* Foot performed notable Service, in putting the Enemy to the Rout by a continual Fire, and regained the Colours which *Row*'s Regiment had lost; and whilst *Row*'s Brigade rally'd, *Ferguson* with his Brigade attack'd *Blenheim* on the Left; but with no better Success: And although both returned three or four Times to the Charge, with equal Vigour and Valour, yet both were still repulsed with the like Disadvantage; so that it was found impossible to force the Enemy out of that Post, without entirely sacrificing our Foot. Our *English* Foot having thus begun the Engagement

on

on the Left, the Horse of the same Wing pass'd the Rivulet *Pell-Mell*, over-against the Center of the Enemies main Battalia: The Horse of our Right Wing also pass'd the Rivulet, having made several Passages with divers Pieces of Wood, which they found at hand; and, in a Word, all pass'd and drew up in Order of Battle, as well as the Ground would permit, on the other Side of the Rivulet. The Enemy gave us all the Time we wanted for that purpose, and kept very quiet on the Hill they were possess'd of, without descending to the Meadow towards the Rivulet; insomuch that even our second Line of Horse had Time to form themselves: And to this Capital Fault of the *French* we ought principally to ascribe our Victory. The Horse of our Left going towards the Hill, that of the Enemy began to move at last, and charged our Men with a great deal of Fury. The *French* Foot at *Blenheim* at the same time, from behind the Hedges, made a terrible Fire on the Flank of our Horse, who were advanced too near to that Village; so that the first Line of our Horse of our Left, from the Head of the Line to the Three Regiments of *Hanover* Troops, *viz.* that of the Elector's, that of *Voigt*'s, and that of *Noyelle*'s, was put into such Disorder, that Part of them retired over beyond the Rivulet. Hereupon, Lieutenant-General *Bulow*, Commander in Chief of the *Lunenburgh* Troops, brought up from the Second Line his own Regiment of Dragoons, and Two others of the Troops of *Zell*, *viz.* Major-General *Viller*'s and Brigadier *Bothmer*'s, who charged the Enemy with such Vigour, that they broke them, and drove them beyond the second Rivulet called *Meulweger*, and from thence to the very Hedges of *Blenheim*. This gave Time to our Men that had given Ground to repass the Rivulet, and to form a second Line behind those Regiments of Dragoons, and some others

others that had joined them; so that those Dragoons remained in the first Line all the remaining Time of the Action. The Horse of our Left having by this Success gained the Advantage of forming themselves entirely in Order of Battle, advanced leisurely to the Top of the Hill, and charged several Times the Enemies Horse, who were always routed; yet, nevertheless, rally'd every Time, though at a considerable Distance, which gave us Opportunity to gain Ground; and as we were preparing for a fresh Attack, Count *Tallard* caused Ten Battalions to advance, and fill up the Intervals of his Horse, in order to make a last Effort; which the Prince of *Hesse Cassel*, General of Horse, Lieutenant-Generals *Lumley*, *Bulow*, *Hompesch*, and *Ingoldsby* perceiving, caused Three Battalions of the Troops of *Zell* to come up, and sustain our Horse; and then we return'd to the Charge: But, by the Superiority of the Enemies Foot, our first Line was put somewhat in Disorder; so that it shrunk back about Sixty Paces distance, and remained for some time, neither advancing against the other. At last, our Men renewed the Charge, and that with such Vigour and Success, that they broke and routed the Enemies Horse; and the Ten Battalions, who were abandon'd by them, were entirely cut in pieces, none escaping, but a few who threw themselves on the Ground as dead, to save their Lives. At this Time Count *Tallard* rally'd his broken Cavalry behind some Tents that were all this Time standing in his Camp; and then seeing Things in this desperate Condition, resolved to draw off his Dragoons and Foot out of *Blenheim*, and sent Orders by one of his Aid de Camps to Marshal *Marsin* at *Overklaw*, to face the Enemy with some Troops on the Right of the said Village, to keep them in Play, and favour the Retreat of his Infantry that was in *Blenheim*; but he reprefented to him by that Meffenger, that he had too much Bufinefs in the Front of his Village, where he had to deal with the Duke of *Marlborough* in Perfon, and the reſt of the Line, to fpare any Troops; he not being victorious, but only maintaining his Ground. In the mean time, Lieutenant-General *Ingoldſby* made the Prince of *Heſſe*, Lieutenant-General *Lumley* and *Hompeſch* fenſible, how eafy it would be to entirely defeat the *French* Cavalry, by charging their Right Flank. The which Advice being put in Execution, with a great deal of Vigour and Courage, the Enemy was prefently diforder'd, and put to Flight, and their Rout was entire: Part of them endeavour'd to gain the Bridge they had on the *Danube* between *Blenheim* and *Hochſtat*; the other Part, among whom were the *Gens d'Arms*, were clofely purfued by *Bothmar*'s Dragoons; and thofe who efcaped being killed, threw themfelves into the *Danube*, where moſt of them were drown'd; and thofe who fled towards *Hochſtat* rally'd once more, making a Shew, to fuccour the reſt; but the Regiment of *Bothmar* faced them, and kept them in Awe for fome time; and being at length join'd with fome other Regiments, the Enemy fled off full Gallop towards *Hochſtat*. The Marſhal *de Tallard* was invelop'd with the Runaways, and taken near a Mill behind *Sonderen* Village by Monfieur *de Boinenburg*, a Lieutenant-Colonel of the Troops of *Heſſe*, and Aid de Camp to the Prince of *Heſſe Caſſel*. Marquis de *Montperous*, General of Horfe *de Seppeville*, *de Silly*, *de la Valiere*, Major-General *de la Meſſilierre*, *St. Palange*, *de Ligondais*, and feveral other Officers of Note, were alfo made Prifoners in this Rout with *Tallard*. Whilſt thefe Things paſs'd at *Blenheim* and in the Center, the Duke caufed *Overklaw* and Marſhal *Marſin*'s Quarters to be attack'd by Prince *Holſtenback*, as

Campaign IV. Anno 1704.

Major-General, with *Berensdorf*'s Brigade of Ten Battalions: The Prince pass'd the Rivulet at the Head thereof, with a great deal of brave Resolution; but as the Imperial Horse, which was to have supported him, was above two Musket-shot from him, he was hardly gone over, when Seven or Eight Battalions of the Enemy fell on him with great Fury before he could form his Two Regiments; so that that of *Goor*'s was entirely cut to pieces, and the Prince himself mortally wounded, and taken Prisoner. Our Men being sustained by some *Danish* and *Hanoverian* Horse, charged a second Time, but with no better Success; but the third Time, the Duke himself having brougbt up some Squadrons, which were supported by others of the Body of Reserve, made them advance with some Battalions beyond the Rivulet: Whereupon the Enemy began to retire; and as soon as he had perform'd this considerable Service, he repaired to the Center; where finding the Action decided in our Favour, he caused part of his victorious Horse to halt, to observe the Motion of that Part of the Enemy, which by that Time was drawn up beyond the Morass of *Hochstat*. During this Halt, the Elector of *Bavaria* was perceived making his Retreat from the Village of *Lutzing*; upon which, Orders were dispatch'd to General *Hompesch*, who was pursuing the Enemy with several Squadrons towards *Merseling*, and who had already overtaken Two of their Battalions, and forced them to lay down their Arms: Orders being sent to him to face about, and march to join those that halted, as well to prevent the Elector's falling on his Rear, as to form a Body to charge the Elector, who march'd in great Haste, but in pretty good Order, with his Squadrons on the Left, and his Battalions on the Right. Before General *Hompesch* returned from the Chace, the Right Wing of our Army was

perceived

perceived at some Distance behind the Elector, and appearing to be a part of his Army, marching in such manner as might easily have flanked us, had the Duke of *Marlborough* immediately charged him. The Duke with great Prudence sent out a Party to view them: During this Time the Elector continued marching off with great Precipitation, till he reach'd the *Morass* of *Merseling*. The *French* Horse being entirely defeated, and our Troops Masters of all the Ground which was between the Enemies Left and the Village of *Blenheim*, the Twenty-eight Battalions and Twelve Squadrons of Dragoons, finding themselves quite cut off from the rest of their Army, and despairing of being able to make their Escape, after a weak Attempt to repulse our whole Infantry that surrounded the Village, they at last capitulated about Eight at Night, laid down their Arms, deliver'd their Standard and Colours, and surrender'd themselves Prisoners of War, on Condition that their Officers should not be searched. By this it appears that not one of the Forty Battalions, with which Count *Tallard* join'd the Elector of *Bavaria* some few Days before the Battle, escaped; Ten thereof were entirely cut to pieces in the Intervals of their Horse, in the Heat of the Action: Two taken in their precipitate Retreat to the other Side of *Hochstat*, and Twenty-eight taken Prisoners of War in the Village of *Blenheim* by our Troops.

Next followeth how Things passed on our Right Wing, in Prince *Eugene*'s Command, against the Elector of *Bavaria* and Marshal *de Marsin*. The Horse of the Right Wing were most of them posted over against *Overklaw*, but the Eighteen Battalions who were to the Right of all, had a great Way to march before they could get up the Hill, and besides the Passage of the Rivulet being very difficult. The Attack could not begin

Campaign IV. Anno 1704. begin on that Side as soon as Prince *Eugene* could have wished; and besides the Troops of our Right, which posted themselves in a Bottom, not far from *Lutzing*, were obliged to remain exposed during three Hours, to the cannonading of the Enemy, without being able to make Use of their Artillery: Till at length a Counter-Battery was raised near the Wood, and though our Right could not charge till half an Hour after, our Left had begun the Attack; yet they were pretty succesful at first, for our Infantry, though much inferior in Number to the Enemy, maintained themselves against them with great Firmness and Resolution, and our Horse broke that of the Enemies first Line, but they were so vigorously repulsed by their second Line, that Part of them were driven in great Confusion beyond the Rivulet; and our Infantry having no more Horse to sustain them, was obliged, notwithstanding the great Resistance they made, to retreat Three or Four Hundred Paces towards the Wood with considerable Loss, especially the Two Battalions that were on the Flanks, insomuch that Things at that Time were in a very ill Condition on that Side. The Infantry stood firm near the Wood, and Prince *Eugene* having rallied the Horse, brought them up again to the Charge; but they were repulsed a second Time. They were rallied once more, and for near three Quarters of an Hour we stood within about Sixty Paces of the Enemy, neither of the two Parties making any Motion. We made Use of that Time to post our Troops advantageously, and to put them in Order, after which we charged a third Time. Our Cavalry had at first some Advantage over that of the Enemy, but were afterwards repulsed by them; whereas our Infantry broke and overthrew that which they had to deal, though they could not march up to the Enemy,

but

but through a most difficult Ground, where a small
Number of Troops was sufficient to stop a great
Number. Hereupon Prince *Eugene* left his Cavalry, seeing no Likelihood of being able to rally
them again, and came and put himself at the
Head of the Infantry, who improving the Disorder into which they had put that of the Enemy,
pursued them over Hills, Dales, Rocks and
Woods; and having charged them again, did entirely rout them, and continued the Chace for above an Hour's March, as far as the Village of
Lutzing. Here Prince *Eugene* caused his victorious Foot to make a Stand, to give Time to his
Cavalry, which had rallied a great Way behind,
to rejoin the Infantry. It was very remarkable,
that at this last Charge, when our Infantry defeated with so much Vigour that of the Enemy, there
remained by them but two of our Squadrons, notwithstanding which they pursued their Advantage,
and gave not the Enemy Time to recover themselves. The *French* Horse daunted with our Success, retired leisurely, ours followed them accordingly, till having joined our Foot, and then the
whole Wing continued the Chace, during an Hour,
as far as the Villages of *Merfling* and *Theffenhoren*,
where the Enemy made a Show to stand their
Ground, that they might have the Time to pass
a great Morass, and reach *Dillengen* and *Lavingen*.

As soon as the Action was decided on our Left
Wing, the Duke disposed himself to march with
Part of that Wing towards *Overklaw*, to charge
the Enemies Left on their Flank, and to succour
our Right; but he was informed by the Way, by
one of *Eugene*'s Aid de Camp, that there was no
more Need of it; that all was recovered on the
Prince's Side, and that the Enemy had abandoned
the Villages of *Overklaw* and *Lutzing*, after setting
them

them on Fire. This Victory, though as great and compleat in itself as any that was ever gained, was still greater in its Consequences. *Bavaria* and *Marsin* having gathered the Remains of their Defeat behind the Morass of *Hochstat*, halted there a few Hours, and that very Night sent over their Baggage to the other Side of the *Danube*, and their Horse towards *Ulm* by *Gondelfingen*; and the next Morning by Break of Day, they drew off the Foot, and passed the *Danube* at *Lavingen*, where they left One Thousand Men, with Orders to retreat as soon as the Enemy should approach, and to burn the Bridge, which was accordingly done. The Elector at the same Time sent Orders to his Troops at *Augsburg* and other Places, to quit them, and to come and join him at *Ulm*, where he march'd with the greatest Precipitation. The Duke and Prince *Eugene* would have followed him with equal Speed, but the great Number of their Prisoners was a Luggage, that retarded their Progress Four or Five Days. That Night after the Battle our Confederate Army drew up, and lay on their Arms near the Morass at *Hochstat*; the Left extended itself towards the Village of *Sonderheim*, and the Right towards *Mersling* The *British* Troops at *Blenheim* formed a Lane, wherein the Prisoners stood all Night, and they on the Watch over the same. The Officers thereof, the Duke out of Compliment, allowed to wear their Swords.

A Computation, which I then received of the Enemies Loss, sustained in that ever memorable Battle at Hochstat, *viz.*

Generals or noted Persons killed in the Field, or drowned in the *Danube*,	9

The Quantity of Thirty Squadrons rush'd into the *Danube*, and drowned, computed,	4400	Campaign IV. Anno 1704.
Killed in the Time of the Battle, Officers included,	6000	
Wounded or disabled therein, Officers included,	8000	
Total killed and wounded, including the Thirty Squadrons drowned, and Ten Battalions cut in Pieces, with the Quantity of Twenty two Battalions otherwise killed and wounded in the Action,	18409	
Deserted in the Battle and precipitate Retreat, otherwise computed,	5000	
Total killed or drowned, wounded and deserted,	23409	

Note, That Three Generals of the aforesaid Nine were assuredly wounded, but no Account could be had of the other Six, whether killed in the Field, or drowned in the *Danube*; but certainly they were left in either of the twain; amongst which there was Four Marquises, Two Counts, and One Duke, whose Names I have here omitted.

Taken, Count *Tallard*, their Captain General, Four Lieutenant Generals, Six Major Generals, and Eight Brigadiers, Three other Colonels of Horse, Three of Dragoons, and Thirteen of Foot; most Counts, Marquises, Princes, Dukes and Barons; besides Three Marquises, and One Prince Captain of the *Gens d'armes.*	41

Besides

Campaign IV.
Anno 1704.

Besides all the Lieutenants, Colonels and Majors of the aforesaid Twenty-eight Battalions, and Twelve Squadrons of Dragoons, each computed to be compleat thereof, — 64

Of Captains and subaltern Officers, computed accordingly, — 1095

In the Twenty-eight Battalions of Centinels, &c. with some Stragglers, that fell into *Blenheim*, — 12200

In the Twelve Squadrons, including also some Stragglers, and otherwise, — 1800

Total of the whole killed or drowned, wounded, taken and deserted, — 38609

By the several particular Accounts of the Enemies Loss, it appears that of the Sixty Thousand Men their Army consisted of before the Battle, there escaped but Twenty-one Thousand Three Hundred and Ninety One. Besides, there were several noted Persons and others taken by the other Allies, which I never found to insert herein. I take the Total of those Accounts of the Enemies Loss in the Battle, to be more real Fact, than that of their own common Account, which discovereth but Thirty Thousand and Two, according to their several following Particulars thereof, *viz.*

Killed and wounded in the Field, and drowned in the *Danube*, Officers included, about — 14000

Taken General Persons Seventeen, other Officers One Thousand Four Hundred and Eighty Five, Centinels Eleven Thousand Five Hundred, in all — 13002

Deserted, or otherwise lost in the Action and precipitate Retreat, — 3000

The

The Enemy were induſtriòus enough in concealing their particular Loſſes, but whether of theſe two Particulars it be, it matters not much; doubtleſs their Loſs was very great in every Reſpect whatſoever; being conquered, beat, and quite defeated; although Eight Thouſand Men ſtronger than the Allies Army, beſides being ſtrongly poſted with the Advantage of the Ground; but by *Tallard*'s own Account, they exceeded in Number but Four Thouſand.

Campaign IV. Anno 1704.

Taken of War Utenſils or Trophies, one Hundred Cannon, Twenty-four Mortars, One Hundred Seventy One Standards, One Hundred Twenty Nine Pair of Colours, Seventeen Pair of Kettle Drums, Fifteen Pontons, Twenty-four Barrels, and Eight Caſks of Silver, Thirty-four fine Coaches, Three Hundred loaded Mules, and Three Thouſand Six Hundred Tents, ſtanding and ſtruck.

In the Confederates gaining this compleat, honourable, glorious, ever-renowned, memorable Conqueſt and triumphant heroical Victory, over and againſt the proud and lofty *French* Army and *Bavarians* at *Hochſtat*, *Auguſt* 2d, their Loſs was computed Twelve Thouſand Seven Hundred and Fifty-eight Men, killed and wounded, including Two Hundred and Seventy-four that were loſt by Deſertion, or otherwiſe taken moroding in the Time of our Army's Abode in *Bavaria*. Killed and wounded Twelve Thouſand Four Hundred and Eighty-four, Officers included, as doth appear by this following Table, each Corp's particular Loſs in brief.

Other

(128)

Campaign IV. Anno 1704.

CORPS.		No. of Batts.	No. of Squa.	Colonels		Lt. Col.		Majors		Captain		Subaltn		Centinels		Total		
				Kd.	Wd.	Kd.	Wd.	Kd.	Wd.	Kd.	Wd.	Kd.	Wd.	Kd.	Wd.	Killed	Wound.	Kd. Wd.
Britains. {	Foot —	14	—	1	2	3	1	6	17	44	26	74	—	509	1220	557	1350	1907
	Horse and Dragoons	—	18	—	1	2	1	3	—	8	10	—	—	101	200	113	214	327
	Total —	14	18	1	2	4	4	3	7	18	47	34	86	610	1420	670	1564	2234
Other Allies. {	Holland's —	14	19	Officers and all Stations included												772	1424	2196
	Lunenberg's —	13	25	Ditto												824	1580	2404
	Wirtenberg's —	7	12	Ditto, Seven Squadrons thereof *Hesse*												450	674	1124
	Danes —	—	22	Ditto												102	200	302
	Ger- { 11 Bats *Prussians* mans. { 7 — *Danes*	18	92	Ditto { Of the Empire, K. of *Prussia*, Circle of *Suabia*, *Wirtenberg*, and other Places												1724	2500	4224
	Total —	66	188	Ditto												4542	7942	12484

We loft in this Action, very few Perfons of Note, except Prince *Holfteinback* and Brigadier *Row,* who were mortally wounded and died thereof, and Lord *North* and *Grey* loft his Right Hand. Doubtlefs each Corp's Officers fuftained great Lofs accordingly as pofted, which I found not.

This Battle being the moft note-worthy Action of any in the whole War, I have therefore been the more particular in writing the larger upon it, than of any other during the War, it being very memorable, by which the Fate of the Empire, or rather *Europe* was decided.

Aug. 3, Or Day after the Battle, our whole Army removed from the Field of Battle rightward paft *Hochftat,* and form'd and pitch'd Camp regularly, with our Right at *Wilifling,* and Left at *Steinbim,* oppofite to *Lavingen* and *Dillengen,* all on the Weft Brink of the *Danube,* with our Front to the River, Seven Leagues Weftward from *Donawert,* to which that Day all our Sick and Wounded were fent, and from thence to our grand Hofpital, then erected at *Narling* in *Wirtenburg.*

5, The Duke and Prince *Eugene* reviewed our Army, and we had a folemn Thankfgiving for the Victory; and at Taptoo, a triple Difcharge of all our Cannon and fmall Arms, as a Rejoycing for the late glorious Succefs obtained over our Enemy at *Hochftat.*

6, The Duke and Prince *Eugene* made a Repartition of the Prifoners taken at *Hochftat,* of which Duke *Marlborough*'s Share, with *Tallard,* and fome others of Note, amounted to Five Thoufand Six Hundred and Seventy Eight, and Prince *Eugene*'s Share amounted to (Officers included) Five Thoufand Five Hundred and Fourteen, which made in all Eleven Thoufand One Hundred and Ninety Two,

Campaign IV. Anno 1704.

Campaign IV. Anno 1704.

Two, including the Ninety-five Officers that were found at *Hochstat*, *Lavingen* and *Dillingen*; besides Three Thousand *Germans* of *Greder*'s and *Surlaben*'s Regiments, who voluntarily lifted themselves in the Service of the Allies, besides some Stragglers that went off otherwise. And next Day Count *Tallard*, with the rest of our Share of Prisoners of Distinction, *&c.* were sent from *Hochstat* under a Guard of Forty *English* Horse, towards *Hanaw* and *Francfort*. Now the Duke and Prince *Eugene* wisely considering that the Face of Affairs in that Country was wholly changed, they imparted to Prince *Lewis* their Sentiments, that to amuse themselves at the Siege of *Ingolstat*, would be but losing Time, and that they believed it would be more advantageous for the Good of the common Cause to join all their Forces, to streighten more and more the Enemy, and oblige the *French* to quit *Germany*, and repass the *Rhine*; for then not only *Ingolstat*, but also the whole Country of *Bavaria*, must fall of themselves: Nor was it long before the Duke and Prince *Eugene*'s Opinion was confirmed, by the Example of the City of *Augsburg*, which the *French* in Garrison there quitted on the 5th of *August*, taking with them Four Hostages, as a Security for Two Thousand Sick and Wounded left there; and the Magistrates thereof at the same Time, sent Four Deputies to the Duke for Protection, whom the Duke gave a kind Reception, and told them, that her *Britanick* Majesty's Troops, and that of the States-General were only sent against the Enemies of the Empire, and their Allies, and need not fear, and thereupon sent a Detachment and took Possession of that City.

8, Our Army decamp'd at, and march'd from *Stenheim*, over the little River *Moad*, and pitch'd Camp, with our Right at *Brentz*, and the Left at *Gondelfing*, two Leagues.

9, Decamp'd at, and march'd from *Brentz* to, and pitch'd Camp between *Langenaw* and *Und-Elchingen*, four Leagues.

10, Decamp'd at and march'd from *Und-Elchingen* Cloister, and pitch'd Camp at *Seslingen* Town, two Leagues; the front Line facing outward, and the Rear, or second Line, facing inward or backward, within about one *English* Mile of *Ulm*; in which the Elector had left a Garrison of Four *French* and Five *Bavarian* Battalions, commanded by Major General *Bettendorf*, which were immediately block'd up. The Elector with the rest of his Troops removed and retired farther up the *Danube*, towards the *Iler*. Here in the Bleaching Yards and Meadows, several of our Men found Plenty of Linnen. That same Morning a Deputy from the City of *Memingen* waited on the Duke for Protection; the next Day the Governor of *Ulm*, justly apprehending a Siege, sent out to the Duke of a Compliment Four Hundred and Thirty Prisoners, which the Enemy had taken of our Army at *Hochstat*, *Dillingen*, and other Places, desiring the Duke at a convenient Time, or when he pleased, to return an equal Number; but being *Germans*, the Duke sent them to Prince *Eugene*'s Disposal.

Now the Elector's Communication being intirely cut off from his own Country, the 12*th* that Night he sent a Letter to the Confederate's Camp, desiring the Favour of the Duke, to give Conveyance of one enclosed to the Electoress, which the Duke sent forward to *Munick* by a Trumpeter of his own; she and her Children being gone thither the Day before, under a Guard of Fourteen Squadrons from *Dutlingen*, whereabouts the Elector then lay.

Aug. 13, Prince *Van Baden* left his Army encamp'd at *Lavingen*, being removed from *Ingoldstat*,

Campaign IV. Anno 1704. ſtat, and came in Perſon to *Seflingen*, to confer with the Duke and Prince *Eugene* for the farther Operations of the Campaign; whereupon the next Day they three concerted thereon, and it was reſolved, ſeeing the Enemy were returning towards the *Rhine*, all the Confederate Forces ſhould likewiſe march that Way, except General *Thungen* with Twenty-three Battalions and Fifteen Squadrons, ſhould be left to carry on the Siege againſt *Ulm*; and that Count *Wratiſlaw* ſhould continue in that Camp, to manage the Negotiations with the Electoreſs, who made ſome Overtures to deliver, not only *Ulm*, but alſo the whole Electorate of *Bavaria*, upon certain Conditions.

Aug. 15, Our Grand Army decamp'd at *Seflingen*, and march'd off from thence in Four Bodies towards *Landawin* different Roads, to eaſe the Country of *Wirtemberg*, viz. The *Germans* with Prince *Lewis* march'd towards the *Rhine*, off by themſelves. The *Dutch* and *Heſſians* another Way apart by themſelves. The *Hanovers* and *Lunenburgers* another Way alſo apart by themſelves. Fourthly and laſtly, General *Churchill*, with the *Britiſh* and *Daniſh* Foot, and our Artillery, march'd off another Way apart by themſelves; and that Day at Night, we pitch'd Camp at *Launſheim*, four Leagues. But the Duke with the Horſe and Dragoons of theſe two Corps laſt mentioned, abode two Days behind at *Seflingen*, giving General *Thungen* his neceſſary Directions for the carrying on the Siege againſt *Ulm*, after which he alſo took another Road, and joined us not till the 20*th* inſtant.

16, General *Churchill*, with the aforeſaid Corps and Artillery decamp'd at, and march'd from *Launſheim*, to and pitch'd Camp at *Groſsſciſſen* in *Lower Suabia*, four Leagues, having that Day
paſs'd

pass'd through *Cyzling Pass*, down between two high steep Hills, and a Wood.

17, Decamp'd at and march'd from *Grossscissen*, to and pitch'd Camp at *Eberspach*, four Leagues.

19, Decamp'd at, and march'd from *Eberspach*, and pitch'd Camp at *Gross-Heppach* in the Dukedom of *Wirtemburg*, near *Eslingen*, on the River *Rems*; where we had pass'd it that Day about Noon.

20, Decamp'd at, and march'd from *Gross-Heppach* to, and pitch'd Camp at *Mundelsheim*, and rejoined the Duke with the Horse and Dragoons, who had come thither a good Way round, and off to the Right Hand of our March; from which the next Morning, the Duke by Invitation went to *Stutgart*, with the Duke of *Wirtemberg*'s Grand Marshal, and was magnificently entertained by the Duke Regent of *Wirtemberg*, and that Evening he returned with several others of our General Officers to *Mundelsheim*.

22, Decamp'd at, and march'd from *Mundelsheim* over the *Necker* at *Lauffeon* to, and pitch'd Camp at *Gross-Gartach*, near to the Town of *Hailbron*, five Leagues.

23, Decamp'd at, and march'd from *Gross-Gartach*, to, and pitch'd Camp at *Eppingen* near *Stetten*, where we had encamp'd going up into *Germany*, three Leagues.

24, Decamp'd at, and march'd from *Eppingen* to, and pitch'd Camp at *Odenheim*; but the Duke with the aforesaid Horse and Dragoons march'd off apart to, and pitch'd Camp at *Steffelt*. The Enemy having then pass'd the *Black* Forest and retired over the *Rhine*; Prince *Eugene* did not go, as intended, to *Rotweil*, but directly to *Rastat*, to draw the Troops together, and march'd to *Philipsbourg*, where he arrived the 22d instant.

Campaign IV. Anno 1704.

Aug. 25, General *Churchill*, with the Troops in his Command, decamp'd at, and march'd from *Oudenheim* to, and pitch'd Camp at *Langenbrick* near *Steffelt*, two Leagues; from which Place, that Morning, the Duke went to *Philipsbourg*, where he was received with all imaginable Joy, under a Discharge of all the Cannon thereof, and dined with Prince *Eugene*; who, after Dinner, went with Count *Nassau Weilbourg*, and several other General Officers of the Palatine Troops, over the *Rhine*, and view'd the Camp at *Spierbach*, and in the Evening return'd to *Steffelt*.

26, The Duke, with our Army, decamp'd at, and march'd from *Steffelt* and *Langenbrick* to, and pitch'd Camp together at *Kurloch*, two Leagues: And having Advice that several Squadrons of the Enemy appear'd on the Rising-Ground over-against *Philipsbourg*, he order'd the *English* and *Danish* Horse to pass over the *Rhine* with all Expedition, to join the *Palatine* Troops, which Prince *Eugene* sent over that Morning; and they immediately advanced towards the Enemy, who thereupon retired over the River *Queich* to *Germersheim*, and our Army encamp'd on this Side.

27, The Duke, with our Foot and Troops, decamp'd and march'd from *Kurloch*, and, with the *Dutch* Troops and those of *Lunenburgh* and *Hesse*, pass'd over the *Rhine*, a little below *Philipsbourg*, and, together with those that were before on this Side, pitch'd and encamp'd on the *Spierbach*, near to *Spires*, three Leagues; where the *French* had defeated the *Germans* under Prince *Lewis* in 1703: And the next Morning Prince *Lewis*, with the Imperial Horse, join'd our Camp, and had Intelligence that Marshal *de Villeroy* and *Marsin*, with *de Cogny*, and the Forces under his Command, were advanced to the River *Queich*, and had possefs'd

themselves

themselves of all the Passes, to prevent our going over that River, in order to invest *Landau*.

29, By Break of Day, our Army being now wholly joined, with also some other Troops, decamp'd at *Spierbach*, and advanced, with Intent to encamp, as nigh to the River *Queich*, as that Ground would permit, near to *Belheim-Pass*, in order to force the Enemy to a second Battle, or to quit the Pass: But they would not give us the Trouble of either; for at the first of our Appearance, they immediately struck Tents, and quitted their strong Camp on the other Side of the River, where they had been several Days fortifying and pallisading all the Fords and Passes, and withdrew and retired from thence with great Expedition, Haste, Confusion, and Disorder, towards the River *Lauter*, and lay on their Arms very alert that Night; which being done in the Dusk, our whole Army advanced, and march'd over the River; the Foot on several Bridges, which the Enemy had broken down, but were soon repaired; and the Horse fording it in several Places, and pitch'd Camp with our Right at *Offenbach* near *Landau*, three Leagues; and Left at *Blenheim*, on the Enemies Old Camp; where, in their Hurry, they left us plentiful Store of Fruits, and all Sorts of Roots for the Use of our Pots, which at that Time were very acceptable. The same Day a Party of the Imperial Horse having been a reconnoitring towards *Landau*, met the Duke *de Montfort* with some Squadrons, with a Major-General who had been conducting Four Battalions and a Sum of Money to *Landaw*, fell upon them with great Vigour, put them to the Rout, and killed upwards of One Hundred of them on the Spot, took several of them Prisoners, and gave desperate Wounds to their Commander, of which he died in a few Days after.

(136)

Campaign IV. Anno 1704.

Ulm surrender'd.

August 30, About Sun-rising, our whole Army decamp'd at *Offenbach*, and again advanced towards the Enemy, where they had lain on their Arms all Night; from which, as soon as they had Notice that we begun our March thitherward, they retired in great Confusion nearer towards the River *Lauter*: After which the Confederate Army, under the Duke's Command, pitch'd Camp with our Right at *Barelroth*, and Left at *Lancandel*, and halted the next Day; in the mean time, the Enemy pass'd the *Lauter*, and march'd to *Haguenaw*; so that they quitted all the Posts from whence they might have obstructed our attacking of *Landaw*: And the said 30*th*, Prince *Lewis*, with the *German* Troops, fell backward somewhat apart nearer towards *Landaw*; and the same Day General *Thungen*'s great Artillery being arrived at *Ulm*, the Garrison beat a Parly, and the next Day, being the 31*st* instant, surrender'd that Place upon honourable Terms; which was granted, that no Time might be lost for the farther Execution of the Projects of this Campaign. The next Day they march'd out thereof, towards the Body of their scatter'd Troops; and the Imperialists took Possession of *Ulm*, in which they found Two Hundred and Twenty-two Pieces of Brass Cannon, and Twelve of Iron; Twenty-five Brass Mortars, Twelve Hundred Barrels of Powder, with great Stores of all other necessary Provisions for our Army's Use, which did very much supply the carrying on the Siege against *Landau*.

Landau Invested.

Sept. 1, Prince *Lewis*, with the *Germans*, march'd apart, with Forty-eight Battalions and One Hundred and Twenty Squadrons, with Ordnance conform, and invested *Landau*; in which there then was Lieutenant-General *de Laubinie*, with a Garrison of Ten Battalions of *French*, computed to be seven Thousand Men, with upwards of Cannon and Mortars mounted: And at the same

same time, the Duke and Prince *Eugene* decamp'd **Campaign** with the rest of our Confederate Troops from *Lan-* **IV.** *candel*, and march'd to, and pitch'd Camp at *Croon-* **Anno 1704.** *Weiſſenbourg*, on the little River *Lauter*, to cover the Siege; and the same Day the Duke sent Brigadier *Ferguson*, with Five Battalions of *English*, for *Mentz*, in order to meet and embark with the *French* Prisoners, and to conduct them down the *Rhine* into *Holland*, which they accordingly did.

9, The Duke detach'd and sent General *Tilly*, with Six Battalions, from *Weiſſenbourg* Camp to *Lauterbourg*, a little Town on the West-Brink of the *Rhine*, to fortify it, and to keep Garrison there, in order the better to preserve our Communication with the Country, on the East-Side of the *Rhine*; which he soon after accordingly did, which proved very serviceable to our Army at that Time, one of our Bridges being brought up from *Philipsbourg*, and there laid over the *Rhine* near the Town.

5, The *Germans* having instantly prepared, and got all Things ready, for the expeditious carrying on the Siege against *Landau*, at Night a competent Number thereof, with and without Arms, opened their Trenches against the Town and Castle, but with great Loss, being discover'd before they got cover'd.

8, The King of the *Romans* arrived in the *Ger-* ***Landau be-*** *mans* Camp before *Landau*; and at the same time **sieged.** the Duke, being recover'd of his Indisposition, went with Prince *Eugene*, and several other General Officers, to wait on his Majesty, who received the Duke with great Demonstrations of Joy and Affection, and sufficiently expreſs'd the high Esteem he had of the Duke's personal Merit, and of his great Services done to his Majesty's Family, and to the whole Empire. There the Duke abode two Days; and, after having view'd the Proceedings of the *Germans* Approaches against *Landau*, he returned to *Croon-Weiſſenbourg*; and from thence, on the 17*th*, he went to wait upon the said King, who that Day review'd the Army before *Landau*: There the Duke ſtaid with his Majeſty that Night, and the next Morning return'd to his Army encamp'd at *Croon-Weiſſenbourg*.

Sept. 20, The Duke having Intelligence before of the King of the *Romans* coming to pay him a Viſit in his Camp, to ſee his victorious Troops, drew up our Army in two Lines Leftward of our Camp, and received his Majeſty at the Left Wing thereof, with preſented Arms, and the uſual Melody of War; and the Duke waited on him all along the Line, and ſaluted him with a triple Diſcharge of all the Artillery and ſmall Arms. The King expreſſing a great Satisfaction at the Entertainment, and the good Condition he found the Army then in.

21, By Break of Day, the *Germans* ſeveral Batteries being erected and compleated, to the Number of Sixty-eight Cannon, and Twenty Mortars and Howitzers, againſt *Landau*, began to play, and that very vigorouſly and ſmartly againſt Town and Caſtle; and afterwards proceeded as gradually as could be expected, conſidering the Badneſs of the Weather, which made it more tedious both to the Beſiegers and Beſieged, and that with great Loſs, whoſe ſmall Particulars I am obliged to wave, none of our Corps being employ'd therein: Nevertheleſs, I could not avoid inſerting ſomewhat of the moſt remarkable Things thereof, for the better Compleatment of my Journal.

26, The Duke return'd the King his Viſit, where he had a long Conference with him and Prince *Lewis* of *Baden*, and return'd: After which, the Duke having received Advice that the *French* intended to ſend a Detachment from the *Netherlands* to ſecure *Triers*, he immediately ſent a Detachment

of

of some Battalions and Dragoons to possess *Hombourg*, &c.

October 2, General *Churchill*, under a Convoy of Four Battalions of *English*, set out from *Croon-Weissenbourg* towards *Holland*, in order for *England*; who the next Day embark'd, in Skiffs, at *Seissenheim*, on the West-Brink of the *Rhine*, and sailed down the same, and in ten Days after arrived at *Nimeguen*; from which, in two Days after, the Four Battalions went to their respective Garrisons, or Winter-Quarters; and then there remained at *Croon-Weissenbourg*, of our Corps, Seven Regiments of Horse and Dragoons, with Five Battalions of Foot, and all our Artillery; maintaining the Field till the 2d of *November*, when the Siege of *Landau* was over, and the Affairs thereof settled, &c.

11, The Duke sent such another after the former Detachment gone to *Hombourg*; and, on the 13th, the Duke follow'd them himself, who on the 17th arrived at *Harmskill*, within six Leagues of *Triers*; where three Deputies of *Triers* waited upon him, and acquainted him that the *French* having still Three Hundred Men in Fort *St. Martin*'s, they were apprehensive of some ill Usage from them, if he did not immediately prevent it: Whereupon, on the 19th, by Break of Day, he march'd with all the Horse and Four Battalions towards *Triers*, and about Eleven appear'd in Sight thereof; and thereupon the *French* immediately quitted and abandon'd the Fort, and his Troops possess'd themselves thereof; and at the same time he summon'd in a great Number of Pioneers, to repair the Fortifications thereof; and on the 20th he view'd the Ground about *Consaarbruck*, for a Camp for his Horse, to cover the Workmen; and on the 21st he went forwards to *Traerbach*, to take a narrow View thereof; and, after having given his necessary Orders and Directions to the Prince of *Hesse*, with those thofe Troops, for the expeditious carrying on the Siege againſt *Traerbach*, he, on the 22*d*, return'd towards *Landau*, where he arrived on the 27*th* in the Evening, and found the *Germans* Maſters of the main Counterſcarp thereof; which, a little before his Arrival, a competent Number of them attack'd vigorouſly and took, after ſeveral ſharp Repulſes to their often Aſſaults: Whereupon, the next Day, the Beſieged beat a Parly, and capitulated to march out thereof, with their ſmall Arms, and ſome other uſual Marks of Honour; and being granted, they march'd out thereof accordingly, and was conducted to their Grand Camp near *Straſbourg*, to which they had retired, as our Army was about forming the ſaid Siege.

During the Siege againſt *Landau*, of eight Weeks, commenced the 21*ſt* of *September*, and ended the 28*th* of *October*, the Beſieged's Loſs was computed to be near Three Thouſand Six Hundred Men killed and wounded. The *Germans*, or Beſiegers, computed inferior, to be about Two Thouſand killed and wounded.

About this Time *Traerbach* alſo ſurrender'd to the Prince of *Heſſe Caſſel*, who ſoon obliged the Garriſon thereto, although it proved ſomewhat tedious; whoſe Particulars alſo I am obliged to wave, according to the aforeſaid Reaſons.

October. 23, The Duke, after his conquering Progreſs, arrived at our Camp at *Croon-Weiſſenbourg*, where Prince *Eugene* commanded in Chief in his Abſence.

November 2, Prince *Lewis* and *Eugene* decamp'd at, and diſpers'd the Imperial Army from *Landau*, towards their Winter-Quarters, which they all ſoon after arrived at: And at the ſame time the Duke of *Marlborough* decamp'd the Army under his Command at *Croon-Weiſſenbourg*; and likewiſe diſpers'd the ſeveral Corps from thence towards their Winter-Quarters,

Quarters, where they in like manner soon after arrived: And the same Day the aforesaid Remainder of our *British* Troops and Artillery march'd off apart by themselves, in order for *Holland*; and that Night pitch'd Camp at *Rhinzabern*, five Leagues.

3, Decamp'd at, and march'd from *Rhinzabern*, and embark'd in Skiffs near *Philipsbourg*, and sail'd from thence down the *Rhine* to *Nimeguen*, in twelve Days Time; where, on the 12*th*, we arrived: But the Horse and Dragoons went the nighest Way by Land down into *Holland*, having left some of our Artillery and Men thereof conform at *Coblentz* on the *Moselle*, ready for a fresh Project on that Side, in the next Spring; of which more afterward. In this Voyage, on the Side of the *Rhine*, I observed Thirty fine Cities and Towns.

16, The Troops and Artillery march'd from *Nimeguen*, cross'd the *Maes* at the *Grave*, and pitch'd a little off to the Westward of the Town, and the next Day to *Bosch*.

19, Dispers'd at the *Bosch*, and Garrison of *Breda* and Artillery march'd to *Walweich*, four Leagues.

20, They removed from *Walweich* into their Winter-Quarters in *Breda*, four Leagues.

The Duke paid a Visit to *Berlin*, *Hanover*, and the *Hague*, before he return'd to *England*.

The tedious, but ever glorious, memorable and victorious Campaign of 1704, was in Length Thirty Weeks and One Day, commenced the 24*th* Day of *April*, and ended on the 20*th* of *November*; of which our Corps, with the Grand Army, and apart, to, in and back from *Germany*, march'd and sail'd Ninety-one Days, and therein Three Hundred Ninety-two Leagues, or One Thousand One Hundred and Seventy-six Miles *English*.

The End of the Fourth Campaign, A. D. 1704.

THE
FIFTH CAMPAIGN,

Begun on the 20*th Day of* April, 1705.

BEFORE I can proceed with my Journal of this Campaign, I muſt ſpeak a little of the Duke's Progreſs (on good Projects, if they had taken) in the latter End of the laſt, &c. After he had ſettled the Affairs of *Landau*, and had ſeveral Conferences with the King of the *Romans* and Prince *Lewis*, of great Conſequence for the Operation of this Campaign, on the 4*th* of *November*, 1704, he ſet out on his Journey; firſt, towards *Berlin*, the King of *Pruſſia*'s Court, where he arrived the 11*th* Ditto; and in going thither, in all the Towns he paſs'd thro' they received him with extraordinary Marks of Reſpect; and at his Arrival at *Berlin*, he was met without the City by the King's Chamberlain, the Head Marſhal, and other Nobility; and that ſame Evening he had Audience of his *Pruſſian* Majeſty and the Queen; and on the 13*th* entertain'd at Dinner by the Prince Royal, who on the 15*th* ſet out with the Duke from *Berlin* for *Hanover*, being infinitely well pleaſed with his Entertainment, and the Succeſs of his Negotiations at that Court. The 19*th* of *November* they arrived at *Hanover*, where the Duke was received by the Elector and Princeſs *Sophia*, and the whole Court,

with

with all imaginable Demonftrations of Refpect: The 24*th* he began his Journey from thence to Holland; and on the 28*th* arrived at *Naerden*, and on the 30*th* fet out for the *Hague*, being faluted with a triple Difcharge of all the Cannon, and the loud Acclamations of the People; and on the 4*th* of *December*, having finifh'd fome Difpatches there, he return'd for *England*, and took over with him Marfhal *Tallard*, and other *French* Generals, and the Colours and Standards taken at *Hochftat*; and at his Arrival therewith at *St. James*'s, he was received by the Queen, Prince, and Nobility, with the higheft Welcome imaginable.

Now, in order to begin this Campaign early on the *Mofelle*, as the Duke before had form'd in his Project, on the 26*th* of *March* he fet out for *Holland*, and arrived at the *Hague* on the 2*d* of *April*; and having there regulated the Operations of the enfuing Campaign, he fet out for *Maeftricht*, where he held a Council of War with Monfieur *Overquerque*, and the other Generals; they to act on the Defenfive in *Brabant*, and he on the Offenfive on the other Side, about or above the *Mofelle*, in order to draw the *French* to a Battle on that Side; which Project, if it had rightly taken Effect, would doubtlefs have decided the Fate of the War on the *Mofelle*, as it had done that in *Bavaria* in 1704: But the *French* Court timely forefeeing the Attempt, ufed all imaginable Precautions and Means to prevent that Blow, which would have entirely opened a Paffage for our Army into *Lorain*, and enabled us to carry the Seat of the War into the very Heart of *France*; and therefore, to prevent the fame, they inftantly fent Marfhal *Villars*, with a powerful Army, to poffefs himfelf of that Part of the Country about *Syrick-Pafs*, near the *Mofelle*; where he foon after was reinforced by two Detachments from Marfhal *Marfin*, where they moft and foon expected

Campaign V. Anno 1705.

Campaign V. Anno 1705.

expected Duke *Marlborough*'s Defign with the Confederate Army; with which I will next begin, and fhew our advancing thitherward, to and from the *Holland* Army at *Maeftricht*, and how returned thither, and what happen'd in our Abfence from them, and what after our rejoining them in the faid Campaign in *Brabant*, &c.

April 20, Generals *Lumley* and *Churchill*, with our *Britifh* Troops and Artillery of the Garrifon of *Breda*, fet out from thence; and that Night canton'd in and about *Waalvyck*, five Leagues: And the fame Day Brigadier *Fergufon*, with the Garrifon of the *Bofch*, fet out therefrom, before our other Troops, all on great Expedition, towards *Maeftricht*; where our General Rendezvous was intended before our Advancement up the Country towards *Triers*, where we were to join all the other Allies intended for the Duke's Command on that Side, &c.

21, The Troops and Artillery march'd from *Waalvyck*, join'd and pitch'd Camp with fome other Garrifons of our Troops at the *Bofch*, three Leagues.

23, Decamp'd at, and march'd from *Bofch* to, and pitch'd Camp at *Carnock*, five Leagues.

24, Decamp'd at, and march'd from *Carnock* to, and pitch'd Camp at *Zelland*, four Leagues.

25, Decamp'd at *Zelland*, and march'd to, and pitch'd Camp at *Boxmeer*, five Leagues.

26, Decamp'd at, and march'd from *Boxmeer* to, and pitch'd Camp at *Griffinfwaert* near *Venlo*, four Leagues; and the fame Day Brigadier *Fergufon*, with the aforefaid Garrifon of the *Bofch*, and thofe of *Venlo* and *Roermonde*, arrived, join'd and pitch'd Camp at *Maefeyck*.

29, The Troops decamp'd, and march'd from *Griffinfwaert* to, and pitch'd Camp at *Chateau de Horn*, five Leagues; and *Fergufon*, with thofe in his Command, removed from *Macfeyck* to *Haught*.

30, Gene-

30, General *Churchill*, with the Troops, decamp'd Campaign
at, and march'd from *Chateau de Horn* to, and V.
pitch'd Camp at *Maeseyck*, five Leagues; and Bri- Anno 1705.
gadier *Fergufon*, with his Command, removed from
Haught, pafs'd *Maeftricht*, and pitch'd at *Buzee*
Village, on the Weft-Brink of the River *Maes*,
half Way between *Maeftricht* and *Liege*, fomewhat
apart from *Holland* Army in Marfhal *Overquerque*'s
Command, who had then join'd, and lay encamp'd
on *Peter's Hill*, near the Citadel of *Maeftricht*;
where they abode the Time of our feven Weeks
Progrefs to and from the *Mofelle*.

May 1, Our Troops and Artillery decamp'd at,
and march'd from *Maefeyck* to, and pitch'd at
Haught, four Leagues.

2, Decamp'd at, and march'd from *Haught*,
pafs'd *Maeftricht* to, and pitch'd Camp, and join'd
with the reft of our Corps, at *Buzee*; where, the
next Day, the Duke, being arrived, review'd all
thereof at the Head of our Encampment; from
which, the Day following, after having fettled the
important Affairs on that Side, he fet out with our
Horfe and Dragoons before, towards the *Mofelle*;
and on the 6*th* he arrived at *Coblentz*; and from
thence he went to *Badftat*, to confer with Prince
Lewis of *Baden*; at the fame Time ordering the
Troops to continue their March to the Neighbourhood of *Triers*; and, after having fettled Matters
with Prince *Lewis*, he on the 16*th* arrived at *Triers*,
where then a confiderable Body of Troops were
affembled, of *Danes*, *Heffians*, *Hanoverians*, *Dutch*,
and other Auxiliaries, in *Dutch* and *Englifh* Pay,
and a Detachment fent from Prince *Lewis*, waiting our Arrival.

4, General *Churchill*, with our *Britifh* Foot and
Artillery, decamp'd at *Buzee*, crofs'd the *Maes*,
and march'd after the Duke, in order to join the
other Allies at, or near *Triers*, as foon as poffible,

for

Campaign V. Anno 1705. for a General Rendezvous, and for Action; and that Night we pitch'd at *Riquelt* Village, four Leagues.

May 5, Decamp'd at, and march'd from *Riquelt* to, and pitch'd at *Herckenrad*, in the Princedom of *Cologn*, three Leagues.

6, Decamp'd at, and march'd from *Herckenrad* to, and pitch'd Camp at *Shaur*, three Leagues.

7, Decamp'd at, and march'd from *Shaur* to, and pitch'd at *Duren*, in the Princedom of *Newbourg*, three Leagues.

9, Decamp'd at, and march'd from *Duren* to, and pitch'd Camp at *Flattine*, three Leagues.

10, Decamp'd at *Flattine*, and march'd to, and pitch'd Camp at *Slyden*, four Leagues.

11, Decamp'd at, and march'd from *Slyden* to, and pitch'd Camp at *Smyttam*, four Leagues.

12, Decamp'd at, and march'd from *Smyttam* to, and pitch'd Camp at *Healfum*, four Leagues; the moſt Part thereof was the next Day accidentally burnt, and ſeveral Perſons therein.

14, Decamp'd at, and march'd from *Healfum* in a great Snow to, and pitch'd Camp at *Shenop*, four Leagues.

16, Decamp'd at, and march'd from *Shenop* to, and pitch'd Camp at *Bibrach*, in the Dukedom of *Luxembourg*, four Leagues.

17, Decamp'd at, and march'd from *Bibrach* to, and pitch'd Camp at *Trierwieler* near *Triers*, four Leagues Weſtward; near which the Duke then lay, with the aforeſaid Troops, on the Eaſt-Side of the City.

22, General *Churchill*, with our Foot and Artillery, decamp'd at, and march'd from *Trierwieler* to, and pitch'd Camp at *Heithell*, two Leagues, on the North-Brink of the *Moſelle* and *Saar*, fronting of both. The Duke at the ſame time, with our Grand Body, removed from the Eaſt-Side of *Triers*

Triers to, and pitch'd Camp at *Kirkcrofs Cloifter*, on the South-Side of the Town, and *Mofelle* fronting it, and General *Churchill*'s Camp; the Left Wing of each extending oppofite to each other, parted by the River. That fame Morning the Duke detach'd Two Companies out of each Battalion of our Corps, and made up thereof Three additional Battalions, in order, as I took it, to countervail the Enemies Number of Battalions, which then lay, as aforefaid, at *Syrick*, and was computed to confift of about One Hundred Battalions of Foot, and One Hundred and Sixty Squadrons of Horfe and Dragoons, Ninety-eight Cannon, Twelve Howitzers, and Thirty Pontons, &c. accounted about Seventy Thoufand Men, under *Villars*'s Command.

The Allies then under the Duke of *Marlborough*'s Command being join'd, including the additional Battalions, were computed to confift of Eighty-four Battalions, and One Hundred and Twenty-fix Squadrons of Horfe and Dragoons, accounted about Sixty Thoufand Men, with Fifty Cannon, and Eight Howitzers, with Twenty-four Pontons, and all other Neceffaries of War conform; the Artillery, which we had left at *Coblentz* the Year before going down the *Rhine*, being join'd.

May 23, Our whole Army decamp'd at their feveral Encampments; the Duke with the aforefaid pafs'd the *Saar* at *Eyll*; and *Churchill*, with our *Britifh* Foot and Artillery, at the fame Time crofs'd the *Mofelle* and *Saar* by *Eyll*; and then both being join'd, the Duke advanced with our Army by the Defile of *Zevern*, towards *Syrick*, where the Enemy then lay; and about Eight at Night arrived within about one Mile thereof, at *Eleft*, where our Army regularly form'd, and lay on their Arms all Night; from which, at the firft of our Appearance approaching thitherward, *Villars* with the
French

Campaign V.
Anno 1704.

French Army retired to the West Side of *Syrick*, and posted himself more advantageously, (for fear of being attack'd by the Duke, though inferior in Number) where the Front of his Army was cover'd by impracticable Defiles, his Right by a Wood, and Left by the *Moselle*, and his Rear by a Rivulet; and thus he was posted, having left Three Hundred Men posted in *Syrick*, which at our Arrival the Duke made Prisoners of War. That Night all Preparations were made, expecting to attack them in the Morning, or that they would have given us Battle; but when Day-light appear'd we found them retired, and strongly fortified, as aforesaid: Whereupon, about Noon, the Duke finding no Opportunity nor Likelihood of any Action, made our whole Army form, and pitch Camp regularly at *Eleft*, seven Leagues, within a Mile on the East-Side, and opposite to *Syrick*, ranging cross that Rising-Ground, with our Right Wing extending downward cross the Bottom, near unto the *Moselle*'s South Brink; and our Left extending near one League Southward from *Eleft*. The Duke of *Lorain* being then alarm'd at the Desolation which his Country was then threaten'd with, sent to the Duke for Protection of his Country, &c. There we lay twelve Days in a profound Silence, and every thing very scarce, and no Sign of any Action on that Side, daily expecting Prince *Lewis* with the *German* Troops to join us, whose Slowness thereto, if not worse, baulk'd our Campaign on that Side, but not in the *Netherlands*; altho', in our Absence, (*Villeroy* being much superior to Marshal *Overquerque*, having Sixty Battalions and One Hundred and Six Squadrons, and Marshal *Overquerque* not above Forty Battalions and Seventy Squadrons, would not venture to attack his entrench'd Camp on *Peter's Hill* at *Maestricht*, but threaten'd much) the *French* Army under *Villeroy*

pass'd

pafs'd the *Maeftricht* at *Bafel*, and invefted *Huy* on the 17th of *May*, by Count *de Gace*, with a Detachment; the Caftle furrender'd to him on the 30th of Ditto, and the Garrifon thereof Prifoners of War; they being numerous, and the *Hollanders* weak; the beft Troops alfo being with the Duke on the *Mofelle*, as aforefaid. They attempted the taking of *Liege* next; and likewife fent Marquis *D'Alegre*, with Eighteen Battalions and Thirty-fix Squadrons, up the Country, in order to reinforce Marfhal *Villars*, left he fhould undergo the fame Fate which *Bavaria*, *Tallard*, and *Marfin* had done already; and the *French* King order'd, that *Villeroy* and *Bavaria* fhould make good Ufe of the Abfence of the Duke of *Marlborough*, with fo many good Troops. The *French* Court in Winter having penetrated into the Duke's Project, in View upon the *Mofelle*, gave out that, to ftop his Progrefs, they would open their Campaign with a Siege againft *Maeftricht*; and thereupon laid up great Stores of Ammunition, &c. in *Namur*. But to that purpofe, they re-enter'd *Liege*, and was about forming a Siege againft that Citadel, in order to retake the fame; and in this very interim, the Duke of *Marlborough* received an Account from the States of the Scheme of their Affairs in the Low Country, the Lofs of *Huy*, and the Siege of *Liege* began, and the Threats that thofe two Generals made, that they would recover all the former Conquefts of the Allies; the Neceffity that there was for him to make a powerful Diverfion to oppofe their Enterprizes; and if that could not be executed upon the *Mofelle*, the States pray'd his Grace that he would return with his Army from thence to *Maes*: Whereupon the Duke, finding no evident Event for the executing of his Project, by any vifible Means on that Side, and the Difficulty in fubfifting his numerous Army in fuch a defert Country, which was

Campaign V. *Anno* 1705.

Campaign V. Anno 1705. likewife ruin'd, and the flow coming of fome German Troops, who were to join him, and the impracticablenefs of attacking *Villars*, who befides his Superiority of Troops in an inacceffible Camp, and no moving of him therefrom, refolved at laft to remarch with his Army to the Relief of *Liege*, with all imaginable Expedition, and for a farther and better Progrefs on that Side; which foon after was glorioufly effected.

June 5, At Taptoo, the Duke of *Marlborough* decamp'd with his Army at *Elfet*, and remarch'd off towards *Maeftricht*, with great Expedition, as aforefaid, and continued our March all that Night without any Halt, till the next Day about Noon; there we recrofs'd the *Saar* and *Mofelle* at *Eyll*, and repitch'd Camp on the North-Side thereof, oppofite to *Kiernyft* near *Triers*; and at the fame time the aforefaid additional Battalions were reduced, each Company to their refpective Regiments; and for the quick Difpatch of our March, our Army received Meal in place of Bread.

7, Here the Duke fet apart Lieutenant-General *Aubach*, with Seventeen Battalions of *Palatines*, Twelve Thoufand *Pruffians*, and Four Thoufand *Wirtenburgers*, in order to remain at *Triers*, and to cover it and thofe Parts of the Country, and to join and reinforce Prince *Lewis* of *Baden* at his Arrival thereat with the *German* or Imperial Troops.

8, General *Churchill*, with all the reft of the Foot of our Army, and a few Squadrons, with our Artillery, decamp'd at *Triers*, and march'd to, and pitch'd Camp at *Banberge*, four Leagues; but the Duke, with the moft Part of our Horfe and Dragoons, abode that Day behind at *Triers*, with Lieutenant-General *Aubach*, giving him his neceffary Directions for the fettling Affairs on that Side, and to maintain the same, if possible, till Prince *Lewis*'s Arrival.

9, General *Churchill*, with the Troops under his Command, decamp'd at *Banberge*, march'd to, and pitch'd Camp at *Nattam* near *Backendorpf*, four Leagues; and the same Day the Duke, with the Horse and Dragoons, set out from *Triers*, and march'd off to the Right of General *Churchill*'s March, void thereof for the Space of seven Days, till our Arrival down the Country at *Duren*.

10, General *Churchill*, with the said Troops, decamp'd at, and march'd from *Nattam* to, and pitch'd Camp at *Budsom*, four Leagues; from which, the next Morning at Eight, he detach'd Lord *Orkney*, with all the rest of our Horse, and all the Grenadiers, and One Hundred Men of each Battalion of our Army, accounted Twelve Thousand Men, to march off immediately before the Body of our Army, to observe the March of a great Detachment of the Enemy, which *Villars* had sent off to the *Netherlands*, as soon as he found our March bent thitherward; and also sent off another great Detachment to reinforce Marshal *Marsin*, who, soon after our Departure, and before Prince *Lewis*'s Arrival at *Triers*, advanced thitherward: Whereupon the *Palatines*, being over-power'd, abandon'd it in haste, and the *French* Troops took Possession thereof, and took therein Forty Pieces of Cannon, and the Magazines, which were not hurt; Lord *Orkney*, and the said Detachment, being march'd on great Expedition before, as aforesaid, in order to observe the March of the aforesaid Body of the Enemy, and to reinforce the *Hollanders* before our Army's Arrival, and to prevent Marshal *Villeroy*'s taking the Citadel of *Liege*, about which they were then form'd; of which they were suddenly prevented: for being instantly inform'd of the Duke's remarching thitherward in several

Campaign V. Anno 1705. veral Bodies, on great Expedition, *Villeroy* and *Bavaria* quickly recalled Marquis *D'Alegre*, with the aforesaid Detachment, from *Moselle*, and sent back their Artillery to *Namur*, abandon'd *Liege*, and retired within their Lines, before the Duke's Arrival to form a new Scheme for the rest of the Campaign, who, in our Absence, had flatter'd themselves with many Conquests, beside the taking of *Liege*; but was now obliged to lodge, and keep within their Lines, and obey the Order of their Court, which was absolutely not to run the Risque of a Battle. But altho' the Duke's returning so soon from the *Moselle* to the *Maes* saved *Lorain*, it caused the Loss of the Low Countries, or at least contributed much to our forcing the Lines: The which Enterprize was a Prelude to the famous Battle of *Ramilies*, no less fatal to *France* than that of *Hochstat*, which decided their Dispute on that Side. But from these Digressions I return to the Particulars of our Remarch.

June 12, General *Churchill*, with the Troops and Artillery under his Command, decamp'd at, and march'd from *Budsom* after Lord *Orkney*, and pitch'd Camp at *Smallab*, four Leagues.

13, Decamp'd at, and march'd from *Smallab* to, and pitch'd Camp at *Steefelt*, four Leagues.

14, Decamp'd at, and march'd from *Steefelt* to, and pitch'd Camp at *Birnsfelt* near unto *Juliers*, a little Town, three Leagues.

15, Decamp'd at, and march'd from *Birnsfelt* to, and pitch'd with the Duke, our Horse and Dragoons at *Birnsdorp* near unto *Duren*, four Leagues; our seventh Day's March downward from *Triers*.

17, All decamp'd at *Birnsdorp*; the Duke with our Horse and Dragoons march'd off apart before towards *Maestricht*, and General *Churchill* with our Foot and Artillery march'd after, and pitch'd Camp at *Aulsdorp*, four Leagues.

18, Gene-

18, General *Churchill* decamp'd at, and march'd from *Aulfdorp* to, and pitch'd Camp at *Harlon*, four Leagues; and the same Day the Duke, with our Horse and Dragoons, arrived and pitch'd Camp at *Esteen*, on the South-East Brink of the River *Maes*, opposite to *Buzee*, (from which we had march'd on the 4th of *May*) half Way between *Maestricht* and *Liege*; and the same Day Lord *Orkney*, with the aforesaid Detachment, arrived at, and reinforced Marshal *Overquerque*'s Camp at *Yarr*, near unto which it had abode during the Time of our going up to, and returning down from the *Moselle*: And now by this Time the *French* had left *Liege*, and retired to their Lines, as aforesaid; of which more afterwards, as it comes in Course.

19, General *Churchill*, with our Foot and Artillery, decamp'd at, and march'd from *Harlem* to, and pitch'd Camp with the Duke, our Horse and Dragoons, where they then lay at *Esteen*, four Leagues; and then all our Troops were nigh, and ready to join the *Hollanders* on the first Occasion.

21, The Duke of *Marlborough* decamp'd, with our whole Army, from *Esteen*, repass'd the *Maes*, march'd to, join'd and pitch'd Camp with Marshal *Overquerque*, with the *Holland*'s Army, at *Yarr*, six Leagues; where, at the same time, the aforesaid Detachment, with Lord *Orkney*, fell into their respective Regiments; and that Day was the first grand Removal of the *Holland*'s Army from *Peter's Hill*, where we had left them as aforesaid; save once, that Lord *Overquerque*, with the main Body, made a small Attempt towards the *French* Lines near *Huy*, in order to baulk the *French* Siege thereof; but the Enemy being much superior in Number to him, he was soon obliged to retire back to *Peter's Hill*: And now the two Armies of the Duke of *Malborough* and Marshal *Overquerque* being again rejoin'd into one, we consisted of One Hundred and Four Battalions of Foot, and One Hundred and Sixty-eight Squadrons of Horse and Dragoons, with One Hundred and Eight Cannon, Twenty Mortars and Howitzers, with Forty Pontons, and all other necessary Utensils of War conform for Action. The *French* Army, on the other Side of their Lines, then, as aforesaid, under Marshal *Villeroy*'s and the Duke of *Bavaria*'s Command, being rejoin'd with the aforesaid Body, and the Marquis *D'Alegre* recalled from *Villars*, and another Detachment besides from him at *Seerich*; they then, I say, was computed to consist of, at *Mayence*, One Hundred and Eight Battalions of Foot, and One Hundred and Seventy-four Squadrons of Horse and Dragoons, with upwards of One Hundred Cannon, Twenty-four Mortars, and Thirty-six Pontons, with all other Utensils of War conform for Action, if Courage would have answer'd their Superiority in Number to the Allies; but it much fail'd them; and more soon after, in not maintaining but losing their Lines by a small Assault.

June 23, The Duke of *Marlborough* decamp'd, with our whole Army, from *Yarr*, march'd and advanced nearer to the Enemy, and pitch'd Camp between *Aelst* and *Tourine*, two Leagues; from which, the next Day, they detach'd General *Schoults*, with Twelve Battalions, Sixty Squadrons, and Ordnance conform, again to invest *Huy*: And the same Day he formed Siege against it, under Cover of our Grand Army; in which Place there was one Major-General *Labadee*, with a Garrison with the Number of Four Battalions of *French*, and Ordnance conform. In a few Days after, they open'd their Trenches, and erected and play'd some small Batteries against the Castle, into which the Enemy was fled; who on the 30*th* surrender'd, and were made Prisoners of War, as *Villeroy* before had made those of the *Hollanders*, when he took it in our Absence.

During

During this small Siege neither Side had above Twenty Men killed and wounded; and when over, General *Schoults* and Lord *Orkney*, with the Troops, return'd to our Grand Camp.

Campaign V. Anno 1705.

26, Our Grand Army decamp'd at, and march'd from *Aelst* to, and pitch'd Camp at *Langaberge*, four Leagues.

30, At Night, our Army was somewhat alarm'd, and the Picquet turn'd out, by Occasion of some lurking Parties of the Enemies Hussars, who had been a skulking in our Front, to make a Prey of some Horses.

July 6, By Break of Day, the Duke having before inform'd himself of the Condition of the Enemies Lines, and that they would not run the Risque to give him Battle, he resolved to attack them before they were made stronger, by farther Detachments from the *Moselle*; and therefore it was resolved that Marshal *Overquerque*, with our Left Wing, should pass the *Meheigne*, and face the Lines, to give the Enemy a Jealousy that they were to be attack'd on that Side, while the Duke should attack them at *Heylishein*; and this Stratagem succeeded according to the Duke's Opinion, tho' contrary to some other Generals, who were against those Measures; but this drew the Enemies main Force that Way, *viz. Overquerque* then, with the State's Troops as aforesaid, inclined Leftward a little from *Vigna Mont*, to alarm their Lines on the other Side of the *Meheigne* near *Meffle*: A Feint which seemed to the Enemy as if all our Army had design'd to advance that Way, to attack and pass that Part of the Line; the which amused and occasioned them to draw their main Body that Way, in order to prevent the same. But the Duke's real and main Design was to pass their Lines at *Heyleshein*, where Count *D'Alegre* was posted with Three Battalions and Twenty-four Squadrons, and Ten Cannon

Campaign V. Anno 1705.

Cannon to defend it, where they least expected to be attack'd. At Six at Night the Duke detach'd Count *Noyelles*, with Twenty Battalions and Thirty-eight Squadrons, who immediately advanced towards *Heylisbein*, on the Van in the Front of the Right Wing of our Army, with which the Duke, at Taptoo, entire decamp'd at, and advanced Frontward from *Langaberge* after Count *Noyelles* very silently; and at the same time Lord *Overquerque*, in order to second the Attempt, in Conjunction with the Duke, inclined Rightward with the Left Wing after the Right Wing, in the Rear thereof: And the next Morning, at Break of Day, Count *Noyelles*, with the Detachment in his Command, being arrived at the Lines, forced his Passage over the same, with little Opposition, near *Tirlemont*; from which the Three Regiments of *French* Dragoons were obliged to retire, and also several other Squadrons, in great Disorder, being suddenly broke at the very first; but immediately after, being join'd with Count *D'Alegre*, and a great Body of Horse and Foot, (that had been posted there for the Security of that Part of the Line, in the Time of the Body of their Army's covering Lord *Overquerque*'s feint Attempt) rallied and advanced, with great Resolution, to a second Charge, in order to attack Count *Noyelles*'s Command: But by that Time, the Duke being already got over the Line, with a great Part of the Horse of our Right Wing, and having immediately form'd them, and attack'd the Enemy with such undaunted Courage and Bravery, that after a sharp Dispute of near two Hours, he obliged them to retire with great Loss; and in a Trice after entirely broke, routed, quite defeated, and put to the Run that Part of their Army; the which so much discomforted the Rest of the main Body of their Army that was then coming Leftward for their Succour, who had been covering *Overquerque*'s feint

feint Attempt at *Mehaigne*, that they likewise inclined Rearward in great Hurry, Disorder, and
Confusion towards *Louvain-Pass* on the *Dyle*, and
stopt not till they got over to the South-Side thereof at *Bethlem*; where, in Time, re-assembled their
scatter'd and disorder'd Army: And, doubtless, if
we could conveniently have push'd them farther a
little than we did, we might have made the same
Conquest that Year which we made the next; but
it was Noon that Day before our Army entire got
up the Line; and then being up, we pass'd it, and
advanced to, and pitch'd Camp on the West-Side
of *Tirlemont*, six Leagues; to which the Duke immediately sent a Detachment, who took therein
Monluc's Regiment Prisoners, consisting of Five
Hundred Men, and immediately dismantled it;
and at the same time another Detachment advanced
to, and seiz'd *Diest*, which the Enemy abandon'd,
and the Magistrates sent to the Duke to beg his
Protection.

In the obtaining of this great and glorious Victory, the Allies Army had not above Two Hundred
Men killed and wounded, Officers included; but
the Enemies Loss therein, killed, wounded, taken,
and deserted, upwards of Six Thousand Men.

*The Particulars of the Enemies Loss in this Skirmish,
Action, or confused Retreat, are as here followeth,*

Lieutenant-Generals taken	2
Major-Generals	2
Brigadiers	1
Colonels	1
Other Officers taken	100
Centinels taken, including One Regiment	3000
Total taken, Officers included	3106

Brought

Campaign V.
Anno 1705.

Brought over	3106
Killed and wounded, Officers included	1000
Total taken, killed, and wounded	4106
Brass Cannon	15
Standards and Colours	20
Kettle-Drums one Pair	1
Trumpets	3

Besides they left a great Part of their Baggage, Ammunition, and Three of their Cannon triple-bored.

That Afternoon the Duke sent the Prisoners off to *Maestricht*.

July 8, Our whole Army decamp'd at, and march'd from *Tirlemont* to, and pitch'd Camp at *Uherbeck-Cloister*, four Leagues, opposite to *Louvain*, and within Cannon-shot thereof, and of the *French* Grand Camp, then rally'd, with the River *Dyle* and City of *Louvain* for a Defence and Cover to their Front, from which they at first threw over several Cannon-shot to the Duke's Quarters, till he threaten'd to burn down the City to the Ground, and then they forbore.

10, About Noon, a little to the Front of the Right Wing of our Camp, by the Brinks of the *Dyle*, there happen'd a small Brush between a small Party of one of our Advance-Guards, and one of the Enemies, from cross the River; in which there was several Men killed and wounded on both Sides, particularly one Captain killed of our First Royal Battalion, who in the very interim had turned out, with some Men of the same Regiment, from the Front of its Encampment, for our Advance-Guards Assistance, it being the nighest thereunto.

18, At Taptoo, the Duke being forward in using all Means to draw the Enemy to Battle, and having concerted with our other Generals, detach'd

Lord

Lord *Orkney*, with Fourteen Battalions of Foot, Campaign Twenty-four Squadrons, Twenty Cannon, and all our *Anno 1705.* Pontons, to go before therewith, and to lay them between *Corbeck* and *Neer Yſche* over the *Dyle*, in order for our Grand Army to paſs thereat the next Morning, if poſſible, that we might attack the *French* Army on the Plain, or elſe oblige them to quit and retire elſewhere from *Louvain Paſs* on the *Dyle*: Lord *Orkney*, according to Order, immediately inclined Leftward, from the Left Wing of our Camp, towards the ſaid Place; where he, after continuing his March all Night, arrived the next Morning by Break of Day; and from thence immediately beat off the Enemies Out-Guards with little Oppoſition, and laid our Tin-Boats over the *Dyle*, and raiſed and erected a Battery of Sixteen Cannon on the North-Eaſt Side of the Marſh and *Dyle*, near *Over-Yſche*, and oppoſite to *Corbeck*, in order to maintain and cover the Paſs till our Army's Arrival, and for our Paſſage thereat as aforeſaid; the which they accordingly did, ſome of his *Dutch* Troops having gone over and poſted on the other Side of the *Paſs*. The ſaid 18*th*, about Midnight, the Duke with our whole Army decamp'd at *Waelbeck*, and march'd after Lord *Orkney*, on great Expedition, towards the *Paſs*; but having a great Round, and a tedious Way, it was Ten the next Morning before the Front thereof could arrive at the *Paſs*, and it was very nigh Noon before our Rear could get up thither; the which baulk'd the Duke's Project in coming too late, our Army having the Bow, beſides a very tedious Way to march, and the Enemy from *Louvain* had the String and a Level to march on, *viz.* immediately after that their Out-Guards were beat off as aforeſaid, they had Intelligence of the Duke's Deſign; whereupon their whole Army being alarm'd, removed by Revally, on great Expedition, towards the ſaid *Paſs*;

where,

Campaign V.
Anno 1705.

where, by Eight in the Morning, they wholly arrived, and advantageously posted themselves, interlining the little Villages and Hedges and Ditches on that Side of the Marsh on the other Side of the *Dyle*, about two Hours before our Grand Army's Arrival: But after that, the aforesaid *Dutch*, at the Time of the Enemy's Arrival, withdrew from the other Side of the *Pass*. In the Time of the Enemies posting themselves, our Battery of Sixteen Cannon all at once humbly greeted them with several smart Rounds, till our Army's Arrival as aforesaid. After which, the Duke having narrowly inspected into the Enemies strong Impostment, to which then there was no visible Possibility of passing to be found for attacking the Enemy without great Loss, and no Prospect thereby of any Victory or Inlet, he immediately order'd, and caused our Tin-Boats and Cannon to be drawn off; after which he withdrew our whole Army from thence, and march'd Rearward to, and pitch'd Camp at *Meldart*, between *Tirlemont* and *Bossut*, six Leagues; where he form'd another Project, in order to force or draw them to Battle, &c. The which, if it had taken Effect, might have proved as fatal to the Enemy as did the Battle at *Hochstat*; and with the same Project I will next proceed, viz.

August 4, The Duke decamp'd, with our whole Army, from *Meldart*, and march'd around over two small Rivers, and pitch'd a little Southward of *Corbeck*, four Leagues; thinking thereby to remove the Enemy from *Louvain-Pass* to Battle, or to put them in a Jealousy of *Brussels*; but they lay more firm and stronger posted than before.

5, We decamp'd from above *Corbeck*, and march'd a little farther round, and over a little River below *Genap*, and there encamp'd, four Leagues.

6, De-

6, Decamp'd at, and march'd from *Genap*, a little more round to, and pitch'd a little below *Waterlowe*, three Leagues.

7, At Break of Day, the Duke detach'd from *Waterlowe* General *Schoultz*, with Twenty-fix Battalions, and Thirty-fix Squadrons, in order to advance on in the Front of our Army towards the Enemy, in order to view their new ſtrong Impoſtments, which they had taken up about one League Weſtward from *Welſwaver*, to which they had advanced the Night before from their old Ground between *Louvain* and *Over-Yſche*, the better to cover it and *Bruſſels*; of which they began to have a Jealouſy. About Eight that Morning the Duke, with the Grand Body of our Army, decamp'd from *Waterlowe*, and march'd after General *Schoultz* on great Expedition, who about One in the Afternoon joined him, and arrived in full View of the Enemy's Army; where they were drawn up in Lines of Battle, prodigious ſtrongly poſted, with a deep muddy River in their Front, and the Wood of *Soigne* in their Rear, and Right towards *Bruſſels*, and a great Scrub beſides on their Right, and another on the Left of their Army at the *Dyle*, and intermix'd in Brigades, in cloſe Grounds with Hedges and Ditches almoſt on the Right and Left of each thereof, almoſt impregnable, beſides a Trench on all Sides to cover them impracticable: And thus they were advantageouſly poſted; and immediately after our Arrival near thereunto, the Duke formed our Army likewiſe in Lines of Battle on the South-Side of the ſaid River, oppoſite to the Enemy in their ſtrong Impoſtments; where we lay the remaining Part of that Day, and all the Night following, on our Arms, hoping for Battle, in order to, and expecting to attack or force them to Battle in the Morning; the which they much doubted;

doubted; but indeed they needed not, considering their great Number and Posture.

August 8, Betimes in the Morning, the Duke again review'd and narrowly inspected into their strong Impostments, as aforesaid; trying, but could not find any visible Means, to attack or battle them, without exposing our Army to prodigious great Danger and Loss, and that without any Sign of Conquest or Victory thereby: He therefore, after having pass'd the Day a soaring thereon, in the Evening, about Six of the Clock, withdrew the Army from thence Rearward, recross'd the River at, and pitch'd Camp on the Hill a little to the East-Side of *Beswaver*; and seeing he had used all imaginable Means to force or draw the Enemy to run the Risque of Battle, but could not prevail, and the Campaign wearing away in Idleness, he projected to spend the Remainder thereof in Sieges, &c.

11, The Duke, with our Army, decamp'd at *Baswaver*, and march'd Rearward to, and again pitch'd Camp a little above *Corbeck*, three Leagues.

15, Decamp'd from *Corbeck*, and march'd to, again repitch'd at *Bossut* near *Meldart*, three Leagues.

18, Decamp'd at *Bossut*, and march'd Rearward to, and pitch'd Camp on the East-Side of *Tirlemont*, near unto that Part of *Brabants*' Line, three Leagues; where we had pass'd and drove the Enemy from, on the 7*th* of *July*, with it in our Rear: And in about fifteen Days after our Army demolish'd a great Part thereof, to prevent a farther Repulse, and to be ready in Order for an Inlet of our Army into the Enemies Country, in the Beginning of the next Campaign; and the said Day the Duke detach'd General *Schoults* to the Siege of *St. Leuwe*, with Troops conform, &c.

19, General

19, General *Schoults*, with Twenty Battalions, and Twenty-four Squadrons, and Ordnance conform, invested it round, in which there was a Brigadier and about Eight Hundred *French*, with upwards of Twenty mounted Cannon; and the next Day they began a preparing their Necessaries for the expeditious carrying on of the Siege against it.

20, At Night, a competent Number of the Besiegers, with and without Arms, open'd their Trenches with very little Loss, by getting into Cover before discover'd of the Enemy.

22, About Seven in the Morning, their several Batteries being erected and compleated, consisting of Thirty two Cannon, and Eight Howitzers, began and play'd very smart, till the 26*th* in the Afternoon, for a grand Breach and sudden Storm on the Town-Walls; so that the Fear and Dread thereof obliged them to beat a Parly, and surrender up the Town and themselves Prisoners of War; who the next Day march'd out thereof, and was conducted to *Antwerp*.

During this small Siege of nine Days, the Besieged had about Forty Men killed and wounded, and the Besiegers Sixty.

27, At Night, our Army had *Feux-de-joye*, with a triple Discharge of all their Cannon and small Arms, for a Victory obtained by Prince *Eugene* over Duke *Vandom* at *Cassano*, on the River *Adda* in *Italy*; of which I had an Account that Prince *Eugene* lost Four Thousand Men killed and wounded, and Duke *Vandom* Six Thousand, and Two entire Regiments drowned.

Sept. 7, Our Grand Army removed from *Tirlemont* to, and pitch'd Camp at *Scherpenheuve*, a famous Cloister near unto the Town of *Diest*, five Leagues.

8, Decamp'd at, and march'd from *Scherpenheuve* to, and pitch'd at *Aerschot*, on the East-Side of the Line, three Leagues; where the aforesaid Besiegers rejoin'd our Grand Army.

[August] 17, Decamp'd at *Aerschot*, recross'd the old Line, and march'd to, and pitch'd Camp at *Herenthal*, where they soon after hutted, being cold Weather; where, the 20*th*, a great Skirmish happen'd between the Cover of our Foragers and a double their Number of the Enemies, which the Night before had advanced from their Grand Camp near *Hanuye*, to which it was advanced, after having found our Army recross'd the Line, and drawing towards Winter-Quarters: But the said Party, by the Alertness of ours, though inferior, were soon obliged to retire from their Ambush back to their Camp, with great Loss.

Sept. 27, About Two in the Afternoon, our Grand Camp was somewhat alarm'd, being *Villeroy* and *Bavaria*, with a great Body of Horse, had advanced within about half a League of the Front of our Camp, gasconading and reconnoitring thereof; whereupon all our Generals, with all our Picquet, and the most of our Horse and Dragoons of our whole Army, immediately advanced out towards those gasconading, faint-hearted Heroes; who instantly, at the Appearance thereof, immediately stopt their Career; in which Time our whole Army was order'd to get ready under Arms for Battle; but before effected, immediately countermanded; for at the very first of our Picquet's advancing, the Enemy hastily retired to their Camp; and soon after our Troops that had advanced fell back to theirs. Indeed that Day, at the first of the Enemies Appearance, they advanced as if immediately design'd to attack our Army, or to give us Battle; to which our Army had been courting them that whole Campaign: But still where ever we advanced in Design thereto, they posted themselves so, that it was impracticable to attack them, being fortified with

with Rivers, Marshes, Woods, Scrubs, Hedges, Ditches, &c.

October 9, Our Army decamp'd at, and march'd from *Herenthal* to, and pitch'd Camp at *Oaest Mael*, three Leagues.

10, Decamp'd at, and march'd from *Oaest Mael* to, and pitch'd Camp at *Brecht*, three Leagues.

12, Decamp'd at, and march'd from *Brecht* to, and pitch'd Camp at *Camulhout*, three Leagues; and the same Day the Duke detach'd Count *Noyelles*, with Sixteen Battalions and Twenty-one Squadrons, with Ordnance conform, to, and laid Siege to *Santoliet Fort*, in which there was a Brigadier and a Garrison of Eight Hundred *French*. The next Day the Besiegers made all Things ready for the carrying on the Siege, and at Night a competent Number, with and without Arms, open'd their Trenches with little Loss.

16, About Eight in the Morning, the Besiegers Batteries being compleated, consisting of Twenty Four Cannon and Six Mortars, began and play'd very smart and furious against the Rampart, and into the Fort, till the 18*th*, about Seven in the Morning, for a sudden Breach and general Grand Storm thereon; so that the Fear and Dread thereof immediately obliged the Enemy to beat a Parly, and surrender up the Fort and themselves Prisoners of War; who the next Day march'd out thereof, and was conducted to *Antwerp*.

During this small Siege of about seven Days, the Besieged had about Fifty Men killed and wounded, and the Besiegers One Hundred.

In two Days after the Besiegers, having demolish'd the Fort, and levelled its Rampart, return'd to our Grand Camp at *Campelhout*.

24, Our whole Army decamp'd at, and march'd from *Campelhout* to, and pitch'd Camp at *Hoghstraat*, three Leagues, somewhat dispers'd by Corps

Campaign in Camp. The Army then was wholly in Lord
V. Overquerque's Command, being then about the
Anno 1705. breaking up of the Campaign, and the Duke gone
for *England*, after having first regulated the Garrisons for the Winter-Quarters of the Army.

October 25, Lord *Overquerque*, about Two in the Afternoon, sent off Seven Battalions of *English*, in order for their Winter-Quarters; and after that they had march'd about two Leagues thitherward, he countermanded them; and they, the same Evening, remarch'd to their former Ground, till all the Army should disperse together at once to their Winter-Quarters.

26, Lord *Overquerque* decamp'd with the whole Army from *Hoghstraat*, and march'd to, and pitch'd at *Turnhout*, two Leagues; and the aforesaid Seven Battalions was again sent off as aforesaid, and march'd two Leagues forward to *Baull*; but was likewise countermanded, as before, and remarch'd to the Army at *Turnhout*; Monsieur *Overquerque* thinking it proper to keep our Army out in Camp and Field somewhat longer, or at least as long as the Enemy, they being not wholly dispers'd.

30, Lord *Overquerque* understanding that the *French* Army was wholly dispers'd towards their Winter-Quarters, he also decamp'd our Army at *Turnhout*, and wholly dispers'd each Corps from thence to their respective Garrisons or Winter-Quarters; into which, in a few Days after, they all arrived: And the same Day General *Lumley* and *Churchill*, with our *British* Troops and Artillery, march'd off apart by themselves towards *Holland*; and that Night canton'd in and about the Villages of *Giveer*, four Leagues.

31, General *Lumley*, with the Garrison of *Breda* and our Artillery, march'd off from *Giveer* by themselves; and at Night they march'd into their Garrison of *Breda*, four Leagues; but the rest or
last

last of our Corps enter'd not their respective Garrisons, or Winter-Quarters, till the 2d of *November*; especially those of the Garrisons of *Worcum* and *Gorkcum*: And here I bring to a Conclusion our Campaign about the Lines of *Brabant*; and as for the rest of the Campaigns on our Side, the Seat of the War was wholly in *Flanders* removed thither by the *French* Defeatment, and quitting their Lines at *Tirlemont*, more especially planted and rooted there by the famous Battle of *Ramilies*; of which I shall speak what relates to it in its proper Place.

Campaign V.
Anno 1705.

The glorious Campaign of 1705, was in Length Twenty Seven Weeks and Six Days, commenced the 20*th* Day of *April*, and ended on the 31*st* of *October*; of which our Corps, with the Grand Army, and apart, to and from the *Moselle* and in *Brabant*, march'd Sixty Two Days, and therein Two Hundred and Twenty Eight Leagues, or Six Hundred and Eighty Four Miles *English*.

The End of the Fifth Campaign, A. D. 1705.

THE
SIXTH CAMPAIGN,
Begun on the 27th Day of April, 1706.

ABOUT the Middle of *April*, the Duke of *Marlborough* arrived in *Holland* from *England*, and had several Conferences with the States-General and others, for the Operations of the ensuing Campaign; and immediately order'd the Troops every where, that were to serve under his Command, to assemble forthwith, with all Expedition, towards *Maestricht*, near unto which he design'd to make his first General Rendezvous: And, after having settled some important Affairs with the States-General, set out to *Maestricht*, in order to meet and join the Troops, in order to put a Stop to a Project of a Council of War held by the *French* Court at *Versailles*; whereby they hoped to drive the Allies out of all their Conquests before made in the Low Countries, and to stop their farther Proceedings; and therefore the Duke of *Bavaria* and Marshal *Villeroy* were order'd to assemble, with all Expedition, with an Army of Seventy Thousand Men at *Ramalies*, pass the *Dyle*, and to cut us out of the Line which we had taken the Year before: Towards which it was design'd our Army should repair as soon as join'd, our several Corps being then on their March thither for the same: And first, I begin

gin with our *English* Troops Affemblement thitherward, *viz.*

April 27, General *Churchill*, with our *British* Troops and Artillery, fet out of their Garrifon of *Breda*, and that Night canton'd at *Wallwick*, five Leagues; and the fame Day the reft of our Corps fet out of their refpective Garrifons, in order to join at the *Bofch*.

28, All our Corps march'd from their feveral Cantonments to, join'd and pitch'd Camp at the *Bofch*, three Leagues, in order to advance from thence, and affemble as foon as poffible, with the other Allies, between *Maeftricht* and *Tongres*, where fome were affembled already.

30, General *Churchill*, with our *British* Troops and Artillery, decamp'd at, and march'd from the *Bofch* to, and pitch'd Camp at *Carnock*, near unto the *Grave*, fix Leagues; and the fame Day, by the Heat and Length of our March, three or four Men fainted and fell down dead on the Road, as we were on our Line of March.

May 1, Decamp'd and march'd from *Carnock* to, and pitch'd Camp at *Buxmire*, fix Leagues; and that fame Day, as we halted on our Line of March, about Noon, the Sun darken'd.

2, Decamp'd and march'd from *Buxmire* to, and pitch'd Camp at *Wandfem*, four Leagues.

3, Decamp'd and march'd from *Wandfem* to, and pitch'd Camp at *Bleerhack* near *Venlo*, four Leagues.

5, Decamp'd and march'd from *Bleerhack* to, and pitch'd Camp at *Chateau de Horn* near *Roermonde*, five Leagues.

6, Decamp'd and march'd from *Chateau de Horn* to, and pitch'd Camp at *Maefeyck*, five Leagues.

7, Decamp'd and march'd from *Maefeyck* to, and pitch'd Camp at *Haught* near *Maeftricht*, four Leagues.

Campaign VI. Anno 1706.

May 8, Decamp'd and march'd from *Haught* to, and join'd and pitch'd Camp with our Auxiliary and *Holland* Troops at *Bilfen* near *Tongres*, three Leagues, in the Duke of *Marlborough*'s and Lord *Overquerque*'s Command.

9, The Duke and *Overquerque* decamp'd, with all our Army, at *Bilfen*, and march'd to, and pitch'd Camp in a more regular Form of Lines between *Borchloen* and *Braught*, three Leagues.

11, Decamp'd and march'd from *Borchloen* to, and pitch'd Camp more uniform, each Corps in their due Poft, between *Corfwaren* and *Chateau de Croon*, three Leagues.

And then our Army confifted of Seventy Four Battalions of Foot, and One Hundred and Twenty Three Squadrons of Horfe and Dragoons, One Hundred Cannon, Twenty Howitzers, and Forty Two Pontons, with all other Neceffaries of War conform in Order for Battle; for which, that Night, all Preparations were made, in full Defign to attack the *French* Army the next Day, they being then in our View join'd at *Judoinge*, threatening us with the fame, and then confifted of Seventy Six Battalions of Foot, and One Hundred and Thirty Two Squadrons, Sixty Six Cannon, Twelve Mortars, and Thirty Six Pontons, with alfo all other neceffary Utenfils of War conform, in Order for Battle, in Marfhal *Villeroy*'s and the Duke of *Bavaria*'s Command; they ftriving, and the Allies alfo, who fhould firft poffefs themfelves of *Ramalies*, and the ftrong Ground thereabout. It is true the *French* having the nigheft Cut, had the Honour, if I may call it fo, in firft poffeffing themfelves thereof; but the Allies had much the greater Honour in attacking and beating them from it; of which more afterwards.

The Battle of Ramalies.
12, In the Morning, about One o'Clock, the Duke fent our Quarter-Mafter-General and Camp-Colours,

Colours, with a few Squadrons, off before in our Van towards *Ramalies*, in order to found the Enemies Intentions, as if defign'd to pitch Camp there; and about Three the Duke and Marfhal *Ov·rquerque* decamp'd with our whole Army, and advanced after in Eight Columns, in a great Fog, towards *Ramalies*: But, two Hours before our Arrival near thereunto, the Enemy being got up, advantageoufly pofted themfelves, *viz*. their Right was cover'd by the Village of *Javieres*, with a Wood in their Rear; their Left extended towards *Judoinge*, and was cover'd by the River *Geet* and a Marfh, and a great Part of their Front by Hedges, and the Village of *Ramalies* in their Center. The Choice of their Troops were pofted on their Right Wing, where the greateft Open was, and all the reft of their Troops ranged accordingly; always, upon fuch Occafions, never failing to make good Ufe of fuch Fortifications. About Ten, the Fog being abated, our Army arrived in full View of the Enemy; and about Noon came in Cannon-fhot thereof; and in a Trice after, our whole Army was form'd ready, and in very good Order for Battle; our Artillery at the fame time getting up, was advanced to our Front, and was pofted as the Duke faw proper, and our Quarter-Colours fell into their refpective Regiments. The Duke and Marfhal *Overquerque* ranged our Army in the Plain towards the Rife of the *Geet*, and gave their neceffary Difpofitions to our other Generals to the carrying on the Attack. Our Right confifted of the *Englifh* and *Danes* Foot; our Left of the *Dutch* Troops, *Holftein*, and the *Swiffers*. The *Danes* Horfe were pofted in the Rear of the Left, to make there a third Line. About Two in the Afternoon, our Cannon being planted as moft proper, they began canonading and playing againft the Enemy, and their's againft us, very vigorous and fmart on both Sides, till a

little

little past Three, and then the Duke and Marshal Overquerque order'd the Attack to begin; the which was begun on the Left by Four Battalions of *Holland*'s Guards, who couragiously attack'd a Body of *French* Dragoons that were posted on Foot amongst Hedges, whom they immediately routed; and then the Left Wing advanced, and attack'd gradually, as the Ground would permit; and the Enemies Foot, which advanced to the Relief of the said Dragoons, were also quickly routed; and then the Horse of both Armies began to engage, and mix'd one with another: *Wirtenberg*, at the same time being arrived with some *Danish* Squadrons, slipt in between the Enemies Left and *Javieres*, and flank'd them; but by a Marsh in the Way, he was obliged to stop a little at the End of his first Line; where after he attack'd, with a great deal of Bravery, the *Gens d'Arms* and *Mousquetaires*, who forced our first Line to give Ground a little, and also repuls'd some others that had advanced to support them; but the Prince of *Hesse Cassel*, with a Body of Horse, seconded them, and disorder'd those of the Enemy, and entirely broke them; and the *Danes* push'd Eight Squadrons into the Marsh: The *Dutch* Guards, and *Holstein*'s and *Doph*'s Dragoons push'd also the *French* Housholds in their Turn; the *French* Horse being then routed, in spite of their two gasconading Heroes, for all the Care they took to rally them: Their Foot were also attack'd on all Sides; those Battalions that were in the open Field suffer'd extremely, and were at last entirely broke: *Ramalies* and *Javieres* were attack'd by Detachments; their Dragoons that were posted in *Javieres* took flight, and abandon'd their Horses: The *Danes* attack'd their Foot, and put them to the Run with Sword in Hand: Those in *Ramalies* were now in their Turn vigorously attack'd by several Battalions of different Corps in

Front

Front and Flank, and was the laſt Scene of the Battle; the Burthen thereof lay moſt on our Left Wing and Center, very hot on both Sides of ſeveral vigorous Aſſaults and Repulſes, of ſmall Shot and Sword in Hand, near three Hours ſharp Diſpute; our Left Wing and Center having ſeveral Times ſhrunk back, and given Way to the Enemies Right and Center, being ſuperior in Number, and ſtrongly poſted; but at laſt defeated their Right: Whereupon the Elector of *Bavaria* and Marſhal *Villeroy* made a Motion with their Left to aſſiſt their Right; the which the Duke obſerving, put a ſudden Stop thereto, by cauſing our *Engliſh* and *Danes* Squadrons from our Right Wing and Body of Reſerve, to ſuſtain our Left, which had ſhrunk back as aforeſaid, and attack'd that Part of the Enemy with ſuch undaunted Courage, Dexterity, Vigour, Fury, and Bravery, that, in ſhort, in about half an Hour after, of hot and ſharp Diſpute, they quite broke the Enemies Right Wing of Horſe, and then fell in upon their Foot and Center, every where putting them in a Trice in great Diſorder and Confuſion: So that by this time, which was about the going down of the Sun, their whole Army was quite broke and defeated, and nothing to be ſeen amongſt them but great Hurry, Diſorder and Confuſion, upon the Run towards *Louvain*. The two Marſhals ſeeing themſelves in this great Neceſſity of retreating, took their Rout accordingly thither, making no Stop till they got to the other Side thereof, and of the *Dyle*. Their Left Wing of Horſe attempted to cover the confuſed Retreat of their Foot, and of the reſt of their Army, which was moſt cruſh'd in the Heat of the Action where it moſt lay; but being ſo hotly purſued by our furious and vigorous freſh Squadrons, with the reſt, the Enemies Horſe were obliged to abandon their Foot, and to ſhift for themſelves with good

Campaign VI. Anno 1706. good Heels, very neceſſary at ſuch a Time; of which there was a great many ſlaughter'd in and about the Village of   , where the Regiment *Du Roy* beg'd and obtain'd Quarters of Lord *Hays*'s Royal Regiment of *Scots* Dragoons, to whom they grounded their Arms, and deliver'd their Colours, but afterwards proved tardy; for when the Dragoons faced to the Purſuit of their Army, they attempted to take up their Arms again; for which they dearly ſuffer'd by the ſame Dragoons, as deſerved: During which, and the whole Night, our whole Army gradually continued their Purſuit by the Way of the Plain of *Judoinge*, till Break of Day, and then we made a little Halt on our Arms, as in the Line of March, between the Villages of *Meldart* and *Hewgar*; from which, about Eight in the Morning, after the Battle, our Army removed, form'd regularly, and pitch'd Camp between *Meldart* and *Buzee*: But that ſame Night Lord *Orkney*, with ſome of the freſheſt of our Squadrons, *&c.* cloſely continued the Purſuit of the Enemy, without any Halt or Stop, cloſe to the *Dyle*, by and oppoſite to *Louvain*, and there ſtopt till the Day after our Army's Arrival; the which cloſe Purſuit kept the Enemy in a prodigious Hurry, Diſorder, and Confuſion, dropping moſt of their heavy Luggage and Baggage on the Road, for their quicker Diſpatch and Safety, in order to get to the other Side of the *Dyle* and *Louvain-Paſs*; where, not thinking themſelves ſecure enough to make any long Stop, or any where elſe that they could depend or expect to rely upon, nearer than *Liſle*, they continued their precipitate Retreat from *Louvain*, for fear of a Relapſe, with all Expedition imaginable, to the Plain on the South-Side of that famous ſtrong City; a Retreat of about thirty ſix Leagues, without ever a Day's Halt, where they made their firſt General Rendezvous after the ſaid Battle;

Battle; in the Heat of which they had upwards of Twenty Battalions cut to pieces, with the Loſs alſo of moſt of their Colours, Cannon, Ammunition, Baggage, Bread-Waggons, and Horſes thereof.

<small>Campaign VI. *Anno* 1706.</small>

Here followeth a nigh Computation of the Particulars of the *French* Loſs at *Ramalies*, according to the beſt Account I could collect thereof, *viz.*

They had Two Lieutenants killed in the Action, beſides many other noted Perſons of Diſtinction, and a great Number of their Commiſſion'd Officers, whoſe Particulars were not given, but caſt in, and ſumm'd up in the General Number of the Total of their killed and wounded, they being always on Actions very apt to conceal their real great Loſs.

Killed in the Battle and precipitate Retreat, Officers included	6759
Wounded or diſabled in Ditto	5328
Taken in and on Ditto, including Two Hundred Commiſſion'd Officers	5729
Deſerted in and on Ditto	4000
Total killed, wounded, taken, and deſerted	21816

Amongſt thoſe that were taken there was One Lieutenant-General, Two Major-Generals, Three Brigadiers, and one Marquis *de la Baume*, Count *Tallard*'s Son, beſides a great Number of other noted Perſons and Officers of Diſtinction of ſeveral Ranks and Regiments, of both Horſe and Foot; but by their moſt publick Computation they had not above Eight Thouſand killed and wounded, with Officers, Three Thouſand Centinels taken, and Two Hundred Officers of ſeveral Ranks; but the greateſt is moſt likely to be righteſt, according to the aforeſaid Reaſons: Of Utenſils and Trophies of War taken, Eleven triple-bored Cannon, Forty-three others, Sixty-five Colours,

lours, Twenty one Standards, Six Pair of Kettle-Drums, and Two Thousand of their Artillery and Bread-Waggons, with several Mortars or Howitzers and Pontons; besides we took the most of their heavy Baggage which they had up in the Battle, and a great Quantity of what they the Night before had left behind them in and about *Judoinge*. If all these Accounts of the Enemies Loss be true, as I believe the most of them are, their Loss was very great, besides thereby giving our Army a free Passage into *Flanders*, leaving most of it behind them to the Allies, abandoning *Louvain*, *Mechlin*, *Bruſſels*, *Antwerp*, *Liere*, *Bruges*, and *Oudenard*; and likewise most of the neighbouring Towns; and in short, the most of *Flanders* in General. All which, in a few Days after, deliver'd up their Keys to the Duke of *Marlborough* in an humble Manner, declaring and acknowledging *Charles* the Third, King of *Spain*, for their lawful Sovereign: And in this Campaign our Army took, by besieging, *Oſtend*, *Menin*, *Dendermond*, and *Aeth*, all with little Loss.

In the Allies gaining and obtaining this glorious Conquest, and ever memorable renown'd Victory, over the *French* Army at *Ramalies*, our Loss was computed but Four Thousand One Hundred and Ninety Two Men killed and wounded, Officers included; as appeareth by this following Table of the Particulars thereof, *viz.* in general and brief.

(177)

Several Stations of our Corps.	Colonels Kd/Wd	Lt. Cols. Kd/Wd	Majors Kd/Wd	Captains Kd/Wd	Subalterns Kd/Wd	Centinels Killed	Centinels Wound	Total Killed	Total Wound	Total Kd.Wd.
Of 126 Squad. Horse and Drag.	2 / 3	/	4 /	3 / 10	14 / 55	351	819	381	907	1288
Of 80 Battalions of Foot	3 / 3	1 /	2 /	4 / 9	20 / 101	867	1848	902	2002	2904
Total of Horse and Foot	5 / 6	1 /	6 /	7 / 19	34 / 156	1218	2667	1283	2909	4192

Besides there were some few killed and wounded of our Artillery, whose Particulars I found not; and there were upwards of Three Hundred and Eighty of our Horse and Dragoons Horses killed and disabled, at the Head of the Royal Regiment of Foot of *Ireland*. The Duke of *Marlborough* had his Horse shot under him, and had a narrow Escape himself. I had in another Account our whole Loss computed to be Six Thousand Men killed and wounded, including some few Men otherwise lost; the which I judge to be most rightest. I had no Account that we had any General Person killed or wounded in this Action.

Note, That in the very Heat of the Battle, Duke *Wirtemberge* join'd and fell in with Six Battalions and Three Squadrons of *Danes* more than in the first Number before given of our Strength; and the *French* had also some more come up, but too late, than the first Number. There were two other different Accounts given of the *French* Strength; the one was Ninety Battalions and One Hundred and Fifty Squadrons, the other was Eighty Two Battalions and One

Campaign VI.
Anno 1706.

One Hundred and Forty Five Squadrons, computed Seventy Thousand Men: Of all which I take the laſt of the third to be the righteſt, neither Armies being quite join'd; each having in a manner but juſt ſet out of Winter-Quarters, and taken the Field. After this, the Elector of *Bavaria* complain'd of Marſhal *Villeroy*, and *Villeroy* of *Bavaria*, &c.

May 14, All the Priſoners and Utenſils that were taken in the ſaid Battle, were ſent away at Break of Day, under a ſmall Convoy of Horſe and Foot, to *Maeſtricht*; and at the ſame time the Duke and Marſhal *Overquerque*, having ſettled the Affairs of the Army, decamp'd therewith from *Buzee*, about Eight that Morning, and advanced after Lord *Orkney*, where he then lay, as aforeſaid, by the *Dyle* near *Louvain*; where, about Two in the Afternoon, our Army being all again join'd, paſs'd the *Dyle*, and pitch'd Camp uniform at *Terbank-Cloiſter*, on *Bethlem-Hill*, with the City of *Louvain* cloſe in our Rear; and at the ſame time the Heads thereof deliver'd up the Keys to the Duke of *Marlborough* in a humble manner, and declared, as aforeſaid, where the *French* and Allies Loſs were regulated and computed as aforeſaid.

15, The Duke and Marſhal *Overquerque* decamp'd, with our whole Army, from *Terbank*, march'd to, and pitch'd Camp between *Beaulieu* and *Filford*, four Leagues, half Way between *Bruſſels* and *Mechlin*; both which, the ſame Day, deliver'd up their Keys to the Duke, and declared in like manner as aforeſaid, &c.

16, Decamp'd at *Beaulieu*, croſs'd the *Senne* near *Filford*, and march'd to, and pitch'd Camp at *Grimberg*, two Leagues; where we had ſtrict and good Orders given, and publiſh'd at the Head of each Regiment of Horſe and Foot of our Army, to prevent and forbid all maroding or plundering the Country,

Country, that our Army thereby might be the better supplied in all manner of Neceſſaries by the Inhabitants.

18, The Duke, about Two in the Afternoon, detach'd Duke *Wirtenberg*, with Two Thouſand Grenadiers, and Twelve Squadrons of Horſe and Dragoons, and who went before all Night towards that famous City of *Ghent*, to prepare and ſee the Way clear thither for our Army to march the next Day; for altho' an Enemy be beat, and made confuſedly retreat, the Beater in his Purſuit can never be too ſecure to prevent Ambuſcadoes or Relapſes.

19, About Eight in the Morning, our whole Army decamp'd from *Greenberg*, and march'd after our Van, who proceeded with their March, and the Army pitch'd at *Alloſt*, on the River *Dender*, four Leagues, half Way between *Ghent* and *Bruſſels*.

20, Our Army decamp'd at, and march'd from *Allort* to, and pitch'd Camp at *Meerlebeck*, five Leagues, near unto the famous City of *Ghent*, on the River *Scheld* and *Ley*; and the ſame Day the Magiſtrates deliver'd up to the Duke the Keys thereof, in a Silver Charger, in a very humble manner, and declared as aforeſaid, &c. And likewiſe by this Time all the aforeſaid Towns and Places had in like manner deliver'd up and declared as aforeſaid; and hereby it appears what great Revolutions the Battle of *Ramalies* made then in *Flanders*; yea, more than I am able to relate, very deplorable and fatal to the *French*: Beſides, as I had an Account, our Army in *Italy* and *Savoy*'s Succeſs was very great alſo over and againſt the *French* Army, whoſe Particulars I muſt wave; ſo that by this Time the *French* Court's Projects, in the opening of the Campaign, by flattering themſelves with great Conqueſts, were all blaſted; and inſtead of

Campaign VI. Anno 1706. of conquering, they were every where defeated and conquered.

May 21, Was a Day of Thanksgiving of our Army to God for the Victory obtained; and at Night we had a *Feux-de-joye*, with a triple Discharge of all our Cannon and small Arms for the same; and also for the Victory obtained by Prince *Eugene* at *Turin.*

24, Our Army decamp'd from *Meerlebeck*, cross'd the *Scheld* and *Lis* above *Ghent*, march'd to, and pitch'd Camp between *Deyuse* and *Nivel*, four Leagues.

25, Decamp'd at, and march'd from *Deyuse* to, and pitch'd Camp at *Arseil*, four Leagues; from which the Duke went to the *Hague*, and had some Conferences with the States-General, for the farther Operations of the Campaign, which as yet was young; and soon after he had concerted proper Matters with them for the same, he returned to our Grand Camp, where he had left it in Lord *Overquerque*'s Command at *Arseil*; where, on the 27*th*, we had another *Feux-de-joye*, in the former manner, for the Victory obtained in *Italy.*

Blockade of *Dendermond.* 29, The Duke detach'd Brigadier *Meredith* to *Dendermond*, with One Thousand Six Hundred Foot, who the next Day block'd it up; in which there was one Lieutenant-General *Grederswish*, and a Garrison of about One Thousand Six Hundred Men, *viz.* Two Battalions, Two Hundred *Spanish* Dragoons, and Seven Hundred detach'd Foot, including a few who rush'd in soon after the Place was block'd up, by Order of a *French* General, who with a great Detachment of about Eight Thousand Men and Five Cannon, drain'd from *Tournay*, *Mons*, and *Aeth*, attempted to surprize, attack, and take the said Brigadier's small Command; but he being, some small Time before their Arrival, aware thereof, put himself into a good Posture of Defence

fence in strong Ground; so that the said General, after he had got a few slipt into the Town, and finding the Brigadier more ready to repulse than he was to assault, immediately retired to the aforesaid Garrisons for fear of an Ambushment from our Grand Camp. After which, the Brigadier lay quiet, till it was taken by a formal Siege, after the taking of *Menen*, the Duke not thinking fit to make any Stop there at first, having an Eye upon *Ostend* and *Menen*, knowing that it must of Course soon after them give up, and only thought it proper that it should be block'd up, till then, from pestering our Roads; by reason that after the Battle, till block'd up, it much pester'd them on that Side of the Country; and, according to the Duke's Opinion, it surrender'd on the 29*th* of *August*, Prisoners of War, &c. Of which more in its Course.

Campaign VI. Anno 1706.

June 3, After that the Duke and Marshal *Overquerque* had held a Consultation about the farther Proceedings of the Campaign, it was agreed; and Lord *Overquerque* march'd off with Twenty Eight Battalions, and Ten Regiments of Horse and Dragoons, in order to lay Siege to *Ostend*, taking with him, and what join'd him, Fifty Cannon, Twenty Six Mortars and Howitzers, with some Pontons, and all other Necessaries conform; but it was six Days after before he could form the Siege, waiting for the Shipping that were to block it up by Sea: On the 6*th* Ditto General *Fagel*, with a Detachment from Monsieur *Overquerque*, block'd it up by Land, and the Fleet by Sea.

Siege of Ostend.

7, The Duke of *Marlborough* decamp'd with our Grand Army from *Arseil*, and march'd to, and pitch'd Camp at *Roaselar*, three Leagues; and the next Day Marshal *Overquerque*, with his Camp apart, removed nearer to *Ostend*, and joined the rest of his Troops for the Siege, where they lay with

Campaign VI.
Anno 1706.

General *Fagel* by *Plaffendal* near *Oftend*, which he had block'd up on the 6th, as aforesaid.

June 9, Lord *Overquerque*, with all the said Troops, being rejoin'd, closed nearer to *Oftend*, ranged and formed a regular Siege against it all round on the Land-Side, assisted by Brigadier *Veglin*, who, with Seven other Battalions and Three Squadrons, cover'd and made good that Side on the Sand-Banks, between *Plaffendal* and *Newport*; and the Sea-side of the Town was inviron'd by Admiral *Fairborn*, with Twelve large War Ships, Twenty Eight lesser Sort, and Two Galleys, all well manned. The Town was defended by Lieutenant-General *La Motte*, with a Garrison of Six Battalions of *French*, Four of *Spaniards*, and One Squadron of Dragoons, with upwards of Twenty Cannon and Ten Mortars mounted, and all other Necessaries conform, for the Defence of the said Place.

12, The Duke of *Marlborough* detach'd from our Grand Camp at *Roufelar* General *Pallant*, with Ten Squadrons of Horse and Dragoons, and all the Grenadiers of the Army, in order to go between, and to take Possession of *Oudenard* and *Courtray*, and to keep that Side of the Country clear of Festerers, while our Grand Army was to cover the said Siege at *Roufelar*; who in a few Days after possess'd himself of the said two Towns, and lay thereabouts till the End of the said Siege, that our Army removed from *Roufelar* to *Courtray*; of which more in its Course.

17, At Night, General *Fagel*, with a competent Number of the Besiegers, with and without Arms, open'd their Trenches against *Oftend*, with little Loss; having in the Time before, after it was invested, provided all Necessaries for the expeditious carrying on of the said Siege; and afterwards proceeded very regularly therewith.

22, About

22, About Eight in the Morning, the Besiegers Batteries being erected and compleated, consisting of in all, and at most, Forty Six Cannon, Eighteen Mortars, and Eight Howitzers, began to play, and play'd very vigorous and furious that Day, and for the five Days following, against the main Wall and Rampart of the Town, for a sudden Grand Breach and General Grand Storm thereon, with all Expedition to the 27*th* at Night, with several small Attacks or Storms in that Time on the Enemies Out-Works, in the Front of their Approaches, too tedious to relate.

25, The Duke seeing the good Success of the Besiegers, and finding that the Besieged could not hold out above one or two Days more, decamp'd with the Army at *Rouselar*, four Leagues, and march'd from thence to, and pitch'd Camp between *Arleberge* and *Courtray*, in order for Plenty of Forage; where, the same Day, General *Palant*, with the aforesaid Squadrons and detach'd Grenadiers, rejoin'd, and all fell into their respective Regiments just as the Army enter'd and pitch'd Camp: And, as aforesaid, the said 27*th* at Night, in the Dusk, the Besieged, fearing a sudden Grand Storm, beat a Parly, and immediately capitulated and surrender'd the Town, and submitted themselves Prisoners of War, to be allow'd to go to their own Garrisons, and there to remain till exchanged for the like Number, Man for Man, or otherwise, as should be afterwards determined at the Allies Pleasure: And the next Day, being the 28*th* Ditto, they accordingly march'd out of *Ostend*, and were conducted by a small Convoy from the Siege, *viz.* the Six Battalions of *French* Prisoners to *Dunkirk*, and the Four Battalions and One Squadron of *Spaniards* were conducted to *Mons*. After that the Prisoners were march'd out of *Ostend*, the Besiegers found therein all Sorts of Ammunition

Campaign VI. Anno 1706. in great Stores, and in the Harbour six Ships of Merchants, and others.

During this brisk Siege against *Ostend*, of Three Weeks and One Day, begun on the 6*th* and ended on the 27*th* of *June*, the Besieged had about Eight Hundred Men killed and wounded, and the Besiegers at Land and Sea about One Thousand Six Hundred Men, Officers included on both Sides, whose Particulars I found not; and in nine or ten Days after Lord *Mordaunt*, with Five Battalions of *English*, and Three others of the Allies of the said Besiegers, embark'd at *Ostend*, and sailed from thence to the *Isle of Wight*, where join'd some more Troops, in order to go in the Fleet with Sir *Cloudsly Shovel* for *Portugal*, to reinforce our Troops on that Side against *Spain*, &c. And Lord *Overquerque* return'd with the Remainder of the said Besiegers from *Ostend* to our Grand Camp, where it then lay at *Courtray*.

June 30, The Duke and Monsieur *Overquerque* decamp'd with our whole Army, and march'd from *Courtray* to, and pitch'd Camp between *Helschen* and *St. Dennis's Cloister*, on the North-Brink of the *Scheld*, on that Part of the *French*'s Old Line, which they had cast up in the former War against King *William*'s Army, at that Time when they march'd ten Days without any Halt, from *Mount St. Andrew*'s to *Arseil* near *Ghent*, from the *French* Army, then commanded by Prince *Vaudemont*.

July 4, The Duke of *Brandenberg*, or King of *Prussia*, with his *Prussian* Troops, and also some *Lunenberg*'s then arriving, fell in and pitch'd apart in the Rear of our Camp at *Helschin*; and then our Army consisted of in all Ninety Eight Battalions, One Hundred and Fifty Six Squadrons, One Hundred Cannon, and Twenty Mortars and Howitzers, Forty Two Pontons, and all other necessary Utensils of War conform. And now by this Time the

French

French Generals *Villeroy* and *Bavaria* had rendezvous'd their mortify'd Troops, and others drain'd together from several Places, assembled about *Lisle* another great Army, computed to consist of about Ninety Battalions of Foot, and One Hundred and Fifty Squadrons of Horse and Dragoons, with an Artillery of upwards of Eighty Cannon, Sixteen Mortars, and Forty Pontons, with also all other necessary Utensils of War conform; accounted in Number again near equivalent to the Allies, but much inferior in Courage and Valour, otherwise they would never have lain by so quiet as they did, and seen their Towns taken.

6, The Duke, Monsieur *Overquerque*, and the King of *Prussia*, reviewed the Front Line of our Army at *Helschen*, drawn out at the Head of our Encampment.

9, They also, in like manner, reviewed the Second or Rear Line of our Army; after which they held a Consultation, and it was agreed upon to lay Siege to *Menin*; and also after to advance the whole Army to *Aeth*, and to finish there the Campaign with the besieging and taking thereof, as soon as possible.

11, About Eight in the Morning, the Duke detach'd to the said Siege Generals *Sallisk*, *Lumley*, *Orkney*, and *Argyle*, with Thirty Two Battalions, Twenty Four Squadrons, and Ordnance conform, who march'd off that Day from the Camp at *Helschen*, and at Night pitch'd at *Lauwe*.

12, General *Sallisk*, with his Troops for the said Siege, removed from *Lauwe*, and invested *Menin* round; in which there was one Lieutenant-General *Caraman*, with a Garrison of Twelve Battalions and Four Squadrons, with upwards of Twenty Four Cannon and Four Howitzers mounted, and all other Necessaries conform: And in a few Days after a famous Train, most by Water, arrived at the Siege,

Campaign VI. Anno 1706.

Siege of Menin.

Campaign VI.
Anno 1706.

Siege, with Monsieur *Mosburger*, Engineer-General and Head Director. This Siege was the regularest and briskest carried on of any Siege in the whole War; and therefore I could not avoid being the more punctual in the Particulars thereof.

July 17, The Besiegers began making and bringing of Fascines, &c. of the like Kind, for the expeditious carrying on of the Siege; and that Night and the next, their Picquet was alarm'd and turn'd out by the sculking of some Partizan Parties of the Enemy and *Hussars*, that had been lurking to steal some of the Besiegers Horses.

22, The Besiegers Line of Circumvallation was begun by a Body of Six Thousand, from the adjacent Country; but in their marching down by General *Lumley*'s Quarters, in fine Order, with their Spades and Shovels, Drums beating, and Pipers playing, I observing the same, saw their Notes immediately changed by the coming of one *Randomer* from the Enemies Mantler, which disinhabited one of his Prime Inhabitants; whereupon the rest, not willing to undergo the like Fate, made about and off, like a Sheep from a Dog; and it was some Days after before they could be rally'd again; but when they rally'd, they took more Care than at the first to keep out of Danger, in proceeding with their Work, which better became them than the Melody of Fighting; letting those that were brought up in that School, humour such Musick.

23, At Night, one Major *Swaran*, with Three Hundred Men of the Besiegers, with Arms, raised a Blind in a Hollow cross a little Morass, on the North-Side of the Town, within Musket-shot of the Enemies Palisadoes, in order for an Inlet and Cover to the Grand Opening of their Trenches, which they maintain'd till the next Night in the Dusk; and then Lord *Orkney* and the Duke of *Argyle*,

Argyle, with Five entire Battalions, and a Detachment of One Thousand Five Hundred Men of the several Regiments of the Besiegers, with Arms, and One Thousand Eight Hundred Men without Arms for Work, open'd their Trenches against *Menin* by one Attack, and that with very little Loss, although somewhat discover'd by the Enemy as begun, and more before that they could get under Cover from their Shot: And the next Morning, being the 25*th* Ditto, about Ten, a great Body of the Besieged sallied very boldly on the Besiegers Approaches, in Design to surprize the Cover thereof, and to level the same; by which, in a Trice, they received a sudden and sore sharp Repulse, and were obliged to retire in great Disorder and Confusion to the Inside of their Works again, and that with the Loss of One Major-General killed, and upwards of Sixty Men killed and wounded.

<small>Campaign VI. *Anno* 1706.</small>

28, The Duke sent from *Helschen* Six Battalions, and that Day reinforced the Besiegers Camp at *Menin*, for the Dispatch thereof.

29, About Seven in the Morning, the Besiegers several Batteries being erected and compleated, consisting of in all, and at most, of about Seventy Two Cannon, Forty Four Mortars and Howitzers, begun to play, and that very vigorous and furious against *Menin*; by which, in a Trice, the Town-House was set on Fire, and also several other Places, and brought as low as the Ground; the Town-House and Bells thereof quite ruined.

August 2, The Duke inclined our Grand Army a little Rightward from *Helschen*, and the Right Wing somewhat extended near to the Besiegers Camp, the better to cover and assist the same, if Occasion should require; being the *French*, as aforesaid, was then again very strong, threatning much, but kept at a Distance.

August

Campaign VI. *August* 3, The Duke, to haften the Siege, sent General *Fagel*, with a Reinforcement of Twelve Battalions more, from *Helfchen* Camp to the Befiegers Camp at *Menin*.

7, About Six at Night, the Duke removed the Grand Army a little nearer to the Siege, and ftood about two Hours at Arms; and in the fame time Lord *Orkney* and the Duke of *Argyle*, with Nine Battalions entire of the Befiegers, vigoroufly attack'd the large Counterfcarp and its Glacis, and feveral others of the Outworks in the Front of their Approaches; and with very fmall Oppofition, in a Trice, beat the Enemy out, and poffefs'd themfelves thereof, but with great Lofs on both Sides, but moftly on our Side after enlodged, by the Enemies firing from off the Walls of the Town on our Mens Flafhes before cover'd; our Men being extream eager a firing at the Enemy on the Walls, could fcarce be reftrain'd, which much laid our Men open to the Enemy; on which General *Ingoldfby*'s and *Lauder*'s Regiments fuffer'd moft; for in a little above half an Hour's Time each loft about One Hundred Men killed and wounded, Officers included; particularly *Ingoldfby*'s had Fifteen Officers killed and wounded: And after that our Men were fenfible of the great Danger they expofed themfelves to, and our Workmen by their unneceffary firing, they were conftrained to ceafe; after which the Enemy ceafed, and our Workmen went on pretty quiet with their Woolpacks, and otherwife, all Night; fo that by Eight the next Morning they had erected and compleated frefh Batteries on the Works which they had taken againft the Town, making up about the fame Number which had play'd at firft: All which, both the former and latter, immediately began again afrefh, and play'd very vigorous and furious againft the main Walls of the Town, that and the two Days following

following, for a sudden Grand Breach and general Grand Storm, to the 10*th*, at the Approach of the Night; so that then the Fear and Dread thereof so terrified the Besieged, that they the next Morning, being the 11*th* of *August*, by Break of Day, beat a Parly, and surrender'd the Town on honourable Conditions, to march out thereof with the usual Marks of Honour to *Douay*; the which the Duke allow'd to be granted, that he might not let the Campaign slip without some farther Conquest, he having a Design on *Aeth*, as aforesaid.

Campaign VI. Anno 1706.

14, About Ten in the Morning, General *Caraman* and Lieutenant-General *Marsin* march'd out of *Menin*, with Twelve Battalions of Foot, and Four Squadrons of Dragoons, Four Cannon, Two Mortars, and Eight Cover'd Waggons, and was conducted from thence by a small Party of our Horse towards *Douay*; and in the Time that they march'd out thereof, the besieging Army stood at Arms in two Lines, one on each Side of the Road, and made a Lane for them till the Rear was quite past the Bounds of the Besiegers Camp: After which the Besiegers found in the Town Fifty Five Cannon of Brass, Ten of Iron, Six Mortars, Eight Hundred and Ten double Barrels of Powder, Three Hundred and Eighty Seven double Barrels of Musket-Balls, with a great Quantity of other Provisions; all which did very much assist in the carrying on the Siege against *Aeth*, after form'd.

During the Siege against *Menin*, of four Weeks and three Days, commenced the 12*th* of *July* and ended the 11*th* of *August*, the Besieged had One Major-General killed, and One Hundred other Officers killed and wounded, and upwards of One Thousand Centinels; Total One Thousand One Hundred and One killed and wounded.

The Besiegers had Two Thousand Six Hundred and Twenty killed and wounded, Officers included,

as

Campaign as doth appear by the following Table of the Particulars thereof, *viz.* in brief;

Their several STATIONS.	Killed.	Wounded.
Lieutenant-Colonels	0	1
Majors	0	4
Captains	13	22
Subalterns	19	53
Serjeants	34	69
Centinels	517	1872
Total —	583	2021

Of the Artillery kill'd and wounded   16

Total kill'd and wounded — 2620

Aug. 20, General *Sallisk* drew the Besiegers Camp closer together, and form'd them into Two Regular Lines on the South-East Side of *Menin*, with their Right adjoining to the River *Lis*, to be the more ready to join the Grand Army on the first Occasion; and the same Day the Duke detach'd General *Churchill* from the Grand Camp, with Nine Battalions and Six Squadrons, in order to march to the Siege of *Dendermond*, which had been block'd up by Brigadier *Meredith* from the 29th of *May*.

22, General *Churchill* arrived thereat, invested it, and was join'd by the said Command.

23, At Night, a competent Number of the Besiegers, with and without Arms, open'd their Trenches, and erected two small Batteries against the Town.

25, The Batteries began to play against *Dendermond*.

28, In the Evening, Lord *Dalrymple*, with a competent Number of the Besiegers, attempted to attack a small Redout in the Front of their Approaches; at the Appearance thereof, the *Spaniards*

ards that were posted thereon abandon'd it, and would not stand to fire any Shot against our Men; whereupon, at the same Juncture, the Governor caused a Drummer to beat a Parly; and that Night Capitulations were made, and the next Morning surrender'd the Town and themselves Prisoners of War; from which, on the 30*th*, the *Spaniards* were sent to *Brussels*, where they took Service; and the rest were sent to *Bergen-op-Zoom*.

During the thirteen Weeks it was block'd up, from the 29*th* of *May* to the 29*th* of *August*, I could not find that either Side sustain'd any Loss; if not, above Twelve by Desertion.

28, The Duke closed our Grand Army and Besiegers of *Menin*'s Camp Leftward, nearer to *Helschen*, two Leagues; where his Quarters had continued during the Siege.

29, He decamp'd our whole Army from *Helschen*, there cross'd the *Scheld*, and march'd from thence to, and pitch'd Camp at *Valut*, three Leagues; and there *Churchill* rejoin'd *Sept.* 2.

Sept. 3, The Duke decamp'd with our whole Army at, and march'd from *Valut* to, and pitch'd Camp at *Gramaz* near *Cameron-Plain*, three Leagues; and the same time Lord *Overquerque* and General *Ingoldsby*, with Thirty Eight Battalions and Twenty Six Squadrons, with Ordnance conform, march'd off apart to, and that Evening invested *Aeth*; in which there was a *French* Major-General, with a Garrison of Six Battalions and Two Squadrons, with Sixteen Cannon and Three Mortars mounted.

6, The Besiegers begun their Line of Circumvallation, and the making and bringing of Fascines, &c.

11, General *Ingoldsby*, at Night, with a competent Number of the Besiegers, with and without Arms, open'd their Trenches with little Loss on

Campaign VI. Anno 1706.

Siege of *Aeth.*

Campaign VI.
Anno 1706.

the South-Side of the Town, by this Stratagem, in first attempting to open them on the North-Side, to which the Enemy drew most of their Strength; so that before the Enemy could discover them, they got under good Cover.

Sept. 13, By Break of Day, the Besiegers several Batteries being compleated, to the Number of in all, and at most, Forty Eight Cannon, and Twelve Mortars and Howitzers, began and play'd very furious against the main Walls of the Town, for the six Days following, for a sudden Grand Breach and General Storm thereon.

15, Our Grand Army had a Thanksgiving and a *Feux-de-joye* for the Prosperity of the Campaign; and the next Night their Picquet was alarm'd and turn'd out to, and drove off some sculking Parties of the Enemy, which had been lurking in their Front to catch some of the Foragers and Maroders and Sutlers Horses.

18, At Break of Day, a competent Detachment of the Besiegers vigorously attack'd, and took a small Redout on the South-Side of the Town; and the next Morning, about the same Time, another competent Number vigorously attack'd, and took the most of all their Out-works in the Front of their Approaches with very little Loss; the which, and fear of a General Storm, so terrified the Besieged, that they the very next Morning, at Break of Day, being the 20*th*, beat a Parly, capitulated, surrender'd the Town, and themselves Prisoners of War.

21, They march'd out thereof, and were conducted to *Mons*.

During this Siege against *Aeth*, of eighteen Days, begun on the 3*d* and ended on the 20*th* of *Sept.* the Besieged had about Sixty Men killed and wounded, and the Besiegers about Two Hundred Men killed and wounded.

25, The

25, The Besiegers Camp was drawn closer together, and regulated into two Lines.

October 1, At Four in the Afternoon, the Duke sent our Quarter-Master-General and Quarter-Colours, with all the Picquet of our Army, before, in order to advance to *Cameron-Cloister*, on that Plain, to take up Ground and Forage for a fresh Camp to our Grand Army and the said Besiegers to join; the which they accordingly did.

2, At Eight in the Morning, the Duke, with the Grand Army, decamp'd from *Gramaz*, and march'd to, and pitch'd Camp at *Cameron-Cloister*, four Leagues; and at the same time Monsieur *Overquerque*, with the Besiegers, rejoin'd us.

7 and 9, Each in the Afternoon, our Army was somewhat alarm'd, and Picquet turn'd out each Time; being the *French* General each Time appear'd with a great many Squadrons from *Mons* in our Front, a reconnoitring our Camp, and gasconading; who each Time, after the advancing of our Picquet thitherward, hastily retired to *Mons*, and our Picquet accordingly fell back to their Post.

15, The Duke and Monsieur *Overquerque* decamp'd with our whole Army from *Cameron*, and march'd Rearward in several Bodies over the *Pass* to, and pitch'd at *Gillengen* near *Anguien* and *Gramont*, four Leagues; where, on the 24*th* and 25*th*, in the Day-time, by tempestuous Winds, a great many of the Tents of our Army were broke, and beat flat down to the Ground; and from thence, at the same time, the Duke went off to the *Hague*, and from that to *England*, leaving the Command of the Army to Lord *Overquerque*.

26, Lord *Overquerque* decamp'd and dispers'd our whole Army from *Gillengen* to Winter-Quarters: Lieutenant-General *Lumley*, with our *British* Troops and Artillery, march'd off to, and pitch'd at *Samber*, four Leagues.

<small>Campaign VI.
Anno 1706.</small>   *October* 27, Decamp'd at, and march'd from *Samber* to, and pitch'd on the Road-Side, North of *Aloft*, four Leagues.

28, Decamp'd at, and difpers'd from *Aloft* to their refpective Winter-Quarters; thefe for *Ghent*, with all our Artillery, to which General *Ingoldfby* was appointed Governor, confifting of Thirteen Battalions of Foot and Five Regiments of Horfe, march'd into *Ghent*, four Leagues: The reft went to *Bruffels* and *Bruges*, and the Two Regiments of Dragoons into *Holland*.

Here ends the glorious Campaign of 1706, which was in Length Twenty Six Weeks and Three Days, commenced the 27*th* of *April*, and ended the 28*th* of *October*; of which our Corps march'd, with the Grand Army, *&c.* apart to, and in *Flanders* Thirty Four Days, and therein One Hundred and Twenty Six Leagues, or Three Hundred Seventy Eight Miles *Englifh*.

The End of the Sixth Campaign, A. D. 1706.

THE

THE
Seventh CAMPAIGN,

Begun on the 7th Day of May, 1707.

ABOUT the latter End of *April*, the Duke of *Marlborough* arrived at the *Hague* in *Holland*, where he had some Conferences with the States-General, and others, concerning Matters for the Operations of this Campaign; and from thence he went to *Bruſſels*, in order to join all the Troops, as ſoon as poſſible, to a General Rendezvous thereabout, that were to ſerve under his Command in this Campaign; of which I have nothing of *Eclat* to inſert, that paſſed on our Side; the other before having run away in a great Current of Conqueſts: So that in this there was a Neceſſity of ſecuring, and not extending them; for notwithſtanding the Enemies great Loſs at *Ramalies*, they had again rendezvous'd another great Army on that Side, ſtill much ſuperior in Number to the Allies, but inferior in Courage. Beſides, in the Spring of the Year, our Army in *Spain* being defeated, the whole Dependance of the Grand Allies lay then on the Duke, and on their Armies; ſo that thereby the Duke was not altogether ſo reſolute as to force them in their ſtrong Encampment, as he had done in the three Campaigns before, at *Hochſtat*, *Tirlemont* and *Ramalies*: Yet, notwithſtanding the ſaid

O   Defeatment,

Campaign
VII.
Anno 1707.

Defeatment, and the Enemies great Superiority in Number, the Duke made two great and fair Offers to draw the Enemy out to Battle; but they took all the Care that could be used to avoid it, to the Duke's great Regret. From which I will pass to my Journal; and first begin the same with the setting out of our *British* Troops and Artillery from their Winter-Quarters to Camp, *viz.*

May 5, General *Lumley*, with our *British* Troops and Artillery, set out of *Ghent*, and march'd from thence, and pitch'd Camp at *Oerdeghem*, three Leagues; and by this Time a great Body of the Allies were assembled at *Brussels*, and all the rest for the Duke's Command was in a moving Posture thitherward, in order to join as soon as possible; the which, in a few Days after, was done.

6, General *Lumley*, with our Corps, decamp'd at, and march'd from *Oerdeghem* through *Aloft* to, and pitch'd Camp between *Afflegbem* and *Ekelghem-Cloister*, three Leagues.

9, Decamp'd at, and march'd from *Afflegbem* to, and pitch'd Camp at *Ternat* near unto *Brussels*, three Leagues; where the Duke was then arrived, and the Allies join'd as aforesaid.

10, Our Corps decamp'd at *Turnat*, and the others of the Allies at *Brussels*, and both march'd from their several Encampments to join and pitch Camp, regularly in two Lines, between *Centurnal* and *Limbeck*, three Leagues; and then our Army, being join'd, consisted of Ninety Seven Battalions of Foot, and One Hundred and Sixty Four Squadrons of Horse and Dragoons, One Hundred and Two Cannon, Ten Howitzers, and Forty Four Pontons, with also all other necessary Utensils of War conform: And by this Time *Villeroy* had join'd the *French* Army between *Mons* and *Soignes*, and was computed to consist of One Hundred and Two Battalions and One Hundred and Sixty Eight Squadrons,

Squadrons, with Seventy Two Cannon, Sixteen Mortars and Howitzers, and Thirty Six Pontons, with also all other necessary Utensils of War conform.

Campaign VII Anno 1707.

14, The Village of *Limbeck* was accidentally burnt down to the Ground.

15, The Duke and Monsieur *Overquerque* decamp'd, with our whole Army, from *Centurnal*, march'd through *Stenkirk*, (where our Army had been defeated in King *William*'s Wars) and advanced to, and pitch'd Camp on the South-Side of *Soignes*, six Leagues, in order and full Design to draw the *French* Army to Battle; who, at the very first of our Armies Appearance, fell back near and closer to *Mons*.

16, We prepared for Battle.

17, Our whole Army, by Break of Day, decamp'd at *Soignes*, and all went to Prayers; after which, we advanced out a little in the Front of where we had encamp'd, in order and full Design to attack or force the Enemy to Battle: But a very heavy Fog having fallen, that we could scarcely see what we were about, or from the Right to the Left of each Regiment, for the Space of three Hours that we stood at Arms; which baulk'd the Duke's Design, but proved very beneficial to the Enemy, who embraced the Opportunity thereof; that instead of giving us Battle, they made off another Way with a fresh Project towards *Louvain*, in Design to possess themselves thereof, and thereby to cut off our Communication from it, *Huye*, *Liege*, *Maestricht*, and in short all the neighbouring Garrisons on that Side of the *Dyle*; of which they were suddenly frustrated; for that very Morning, immediately after the Fog, and Return of our Spies with Intelligence thereof, our whole Army remarch'd Rearward from *Soignes*, on great Expedition,

tion, and repitch'd Camp at *Notredame Hall*, six Leagues, without any Halt.

May 18, Decamp'd at, and march'd from *Notredame* over the *Senne*, and went through the Out-Skirts of *Bruſſels*; and in that Evening pitch'd Camp between *Beaulieu* and *Diegem-Cloiſter*, five Leagues, without any Halt.

19, At Break of Day, decamp'd at, and march'd from *Diegem*, and about Noon arrived and pitch'd Camp at *Turbank-Cloiſter* on *Bethlem-Hill*, on the South-Side of *Louvain-Paſs*, four Leagues; and thereby fruſtrated the Enemy of their Deſign: So that although they almoſt had the String, and we the Bow, they were obliged to ſtop, and pitch Camp at *Gemblours*, three Leagues ſhort of their Intention, where they kept cloſe, and lay firm for the Space of ten Weeks after; and our Army lay very quiet, waiting their Motion, at *Meldart*: And at the End thereof, at their next Removal, the Duke again uſed all the Means that could be expected to draw them to Battle, but could not prevail.

21, The better to cover the Enemy, and to preſerve our Communication with the aforeſaid Garriſons, *Holland* and *Flanders*, finding no Sign of bringing the Enemy to Action, but the Sign of a ſettled Camp; the Duke decamp'd, with our whole Army, from *Turbank*, re-croſs'd the *Dyle*, and march'd from thence to, and pitch'd Camp between *Meldart* and near to *Tirlemont*, five Leagues; where we lay, as aforeſaid, firm for ten Weeks, without any Motion of Action; where we had the Account of our Army's Defeatment at *Almanza* in *Spain*, on the 14*th* of *April*: And then, as aforeſaid, the whole Dependance of the Grand Allies lay upon the Duke of *Marlborough*, and their Troops in his Grace's Command in the *Netherlands*.

22, The

22, The Duke detach'd and sent back Lord Orkney, with Seven Battalions of Foot, from *Meldart* to the *Pass* of *Louvain*, in order thereby the better to preserve our Communication therewith, and on that Side with *Flanders*, and in Case of Surprizals to prevent the same; the which he accordingly did, and there abode during the Time of our Army encamping at *Meldart*.

30, The Duke of *Marlborough* review'd all the *British* Corps, who exercised and fired four Rounds gradually before him, and that by the Signal of the waving of a Pair of Colours for each Word of Command, perform'd by Colonel *William Blakeney*, on the Top of one of our Pontons, posted a little in the Front thereof; attended by each Drum-Major, with a Drum, in the Front of their respective Regiments, who, at each wave of the Colours, gave a Tap on his Drum, answerable to and for each Word of Command; the which each Regiment observed to perform accordingly: And soon afterward he review'd each other particular Corps of the Army, who also in like manner exercised and fired gradually before him.

June 1, By the Duke's Orders, all the Baw Horses of the Foot of our Army, besides several others of our Horse and Dragoons, were sent out a grassing up and down about the *Dyle* Side near unto *Louvain*, and at several other Places, where Grass was most Plenty, within two or three Leagues of our Camp, under the Cover of several of our Guards.

6, A little before Taptoo, there fell a great and heavy Shower of Rain in our Camp; the which, by its Violence, broke down and removed several Tents and Bells of Arms, carrying and driving them before it, it running in several hollow Places of our Camp like unto little Rivers, where it was dry before, without any Sign of any such Passage.

Campaign VII.
Anno 1707.

During the Time of our Abode at *Meldart*, there happen'd several small Skirmishes between ours and the Enemies foraging Parties, but neither of great Moment.

July 30, About Six at Night, after that the Duke and *Overquerque*, and the other Generals, had held a Conference among themselves, to use what Means possible to draw the Enemy from *Gemblours* to Battle, and not to let the Campaign slip wholly away without some note-worthy Action of so many brave Troops, it was concerted to make a Motion toward the Enemy, to sound their Intention; whereupon they immediately decamp'd our whole Army from *Meldart*, and advanced Frontward in Order and Design to move the Enemy from *Gemblours*, and to draw or force them to Battle, or to get, as I suppose, between them and *Mons*; and thereupon continued our March all that Night; and the next Morning, by Break of Day, we repass'd the *Dyle*, and another little River a little above *Corbeck*; and by Six at Night our whole Army, being on great Expedition, got up to, and pitch'd Camp at *Genap*, a little off to the South-Side of the *Dyle*, a Round Westward from *Meldart* of ten Leagues, of twenty four Hours March, without any Halt. Now by this Time the *French* removed from *Gemblours*, in order to cover *Mons*, but very careful to avoid Battle, as in my next Section is declared, according to what I saw and learned therefrom, *viz.*

August 1, The Duke, with our Army, decamp'd at *Genap*, and advanced therewith to, and about Six at Night pitch'd Camp at *Nivelle*, three Leagues, within about Two *English* of the *French* Army, where they were just arrived, a covering of *Mons*; but being in a great Hurry, they pitch'd no Camp: Thereby it was thought that they would have given us Battle in the Morning following, where they were also, as often before, strongly fortified with Hedges,

Hedges, Ditches, Woods, and Scrubs, and other strong Ground: Whereupon the Duke immediately that Evening detach'd Lord *Orkney*, with Twelve Battalions of Foot, and Thirty Squadrons of Horse and Dragoons, with all the Grenadiers of our whole Army, who advanced a little out in the Front of our Army, and lay on their Arms in the Van all that Night, within Cannon-shot of the Enemy, waiting their Motion, and to found their Intentions, they being a gasconading as design'd to give us Battle in the Morning, which was the very least of their real Thoughts or Design; for in the Twilight of the Evening, their main Body was perceived drawing Rearward through the Wood toward *Mons*, embracing the Opportunity of the Canopy of the Night, which often favoured them at such Times, leaving a few Battalions and Squadrons to cover their Retreat, who in the Morning falsified and gasconaded, as if their whole Army had been a posting for Battle: But as soon as Lord *Orkney* discover'd their Falsity, he boldly advanced thither with his Detachment, from which the Gasconaders retired after the main Body of their Army, and he couragiously charged and pursued the Rear upward of a League and a half, and killed and disabled, and caused to desert, upwards of Four Thousand of the Enemy, according to the Report of some of their Deserters, and several others; the which did very much redound to his Honour, and to the Enemies great Dishonour. After which, being recalled, he returned to our main Body; and then our whole Army, which had that Morning betimes advanced a little in the Front of their Camp, and lain on their Arms in the Time thereof, in order to assist Lord *Orkney*, and to fall on the Enemy, if Occasion and Opportunity had served; but the heavy Fog and Rain, with the Enemies retiring, prevented it; and we fell back again

Campaign VII. Anno 1707. to our Tents, which we had left standing firm in the Time thereof: And this same Morning General *Villeroy* had a narrow Escape out of his Quarters from *Orkney*'s Command, who enter'd that Village before he got out thereof; but they expecting none such to be there, he got safe off to his Army. Now this was the second Attempt and Offer which the Duke made to draw and force the Enemy to Battle, but could not prevail.

August 3, The Duke decamp'd our Army from *Nivelle*, about Eight in the Morning, and march'd in a very great Rain and deep Road to, and pitch'd Camp at *Soignes*, five Leagues; and the same Day, by the Heaviness of the Rain, and Tediousness of the deep watry Road, to speak within Bounds, the Quarter of our Foot scarce got up with their Colours till the next Day about Noon, and then all got up; they falling at the same time back closer to *Mons*.

4, About Noon, and at Night, our Camp at *Soignes* was each Time somewhat alarm'd, and our Picquets each Time turn'd out; being the *French* General, with a great Body of their Horse were seen a reconnoitring and gasconading a little out to the Front of our Camp; the which then, as often before and after, the more they saw or view'd it, the greater they feared and dreaded it, but would never venture to attack it, nor give or force us to Battle, as we did often them, although always inferior in Number to them.

20, The Duke decamp'd our Army from *Soignes*, and march'd past *Cameron* to, and pitch'd Camp between *Sheath* and *St. Dennis's-Cloister* near *Aeth*, four Leagues; and the same Day, at the first of our Army's Appearance, the *French* Army abandon'd *Cameron-Plain*, and retired from thence to, under the Cover of, *Tournay*.

23, De-

23, Decamp'd at, and march'd from *St. Denis*'s to, and pitch'd Camp between *Newburge* and *Arburge Cloister*, near unto *Enghien*, four Leagues.

<small>Campaign VII. *Anno* 1707.</small>

24, Decamp'd at, and march'd from *Newburge* to, and pitch'd Camp at *Genham Cloister*, on the East-Side of the *Scheld*, near *Oudenard*, four Leagues.

25, Decamp'd at *Genham*, and there pass'd the *Scheld*, and pitch'd at *Alsgham Cloister*, two Leagues.

27, Decamp'd at, and march'd from *Alsgham* to, and pitch'd Camp at *Helschen*, three Leagues, with the Right of our Right Wing extended near unto *Courtray*.

Sept. 3, At Taptoo, the Duke detach'd Lord *Orkney*, the Duke of *Argyle*, and several other General Persons, with Twenty Six entire Battalions, and Twenty Squadrons of Horse and Dragoons, and all the Grenadiers of our Army, with Fifteen Cannon, and Six Pontons, in Order, and advanced to *Turquony*, three Leagues Frontward of our Army, as only design'd to forage by the *Scheld*; but it was a Decoy, with a real Design to draw the Enemy thitherward from *Tournay* to Battle, and to get between and the City; and in Case the Enemy drawing out from thence, at the firing off three Pieces of Cannon, all the rest of our Army was immediately to advance gradually Frontward, or otherwise, as Opportunity should serve, in order to assist the said Detachment, and to fall on and battle the Enemy: But they having some private Intelligence of our Design, lay very firm, close to, and covered the City, and that more alertly than before; so that thereby the Duke finding no visible Sign of putting his Project in Execution, he therefore caused the said Detachment to remarch to their former Camp, into which they the next Night after arrived, about the same Time which they had left it the Night before; having

<small>Third Attempt to draw the Enemy to Battle.</small>

that

Campaign VII.
Anno 1707.

that Day first foraged close by the Enemies Advance or Out-Guard, and that without any Opposition or Interruption. Now this was the third Attempt which the Duke made in this Campaign to draw or force the Enemy to Battle, but could not prevail with neither; they being each Time as careful to avoid fighting, as he was forward in the using of Means to draw them to it, both at *Soignes*, *Nivelle*, and *Helschen*, as of each before prescribed: So that altho' we had neither battling nor sieging in this Campaign on our Side, we were somewhat employ'd in marching and countermarching to and fro from one Encampment to another. But after this last Attempt, our Army lay pretty quiet up and down by the *Scheld* Side, the remaining Part of the Campaign; but in the next we were much hotter employ'd, as it doth appear in the Journal thereof, in its Course.

Sept. 17, The Duke neither finding, nor seeing any visible Sign of any Action to be made on our Side, dismiss'd and sent off the Recruiting-Officers for *England*, and elsewhere, in order the sooner to have the Troops compleated, and ready for an early Campaign in the next Spring following, &c.

30 The Duke decamp'd our Army from *Helschen*, and march'd to, and pitch'd Camp between *Pegham* and *Alsgham* near unto *Oudenard*, three Leagues, for more Plenty of Forage, it being then grown very scarce about *Helschen*.

October 1, Decamp'd at, and march'd from *Pegham* to, and pitch'd at *St. Peter's Cloister*, two Leagues.

2, Decamp'd at, and march'd from *St. Peter's Cloister* to, and pitch'd Camp at *Wesenham*, two Leagues.

3, Decamp'd at, and march'd from *Wesenham* to, and pitch'd Camp at *Afflegbem* near *Alost*, three Leagues.

20, The

20, The Duke decamp'd and difpers'd the whole Army from *Affleghem* to their Winter-Quarters; and the fame Day General *Lumley*, with thofe of our *Britifh* Troops and Artillery that were for the Garrifon of *Ghent*, march'd from *Affleghem* into *Ghent*, four Leagues; and from thence the Duke went off from the *Hague*, and fo for *England*, &c.

Campaign VII. *Anno* 1707.

Here endeth the Journal of our Seventh Campaign in 1707, which was in Length Twenty Four Weeks and One Day, commenced the 5*th* Day of *May*, and ended on the 20*th* of *October*; of which our Corps, with the Grand Army, and apart, march'd in all Twenty Three Days, and therein Eighty Six Leagues, or Two Hundred and Fifty Eight Miles *Englifh*.

The End of the Seventh Campaign, A. D. 1707.

N.B. Before that I can begin in the tracing of any thing in the next Campaign in 1708, I muft touch a little at fomewhat of a Tranfaction that happen'd in the Way before it began, according to the beft that I know thereof, and wave the reft, *viz.*

About the 1*ft* of *March*, the ufurping King of *France*, infufed of Mifchief, caufed a great Fleet to be affembled at *Dunkirk*, and Twelve Battalions and feveral detach'd Troops, with the pretended Prince of *Wales* on Board thereof, with his Project, in Defign to make an Invafion upon *Scotland*, yea *England* and *Ireland* alfo, towards which they then accordingly failed; but was fuddenly interrupted by our Queen and Council's good Care, who having timely Intelligence thereof, order'd and fent out Admiral *Byng*, with Thirty Two War-Ships, immediately to wait their Motion: Admiral *Baker*, with Twelve thereof, at the fame Time failed to *Oftend*, in order to take in, and convoy from thence Major-

Major-General *Sabine*, and Ten Battalions of our *English* Foot, most readiest, who then were assembled from *Ghent* and *Bruges* at *Ostend*, on the 15th Day of *March*, and the same Day embark'd in the said Fleet and some Transports; who all, on the 17th, set Sail from *Ostend* after the Pretender toward *Scotland*, in order to stop his and the *French* Career, and to frustrate their landing there, or any where else within the said Dominions. The 20th Ditto our Fleet arrived near unto *Tinmouth Castle*, and near unto *Sheils*; where, on the 21st Ditto, in the Morning, all our Transports went in and cast Anchor in that Harbour, and there to abide till call'd for; but the War-Ships, with those aboard thereof, in order to join Admiral *Byng*, or otherwise, sailed on in Pursuit of the Enemy to the Firth of *Leith*; where the Enemy, finding no Opportunity nor Encouragement for Landing, sailed from thence round the Northern Part of *Scotland*, where they all along retained likewise a great Fear to put their Project in Execution: So that they could find no safe Opportunity or Inlet for Landing, and therefore they only plunder'd some of the Northern Parts thereof, where there was no Power to resist them; and after having so done, they instantly resailed back to *Dunkirk*, to avoid our Fleet that was in Pursuit thereof; having for their Pains only a View round *England*, *Scotland* and *Ireland*, with their Loss of the *Saulsbury* Prize, taken by our Fleet in the Firth of *Leith*, as she was about making her Escape under the Cover of *English* Colours; in which there was taken several noted Persons of Distinction: After which, the Enemy being resailed to *Dunkirk*, and elsewhere in *France*, our Fleet also resailed, those with Admiral *Baker* to *Sheiles*; from which, on the 16th of *April*, they, with the aforesaid Transports, set Sail, and resailed toward *Ostend*; where all, on the 19th Ditto, arrived safe at Anchor; and on the 20*th* the Transports went into that Harbour, and the Major-General, and the Ten Battalions that were on Board thereof, and of the Fleet, disembark'd off them, and went on Board of Ships or Bilanders, and sailed up to *Bruges* on that Canal of the *Leys*; from which, on the 22*d* Ditto, Brigadier-General *Sabine*, with the Seven Battalions of the Garrison of *Ghent*, re-sailed up the said Channel into *Ghent*, the which he had left on the 8*th* Day of *March*. This was a Round of Sixteen Days sailing, accounted about Three Hundred Leagues, or Nine Hundred Miles *English*.

THE

THE EIGHTH CAMPAIGN,

Begun in the Year 1708.

IN the latter End of *April*, the Duke of *Marlborough* arrived at the *Hague* from *England*, where he had several Conferences with the States-General, &c. about important Affairs, concerting of Measures for the Operations of the ensuing Campaign; and from thence he went to *Brussels*, in order to hasten the joining all the Allies Troops that were to serve on this Side, towards which they were then assembling on great Expedition; so that by the 10th of *May*, the most Part of all thereof were there assembled with the Duke. In the foregoing Winter, the *French* Court stated two great Projects, but neither thereof took Effect: The first is past already; the second, in brief, was to outwit the Allies out of their Conquests in *Flanders* by Policy, which they could not do by Power of Arms, although still superior in Number; of which in its Course, as I go along in my Journal; the which of this Campaign I here begin, *viz.*

May 11, General *Lumley*, with our *British* Troops and Artillery, set out of *Ghent*, and march'd from thence to, and pitch'd Camp at *Oudengham* Village, three Leagues; leaving behind a Detachment of

Seven

Seven Hundred Men, with Major *Dillabane*, to keep Garrison in the Castle of *Ghent*; who, in a few Days after, proved of great Consequence to the Allies.

Campaign VIII. Anno 1708.

12, Decamp'd at, and march'd from *Oudengham* to, and pitch'd Camp at *Sandburg*, near unto *Gramont*, four Leagues; our other Allies being some few Days before join'd, lay then apart from us at *Bruffels*, where the Duke of *Marlborough* first arrived.

14, Our *British* Corps and Artillery decamp'd at *Sandburg*, and all the other Allies at *Bruffels*, and both march'd from their several Encampments and join'd, and regularly form'd and pitch'd Camp at *Bellinghen*, three Leagues; where then our Army consisted of in all One Hundred and Twelve Battalions of Foot, and One Hundred and Eighty Squadrons of Horse and Dragoons, One Hundred and Eight Cannon, Twenty Four Mortars and Howitzers, with Forty Four Pontons, and all other necessary Utensils of War conform. The *French* general Rendezvous was then on the South-Side of *Soignes*, between it and *Mons*; and were computed to consist of One Hundred and Thirty Two Battalions of Foot, and Two Hundred and Seven Squadrons of Horse and Dragoons, Ninety Four Cannon, Sixteen Mortars, and Thirty Six Pontons, with also all other Necessaries of War conform, in Order for Battle, as was expected.

18, The Duke decamp'd, with our whole Army, from *Bellinghen*, and advanced Frontward somewhat nearer to the Enemy, to found their Intentions, and pitch'd Camp between *Centurnal* and *Notredame Hall*, three Leagues.

22, By Break of Day, the most of all our Horse and Dragoons being gone a foraging, the Enemy, having present Intelligence thereof, embraced that Opportunity to get the Start of our Army, and

march'd

Campaign VIII. Anno 1708.

march'd from *Soignes* round toward the *Pafs* of *Louvain*, on great Expedition, to cut us off from thence, and all that Side of the Country, and to prevent Prince *Eugene* joining us, who was then on his March from *Germany* thitherward, with about Thirty Thousand *Germans*; of all which they were suddenly frustrated, to their great Regret, *viz.* That Morning, by Eight, the Duke having Intelligence of their being march'd, and penetrated into their Designs, caused immediately Three Pieces of Cannon to be fired, by which, in a Trice, all our Foragers was return'd; and then our whole Army decamp'd from *Centurnal*, and march'd Leftward paſt *Notredame Hall*, and in the Night crofs'd the *Senne* at *Bruſſels*, and pafs'd through the Out-Works thereof in a heavy thick Rain; and in the Morning, about the Rifing of the Sun, we got quite clear off the Town, and about Noon our whole Army arrived up, and pitch'd Camp at *Turbank-Crofs*, *Bethlem-Hill*, on the South and Eaft-Side of *Louvain*, eight Leagues; and thereby baulk'd the Enemy of that Project, and obliged them to pitch three Leagues ſhort at *Gemblours*, where they had their long Camp in the Year before, when they came ſhort of *Louvain*; of which it was ſaid, and it was very likely, that the *French* General had Invitations, and alfo of *Bruges* and *Ghent*, and of moft of the noted Cities and Towns in *Flanders*, by Articles figned by the Heads thereof, in *Mons*, the Year before, as aforefaid, to and by the Prevailance of the Duke of *Bavaria*, and ſeveral other Sticklers for the Houfe of *Bourbon*, on the Levity and Reſtlefs Spirits of the fickle Inhabitants of *Bruges* and *Ghent*, &c. to deliver up to the *French* at any Time after, as foon as poſſible they could put in Forces there for their and their own Security; and by this Stratagem thought to weary the Allies quite out of *Flanders* again, without ever a Stroke: All which

which soon after proved far contrary to their Expectations; for before the Campaign being over, although tedious, instead of driving us out of Flanders, we beat and defeated their Army, and advanced much farther into the Heart thereof, and, to their great Regret, took the Metropolitaneſt City thereof: So that at laſt they were inſnared in their own Trap, and all by the good Conduct of the Duke, and our other Generals and couragious Soldiers, under the providential Care and Goodneſs of God, contrary to Merit.

Campaign VIII. Anno 1708.

June 4, Prince *Eugene* in Perſon came privately on great Expedition to the Duke, and had ſome few ſecret Conferences of important Affairs with him, about the Operations of the enſuing Campaign; after which he immediately return'd to his Troops on the *Rhine*, in order to haſten therewith from thence, to join the Duke as ſoon as poſſible. The Duke of *Berwick* was alſo on his March at the ſame time from *Alſace*, with a great Body of Troops, to join *Vendoſme*, before the Conjunction of the Duke of *Marlborough* and Prince *Eugene* with the Confederates, but was not ſo forward on his Journey as Prince *Eugene*; both which came ſhort of the Battle that ſoon after happen'd; wherein the Duke of *Marlborough*, with the Troops in his Command, quite broke and defeated the proud *French* in lofty *Vendoſme*'s.

6, The Duke of *Marlborough* review'd the whole Army under his Command.

23, At Break of Day, the Duke having Intelligence that in the Night the *French* Army was march'd off from *Gemblours*, on great Expeditions toward *Ghent*, in order to embrace its and *Bruges* Invitations; whereupon he immediately decamp'd our Army from *Terbank*, and alſo march'd after the Enemy on great Expedition, in order, if poſſible, although inferior much in Number, to fruſtrate them

Ghent and *Bruges* taken.

them of *Ghent*, or to draw them to a pitch'd Battle; but came somewhat short thereof, they having the Start of us, with also the String to march, and we the Bow; for which after they paid dearly. About Noon our Army pass'd *Bruffels*; and about Ten at Night, the Enemy having made a small Stop or Halt, our Front by that Time coming up near to their Rear, our Army halted also, and pitch'd Camp at *Centurnal*, with our Right opposite to the Enemies Right in our Front, about one Mile asunder. They unpitch'd, and gasconading, as designing to give us Battle in the Morning; but, unwilling to give us Battle, and to accomplish their real Intention, they embraced the Favour of the Canopy of the Night; for by the Time that we had pitch'd Camp, their Left began their March; so that by Break of Day, their manly great Expedition got over to the West-Side of *Aloft*, and a Part thereof went on to *Ghent*, without any Halt, leaving a few Battalions and Squadrons in their Rear to cover their Retreat, which also served for a Decoy, as if design'd for Battle: So that thereby most of our Army kept all that Night in a moving Posture, expecting the same; and the next Morning, being the 24*th* of *June*, they falsified and flourish'd their Colours apace in the Scrub in our Front, as if all their Army had been there a posting to give our Army Battle; the which Falsity did very much detain and frustrate our Expectations, and of the truly securing or preventing them of *Ghent*; for it was very near Noon-Day before that our General fully found out that their main Body was really gone off, and intended not Battle: After which, the Duke immediately advanced, with the most of our Horse and Dragoons, after that Part of the Enemy that had been so a falsifying, and with undaunted Courage and Bravery charged and pursued their Rear to the other

ther Side of the *Pafs* of *Aloft*, and killed, wounded, took, and caufed to defert thereof, by their own Computation, upwards of Four Thoufand Men, befides took a great Quantity of their Baggage; the which did much more redound to his Honour, than theirs in flipping off from Battle, and ftealing off *Ghent* by their Marches and Countermarches: And after that he had drove them over the faid *Pafs*, Night coming on apace, he withdrew, with the Horfe and Dragoons from their Purfuit, to the main Body of our Army, who by that Time was got up to *Afch* Village, three Leagues, where then our whole Army form'd and pitch'd Camp on that Road-Side, half Way between *Bruffels* and *Aloft*: And the next Day the *French* Army re-enter'd *Ghent*; but *Delabane*, with his Garrifon in the Caftle of Seven Hundred Men, ftood them a Difpute three Days after; and at laft obtained honourable Conditions to march out to *Safs-Gand*; the which Detainment to their powerful Army proved very fatal, and was a great Prelude to the Battle at *Oudenard*: For although they had poffefs'd themfelves of *Ghent* and *Bruges*, yet they thought not themfelves fecure; and therefore defign'd again to quit them, and to retire toward their Lines and ftrong Towns, before the Conjunction of Prince *Eugene* and the Duke; the which they had Intelligence would be long before *Berwick*'s Arrival, which might enable them to cope with us, and to preferve their late Conquefts; of which the Duke foon projected a Way to difinherit them thereof, to draw them to Battle, by paffing the *Scheld* at *Oudenard*, and to get between them and their own Country, believing he was able to cope with them, notwithftanding their Superiority in Number, before their retiring to their Lines, as aforefaid.

(214)

Campaign VIII. Anno 1708.

June 28, About Break of Day, the Duke, in order to put his Project in Execution, decamp'd our whole Army from *Asch*, and march'd off from thence with all the Grenadiers in our Rear, and continued our March all that Day and Night following, on great Expedition, without any Halt, round toward *Oudenard*, till the next Morning about Sun-rising, that we arrived at *Aeth*; where we halted a little on our Arms, to bring up our long Rear: After which we proceeded with our March from thence, and about Noon pitch'd Camp between *Lessines* and *Hisberg* Villages; a Round, or wonderful swift March, of ten Leagues, in order for Battle, to prevent the *French* of *Oudenard*, which they design'd to reduce in their Retreat to their Lines, toward which by this Time they were now about to repair with Speed, but soon intervened, as by my following Account of the Battle that then ensued thereby doth appear, both Armies consisting of Strength much as aforesaid, *May* 14; the *French* computed, by their own Computation, Twelve Thousand Men in Number stronger than the Allies, besides the Advantage of the Ground, and their whole Army being first up, and strongly posted, before the Allies Arrival; of which more afterward in its Course, *&c.*

Battle of Oudenard.

30, At Break of Day, the Duke of *Marlborough* detach'd and sent off, in the Van of our Army from *Lessiner* Camp, toward *Oudenard*, Lieutenant-General *Ranzaw* and *Cadogan*, with Twelve Battalions of Foot, Fifteen Squadrons of Horse and Dragoons, and all the Quarter-Colours of our Army, with Thirty Two Cannons, and our Pontons, in order to lay and to cover the laying thereof over the River *Scheld* at *Oudenard*, for our whole Army there to pass, if possible, to pitch on the other Side thereof for Battle. About Eight in the Morning our whole Army decamp'd from *Lessiner*,

and

and march'd on great Expedition after General Ranzaw's Command; who about Noon arrived at, and laid the Tin-Boats over the *Scheld*, a little below *Oudenard*, and immediately quietly pass'd the same, and advanced to *Amberge* Village, near unto which, at the same time, the *French* Army being now removed from *Ghent* thitherward, on great Expedition for Battle also, had posted in the said Village Four Battalions for the Extent of their Left Wing to range near the *Scheld*, to which it was then expeditiously inclining to join the same for Battle: But they seeing our said Detachment, as if our whole Army had been up, advancing thitherward with undaunted Courage, they faced and inclined Rightward; whereupon General *Ranzaw*'s Command immediately advanced up to, and took all those that were posted at, and had otherwise got into *Amberge*; and from thence advanced a little farther with our Quarter-Master-General, and beat back a few Squadrons of the Enemy, which at first had been somewhat too hard for our few Squadrons that had been a reconnoitring the Ground for our Army, when up, to form and draw up upon in proper Lines, in order for Battle: After which, General *Ranzaw*'s Detachment inclined a little Leftward to, and halted a little at, and in the Wood-Side, longing and waiting for the Arrival of our Army thither, whose Front by this Time had arrived near unto the *Scheld*; in which Time the Enemies main Body being up from *Ghent*, they, with all the Expedition imaginable, strongly and advantageously posted themselves on the other Side of the Wood and Scrub, and amongst Hedges and Ditches, with a Defile in a Part of their Right Wing's Front, in Order for Battle, within Cannon-shot of General *Ranzaw*'s Command: The which, I must needs say, that if the *French* had rightly managed their Matter, they might have easily

Campaign VIII. Anno 1708. easily prevented our passing the *Scheld*; and after that we had pass'd it, they might with their huge Body attack'd and taken them, or drove them back over the *Scheld* again, being but such a small Number, and that long enough before the Duke of *Marlborough*'s Arrival with the main Body of our Army. But to make short of it; about Two in the Afternoon, the Duke, with about one Half of our Army, got up to, and pass'd the *Scheld* in two Places at, and below *Oudenard*, and that with all imaginable Expedition, for General *Ranzaw*'s Relief and Assistance; and as soon as they arrived thereat, and in Line formed for Battle therewith, the Duke immediately caused some few Cannon, that had got up, to be posted as most proper, and begun a saluting and cannonading the Enemy therewith, and they our Army in like manner with theirs: But the Duke, on this Occasion, having no Time to give exact Dispositions for attacking the Enemy, order'd what was up, as they were, to begin and attack, and the rest as they came to fall in accordingly; whereupon all that was up, which was little above the Half of our Army, immediately advanced on with undaunted Courage, and vigorously attack'd the Enemies Right Wing next to them, and most open, and elsewhere, with small Shot, as regular and gradual as the Time and Ground would permit; in which Time the Duke was very busy every where giving his necessary Directions; and as the rest got over the Pass, and up, they fell in and on in their regular Places, smartly also with their small Shot: All which Particulars are too tedious for me to relate, or any one else, both in a manner being taken on their March; but, in short, small Shot continued very brisk and smart on both Sides, with several sore Assaults and Repulses, from about Three in the Afternoon till past Nine at Night, before it was fully ceased, or

the

the Dispute decided: In which Time, with much to do, to speak the Truth, we drove the Enemy from Ditch to Ditch, from Hedge to Hedge, and from out of one Scrub to another, and Wood, in great Hurry, Disorder, and Confusion; so that the Night being approached, the Enemy, as often before, most joyfully embraced the Shade of its Canopy, under which they retired from the Place or Field of Battle, on very great Expedition, Disorder, and Confusion, to the North-Side of *Deinse* and the River *Lys*, and broke down the Bridge thereof, to prevent the Passage of the Pursuers: In which Time, of this their disorderly Retreat, the main Body of our Army lay on their Arms very alert all Night, in a very soaking Rain; and in the Morning our whole Army, with the most of our Horse and Dragoons in the Front, march'd after the Enemy towards *Deinse*; the which so closely pursued their Rear, that they killed and destroy'd, and took thereof, upwards of One Thousand Men; besides, they had a great many deserted and drowned, that could not get up and over the *Lys* with the Grand Body of their Army in the Night, the Bridges being broke down to prevent our Armies farther Pursuit of them, as aforesaid; the which deceived a great many of them, to the Loss of their Lives. After which, that same Day, being the 1*st* of *July*, about Noon, our whole Army return'd from the Pursuit to, and pitch'd Camp on the same Ground where we, the Day before, had fought the Battle near *Oudenard*, four Leagues; and the *French* Army retired from *Deinse*, and remarch'd through *Ghent*, and repitch'd Camp at *Bellen*, and entrench'd between *Ghent* and *Bruges*, beyond that Canal, where they had their first general Rendezvous of their broken Troops; their Generals in great Discontent one with another; but ours, as at *Hochstat*, gained never-fading Laurels,

Campaign VIII.
Anno 1708.

P 4 &c.

Campaign VIII. *&c.* Now by that Time they had bought *Ghent* Anno 1708. and *Bruges* fomewhat dear, but much dearer before the End of the Campaign; by, and in which, if rightly computed one way with another, they loft upwards of Forty Thoufand Men: But as to the Total of their Lofs in this Battle, it was computed to amount to, of taken, killed, wounded, drowned, and deferted, in all Sixteen Thoufand Four Hundred; as appears by the following Table of the Particulars thereof, as given, *viz.*

Lieutenant-General	1
Major-Generals	3
Brigadiers	4
Colonels	7
Lieutenant-Colonels	8
Majors	8
Captains	189
Lieutenants	173
Cornets and Enfigns	174
Quarter-Mafters of Horfe	47
Of their Houfhold	186
Taken of Centinels	9000
Taken, Officers included	9800
Killed and wounded	4200
Deferted	2400
Taken, killed, wounded, and deferted	19400
Taken Pieces of Cannon	10
Pairs of Colours	56
Standards	52
Pairs of Kettle-Drums	8
Horfes	4500

Another

Another Account, differing much, of the Enemies giving, *viz.*

    Taken by the Allies.
Officers	700
Centinels	5000
Killed	4000
Wounded	5000

    Another.
Prisoners	8000

Either of which, their Lofs was very great, much fuperior to the Allies Lofs; which, in the gaining of this glorious Victory, had but Three Thoufand and Forty One killed and wounded in all, as appears by the following Table of their Particulars, *viz.*

(220)

Campaign VIII. Anno 1708.

	Lt.Gen. Kd.|Wd.	Ma.Gen. Kd.|Wd.	Colonels Kd.|Wd.	Lt.Col. Kd.|Wd.	Majors Kd.|Wd.	Captains Kd.|Wd.	Subalterns Kd.|Wd.	Serjeants Kd.|Wd.	Centinels Kd.|Wd.	Total Killed.|Wound.	Total Kd.Wd.
Of the Britains				2 |	|	6 | 4	|	9 | 5	9 | 49	151 | 53	173 | 226
Prussians ——			1 | 1	|	|	2 |	4 |	12 |	50 | 119	51 | 139	190
Hanovers ——			1 | 1	2 |	3 |	4 | 1	1 | 11	1 |	106 | 320	111 | 339	450
Danes ——		1 | 1	1 | 1	| 2	2 | 1	5 | 4	18 | 26	201 | 345	207 | 398	605
Hollanders ——	2 | 2	1 |	2 |	3 |	9 | 3	124 | 62	1638 | 350	1006 | 402	1144 | 1546
Total ——	1 | 1	2 | 3	6 | 1	6 | 1	9 | 14	45 | 53	100 | 1686	756 | 1941	824 | 2193	3041

In the general Total of killed and wounded, the Four Generals, with Twenty killed and wounded of our Artillery, cast in Two of our Brigadier-Majors that were taken as going in the Action from Left to Right Wing, with Orders, the said Day: The Action was quite over, and it was dark Night, before the Rear of our Army got up and over the *Scheld*; nay, all got not quite over till the next Morning.

Now

(221)

Now the Dispute of the Battle being over, decided in our Favour, and Matters somewhat settled, and the *French* thereby debared Entrance into *French Flanders*, and forced to be content to embrace and inhabit with the Fruit of their new dear Conquest for a Time, and to make the best of their late Defeatment, one General reflecting against the other; whilst, in the mean time, the Duke of *Marlborough* (whose heroical Spirit was ever prone for further Conquests, and to keep the Enemy in Confusion before reinforced) next bent his Intention to level the Lines of *French Flanders* before the Duke of *Berwick*'s Arrival thereat, who was then on his March thitherward, on great Expedition, with a Body of Troops from *Alsace*, as aforesaid; and next after the levelling of the said Lines, the Duke fully design'd to reduce *Lisle*, and that as soon as possible; both which was bravely effected, although with a great deal of Difficulty and Loss, yet the more honourable.

<small>Campaign VIII. *Anno* 1708.</small>

July 2, At Night, the Duke, when after some Conferences with our other Generals for the carrying on these Projects, detach'd and sent before, from our Camp at *Oudenard*, towards the said Lines, Count *Lottum*, with Thirty Battalions and Fifty Squadrons, and some Field Cannon, in order to pass the same near *Warneton* and *Werweick*; who thereupon immediately march'd Leftward, and halted a little of that Night on their Arms, near unto *Helschen*; and also that same Evening the Duke decamp'd the Grand Army from *Oudenard*, and march'd slowly after Count *Lottum*, and likewise lay on their Arms that Night, a little in the Rear of the Count's Command.

<small>The passing of the Lines.</small>

3, By Break of Day, Count *Lottum*, with the said Troops, proceeded on with his March, and about Noon pass'd *Courtray*, where they halted a little to bring up the Stragglers, and then march'd

on

Campaign VIII. Anno 1708. on from thence to *Menin*, where that Night alſo they lay on their Arms; and the Grand Army alſo having continued their March after, pitch'd Camp near *Courtray*, four Leagues, but not join'd.

July 4, Count *Lottum*, with his Detachment, proceeded on with his March from *Menin*; and about Ten in the Morning arrived near unto the ſaid Line, and advanced up to it, and broke down a Part thereof, and paſs'd the ſame near unto *Commines*, without any Oppoſition; for at the very firſt of his Appearance approaching thither, the Enemies Out-Guard, that had been poſted thereon from their Garriſon at *Warneton*, immediately abandon'd the Line, and retired in great Haſte and Diſorder to *Werweick*, unto which next the Count advanced, and took it, and thoſe therein Priſoners of War, *viz.* one Lieutenant-Colonel *Burch*, with Twelve other Commiſſion'd Officers, and Three Hundred and Seventy Centinels, including Non-Commiſſion'd Officers, and found therein Ten Cannon of Iron; the which being done, the ſaid Count, with his Command, pitch'd Camp on the Weſt-Side of the Town; and that Morning, at Break of Day, the Duke, with our Grand Army, decamp'd from *Courtray*, and expeditiouſly march'd after the ſaid Count; and about Two in the Afternoon, being arrived, pitch'd Camp at *Werweick*, on the other Side of the Line, near unto where the ſaid Count had paſs'd it, about half a League aſunder, about two Leagues Weſtward of *Menin*, and five Leagues Weſtward of *Courtray*, and poſſeſs'd their Lines; and the next Day Count *Lottum*, with his Command, removed his Camp from the Weſt to the South-Side of *Warneton*.

10, The Duke, with our Grand Army, decamp'd from the other Side of the ſaid Line, and regularly form'd, join'd, and pitch'd Camp into one Croſs-Way of the ſaid Line, with our Right adjoining to *Werweick*, and Left extended to *Pont Roufe*, or Pafs of *Redbridge*, for the Security thereof, and Plenty of Forage: No Enemy can ever be too fecure in another's Country; we and the *French*, for a Time, having there in a manner made an Exchange.

Campaign VIII. Anno 1708.

14, The Duke detach'd and fent off Count *Tilly*, with Twenty Five Battalions and Thirty Eight Squadrons, with Nine Hundred Grenadiers, in order to advance from *Werweick* into the *French* Country about *Arras*, in the Province of *Artoife*, to raife Contribution, and to caufe the Inhabitants to bring in Provifion for our Army, whilft the Enemy was ravaging the Country about *Ghent* and *Bruges*; the which, in a fhort Time, they accordingly did.

16, The Duke detach'd and fent after Count *Tilly* Lord *Orkney*, with a Reinforcement of Twelve Battalions and Twenty Five Squadrons, left the Duke of *Berwick*, who was all this while expected, fhould interrupt him, or be otherwife over-power'd in or by the Country; but neither thereof oppofed them: So that after feven Days Progrefs, having accomplifh'd their Defign, they arrived back to our Grand Camp on the 23d inftant, leaving feveral of thefe Villages, and other Places about *Arras*, in Afhes, who did not contribute and fubmit to their Demands.

22, In the Night, in our Camp at *Werweick*, there happened great Lightning, Thunder, and Rain, the Violence thereof broke down feveral Tents flat to the Ground; and I had Account that the fame Day General *Earle*, with Nine Battalions, from *England*, was landed at *Oftend*, and pitch'd Camp on the Weft-Side of the Town; where, foon after, he was reinforced by Two Battalions more from *England*, in order the better to preferve the Communication of our Grand Camp with *Oftend* and that Side, our Paffage therewith being
then

<small>Campaign VIII.
Anno 1708.</small>
then mostly block'd up, and pester'd by the *French* Grand Army, which then inhabited on that Side, who then thought that they had our Army in a Pound; but searching into the Depth thereof, they at last found themselves mostly snared therein.

July 23, Count *Tilly* and Lord *Orkney* being return'd, as aforesaid, the Duke detach'd and sent Count *Lottum*, with Twenty Four Battalions and Forty Squadrons, in order to convoy up our heavy Train from *Bruffels*, for the carrying on of the Siege against *Lifle*, on which the Duke's Intent was fully bent, waiting for Prince *Eugene*'s joining.

24, The Duke caused the Right and Left Wing of our Army to close to the Center, and filled up the Interval of those Troops that were gone off with Count *Lottum*.

<small>The Siege of *Lifle*.</small>
This Siege was the longest, and most note-worthiest of any during the War; and therefore I could not, if I would, avoid inserting the larger on the Matters thereof; being, that very soon after that it was form'd, the Duke of *Burgundy* and *Vendofme* having rendezvous'd a puissant Army, reinforced by the Duke of *Berwick* with the aforesaid Troops, and by Order drain'd down with him several Troops from *Namure*, *Mons*, *Valenciennes*, *Charleroy*, and several other Garrisons together; who, in Conjunction with the two defeated Heroes, made several faint Attempts or Gasconades to relieve or reinforce the City, and as if design'd to attack the Army in the Duke of *Marlborough*'s Command, who cover'd the Siege; but each Time, by his and Prince *Eugene*'s good Conduct from the besieging Army, who were more ready to repulse, than they were to assault, their Attempts were blasted, and they also abashedly fell back, and at last repassed the *Scheld*, and entrenched along the Brink thereof from the Hill above *Oudenard*, near unto *Ghent*, with a Project to cut off our Armies Communication from *Bruffels*,

Bruſſels, &c. The which, in ſhort, they put in Execution; and not only that, but in a manner, nay wholly and quite cut off our Communication of all manner of Succour from our own Countries for a Time, till Providence order'd it otherwiſe on our Side, to the Enemies great Abaſhment, and the Allies great Honour and Praiſe, ever renowned; and from theſe Digreſſions I paſs, and proceed with each Thing as it happen'd in Courſe, *viz.*

Campaign VIII. *Anno* 1708.

31, The Duke having Intelligence that Prince *Eugene*, with the aforeſaid Imperial and Palatine Troops of Thirty Thouſand Men, were within four ſmall Days March, on the other Side of *Liſle*, for which we had been ſeveral Days waiting and expecting, detach'd from his Army at *Werweick*, out of our ſeveral Corps, in order to join Prince *Eugene* for the ſaid Siege, the Prince of *Orange*, with Thirty One Battalions of Foot, and Forty Four Squadrons of Horſe and Dragoons, with ſome of the beſt and moſt proper of our Artillery, for the North and Weſt-Side of the City; and Prince *Eugene*, with his Eighteen Battalions and Forty Three Squadrons, for the South and Eaſt-Side of the City; and thus they were diſtinguiſh'd: And the ſaid Day the Prince of *Orange*, with thoſe in his Command, at Six at Night, march'd off towards *Liſle*, and in the Duſk paſs'd through *Menin*, and in the latter Part of the Night made a Halt on their Arms, on the Weſt-Side of the Road, half Way between *Menin* and *Liſle*; and the ſame Day our heavy Train arrived at *Menin*, which came from *Bruſſels* by the Way of *Soignes*, aſſiſted by the *German* Troops.

Auguſt 1, Betimes in the Morning, the Prince of *Orange*, with his Command, advanced from the ſaid Ground, where they had lain the remaining Part of the ſaid Night, near to, and oppoſite *Marquet Cloiſter*, which is on the Weſt Brink of the *Lys*, within Cannon-ſhot of the City of *Liſle*; and

Campaign VIII.
Anno 1708.

at the same time the Enemies Out-Guards that had been posted on *Marquet Bridge*, abandon'd it, and retired to the City in great Hurry and Disorder; After which Serjeant *Littler*, in *Godfrey*'s Regiment, swam over the River, and cut and let down the Bridge for the Passage of the Troops; and a Party thereof immediately passed over, and secured the said Pass, which the Enemy attempted to repossess, but came short; for which singular Piece of Service Serjeant *Littler* had Colours bestowed on him, in the Duke of *Argyle*'s Regiment: And the said Day General *Bouffler*, with the most of his strong Garrison, issued out, and advanced a little from the City, making a great Show, and gasconading as if they would have given the Prince of *Orange* Battle, of which Courage failing them, they soon retired to their wonted Post; and we of the Prince of *Orange*'s Command, lay all that Night after on our Arms by the said Pass of *Marquet-Bridge*: And also that same Day our Grand Army decamp'd from *Werweick*, and march'd to, and pitch'd Camp at *Helschen*, six Leagues, to attend or wait the Enemies Motion, in Case that they should attempt to make any from *Ghent*, being strong.

August 2, The Duke, with our Grand Army, decamp'd at, and march'd from *Helschen* to, and pitch'd Camp at *Amogis*, two Leagues, the better to cover the said Siege that we were now about forming; and the same Day the Prince of *Orange*, with his Command, cross'd the River *Lys*, on the said Bridge at *Marquet Cloister*, and ranged his Troops along that Bottom between it and Abbey *de Low*; and thereby block'd up the City and Citadel of *Lisle*, and lay on our Arms that Night, and the two following Days and Nights, very alert, waiting for the coming of Prince *Eugene*, with the *German* Troops, as aforesaid, to join us, before that we could invest or form a regular Siege against

the

the City and Citadel, it being of a very great Compass round: Besides it was strongly manned with a Garrison, consisting of in all Twenty One Battalions of Foot, and Six Squadrons of Dragoons, One Hundred and Forty Horse, and Eight Hundred Invalids, fit for Service, with upwards of One Hundred and Twenty Cannon and Thirty Mortars, mounted on City and Citadel, with all other necessary Utensils of War conform, for the standing of a strong Siege, commanded by Monsieur *Bouffleurs*, Lieutenant-General *Sourville* and *Lee*, &c.

5, Prince *Eugene* being arrived with the aforesaid Troops, and join'd with the Prince of *Orange*'s Command, they immediately invested the City regularly, Prince *Eugene* at *Abeg de Low*, and *Orange* at *Marquet-Cloister*, in Form as aforesaid ; and carried on the Siege by two Attacks, the Right by Prince *Eugene*, with Twenty Seven Battalions, and Sixty Two Squadrons ; the Left by the Prince of *Orange*, with Twenty Two Battalions, and Twenty Five Squadrons ; both consisted of Forty Nine Battalions, and Eighty Seven Squadrons: The two Head General Engineers were Monsieur *La Roque* and *Du Mey*. And thus the Siege was formed, and afterward carried on as regular as could be expected, and as the Ground would allow ; but with a great deal of Difficulty, and the Loss of a great many brave Men. In the two Days that the Prince of *Orange*'s Command lay on their Arms near *Marquet-Cloister*, on the upper Road we erected a small Sconce, with Seven small Cannon thereon, in order to prevent its being surprized ; the Regiments lying thin, and each taking up the Ground of two Regiments.

6, The Besiegers Line of Circumvallation was begun, and carried on by a Body of between Seven or Eight Thousand Boors, of that and the adjacent Countries ;

Campaign VIII. Anno 1708.

Countries; and that same Day also the Besiegers began making and bringing of Fascines, long and short; Gabions, big and little, with Baskets for Mortars and Hurdles, with Picquets and Mauls, and also all other Necessaries of that Kind, for the expeditious carrying on of the said Siege, on which the Eyes of all the Kings, Princes, and other Potentates of the Grand Confederacy and *France*, were then fix'd; nay, I may lawfully say, all *Europe*, without Offence.

August 11, About Noon, the aforesaid small Batteries of Seven Cannon began to play, and that smartly, from the said Sconce, and drove in a great Party of the Besieged, who had been erecting some Fleches, and other Out-Works, in order to keep the Besiegers at as great a Distance from the City as possibly they could, and as long, and to prevent and frustrate their sudden encroaching thereon, but in vain; for the same Day, at Night, the Prince of *Orange*, with several other General Persons, with Sixteen entire Battalions, and a great and competent Number of Men, with and without Arms, of the Besiegers, opened their Trenches, by two Attacks, against and on the North-East Side of the City, and that with very little Loss, by getting into Cover before discover'd: But as for the Right, or general Opening of the Trenches on the *Germans* Attack, it was not till the next Night, about the same Time, when our Grand Batteries was erected, and the several other Batteries, on both Attacks consisting of, *viz.* the Grand Battery, where the *English* were employ'd, of Forty Eight Cannon; the small ones, one of Eleven Cannon, one of Twelve, one of Seventeen, one of Eight, and one of Five; of Mortars, one of Eight, and Eight Howitzers; and another of Eight Mortars, and Eight Howitzers; and thus they were distributed at first, and amounted to in all One Hundred and

One

One Cannon, with Thirty Two Mortars and How- *Campaign*
itzers: And afterward, as we gained Ground, our *VIII.*
Anno 1708.
Batteries were gradually advanced, and placed
nearer to, and against the City, in small Parcels,
as the Ground would best allow or permit; and at
the last erecting of our Batteries on the Glacis and
Inside of the Palisadoes, they stood thus, *viz.* one
of Seventeen Cannon, another of Fourteen; three
Batteries, each of Eight, one of Six, one of Five,
one of Four, and one of Three; the Mortars and
Howitzers stood thus, one of Eleven, two of Nine,
one of Six, and one of Five; and thus they stood,
and were distributed at last, and amounted to in
all Sixty Six Cannon, and Forty Mortars, against
the City when surrender'd.

14, Our heavy Train that were, as aforesaid,
arrived from *Brussels* to *Menin*, now arrived at the
besieging Camp, with great Stores of Provisions,
and were then posted near *Marquet-Cloister*; and
the next Day each of the first aforesaid Batteries
were compleated.

16, At Seven in the Morning, the first of our
Batteries, as before stated, began to play, and
play'd very vigorous and furious against the main
Wall of the City, for a Grand Breach thereon;
but being at too great a Distance, it was a considerable Time after before that there was any great
Impression made thereon, for a firm Breach or general Storm.

20, The Duke of *Marlborough* decamp'd our
Grand Army at, and remarch'd from *Amogis* to, and
again repitch'd Camp at *Helschen*, two Leagues.

21, Decamp'd at *Helschen*, and march'd to, and
pitch'd Camp at *Templere*, three Leagues, the better to cover the Besiegers; and that Night a competent Number thereof attack'd and took a small
fortified Chapel and Windmill, which before somewhat flank'd and gall'd a Part of the Left of our
Approaches,

Campaign VIII.
Anno 1708.

Approaches, and beat the Enemy out thereof into their main Works, with the Loss of one Major-General, and Eighty Men killed.

August 22, The Duke decamp'd our Grand Army at, and march'd from *Templere* to, and pitch'd Camp at *Peron*, two Lergues, covering the Enemy that were then in a Motion for great Matters.

24, Decamp'd at, and march'd from *Peron* to, and Camp at *Fretin*, three Leagues, on the Plain Side, on the South and East-Side of *Lisle*, near thereunto, the better still to cover the Siege thereof. The Enemy being now come to a very great Head, as aforesaid, and consisting of One Hundred and Thirty Six Battalions of Foot, and Two Hundred and Forty Squadrons of Horse and Dragoons, with Ordnance conform, march'd round the Country by *Tournay*, and advanced to the other Side of *Londway*, within about one League of our Grand Army, a gasconading, and threaten'd, as if fully design'd to attack our Army, and to relieve or reinforce the Besieged the next Day, if possible; of all which they fell far short, by the judicious Care and good Conduct of our warlike and heroical Generals, and undaunted, triumphant, couragious Army: At this Time the Army in the Duke's Command, consisting but of Eighty Three Battalions, and One Hundred and Thirty Seven Squadrons, far inferior in Number to the Enemy, as aforesaid, caused, the said Night, a running Trench to be cast up in the Front of our Army, for their better Security, with several Batteries thereon, to prevent the Surprizals of those now three gasconading Heroes, as it stood him upon, for the maintaining this important Siege; at which there was, as aforesaid, a considerable Part of the Army, Forty Nine Battalions, and Eighty Seven Squadrons; of which, the next Morning betimes, Prince *Eugene* and the Prince of *Orange* brought from thence, to

the

the Duke's Affiftance, Fifteen Battalions, and the moft of the Horfe and Dragoons, leaving the reft very alert, to keep the Befieged in Play and Awe till their Return.

25, About Ten in the Morning, the faid three gafconading Heroes advanced out with three huge Armies from the Side of *Londway*, from their Encampment, towards our Army, as immediately defign'd to attack or force the fame, and came within Cannon-fhot thereof; but finding our Army in better Order, and much readier to repulfe than they were to affault or oppofe them, it put them to a fudden Stand and great Confternation: So that after their reconnoitring and gafconading all Day, with brifk cannonading each other, their hot fiery Fury was abated, and Courage cool'd: They, in the Dufk of that Evening withdrew, and fell farther back to, and pitch'd their Camp on the far Side of *Loudway*, at fomewhat greater Diftance from our Army than before, on the other Side of the Plain, and fully without the Random-fhot of our Cannon, to confult and form fome new Project for the fomewhat Prefervation of their blafted Honour, that it might not quite die. After which, that Evening, our Army again repitch'd Camp on the Infide of their Entrenchment; and at the fame time Prince *Eugene* and the Prince of *Orange*, with the aforefaid Troops, return'd to their Poft at the Siege, where, that Forenoon, in their Abfence, a great Body of the Befieged, in a great Fog, fallied out on the Befiegers Approaches, thinking thereby to furprize the fame; but by the Alertnefs of the Cover thereof, beyond their Expectations, they were fuddenly and fharply repulfed, and beat from thence, and obliged to retire in again within their wonted Poft, in great Diforder and Confufion, and that to their great Lofs; the like not to be done without.

Campaign VIII. Anno 1708.

August 27, About One in the Afternoon, Prince *Eugene* and the Prince of *Orange*, with all their Grenadiers, and a great Detachment besides of the Besiegers, with also a Detachment of Grenadiers and Musketeers from our Grand Army, vigorously attack'd a high Counterscarp in the Front of their Approaches; and after about half an Hour's hot and sharp Dispute of Assault and Repulses, they took it with Sword in Hand, but with very great Loss on both Sides: The Defendants had upwards of One Thousand Men killed and wounded; and the Offendants in all Two Thousand Three Hundred and Fifty Eight, Officers included, *viz.* Three Hundred and Fifty killed, and Two Thousand and Eight wounded; yet, notwithstanding of this great Loss, I must needs say in Truth, that it was the best and regularest carried-on Attack or Storm of any one that was made or carried on, at or against any other Place, during the whole Siege.

31, The aforesaid *French* Generals, with their huge Army, advanced with a second Gasconade, or last Effort, on Design as aforesaid; and after cannonading on both Sides very smartly all that Day, and the two Days following, of each other, each Day from Morning to Night, the Enemy fell back at last, as aforesaid, on the 25*th* Ditto, and repitch'd on their former Ground, and our Grand Army again repitch'd on the Inside of their Entrenchments; and at the same time Prince *Eugene* and the Prince of *Orange*, with the aforesaid Number of Troops, which came the said 31*st*, by Break of Day, from the Siege, to assist the Duke, as on the 25*th*, return'd again to the Siege the said 31*st* at Night; and the said Day a great Body of the Besieged, about Noon, in their Absence, sallied as they had done the Time before, and had the like Loss, and no better Success than before.

Sept. 3, The *French* Generals concerted another Stratagem and Project for relieving *Lifle*, viz. they inclined a little Leftward, with their Army, toward *Oudenard*, a Feint or Decoy to get or flip in between our Army and the Town, if moved Leftward; but our judicious General being somewhat aware thereof, and penetrating into their projected Defign, lay firm with our Army, maintaining their Ground and the Siege, in Oppofition of that and all the Projects and Stratagems which they had or could ufe; and in the Time of this Feint Rightward, General *Cadogan* fail'd not to advance with a few Squadrons to, and removed away moft of their Forage from the Encampment of their Left, to the Encampment of our Right Wing; fo that if they were idly employ'd with their Time, he was not. After which the *French* General, finding that this Project or Feint took no Effect, they remarch'd their Army Leftward, and again repitch'd Camp on their former Ground, and found it empty and clean fwept of Forage by our Army; and the next Day the *French* Generals, feeing that they could do nothing of Effect on that Side, having another Project in Hand, that for a Time took great Effect, they remarch'd their Army from near *Loudway*, round again by *Tournay*, to a little Eaftward of *Oudenard*; and from thence, as aforefaid, they drew up a Line on the Eaft-Brink of the *Scheld*, near unto *Ghent*, with a great Body alfo between *Ghent* and *Bruges*, and thereby cut off quite our Armies Communication with *Bruffels*, *Antwerp*, &c. on that Side, and almoft *Oftend*; the which alfo they foon after cut off for a Time. General *Earle*, with the aforefaid Nine Battalions that had been for a Time alarming the Coaft of *France*, being now, by the Duke's Order, pofted between *Oudenberg* and *Leffinghen*, we obtained a free Communication with *Oftend*; a confiderable Convoy of all Necef-

Campaign VIII. *Anno* 1708.

Campaign VIII. Anno 1708. faries were sent thither, with great Expedition, by General *Webb*.

Sept. 5, The Duke decamp'd our Grand Army from *Fretin* near *Loudway*, and march'd Leftward somewhat after the Enemy, observing their Motion, to, and pitch'd Camp at *Sainghin*, two Leagues.

7, Decamp'd at, and march'd from *Sainghin* to, and pitch'd Camp at *Templew*, three Leagues.

9, Decamp'd at, and march'd from *Templew* to, and pitch'd Camp at *Lannoy*, four Leagues.

16, Decamp'd at, and march'd from *Lannoy* to, and pitch'd Camp at *Runck*, two Leagues, the better to preserve theirs and the Besiegers Communication with *Ostend*; all other Sides, as aforesaid, being block'd up, but that by the *French* Grand Army.

Now our Army, as aforesaid, being block'd up closely on all Sides, but that of *Ostend*, and Provisions began to be scarce, but especially Ammunition, at the said Siege, of which we were too lavishing at first by ill Husbandry, in the Misunderstanding of our Engineers in throwing it away, by the erecting of their Batteries at such a vast Distance, to no Effect worth speaking of; the Duke detach'd and sent off General *Webb*, with Twenty Two Battalions and One Hundred and Fifty Horse, some few Days before, to convoy up the aforesaid Provisions from *Ostend*, for the Use of our Grand Army and the Besiegers; and in his returning again therewith, he was met on *Winnendale-Plain* by Count *La Motte*, with the aforesaid Body from *Ghent*, and vigorously attack'd him on his March, as he just enter'd the Plain; and although he was so much inferior in Number to the Enemy, yet posting his Men at the best Advantage, undauntedly and courageously, most firmly maintained his Ground and Convoy with all imaginable Bravery of himself and Troops, and that by several sharp

and

and smart Repulses to and against the Enemies often furious Assaults or Attacks; so that at last *La Motte*, with his great Body, was obliged to retire toward *Ghent* again, abashedly leaving the Field and Nine of his Cannon behind him, and the Quantity of Four Thousand Men killed and wounded, besides a great many of his Men deserted, both in the Action and Hurry of their Retreat: And that same Night the Convoy arrived at *Roslaer* unmolested, and the next Day at *Menin*, and from thence to the Siege, and that through a very critical Victory, attributed to the Conduct of General *Webb*, and the Bravery of those small handful of Troops with him, against above Triple the Number.

In the obtaining of this brave, great, and glorious Victory by General *Webb*'s Command (which was one and the most note-worthiest Exploits of any one done in the whole War, considering the vast Difference between the Number of Offendants and Defendants, near Four to One, besides fought on a Plain) they had in all Nine Hundred and Thirty Eight Men killed and wounded, Officers included, as followeth in this Table of the several Particulars of each Station's Loss, *viz*.

Their several STATIONS.	Killed.	Wounded.
Colonels	0	3
Lieutenant-Colonels	0	2
Majors	2	1
Captains	4	18
Subalterns	6	58
Serjeants	15	38
Centinels	111	680
Total	138	800

Total kill'd and wounded — 938

Sept.

Campaign VIII.
Anno 1708.

Sept. 17, At Night, the Chevalier *de Luxemburge*, with a Body of about Four Thousand Horse and Foot, double mounted, with a great Quantity of Powder, made a very bold Attempt to reinforce the Besieged in *Lisle*; and a great Part thereof, before discover'd, pass'd our Out-Guards on the *Germans* Side of the Circumvallation Line, by having privately got our Watch-Word, and pass'd in the Name of a Party going with some Prisoners to Prince *Eugene*'s Quarters; but a little after that a good many of them had got past the Overture and Camp-Line, a Centinel at his Post, on the Flank of the Battalion, heard one of them say to the other in *French, The Besiegers let us pass in very quietly, contrary to our Expectation*; and thereupon the Centinel, pausing a little on their Words, conjectured what they meant, and thereby suspecting them to be what they were, the Enemy; and upon the same he immediately discharged his Piece amongst the Thick of them, whereby they were then fully discover'd, and our whole Camp alarm'd, and the Regiment next thereunto on the said Line instantly turn'd out of their Tents, in only their Shirts and Cartridge-Boxes, with their Ammunition, and seiz'd their Arms from their Belts, and in a Trice form'd themselves in as good Order as could be expected, and with undaunted Courage, though in the Dark, fired amongst the thickest of the Enemy, putting them in great Disorder and Confusion; so that in the Hurly-Burly thereof, several of the Bags of Powder which they had behind them on Horseback fell off on the Causeway near *Abey de Low*, and was broke; the which, by the prancing of the Horses Feet, took Fire, and thereby blowed up and tore to pieces upwards of One Hundred Men of them, and likewise destroy'd a good many of their Horses; but in the interim thereof, a few of them slipt into the City, with some Ammunition also;

also; but the major Part was obliged to retire, and that in very great Haste, Disorder, and Confusion, back again to *Tournay*; and as some of them were repassing of the Circumvallation, several Officers and Soldiers were taken Prisoners of Discretion: The same Night, when alarm'd, the besieging Army was turn'd out, and lay on their Arms the remaining Part of the Night, very alert, and in the Morning turn'd in. The Besieged made a great Huzzaing that Night, because they had got those few in, with some Relief of Powder.

Vendosme, enraged at Count *La Motte*'s shameful Defeatment, march'd himself, with the best Part of his Army, to *Oudenburgh*, and caused the Dykes between *Bruges* and *Newport* to be cut down in several Places, in order to lay the Country under Water, and to cut off our Communication with *Ostend*; yet, notwithstanding that great Inundation, Major-General *Cadogan*, with a Party from our Grand Camp, assisted by our said Troops at *Leffinghen*, found Means to carry through the Water a considerable Quantity of Ammunition, and other Necessaries, for the Relief of our Army and the said Siege: After which, and last of all, to quite deprive us of Succour from *Ostend*, the Duke of *Vendosme* caused Eight Thousand Men to advance and form a Siege against *Leffinghen*, in which there was Colonel *Caufeild*, with a Garrison of about One Thousand Men from General *Earle*'s Camp, near unto *Ostend*, for Assistance to our Army and Besiegers on that Side, as aforesaid; who, after eight Days open Trenches, and several warm Repulses, gained it through the Supineness of some Officers, and made the Garrison Prisoners of War, after having attack'd the Sconce with little or no Opposition at all, being very ill defended; the which required to have been maintained to the last Man, in a manner, considering the Posture

that

Campaign VIII. Anno 1708.

that our Armies were then hem'd up in, too tedious to relate herein; of which I have hinted in several Places before, as it fell in Courſe: Nevertheleſs, it proved but of ſmall Advantage to them; for two Days before, General *Bouffleurs* capitulated for the City of *Liſle*.

Sept. 18, At Night, a competent Number of the Beſiegers of *Liſle* attack'd, and took only a Part of the ſecond Counter-Guard and *Tenaille*, next to our Grand Breach at the Water-Port.

20, At Night, another Detachment of the Beſiegers attack'd, and took the remaining Part of the ſaid Counter-Guard. Each Attack thereon was with great Loſs on both Sides.

22, In the Duſk of the Evening, a great Party of Grenadiers and Fuſileers vigorouſly attack'd, and took, with great Loſs, the Counter-Guard and *Tenaille*, call'd *The Unfortunate One*; being often repulſed thereby before that it was fully taken.

24, At Night, another competent Number of the Beſiegers attack'd, and took an Out-Flanker, and a Part of a ſmall Glacee, with alſo as great Loſs as of the reſt.

27, At Night, another competent Number attack'd, and took a Corner only of the Sconce call'd *The Black Sconce*; and the ſame Night, a little after, as a Party of Fuſileers were about to attack the reſt thereof, our Engineers, in ſearching for Mines, found and drew two great ones, which lay under a Glace, (the which ſaved ſeveral of our Mens Lives) that the Enemy was ready to ſpring, when attack'd: And that ſame Day the Duke decamp'd our Grand Army from *Roncq*, and march'd from thence to, and pitch'd Camp at *Rouſlaer*, four Leagues.

28, Decamp'd at, and march'd from *Rouſlaer* to, and pitch'd Camp at *Tournhout*, four Leagues.

29, De-

29, Decamp'd at, and remarch'd from *Tourn-* *bout* to, and again pitch'd Camp at *Rouflaer*, four Leagues.

30, Major-General *Sancko*, Governor of *Oudenard*, with Ten Squadrons, amongſt which there was a few *Engliſh*, advanced from thence couragiouſly to *Gramount*, and ſurprized and took therein of the Enemy, One Hundred loaded Waggons of Corn, as they were going from thence, under a ſmall Convoy, to their Grand Army then at Camp near *Ghent*; for at the very firſt of General *Sancko*'s Appearance thitherward, with his Command, the Enemies Convoy abandon'd it, and ours brought off the Booty; the which, by that notable Piece of Service, did very much aſſiſt our Camp, Things then being very ſcarce in both Grand and Beſiegers.

October 2, At Night, another competent Number of the Beſiegers attack'd, and took the remaining Part of the aforeſaid *Black Sconce*; and at the ſame time Monſieur *Bouffleurs*, fearing a Grand Storm on the Walls of the City, made a Fire on the Grand Breach at *Water-Port*, of great Trees and Loggs of Wood, prepared and placed thereon beforehand for the ſame Purpoſe, faſten'd and link'd together with great Chains, Bars, and long Spikes of Iron, to prevent the Beſiegers ſudden approaching thereon; and always fed the ſame Day and Night for a long Time, without ceaſing or extinguiſhing.

4, In the Night, a great Body of the Beſieged boldly ſallied towards the Beſiegers Approaches; from which, by the Cover thereof, they were ſoon ſharply repulſed, and beat in again to their Lodgements, to their great Loſs: After which, the Beſiegers daily and ſpeedily approach'd and encroach'd ſucceſsfully nearer and nearer apace in the gaining of Way or Ground to the Grand Foſſee, &c.

Campaign VIII. Anno 1708.

October 11, By Break of Day, the Besiegers had finish'd five Bridges and a half of Fascines quite over the Grand Fossee, to the very Foot of the said Grand Breach, which was by that Time enlarged by several fresh Batteries, and others raised and erected, with their Muzzles over the very last Palisadoes, pointing over the last and Grand Fossee, all ready and in very good Order to play, and to clear away the Rubbish of the Grand Breach, for sudden and general Grand Storm on the main Walls of the City, for Passage thereto; having by that Time received up from *Ostend* a fresh Relief or Supply of some more Ammunition for that purpose, without Delay; and the Batteries stood in Number and Parcels, as I have before prescribed: All which so terrified Monsieur *Bouffleur*, and his Besieged, that he that very Morning beat a Parly, and capitulated for the City; that he and all his Troops should forthwith, in two Days after, march out of the City into the Citadel for a second Siege, if he thought fit to stand it according to his Demands; 2*d*, That all his sick, wounded, maimed, or decrepid Soldiers, with the most of his Horse and Dragoons, should be admitted to go from thence, under a Convoy of our Horse, to their Garrison of *Douay*.

12, At Break of Day, Monsieur *Bouffleurs*'s Demands being accordingly granted, he immediately deliver'd one of the Gates in Possession of the City to a Party of the Besiegers.

13, The aforemention'd were sent, as aforesaid, from *Lisle* to *Douay*; and Monsieur *Bouffleur*, with the rest of his effective Troops, march'd entire out of the City into the Citadel, in order, as aforesaid, to stand a second Siege, but with some heavy Hearts: And at the same time a great Party of the Besiegers march'd into, and took full Possession of the City; and from thence, to the 18*th* Ditto, the

the Besiegers, at the Request of the now Besieged in the Citadel, continued their Parly, to see whether they would also come to a Composition, they being in great Consternation what they had best to do; so that at last, the Besiegers finding that no fair Means would prevail with the Besieged, designed to force them to a Composition by Arms, and the Invitation by Cannon and Mortars, and other such like Courtiers, as the usual Melody of War affords, fit for such obstinate Spouses; and therefore, about Four o'Clock that Afternoon, the Parly broke off, and the Besiegers and Besieged began briskly saluting each other with the said usual Melody as belongs to the Heat of a Siege: And also that same Night the Besiegers made a General opening of their Trenches against the Citadel, toward which they had been secretly encroaching in the two Days before on the two Sides of the *Esplanade*, under the Cover of the Running *French*, which was allow'd by both Parties to be made between the City and Citadel, in the Time of the Parly, to prevent Surprizals on both Sides. After which the Besiegers proceeded gradually, as the Ground would allow, through the *Esplanade* to the River *Ley*'s Part that runs through the Midst thereof between the City and Citadel. Now, as aforesaid, the *French* used all Means, by their Inundations between *Bruges* and *Newport*, and their Entrenchments along the *Scheld*, to distress and cause the Allies, as they thought, to abandon *Lisle*; but our heroical Generals being so indefatigably Intent upon their Purpose and proper Business, that they could not; the Duke of *Marlborough* in providing Corn out of *Artoise* and the Districts of *Furnes* and *Dixmude*, and Prince *Eugene* in the husbanding of what the Duke sent him, that both our Armies lived in indifferent Plenty: So that the Siege against the Citadel of *Lisle* was also carried on with all the Vigour imaginable, consisting

ing with the cautious Methods of Sappings now become more customary; and hereupon the Enemy opened two new Sconces, and sent off great Parties to, and made Incursions into the District of *Bois-le-Duc*, burning and ravaging that Part of the open Country for some small Time.

November 5, A competent Number of the said Besiegers, with and without Arms, laid their Bridges over the Middle of the said River; and from thence, Day and Night, by Sapping and otherwise, expeditiously encroach'd and approach'd to the farthest Extent that possibly they could, till at last they erected their Batteries on the Glacis, with the Muzzle of their Cannon quite over the very Top of the Palisadoes: And the said 5th, at Night, a great Party of the Besiegers vigorously attack'd, and took a Glacis, and the most of the Palisadoes in the Front of the Center of their Approaches, by the nearest Barrier cover'd Way and first Bridge, which leadeth from the City to the Citadel, and that with very little Loss, the Besieged being careless and wearied thereof, being greatly fatigued.

8, 9, 10, 11, 12, and 15, Each thereof by Break of Day, small Parties of the Besieged made small Sorties or Sallies on the Besiegers Approaches, and had but little Success on either thereof, being each Time sharply repulsed by the Cover of the Approaches, beat off, and obliged to retire in great Haste, Disorder, and Confusion into their former Posts and dismal Enlodgements; and that each Time with very great Loss.

11, The *French* last Scene, and last of the two aforemention'd, the Duke of *Bavaria*, with Fifteen Thousand from their main Body, invested *Brussels*; in which there was but Four Battalions, and One made up of sick Men, computed to consist of, sick and well, but in all about Five Thousand Men, commanded by Major-General *Paschal*, who made
a noble

a noble and resolute Defence, being very much encouraged by the Duke that he would relieve him sooner than expected. The Duke and Prince Eugene concerted Measures to pass the *Scheld*, and caused several *British* Regiments and *Dutch* to be transported from *Ostend*; and having sent and signified to General *Paschal*, that he would relieve him, the States Deputies abode there; and no less were the States-Generals solicitous for the Security of *Antwerp*, who sent General *Freisham* thither, with a Reinforcement of Troops from *Naerden*, *Heusden*, *Grave*, and several other Places.

12, The Elector of *Bavaria* sent in General *Paschal* a Summons to surrender, who answer'd the same like a Man of Honour, and made necessary Dispositions for a resolute Defence, in Concert with Major-General *Murray*, Baron *Wrangel*, and the States Deputies, and the Council of State: From which I will pass a little, to shew that the Duke of *Marlborough* was as good as his Word to General *Paschal*, viz.

14, He decamp'd with his Army from *Rouslaer*, and march'd to, and pitch'd at *Arleberge* near *Courtray*, four Leagues, in Order and full Design to use all possible Means to again repass the *Scheld*, and to attack or remove the *French* Army from their strong Impostments near *Oudenard*, and to open our Passage into our own Countries, from which we were then entirely block'd up, and to relieve the Besieged in *Brussels*; the which, in two Days after, was effected, and that effectually, much easier than could be expected, and that with very little Loss, contrary to ours and all Peoples Expectation, considering the Enemies huge Superiority in Number, and strong Impostments, and our Armies Weakness through the Tediousness of the Siege, and otherwise: The which great Victory must wholly be attributed to the Providence and great

great never-failing Goodness of the All-sufficient Almighty God, who work'd with and without Means; and in animating the Duke and Prince *Eugene* with good Conduct, then and often before, and after, in the leading on of our valiant and ever couragious and triumphant Armies, who still strove to imitate the Steps of their famous and brave heroical Leaders, in all their Enterprizes and good Undertakings, of which this was one of the chief and most admirable of all the said War.

<small>Campaign VIII.
Anno 1708.</small>

<small>The passing the *Scheld*.</small>
November 15, At Night, the Duke decamp'd with our Grand Army from *Harlebeck*, and march'd from thence toward the *Scheld*, and was join'd on their March by Prince *Eugene*, with Thirteen Battalions, and most of the Besiegers Horses and Dragoons, which had left *Lisle* that Morning; and all continuing on their March all Night, by Break of Day, in a great Fog, arrived at the *Scheld*, and laid their Bridges immediately over the same, near *Oudenard*, and a little above it at *Kirk-Hoven*, four Leagues; and at that same Juncture, the Duke sent Lord *Orkney* over first on the Van, with Twenty Four Battalions, to discover the Enemies Alertness, whom he found very quiet; and thereupon gave a Signal by Fire to the Duke and Prince *Eugene* that all was safe, and no Opposition made: Whereupon they, with incredible Expedition and Secrecy, pass'd the *Scheld* in a Trice, with our whole Army, and that without almost any Opposition; and with undaunted Courage boldly advanced up to the Enemies Entrenchments before they were aware thereof, the Fog favouring us; at which Appearance they, being suddenly surprized and terrified in a panick Fear and Distraction, abandon'd their Lines and Entrenchments, the Works of three Months past, and that to their eternal Reproach, without giving any Repulse; and retired from thence in great Haste and Hurry, Disorder and Confusion,

Confusion, in four several Bodies; their main Body to *Ghent* and *Bruges*, the other to *Tournay* and *Mons*: And thus they were separated from each other, and our Army regain'd a free and easy Passage thereby to our own Garrisons and Countries; and that same Night our Grand Army pitch'd Camp a little above *Oudenard*, by the *French* old Entrenchments, two Leagues. That Morning, by Ten, the Duke of *Bavaria* having Intelligence of their Armies shameful Defeatment, turn'd his Siege against *Brussels* into a Blockade, and instantly retired from thence also in great Disorder, Hurry and Confusion towards *Mons*, for fear of our Grand Armies approaching thither, leaving their Batteries of Twelve Cannon and Four Mortars on their Platforms standing behind them, &c. with the Loss of about Eight Hundred Men of his killed and wounded, and left his wounded Men behind him, besides as many deserted from them, &c. And the Besieged, with Major-General *Paschal*, had One Hundred and Seventy One Men killed, and Two Hundred and Forty Two wounded; Total killed and wounded Four Hundred and Thirteen, Officers included. Now by this Time it appears, that the Duke was as good as his Word to General *Paschal*, of whom I must speak a little more, viz.

The 15th instant, by Break of Day, the Elector of *Bavaria*'s Batteries begun to play, and play'd very smart against *Brussels* all that Day; and about Nine at Night the Enemy begun attacking the Besieged in their Out-Works, and made three sore and furious Attacks, by whom they were each Time as furiously and sharply repulsed, beat back, and obliged to retire to their great Loss, and to no Effect, without gaining one Foot of Ground; the which continued with great Obstinacy on both Sides, with great Slaughter, till about Ten the next Morning, that the *French* being daunted by the Garrison's

Garrison's stout Resistance, and superior Bravery, animated by their General, the Enemy retired on all Sides, as aforesaid: The main Preservation thereof may justly be attributed to the good Care and Conduct of the Duke and Prince *Eugene*, in their incredible Expedition and Secrecy in the passing the *Scheld*, as aforesaid, and overturning all the *French* Schemes and Projects; and they fell in their own Snare, and lost their Lines shamefully, which before they brag'd much of, and upbraided us with starving; but neither of their Attempts had any Success. The Governor of *Brussels* deserves a good Applause for having made such extraordinary good Defence in that important Place, so large and unfortified, with his weak but brave spirited Garrison, gave as many sharp Repulses as the Enemy gave Assaults; and in Acknowledgment for their good Service, each Man had *gratis* a Month's Pay for their farther Encouragement.

November 17, Our Grand Army decamp'd at, and march'd from *Oudenard* to, and pitch'd Camp at *Humbergin*, two Leagues.

19, Decamp'd at, and march'd from *Humbergin* to, and pitch'd Camp at *Beerlegm*, two Leagues, where they lay firm and now quiet for the Remainder of the Siege against the Citadel of *Lisle*; to which, the same Day, Prince *Eugene* retired, with the aforesaid Troops, and Seven fresh Battalions, in order to hasten the same; where, that same Evening, all the Besiegers Batteries that were compleated and finish'd, saluted the Citadel with three Rounds thereof, for the said Victory obtained by our Grand Army, as aforesaid, over the *French* Army; the which Defeatment did very much discomfort the Besieged; and that same Night the Besiegers Camp was somewhat alarm'd by some skulking Parties of the Enemies from *Ypres*, that had been lurking for a Prey of Horses: After which the

the Besiegers gradually proceeded with their Approaches, and advanced their Batteries apace, with all Expedition, for a Grand Breach and sudden General Storm on the Citadel; Winter now approaching apace, and two other Sieges to be begun and carried on against *Ghent* and *Bruges*, before that our Grand Army could well finish this glorious, but tedious and difficult, but ever memorable Campaign.

22, All the Besiegers Dragoons that were on the South-Side of the City, were removed closer together to the East-Side thereof, in order the better to prevent *Ypres* Surprizals on that Side of the Siege, which could not be too secure.

26, At Night, the Besiegers several Batteries were erected and compleated afresh against the Citadel, with their Cannons Muzzles quite over the Palisadoes, pointing directly over the Moat or Grand Fossee, and stood thus; one of Thirteen Cannon, one of Eleven, one of Six, one of Three, and another of Three Cannon; one of Twelve Mortars, and another of Twelve Howitzers, all ready and in very good Order to begin to play the next Morning, at Break of Day, for a Grand Breach and sudden general Grand Storm against, and on the main Walls of the Citadel, with also the Advantage of the Frost hastening apace to serve in Place of many Bridges to accomplish the same: The Fear and Dread thereof so terrified Monsieur *Bouffleur*, and his Garrison also, and the Discouagement of their Armies other Defeatment, and lest they should be made Prisoners of War, immediately beat a Parly, on the 27*th*, at Break of Day, and capitulated, and surrender'd the Citadel on honourable Terms, to march out thereof to *Douay*, with the usual Marks of Honour; the which was accordingly granted, our Generals having

Campaign VIII. Anno 1708. ing those further important Matters in hand, as before prescribed.

Nov. 30, General *Bouffleur*, with the Remainder of his Garrison, as afore specified, march'd out of the Citadel of *Lisle*, with Drums beating and Colours flying, with also Six Cannon and Two Mortars, and Twelve Cover'd Waggons; and was conducted by a Party of the Besiegers Horse on their Way to *Douay*.

We must do Monsieur *Bouffleurs* the Honour and Justice to say, and that truly, that he made a very good Defence; but our Armies Courage and Valour overcame the same, as we had otherwise done on such like Occasions.

During this tedious Siege against the City and Citadel of *Lisle*, of seventeen Weeks, commenced the 1*st* Day of *August*, and ended the 27*th* of *November*, the Besieged or *French* Loss was computed to amount to upwards of Six Thousand Men killed and wounded, Officers included, with some few Deserters. The Besiegers or Allies Loss was computed to amount to in all about Sixteen Thousand Men killed and wounded, Officers included, and also some few Deserters, as often are on such Occasions, according to the following permanent Account thereof; and first, *viz.*

A Table of the Particulars of each Corps of the Allies Loss, in their Siege against the City of ten Weeks and two Days, begun on the 1*st* of *August*, and ended on the 11*th* of *October*; they had Eleven Thousand Nine Hundred and Forty Seven Men killed and wounded, as here followeth.

(249)

Of Engineers lost ——— ——— ——— 9   Campaign VIII. Anno 1798.

CORPS.	Batt[s]	Colonels. Killed	Colonels. Wd.	Lieut. Col. Killed	Lieut. Col. Wd.	Majors. Killed	Majors. Wd.	Captains. Killed	Captains. Wd.	Subalterns. Killed	Subalterns. Wd.	Serjeants. Killed	Serjeants. Wd.	Centinels. Killed	Centinels. Wd.	Total Killed	Total Wd.	Total K.W.
Germans	4		1		1		1	3	9	4	17	11	23	360	740	379	792	1171
Hessians	9							5	10	13	11			290	640	308	662	970
Prussians	4		2	1		1		4	3	6	13	11	23	269	527	292	568	860
Palatines	6						3	9	17	13	19			664	1110	689	1153	1842
Danes	3						5	1	3	4	23	14	24	186	435	205	480	685
Hanovers	3						1	3	7	4	9	11	25	216	477	232	519	753
Hollanders	15		2	2		1	1	16	21	25	56	38	89	960	2491	1041	2662	3703
Britains	5			1		1	1	4	18	11	24	23	54	424	1039	464	1136	1600
The Detach[t] from Gr. Army, Aug. 27		1						1	9	7	9	1	12	51	273	60	303	363
Total	49	1	5	3	6	7	10	46	97	87	181	109	250	3420	7732	3672	8275	11947

Campaign VIII, Anno 1708.

As to the Particulars of the Besiegers Loss against the Citadel, I could not find them so exactly as those against the City, because of several Battalions going to and fro, at several Times, in the Time thereof, as Occasion required; but as to the Total thereof, in the six Weeks and five Days Siege against the Citadel, begun the 12th of *October*, and ended the 27th of *November*, the Besiegers Loss was computed to amount to in all — } 1044

Total against City and Citadel — 13000

To which the Loss on General *Web*'s Command at *Winnendale* is properly added, being it was on its Account in conveying up of Ammunition thereto, and was — } 938

Of our Grand Army otherwise at *Londway, &c.* in the maintaining the Besiegers, and including some few Deserters, lost at several Times in all ——— } 2062

Now, by those brief Accounts, it appears that at, and maintaining the two Sieges, the Besiegers and Grand Armies Loss amounted to in all — — } 16000

Soon after our investing of *Lisle*, it was said that Monsieur *Bouffleur* said, that if the Allies must needs take *Lisle* before that they left it, that they must gain it Inch by Inch; and indeed we may safely say that he in a manner was as good as his Word; and no Wonder, the great Hindrance of the want of Ammunition was a great Baulk to the Besiegers vigorous Proceeding, all our Passes most of the Time thereof being obstructed by their huge Army dispers'd up and down between us and our Garrisons, as I have already hinted of in several Places before. Nevertheless, the Valour, Vigilance, Activity, consummate Skill, and Unanimity of the
Duke

Duke and Prince *Eugene*, with our other Generals, together with the Resolution, Courage, and indefatigable Labour of the Troops, in their good Conduct and Care, did at last overcome all Difficulties. Prince *Eugene* having received a small Wound in his Head, caused the Duke to bear the Weight of both Armies for some Days, about the Time that the *French* Heroes made their most gasconading Attempts to relieve the Besieged. The *French* Army being now, as aforesaid, scatter'd, their Generals thought that the Conquest of *Lisle* would now have satisfied our conquering Generals, withdrew most to *Paris*; but the Duke and Prince *Eugene* did not design to end their Campaign so, till recover'd *Ghent* and *Bruges*.

Campaign VIII. *Anno* 1708.

December 1, Prince *Eugene* having settled a sufficient Garrison in *Lisle*, and the Affairs thereof, prepared to remove the Besiegers from thence, that a Part thereof might join the Duke, in order to lay Siege to *Ghent*; who, the same Day, decamp'd with our Army from *Beerlegen*, and march'd to, and pitch'd at *Meel*, two Leagues.

2, The Besieging Army decamp'd from *Lisle*, and march'd from thence by the Way of *Menin* to, and pitch'd Camp at *Courtray*.

3, They decamp'd from *Courtray*, and Prince *Eugene*, with the *Germans*, march'd off apart toward *Oudenard*, and the rest, amongst whom our *British* Quota was, march'd to *Deinse*, where they halted three Days, all waiting the Duke's Motion with our Grand Army, in order to lay close Siege to *Ghent*.

7, The Duke, with our Grand Army, decamp'd from *Meel*, and march'd to, and pitch'd Camp at *Meerleberge*, two Leagues; and the aforesaid Besigers removed from *Deinse* to, and pitch'd Camp at *Marykirk*; all Round-ways of the famous City of *Ghent*, and block'd up it and the Citadel; in

Siege of *Ghent*.

both

Campaign VIII Anno 1708. both which there was a large Garrison of the scatter'd *French* Troops, consisting of Thirty Seven Battalions of Foot, and Nineteen Squadrons of Horse and Dragoons, and a great Quantity of their Armies Artillery, &c. commanded by Count *La Motte*, &c.

Dec. 8, The Duke decamp'd both our Armies from their several Encampments, join'd and pitch'd Camp closer to, and regularly entire invested *Ghent* round; and our Grand Army immediately begun making and bringing Fascines, &c. of the like Necessaries, for the expeditious carrying on of the said Siege, of which some were prepared aforehand, having then both it and *Bruges* to disinherit or weed of the Enemy, before that our Army could conveniently be dispers'd to their Winter-Quarters, they being commonly the *British* Troops Winter Residence: There we made a small Countervallation Line, in Places most open, to prevent the Garrisons sudden Surprizals; and afterward our Grand Army proceeded gradually on with the Siege by three Attacks against the City and Citadel, *viz.* General *Fagel* carried on two against the City, both between *St. Peter*'s and *Courtray* Port, opposite to that Advance on its South and West-Side; and General *Evans* carried on the other against the Castle, on the East-Side thereof: And thus the Siege was formed and carried on.

13, General *Fagel*, at Night, under the Cover of Nine Battalions, and Six Hundred Horse, with a competent Number of Workmen, open'd the Trenches on both the said Attacks against the City; and also at the same time General *Evans*, with another competent Number of Men, with and without Arms, open'd their Trenches in like manner against the Castle; and that by very little Loss on all three Attacks, by getting fully into the Cover before discover'd of the Besieged.

15, About

15, About Nine in the Morning, with the Opportunity of a very great Fog, a great Body of the Besieged boldly sallied out on Brigadier *Evans*'s Attack, and some Part of them got into some Part of his Approaches before discover'd; the which at first somewhat surprized the Cover thereof, and took a Brigadier and a Lieutenant-Colonel, with several others, before aware thereof: Nevertheless, they were soon sharply repulsed by the rest of the Cover next thereunto, and beat into their former Lodgments, to their great Loss.

16, At Break of Day, the Duke detach'd and sent off Brigadier *Veglin*, with Seven Hundred Foot, with Six Cannon, and Two Mortars, to reduce a small Reduct on the East-Side of the *Scheld*, half Way between *Ghent* and *Sass-Ghent*, in which there then was a *French* Captain and One Hundred Men; the which, about Noon the said Day, he took and made the said Garrison Prisoners of War, and that with very little Opposition, and no Loss; and then the River *Scheld* was fully and clearly open'd of and from all Pesterments, between our Grand Camp and *Holland*, and all other Passages that Way.

19, At and in the Night, all the several Batteries on the aforesaid three Attacks, were fully erected and compleated against the City and Castle of *Ghent*; and, in short, consisted of in all Eighty Cannon and Thirty Mortars, all ready and in very good Order, against the next Morning, to begin to play, and from thence to play both Day and Night, without ceasing, till finish'd a competent Breach for a sudden and general Grand Storm on both; it being then too late of the Year for any farther Prolongment thereof, and for our Army lying any longer in Tents, the Middle of Winter being approach'd with prodigious cold Frost: All which the more desperately enraged our Armies Fury and Rage against both the Besieged and Citizens,

Campaign VIII. *Anno* 1708. zens, that if it should have come to a General Storm, neither could have expected but very little Favour from the Hands of our undaunted couragious Army, if once got in amongst; whereupon Count *La Motte*, &c. of his General Officers in Concert with the Magistracy of the City, considering aright what was likely to be the real Event of their withstanding our Force any longer, and that the Severity at last of all would fall somewhat the heavier upon themselves, by their obstinate Stiffness or Stubborness, and the Fury of our Armies Desperateness, and the great Service the Frost would be to our Army, which was then begun and approaching apace, to serve in Place of many Bridges over the Grand Fossee to their Ramparts, for a general Grand Storm thereon; and thereupon the Fear and Dread thereof so terrified the Thoughts of the Besieged, that they, to prevent all the Calamity that was ready to fall upon them, called a Council what was to be done. Count *La Motte*, after his Night's Consultations, the very next Morning, by Break of Day, being the 20*th* Ditto, caused a Parly to be beat, and capitulated, and surrender'd the City and Castle of *Ghent* to the Duke of *Marlborough*, on honourable Conditions, to be admitted to march out thereof with the usual Marks of Honour to *Mons*, &c. The which accordingly being granted by the Duke, to put an End to the long and tedious Campaign, the *French* Garrison, on the 22*d*, march'd out thereof, *viz*. Count *La Motte*, with Thirty Seven Battalions and Nineteen Squadrons, Six Cannons, and Four Mortars, toward *Mons*, as aforesaid, without any Escorte; and at the same time a Detachment of our *British* Troops took full Possession of the City and Citadel, having had the Day before Possession of one of the Gates of each.

During this Siege against the City and Citadel of *Ghent*, of fourteen Days, begun on the 7*th*, and ended

ended on the 20*th* of *December*, the Besiegers Loss was computed to amount to upward of Four Thousand Men killed, wounded, and deserted, Officers included; but the most Part thereof were Deserters: The Allies Army's Loss in general was computed not to exceed Four Thousand Eight Hundred killed and wounded, Officers included.

<small>Campaign VIII. Anno 1708.</small>

Our last great Effort was attended with the Recovery of *Bruges*, *Plaſſendale*, and *Leffinghen*, which the *French* were instantly obliged to abandon.

Note, That same Day which *Ghent* surrender'd, the Duke at Night order'd Troops to be ready the next Morning to invest *Bruges*; but there was a Project laid, that suddenly put a Stop thereto, by the Duke and Prince *Eugene*, to baffle them out thereof, &c. viz. Count *La Motte* not having made Conditions with Prince *Eugene* in the Emperor's Name, as well as with the Duke of *Marlborough* in the Queen of *Great Britain*'s Name; whereupon Prince *Eugene*, with the *German* Troops, met Count *La Motte* and the *French* Troops by the Way, and stopt them in the Emperor's Name; telling *La Motte* that he and his Troops should go no farther till *Bruges*, &c. were immediately deliver'd up, as well as *Ghent*; he having in his Conditions (for *Ghent*) with the Allies made none for *Bruges*, either to remain there or march out thereof; and in Case he would not immediately grant the same, without any further Dispute, both he and his Troops must submit themselves Prisoners of War: The which put *La Motte* to a sudden Stand and strange Consternation, conjecturing which of the two Proposals he had best embrace of to do; and thereupon he instantly granted that *Bruges* the next Day should be deliver'd up to the Allies, and those therein should march out to *Ypres*; and therefore *La Motte* accordingly immediately sent an Express to *Bruges*, who, the next Day, as aforesaid, march'd out thereof

Campaign VIII. Anno 1708. thereof to *Ypres:* And after the Report thereof, Count *La Motte,* with the aforesaid Troops, proceeded on with his March to *Mons.*

Dec. 25, The Duke dispers'd the most of the Army from his Camp at *Meerlebeck* near *Ghent,* to repair to their Winter-Quarters; and the next Day the remaining Part of our Army decamp'd from thence, and dispers'd off toward their respective Winter-Garrisons and Quarters; and the same Day those of our *British* Troops and Artillery for the Garrison of *Ghent,* march'd into *Ghent.*

After which the Duke of *Marlborough* went to the *Hague,* and from thence to *England.*

Here ended the Journal of our Eighth glorious but tedious Campaign in 1708, which was in Length Thirty Two Weeks and Six Days, commenced the 11th Day of *May,* and ended the 26th Day of *December*; of which our *British* Corps, with the Grand Army, and apart, march'd in all Thirty Eight Days, and therein One Hundred and Twenty Nine Leagues, or Three Hundred and Eighty Seven Miles *English.*

THE

THE NINTH CAMPAIGN,

Begun in the Year 1709.

ABOUT the Middle of *May*, the Duke of *Marlborough* arrived from *England* at the *Hague*; where there was Preliminaries of a Treaty of Peace concluded the 17*th* Ditto, and sign'd by the Plenipotentiaries of the Emperor of *Germany*, and Queen of *Great Britain*, and of the States-General of the United Provinces, with the Ministers Plenipotentiaries of the King of *France*, digested into Forty Articles.

Eugene of *Savoy*.
Prince and Duke of *Marlborough*.
Philip Lewis, Count of *Sinzendorf*.
Townshend.
Waldern à Heinsius.
Boninna, Baron *de Reed van Rensweude*.
Goslinga.
Ittersum.
Wickers.
Wil. Buys van Dussen.

Campaign IX. Anno 1709.

The Restoration of the whole *Spanish* Monarchy being stipulated by one of the Articles, which the *French* King could not digest, who, upon Marquis de *Torcy*'s Return to *Paris*, refused to ratify the said Preliminaries, which was to be done in the Space of Two Months after the said Conclusion, and to be done against the 1*st* of *July* next; the Congress, to hasten the said General Peace, to begin at the *Hague* the 15*th* of *June* next: But the Allies being justly incensed by the *French* Refusal, that it was only a Prolongment, and put off for farther Advantages, and not real Fact for a General Peace; they therefore further vigorously prosecuted or proceeded on with the War, to bring the *French* to that with Force of Arms, that they could not do otherwise by fair Means and Terms; and for that End the Duke and Prince *Eugene* instantly caused the Allies Troops, for their Command, to assemble, and took the Field about *Gaver*, on the West-Side of the *Scheld*, opposite to, and near unto *Oudenard*, in the latter End of *April*, and lay in their several Corps somewhat apart, but join'd not regularly in one Camp, nor advanced any further, till Prince *Eugene*'s Arrival, and till the Duke of *Marlborough* in Person, with our *British* Troops and Artillery, set out for *Ghent*, Forage being then very scarce, because of the extream hard Winter before, and of the long and tedious Campaign of the two powerful Armies so long on that Side in Camp.

June 2, The Duke and Prince *Eugene* arrived at *Ghent*, and were highly entertain'd at the *Stadthouse* by the Magistrates of the City: And from these Digressions I pass to, and proceed on with my Journal of this Campaign, of every Thing note-worthy thereof, as fell in Course, *viz.*

6, The Duke in Person, with our *British* Troops and Artillery, set out of *Ghent*, and march'd from thence to, and pitch'd Camp at *Gaver*, three Leagues;

Leagues; from which, that Morning, the other Allies removed, and advanced on before our Corps toward *Lisle*, where our general Rendezvous was then soon intended, in order to draw the *French* to Battle on the Plains of *Lens*, to which *Villars*, with the *French* Army, was then assembling.

7, Our Corps decamp'd from *Gaver*, and march'd to, and pitch'd Camp at *Harlebeck*, five Leagues; and the other Allies pitch'd somewhat apart a little to the South-Side of *Courtray*.

10, Our Corps decamp'd at, and march'd from *Harlebeck* to, and pitch'd Camp at *Turcoin*, three Leagues, and join'd our Auxiliaries, and some other Troops of the Allies, and the *Germans*, and some others pitch'd somewhat apart therefrom.

12, Our Corps decamp'd from *Turcoin*, and each other of the Allies from their several Encampments, and all march'd and advanced from thence to, join'd and pitch'd Camp near *Loudway*, on that Plain on the South-Side of *Lisle*, within about one League in the Rear of the Center of our Army: Prince *Eugene*, with the *Germans* on our Right, extended past *Fretin*, pointing and extending toward *Tournay*, where our Design then lay most, if Battle prevented it not; and here our Army consisted of the greatest Strength of any Campaign in the whole War, either in *Holland*, *Germany*, and *Flanders*. Thus our Right Wing of Imperialists in Prince *Eugene*'s Command, consisted of Sixty Five Battalions of Foot, and One Hundred and Twenty Three Squadrons of Horse and Dragoons, including some *Hussars*: The Left Wing in the Duke of *Marlborough*'s Command, made up of *Britains* and their Auxiliaries, *Hollanders* and their Auxiliaries, and others of the Allies, consisted of One Hundred and Twenty Nine Battalions, and One Hundred and Ninety Seven Squadrons of Horse and Dragoons, also including some *Hussars*; the which

Campaign IX.
Anno 1709.

which amounted to in all conjointly, One Hundred and Ninety Four Battalions and Three Hundred and Twenty Squadrons, with One Hundred and Four Cannon, Twenty Four Mortars, and Forty Two Pontons, with also all other necessary Utensils of War conform. On the other Side the *French* Grand Army, wholly in Marquis *Villars*'s Command, being then assembled and rendezvous'd on the Plains between *Vitre* and *Lens*, about half Way between *Arras* and *Douay*, was computed to consist of upwards of Two Hundred Battalions, and Three Hundred and Forty Squadrons of Horse and Dragoons, with Ninety Eight Cannon, Twelve Mortars, and Thirty Six Pontons, with also all other Necessaries of War conform; both Sides waiting and expecting Battle. But their General desisted therefrom, and most advantageously and strongly posted and fortified his Army about the Scarp, to avoid the same; that it was impossible for our Heroes to attack them, without great Disadvantage, Hazard, and Loss; and therefore inclined their Army contrary and Leftward, and laid Siege to *Tournay* in the following manner, *viz.*

June 15, At Taptoo, the Duke and Prince *Eugene*, with our whole Army, decamp'd from the aforesaid Plain by *Lisle*, and march'd off from thence in order and full Design to invest *Tournay*, if possible, before the Enemy could rightly cover it; our Right Wing and Center at first inclined a little towards the Front: A Feint as if our whole Army design'd to advance towards the Enemies strong Encampment, and to attack the same near unto *Douay*; at the same time the Left Wing of our Army inclined exactly and wholly Leftward, to accomplish our General's real Design, and to slip in between the *French* Grand Army and *Tournay*, and to cut off their Communication from thence; the which, the next Morning by Eight o'Clock, we accord-

accordingly eafily effected, and that without any Oppofition; and then our whole Right Wing and Center inclined and march'd wholly to the Left: After which our Army form'd, join'd, and regularly pitch'd Camp at *Elmew*, fix Leagues, within Cannon-fhot of *Tournay*, and immediately block'd up the faid City and Citadel; and at the fame time Lord *Orkney* was fent off by the Duke, with Nine entire Battalions and Twelve Squadrons, Six Cannon and Two Mortars, to *St. Amand* and *St. Martin*'s Sconce; and immediately after his Arrival at the faid Sconce, and after the firing Three Cannon, which then broke down the Enemies Draw-Bridge, they that had been pofted thereon from *Valenciennes* retired thither, all but Twenty, which were taken in their confufed Retreat, and *Orkney* poffefs'd himfelf of the faid Sconce; and at this Difafter, in the fame Juncture, thofe that had been pofted in *St. Amand* abandon'd it, and alfo retired inftantly from thence to *Valenciennes*: After which, the next Day, Lord *Orkney* pofted fome fmall Guards on the Sconce, and in the faid Town; and in the Evening he return'd with the reft of his Troops to our Grand Camp at *Elmew*.

20, The Duke and Prince *Eugene* fet apart, for the carrying on of the Siege againft the City of *Tournay*, Count *Lottum*, Lieutenant-General *Schulenberge*, Lieutenant-General *Fagel*, and Lieutenant-General *Meredith*, with Sixty Battalions of Foot, and Sixty Squadrons of Horfe and Dragoons, and Artillery conform; who immediately invefted the City and Citadel round; in which there was one Lieutenant-General *Surville* and Lieutenant-General *Megrigny*, with Two Major-Generals and Two Brigadiers, with Eleven Battalions and Two Squadrons of Horfe, Seventy Eight Cannon and Twenty Mortars, all mounted fit for Service.

Campaign IX. Anno 1709.

June 21, The said Besiegers begun their Line of Circumvallation from the East-Side round by the South, to the West-Brink of the River *Scheld*, in order to prevent sudden Surprizals; the *French* Army, as aforesaid, being very powerful, and Prince *Eugene* with the *Germans* lying a good Way off, to the Right of the rest of our Army, the better to preserve all our Communications with *Lisle*, &c. and for the Enlargement of Forage to all; and likewise, the same Day, begun making and bringing of Fascines, and all other Necessaries of the like Kind, for the expeditious carrying on of the Siege, much assisted therein by our Grand Army.

22, Our Grand Army was regulated a little Leftward, and filled up the Intervals of those Troops that were set apart to, and for the carrying on of the said Siege; but Prince *Eugene*, with the *Germans*, lay firm, as aforesaid, about one League to our Right.

24, By Break of Day, the Governor of *Ypres*, and from several other Places, issued out with a great Body, computed Twenty Five Battalions and Thirteen Squadrons to, and retook *Warneton*, and therein a Garrison of about Six Hundred detach'd Foot: And the same Day, about Three o' Clock, the Duke, having Intelligence that the said Troops were out, but not that *Warneton* was taken and surprized, detach'd immediately, and sent thitherward, General *Sparr*, with Six Thousand Grenadiers and Eight Squadrons, in order to prevent the said Six Hundred from being taken, or if taken to restore them, if possible, before the Enemy re-enter'd their Garrison therewith; but lying too wide before *Sparr*'s Arrival thereat, the next Morning at Eight, the Enemies Rear was seen a retiring, on great Expedition, out of the Sight and Reach thereof, and would not so much as stand one Encounter with *Sparr*, although double his Number: After which

which General *Sparr*, with his Command, withdrew from thence that Evening (the 25*th* Ditto) towards our Grand Camp, to which he arrived on the 26*th* in the Evening.

 26, At Night, Count *Lottum*, General *Schulenberge*, and General *Fagel*, with a competent Number of the Besiegers, with and without Arms, open'd their Trenches, as here placed, by three Attacks against the City of *Tournay*, and on one Side of the Citadel, each with very little Loss, by getting into Cover before discover'd by the Enemy: After which the Besiegers, on all Sides, proceeded as gradually as the Ground of their Approaches would allow or permit; General *Schulenberge*'s Attack, with the *Germans* on the Right, was on the North-Side of the City; Count *Lottum*'s, with the *Britains*, *Prussians*, and *Hanovers*, or third Attack, was on the East-Side of the City; and that of General *Fagel*, with the *Hollanders*, &c. or second Attack, was on the West-Side of the City: And thus the Besiegers were regulated into three Attacks, and carried on the Siege.

 July 2, By Break of Day, some small Batteries on Count *Lottum*'s Attack being compleated, begun to play against their Flankers; and in a few Days after they dismounted all thereof, and soon after gradually advanced and placed their other larger Batteries on the Glacis, with their Muzzles almost over the Palisadoes; in which Time the other two Attacks had also advanced their Batteries near enough, and compleated them fit for present Execution, amounting to in all, on the three Attacks, at most, of One Hundred Eighty Cannon, and Fifty Mortars and Howitzers; all which having begun, as aforesaid, and encreased by Degrees, play'd on from thence very smart and vigorous, in their Times, against the Counterscarp's Counter-Guards,

<small>Campaign IX.
Anno 1709.</small> Guards, and Ravelin, and Bastions, and to the End of all.

July 9, By Break of Day, a great Party of the Besieged boldly sallied out on the Approaches of General *Schulenberge*'s Attack, by whom they were soon sharply repulsed and beat into their Lodgements, to their Loss.

10, At Night, such another Party in like manner sallied out on the same Attack, where they met with no better Success, after three Assaults, than the others had done the Day before: And that same Morning, by Two o'Clock, a Major-General, and about Four Thousand Men from the Enemies Grand Camp, surprized and took, in *Hanna-Chateau*, a Captain and Two Hundred Men of our Grand Camp, who had been posted there some few Days before. The Duke having some Intelligence thereof, sent off General *Sparr*, at Break of that Day, with all the Picquet of our Army thitherward, in order, if possible, to rescue the same before the Enemy got off therewith; but, about an Hour before his Arrival thereat, the Enemy got off to *Valenciennes* in great Haste: After which General *Sparr*, with his Command, return'd through *St. Amand* to our Grand Camp at Six that Evening.

11, At Night, a competent Number of General *Fagel*'s Attack couragiously attack'd, and took a small Counterscarp in the Front of their Approaches, and that with very little Loss.

16, At Night, in the Dusk, a competent Number of Count *Lottum*'s Attack vigorously attack'd, and took a little Spure and Horn-work in the Front of their Approaches, and that also with very little Loss.

<small>Tournay taken.</small> 17, At Break of Day, a competent Number of General *Schulenberge*'s Attack vigorously, and with undaunted Courage and Fury, attack'd the high Counterscarp in the Front of their Approaches, and

and foon, after feveral sharp Repulses to their couragious Assaults, beat the Enemy therefrom, and took it, but with very great Loss on both Sides; and by that Time all the three Attacks had storm'd and sap'd the Besieged out of the most of the Out-Works in the Front of their Approaches, and had made two Breaches in the main Wall, in order for a General and Grand Storm, the Fear and Dread thereof so terrified the Besieged, that the Governor that Evening beat a Parly, and immediately capitulated for the City, much after the Conditions of *Lisle, viz.* 1*st*, That the Governor-General *Megrigny*, and all the effective Troops, should march out of the City into the Citadel, in order for to stand a second Siege, if he thought proper and fit to stand it, according to his Demands; 2*d*, That the sick and wounded, maimed and decrepid of his Garrison, and Baggage, should be admitted to go from thence under a small Convoy of our Horse to *Douay:* All which being accordingly granted, they, on the 19*th* Ditto, at Break of Day, deliver'd up to the Besiegers one of the Gates of the City; and the next Morning the Enemy, to the Number of Four Thousand Men, march'd out of the City into the Citadel, for a second Siege; and at the same Time the Besiegers took full Possession of the City: And that same Day Marquis *Surville* dined with Prince *Eugene*, and in the Afternoon went after his Garrison into the Citadel; but a great many concealed themselves in the City, and Two Captains, Four Lieutenants, and about One Hundred and Fifty Men, came out to the Duke's Camp; and their sick and wounded, &c. to the Number of Eight Hundred, was conducted from thence to *Douay*; and Lord *Albemarle* was appointed Governor to the City of *Tournay:* And the said 20*th*, at Six at Night, the Parly broke off, and the *French* begun the first Act of Hosti-

S 4   lity

<small>Cmapaign IX.
Anno 1709.</small> lity with Cannon and small Shot, and the Besiegers throw'd a great many Bombs into the Citadel, in Answer from the Batteries on the Left of Count *Lottum*'s Old Attack, which had been secretly encroaching thitherward all the Time of the Parly.

<small>Citadel besieged.</small> *July* 22, The Duke and Prince *Eugene* dismiss'd those Troops which had been employ'd in the Siege against the City of *Tournay*, and set apart Thirty fresh Battalions to carry on the Siege against the Citadel by two Attacks; the which of the Old was already begun, *viz.* The Left of Count *Lottum*'s having, as aforesaid, encroach'd close to the Out-Works of the Citadel, and was, and stood ready, for further Action, as soon as required; the Right of General *Schulenberge*'s Attack having also, in the Time of the Parly, in like manner encroach'd on that Side nearer unto the Works of the Citadel, also ready for Action: So that thereby, in short, every Thing was ready, and in very good Order, on both Sides, to carry and proceed on with the second Siege, as if it had been proceeding on only with the first Siege; for on the 21*st*, being the Day after the Parly broke, the Besiegers several Batteries, by their smart Firings dismounted most of the Flankers of the Citadel, which most flank'd their Approaches: After which (although tedious, by reason of their many Minds) the Besiegers proceeded very regular with the Siege.

26, The Duke advanced our Army from *Elmew* to, and pitch'd at *Orchies*, three Leagues, in order to enlarge the Besiegers Forage, and to forage nearer to the Enemies Grand Camp, which then lay between *Bouchain* and *Marchienne* very quiet, and seeing their Garrison taken.

27, In the Dusk of the Evening, a great Party of the Besieged sallied out a little on their Glacis, where they stood firm a short Time; a Decoy, daring the Cover of the Aproaches to advance thereon, on, who, not confidering their Troops of Mines, advanced thereon, but was fuddenly obliged to retire back to their Approaches with great Lofs; the Enemy, at their Advancement, having immediately fallen back, and fprung the Mines under the Glacis, which fuddenly furprized them; for which Decoy they were fully rewarded in the next Sally on Count *Lottum*'s Attack.

28, About Two in the Afternoon, the Duke having a Defign, if poffible, to cut the *French* Army out of *Marchienne-Pafs*, to prevent Surprizals, and to make Paffage for our Army to the other Side of the Scarp, detach'd and fent off thitherward Lord *Orkney*, with all our Grenadiers of our Army, and Twelve Squadrons, in order to attack a fmall Body of the Enemy pofted thereon from their Grand Camp, to prevent our Armies fudden Surprizals, or Paffage to that Side; near unto which Lord *Orkney*, with his Command, approach'd that Evening, where they lay on their Arms all that Night very alert, and in the Morning, by Break of Day, the Duke and Prince *Eugene* in Perfons reinforced Lord *Orkney* with Eleven Battalions, and a few more Squadrons, in order to begin the Attack on the faid Pafs; but firft they took a full View of the Situation thereof, and could find no vifible Poffibility of attacking it without great Hazard and Lofs, and no Sign of gaining the fame thereby, it being prodigioufly ftrongly feated on the South-Side of the Scarp, in a great Marfh; and befides, that Night, before Lord *Orkney*'s Arrival thereat, the Enemies Grand Camp, lying near thereto, reininforced the Pafs with Thirty Battalions, which ftrongly interlined it: Whereupon the Duke and Prince *Eugene*, after a little reconnoitring of their ftrong Impoftments, and not willing to throw away their Men, without Honour and Victory, withdrew their Troops, and caufed them to remarch to

their

<small>Campaign IX.
Anno 1709.</small> their respective Corps, and consulted to put another Project in Execution after the said Siege then in Hand; the which Project took Effect, but with a great deal of Loss on both Sides; of which more in its Course.

July 30, The Duke detach'd, and sent off from his Camp at *Ochis*, a Reinforcement of Ten Battalions to the Besiegers of the Citadel of *Tournay*, in order to hasten the same; and that same Evening, in the Dusk, a great Party of the Besieged sallied out towards the Besiegers Approaches; with a Decoy, as on the 27*th*, to draw the Cover of the Approaches on their Mines, in full Design to spring the same thereon, as before; but the Besiegers being expensively before warn'd of the Enemies political Design or Decoy, stood firm in their Approaches, and trap'd them in their own Kind, having before prepared a Counter-Mine under theirs, the which our Engineers instantly sprung, and blow'd up thereby theirs, and a great many of the Salliers, and caused the rest to retire in great Haste, Hurry, Disorder, and Confusion, to the Inside of their Palisadoes, or dismal Enlodgements, with great Loss.

August 4, By Break of Day, a competent Number of General *Schulenberge*'s Attack attack'd, and took a little Spur in the Front of their Approaches, close by the Sides of the Palisadoes, and immediately erected and compleated thereon three small Batteries, one of Six Cannon, one of Eight Mortars, and the other of Eight Howitzers; the which, the same Day, begun to, and play'd smartly into the Citadel, and dismounted a Battery of Five Cannon, the which before did very much Injury for some time to the Besiegers Camp, and by flanking their Approrches.

10, About Noon, the Engineers, by their careful Inspections, found and drew a Mine of the Enemies,

nemies, confifting of upwards of Six Barrels of Powder, that they had placed under the aforefaid Spur and Batteries, in order to blow them up that Night, and would, if had not been fo prevented.

14, The Befiegers found and difcover'd a Mine of the Enemies, erected under the Corner of their main Counterfcarp, in order to blow it up for a Grand Attack, being by that Time they had ftorm'd aad fap'd the Enemy out of the moft of the Out-Works, in the Front of their Approaches, and advanced, raifed, and erected their Batteries nigh and low enough for a Grand Breach in the main and triple Wall of the Citadel.

18, The Befiegers Batteries play'd very vigorous and furious for a Grand Breach on the faid Wall; in which Time the Befieged fprung a large Mine, and thereby blow'd up a great Part of the Befiegers two Fore-Trenches, and alfo a fmall Platform and a Gallery, but no great Lofs thereon.

Note, That before I proceed any further, I muft here infert a Propofal made by *Surville* for the Surrender of the Citadel, foon after that it was clofely attack'd or befieged apart, *viz*.

24, Governor *Surville* propofed a Surrender, and two Perfons were appointed to treat thereon; the Duke and Prince *Eugene* appointed Brigadier *Lallo*, and *Surville* appointed Brigadier *Ravignan*, who conferred and agreed together, and fubfcribed to Seven Articles approved of by both Parties, and then fign'd, to march out to their neareft Garrifon on the 25*th* of *Auguft*, with their Arms, Baggage, and Honours of War, and the Citadel deliver'd up (in Cafe the Siege was not raifed before) on the 28*th* of *July*, if *Ravignan* returns from Court with the Ratifications thereof; fufficient Hoftages to be given on both Sides; a Gate fhall be deliver'd up on the 28*th* or 29*th* of *July*, after the Capitulations fhall be fign'd; the which the *French* King refufed,

Campaign IX. Anno 1709. fused, unless a Cessation of Arms in the *Netherlands* till the 25th of *August*, which was only a Prolongment to hinder our Armies further Progress; the which being rejected by our Generals, the Besiegers, as aforesaid, went on with all imaginable Vigour, notwithstanding the great Difficulty we met with by the Enemies numerous Mines, &c.

August 19, The Besiegers several Batteries play'd all that Day and Night very vigorous and furious, for a sudden Grand Breach and general Grand Storm on the Citadel; the Fear and Dread thereof so terrified the Besieged, the Governor the next Morning, by Break of Day, beat a Chamade, and proposed Eleven Articles; the main Substance was, to march out thereof in three Days to any of their nighest Garrisons, with all their usual Marks of Honour of War, Drums beating, Colours flying, &c. with Twelve Cannon and Six Mortars, and all their Baggage, and each Man Twenty Charges of Ammunition, and Horses and Waggons, and their Necessaries to be furnish'd them by the Besiegers: But the Duke and Prince *Eugene* would allow them no other Conditions than to be Prisoners of War, for our Honour; and the *French* King's refusing to agree to the former Capitulations; whereupon the said 20th, at Four in the Afternoon, the Parly again broke off, and all the Besiegers began again afresh, and play'd more vigorous and furious than at any Time before, from both Attacks, for a sudden Grand Breach and general Grand Storm, as aforesaid, to the 23d, about Three in the Morning; and then, to prevent those Things that was hastening apace, the Governor again, and at last, beat a Parly to surrender, on such Terms as should be allow'd them: Whereupon the Duke and Prince *Eugene* came, after that Lord *Albemarle* had that Morning acquainted them therewith, and sign'd the Articles with *Surville*;

Citadel taken.

by

by which all the Officers and Soldiers were only to retain their Swords and Baggage, and permitted to return into *France*, on Conditions that they should not serve till they were actually exchanged against the like Number of Officers and Soldiers of the Allies, Man for Man, and those which the *French* had surprized and taken at *Warneton* to be immediately sent back; and, according to the Capitulations, the said Day, about Four in the Afternoon, the Besieged deliver'd up to the Besiegers one of the Gates of the Citadel, and discover'd their Mines.

25, They march'd out thereof, and were conducted to *Condé*, in Number Three Thousand Three Hundred and Thirty Five Centinels, besides upwards of Three Hundred Commission'd Officers, according to this following Table of the Particulars of the Prisoners, *viz.*

Commission'd Officers	300
Gunners	15
Miners	30
Dragoons	328
Invalids	358
Artagant Battalions	301
Villamours	248
St. Valliers	279
St. Vicars	123
Voixins	339
Swiffes	18
Bourbons	426
La Faile	49
Vendosmes	468
Grenadiers	353
Total	3635

Here

Campaign IX.
Anno 1709.

Here followeth a Table of the Particulars of the Besieged's Loss in both Sieges, viz.

Their several STATIONS.	Killed.	Wounded.
Colonels	0	1
Lieutenant-Colonels	0	1
Captains	17	45
Subalterns	22	31
Centinels	1668	1398
Total	1707	1476

Total kill'd and wounded — 3183

In all $\begin{Bmatrix} 300 \\ 3335 \\ 3183 \\ 800 \\ 150 \end{Bmatrix}$ 7768

By these Accounts the *French*, when first besieged, consisted of in all Seven Thousand Seven Hundred and Sixty Eight, besides no Account of those which abandon'd them when they went out of the City into the Citadel.

During the Siege against the City of *Tournay*, of four Weeks and six Days, begun on the 16th of *June*, and ended on the 19th of *July*, the Besiegers had Three Thousand Two Hundred Men killed and wounded; and from the 20th of *July*, to the 23d of *August*, against the Citadel, being five Weeks, both Days included, the Besiegers had Two Thousand One Hundred Men killed and wounded; or during both, or one continued Siege of nine Weeks and six Days, commenced and ended as aforesaid, the Besiegers Loss amounted to in all Five Thousand Three Hundred and Forty Men, killed and wounded, Officers included, according to this following Table of the several Particulars thereof.

(273)

ATTACKS	CORPS	Colons Kd/Wd	Lt Cols Kd/Wd	Majors Kd/Wd	Capts Kd/Wd	Subalts Kd/Wd	Serjeants Kd/Wd	Centinels Killed/Wd	Total Killed/Wd	Total K.W.
Count *Lottum's* on the Left against the City	Britains				2 / 5	— / 4	3 / 16	110 / 293	115 / 318	433
	Prussians			1 / —	1 / 1	— / 4	— / 6	22 / 150	27 / 157	184
	Hanovers			1 / —	1 / 2	— / 6	— / —	30 / 182	32 / 190	222
His the Third	Suma				4 / 5	2 / 7	6 / 28	162 / 625	174 / 665	839
General *Fagel's* the Second	Suma		1 / —	2 / 4	4 / 23	— / 5	— / 20	220 / 782	231 / 830	1061
General *Schulenberge's* First	Suma	1 / 1		3 / 7	6 / 16	8 / —	9 / —	268 / 956	286 / 989	1275
On the Third against the City	Total	1 / 1	1 / 1	9 / 16	12 / 46	19 / —	57 / —	650 / 2363	691 / 2484	3175
Count *Lottum's* on the Left against the Citadel	Britains				1 / 1	2 / 4	— / 12	59 / 185	63 / 203	226
	Prussians				— / —	— / 1	6 / 6	72 / 81	77 / 87	164
	Hanovers				— / —	1 / —	6 / —	44 / 101	46 / 107	153
	Hollanders			1 / —	2 / 5	2 / 8	8 / —	137 / 337	147 / 352	499
His the Second	Suma			1 / —	2 / 3	3 / 10	16 / 32	312 / 704	333 / 749	1082
General *Schulenberge's* the First	Suma				1 / 4	8 / 15	6 / 21	193 / 782	209 / 822	1031
On the Second against the Citadel	Total		1 / 1	1 / 1	3 / 7	11 / 25	22 / 53	505 / 1486	542 / 1571	2113
At both Sieges	Total	1 / 1	1 / 1	1 / 1	12 / 23	17 / 41	110 / 135	849 / 1233	1405 / 5285	5285

<small>Campaign IX.
Anno 1709.</small>

Besides those in these two Tables, against the City, Engineers Six killed, and Nine wounded; Gunners Two killed, and Two wounded; Miners Five killed: Against the Citadel, Director Monsieur *Du Mey* and *De Bouch*, Head Engineers of the Trenches, killed; of the Artillery Two killed, and Six wounded; of Sappers One Serjeant and Eight Men killed, and Eight wounded; Total killed and wounded Five Thousand Three Hundred and Forty. When the Citadel surrender'd, there was mounted in all, and at most against it, on the Batteries of the two Attacks, Eighty Cannon, Forty Mortars and Howitzers; and in the Citadel there was found several necessary Stores. On Count *Lottum*'s Attack against the Citadel, there were Four Lieutenant-Generals, Four Major-Generals, and Four Brigadier-Generals, with Thirty Battalions and Ten Squadrons, including the Garrison of *Tournay*.

August 20, The Duke, in order to clear his Way towards *Mons* that Evening, detach'd and sent off before Lord *Orkney*, with all the Grenadiers of our Army, and Twenty Squadrons from his Camp at *Orchies*, toward *St. Guillian-Pass*, on the River *Heine*, two Leagues Northward of *Mons*, in order to attack and take the same, for the better Passage of our Army to *Mons*.

23, At Taptoo, on the Day that the Citadel of *Tournay* surrender'd, General *Dedem* and Prince of *Hesse-Cassel* was detach'd from the said Siege, with Four Thousand Foot from the several Regiments, and Sixty Squadrons on the Van, on great Expedition to assist Lord *Orkney*, if Occasion required, and to attack and pass the *French* Lines between the *Hague* and the *Sambre*, as soon as possible, and then to block up *Mons* against our Grand Armies Arrival thereat; and at the said Night, about Nine o'Clock, the Duke detach'd and sent after, at some Distance,

Diftance, in the Rear of the faid Command, General *Cadogan*, with Forty Squadrons, all ready and nigh to affift each other, as Occafion fhould require; and at Midnight the Duke and Prince *Eugene* decamp'd their Armies from *Orchies* paft the *Scheld*, and march'd after the aforefaid three Bodies; and the next Day, being the 24*th* of *Auguft*, pitch'd Camp at *Briffoeil*, five Leagues; and from thence, for the Space of nine Days following, our Army continued in a conftant Motion, without ever a Day's Halt, till after the Battle that was fought at *Malplaquet*: And the faid 24*th*, by Break of Day, Lord *Orkney*, with his Detachment, arrived near unto the faid Pafs, but the Night before it being reinforced from *Villars*'s Army by Seven Battalions; the which fo ftrongly interlined it, that he was obliged to withdraw from attacking it, and lie by for our Grand Armies Arrival: And that fame Night the Prince of *Heffe*, with his Command, which had left *Tournay*, and there pafs'd the *Scheld* the Night before, and continued on with his March, paffing by the faid Pafs of *St. Guillian*, leaving it a little off to their Right Hand; on great Expedition, as aforefaid, that Night, and the next Day and Night following, without any Halt, or very little, notwithftanding the violent Rain, till the 26*th*, about Two in the Morning, that we pafs'd the *Haifne* a little below *St. Denis*'s Village, and came to a Point on the South-Side thereof, and of the City of *Mons*, where we halted on our Arms a little in Orchards on marfhy Ground; where the Prince of *Heffe* made his Difpofitions to attack the aforefaid Line from the *Haifne* to the *Sambre*; toward which, about Seven that Morning, he, with his Command, advanced gradually over a fmall Hill to *Alfpenas*, in a Bottom, on that Part of the *French* Line, over which we pafs'd about Noon, without any Oppofition; for at the very firft of

T our

Campaign IX. Anno 1709. our Appearance, advancing over the Hill thitherward, the Three Regiments of Dragoons, and some Foot-Guards, that had been posted thereon from *Mons,* immediately abandon'd the Line, and retired from thence in great Haste, Hurry, and Disorder, the Foot-Guards Leftwards to *Mons,* and the Dragoons with the Intelligence of the Disaster to their Grand Army; to assist which Duke *Luxemberge,* with upwards of Thirty Squadrons, soon after arrived near unto the Lines, and was follow'd by *Villars,* with their Grand Army, from their Lines behind the Scarp; but finding that their Troops had quitted and abandon'd their Post, and ours taken Possession thereof, they remarch'd to their former Ground at *Quievrain,* and the Prince of *Hesse* with his Detachment advanced to *Bellin* Village, and extended his Right to *Jennapp,* and Left to *Tremiers,* whereby *Mons* was in a manner block'd up, where they stood all that Night at Arms, and also the Days and Nights following very alert, till ten Days after the Battle of *Malplaquet,* that all necessary Matters were regulated, and Siege laid to *Mons;* in which there was a Garrison of Eleven Battalions, and One Regiment of Dragoons, commanded by Lieutenant-General *Grimaldie, &c.* who, although superior in Number, made no Attempt to come out in all that Time: But to return to our Grand Army, who was also pressing thitherward on great Expedition for the Prince of *Hesse*'s Aid and Assistance, *viz.*

August 25, The Duke and Prince *Eugene* decamp'd with the Army from *Brisfoeil,* and march'd to, and pitch'd Camp at *Siraut,* four Leagues; and Lord *Orkney* rejoin'd within about One League of the *Haisne.*

26, Decamp'd at, and march'd from *Siraut* betimes in the Morning to, and pitch'd Camp at *Havre,* four Leagues, and that Part with Prince *Eugene,*

Eugene at *St. Denis*, where the Duke had an Account that that Morning the Prince of *Heſſe* had paſs'd the Lines aforeſaid.

27, About Noon, the Duke having Account that the *French* Army was then on their March, on great Expedition, to attack that Body under the Prince of *Heſſe*, before his Arrival thereto with our Army; whereupon the Duke decamp'd our Army immediately from *Havre*, and left their Tents ſtanding, and Baggage behind them, paſs'd the aforeſaid Line at *Eſpion*; and form'd and pitch'd Camp on that Side of the Line, a little in the Rear of the Prince of *Heſſe*'s Command, four Leagues; who then being very ſafe, advanced a little paſt *Bellin*, on that Riſing-Ground within leſs than Cannon-ſhot of *Mons*, giving the more Room for our Grand Army to range, who in the Duſk of that Evening, again leaving their Tents and Baggage ſtanding behind them, march'd paſt the ſaid Prince's Command at *Bellin*, advanced a little further, and made a Halt on their Arms moſtly the remaining Part of that Night on them Hills, but in Order of Battle; having an Account that the *French* Army had not yet paſs'd the Defiles of *Waſmes*; and thereupon our Army pitch'd Camp between *Kievren* and *Sern*, the Duke conjecturing that *Villars*'s chief Deſign was to draw all our Body together into the Plain, and thereby ſlip in a Reinforcement into *Mons*, there being then in it as aforeſaid, and that but weak; and to prevent the ſame, the Duke ſent ſome Troops off toward *St. Guilian-Paſs*; the which they took on the 30th Ditto, with Sword in Hand, and therein Two Hundred Men Priſoners of Diſcretion.

28, The Duke and Prince *Eugene* ſpent it wholly in viewing the Ground between the two Armies where they then lay.

29, In the Morning, the Enemy made a Motion as if they would march towards *Boſſu*; but the

Campaign IX.
Anno 1709.

the Duke, with several other Generals, taking then a narrow View of their Army, perceived that the Motion of their Left was only a Feint to cover the March of their Right, which foil'd off at the same time; whereupon the Duke, not willing to lose any Time, caused his Army to march Leftward; and by that Motion the two Armies were so near, by Two in the Afternoon, that they began and cannonaded each other till the Evening, and continued all that Night in the same Situation. The *French* Army were posted behind the Wood of *La Merte* and *Faisniere*, near unto *Taisniere* and *Malplaquet*, where they strongly entrench'd themselves that Night, and the next Day and Night triple, &c. Our Army lay with their Right near *Sart* and *Bleron*, and Left on the Edge of the Wood *Lagniers*, two Leagues; and our Head Quarters being near the Center of *Blarignies*, our two Heroes, in Concert with the States two Field Deputies, resolved to attack the *French* Army, notwithstanding their advantageous Post and Entrenchments. The Troops, with Count *Lottum* from the Siege of *Tournay*, were order'd to join our Grand Army with all Expedition; the which accordingly was done (being three Leagues Westward of *Mons*); and the said Morning, by Break of Day, the said Troops set out from *Tournay*, and march'd with all Expedition imaginable, till join'd in the Battle. The *French* Army, then in *Villars* and *Bouffleur*'s Command, computed to consist of One Hundred and Sixty Battalions of Foot, and Three Hundred Squadrons of Horse and Dragoons, amounting to nigh One Hundred and Twenty Thousand Men, with Eighty Cannon, &c. in Order for Battle. We of the Allies Armies, in the Duke of *Marlborough*'s and Prince *Eugene*'s Command, including the Besiegers from *Tournay*, as aforesaid, consisted of One Hundred and Fifty Two Battalions of Foot, and Two Hundred and Seventy

Seventy One Squadrons of Horse and Dragoons, with Eighty Eight Cannon, &c. also in very good Order for Battle; which the *French*, if they would, could not then well avoid, both Armies lying then within less than Cannon-shot of each other.

30, A little after Noon, the Duke and Prince *Eugene* advanced our Army in Lines of Battle a little nearer to the Enemies Entrenchments, over which they had made a small Motion the Day before; but at our Armies approaching somewhat closer thereto, they immediately fell back, and triple entrench'd as aforesaid; and the said 30*th* Day, and at, and in the Night, erected five Batteries thereon against our Front, *viz.* one of Twenty against our Center, one of Sixteen, one Eight, one of Seven, and another of Six Cannon, as they thought most proper for their own Safety, and our Prejudice. Our Generals spent the Remainder of that Day and Night also a viewing the Enemies strong Impostments, and in making all necessary Preparations and Dispositions to attack the same in the Morning following; in which Time our Army lay on their Arms in about Musket-shot of the Enemies Entrenchments, against which they erected five Batteries, two each of Twenty Cannon, and Three small ones, one of Five Cannon, one of Ten, and the other of Two; in all Fifty Seven: And in that Night the two Armies lying too close to each other, several of both Sides had frequent and friendly Commerce and Conferences with one another, as if we had been in an Alliance together; but at last each Man being called to his respective Post, our Commerce was turn'd to, and swallow'd up, and drowned in Blood, as in the Salutations of the Day after appear'd. That Night the most of the Besiegers Horse and Dragoons got up, and join'd our Army; and in the Morning, before and in the Heat of the Battle, the Foot, as they could get

get up, join'd and fell in during the Battle, as Ground allow'd, and Occafion required: And that fame Night the Duke and Prince *Eugene* regulated and made Difpofitions, in order for Battle, to be carried on in Six Attacks: Thus in brief;

Campaign IX.
Anno 1709.

	Battalions.
The Firft Attack to be led on by General *Schulenberge*, with ———— ————	36
The Second by Count *Lottum*, with *Britains*, *Pruffians*, and *Hanovers* ——	22
The Third by Prince *Eugene*, with feveral Corps of the Allies ————	36
The Fourth by General *Withers*, of Ditto —	19
The Fifth by General *Fagel*, made of *Hollanders* ———— ————	15
Total of the moft of the Foot which was then up when begun ——	128

The Sixth by Prince *Auvergne*, with Thirty Squadrons of Horfe and Dragoons.

The which was all that Night fully engaged thereof in the Battle; the reft fhared but very little therein, by reafon of the Marfh, and other Croffnefs of the Ground; whereby the whole Burthen of the Battle fell wholly and folely on our Foot, as it often and commonly happen'd to do in the late War.

Battle of *Malplaquet.*

That Morning, by Break of Day, after our two Heroes and the States Deputies had gone along the Lines between the two Armies, and view'd the fame, and pofted the Detachment that came from *Tournay* the Night before, on the Right Wing oppofite to the Enemies Left, both Armies begun cannonading each other very vigorous and furioufly, till a little paft Eight in the Morning, and then the General Signal was given for the Battle to begin, by a General Difcharge of all our Artillery;

after

after which immediately the Duke and Prince *Eu-* *Campaign*
gene, and the reft of our Generals, boldly and gra- *IX.*
dually advanced on with our Army, and attack'd *Anno 1709.*
the Enemy in their Entrenchments in three different Places, as regular as poffibly the Ground would allow, with the ufual Salutations and Melody of War. It is impoffible to exprefs the Violence of either Side's Fire; befides the Enemies advantageous Situation, they defended themfelves like brave Men, and made all the Refiftance that could be expected from the beft of Troops; but there could nothing be braver than to fee our Foot furmount fo many Obftacles, refift fo great a Fire, force the Enemies Entrenchments, beat them from thence, and drive them quite out of the Wood; and after all, to draw up in very good Order of Battle on the Plain, in the Sight of our Enemies, and that before their third Entrenchment: All which was effectually done in the Space of about five Hours, by the Courage and Valour of our undaunted, triumphant Troops, the Conftancy of our Generals, and the continual Prefence of our two chief heroical Commanders. The Battalions which firft attack'd were entirely defeated; but being ftill fuftained by frefh Troops, the Enemy were every where forced out of their Entrenchments, and purfued into the Wood, through it, and from it, into the Plain: Hereupon their Horfe and Foot drew up behind a third Entrenchment, more refolute and firm than ever, and made a dreadful Fire on our Men, as they came out of the Wood to form themfelves. Neverthelefs, by the conftant Experience of our Generals and couragious Troops, they foon made the Enemy again fenfible of their Valour and Bravery; for after that they had for feveral Times repulfed the bold Affault of our Battalions, Prince *Eugene* having put himfelf, with Sword in Hand, on Foot at the Head of the *Dutch* Infantry, the laft

Entrench-

Campaign IX. Anno 1709.

Entrenchment was carried on all Sides, and the Infantry which defended it pursued by several of our Battalions, at the same time Three Regiments of *Danish* Horse falling on the Enemy, made a terrible Saughter; till they having a second Wood, thereby found Means to escape: So that it was out of our Power to insult them any more. In the mean time, our Horse attack'd their Right Wing, some of which at first were somewhat disorder'd by the *French* Houshold; the which the Duke perceiving, immediately repaired thither, and in Person rallied, and brought the said disorder'd Squadrons to the Charge again; and that with such good Success, that they made the Enemy give Ground, and entirely broke them; so that they retired in great Disorder towards their Infantry, which had gain'd the little Wood; by the Favour whereof they retreated with Precipitation, abandoning and leaving to us the Field of Battle, their wounded Artillery and Ammunition, having no Baggage with them to lose: After which Eighteen Squadrons were detach'd to disperse a Body of the Enemy that retired toward *Quievrain*, who met the Enemies whole Left Wing, of about One Hundred Squadrons, commanded by Monsieur *Bouffleur*, about one League of this Side of the little River *Haisne*. Ours at first perceived but their Rear posted at the Corner of the Wood, from which they drove them without Resistance; but Colonel *La Lippe*, and a Cornet thereof, advancing too far, were taken without being perceived by our Men. The Wood being forced, our Eighteen Squadrons having advanced into the Plain, saw the Enemies said whole Left Wing before them in three Columns, one of which retreated in good Order, but the other two in Confusion. At the Sight of such a great Number of Men, made a short Halt, and were surprized to see them face about, and draw

up

up in Order of Battle: However, we kept our Ground, and posted ourselves on the Height, with the Wood of *Elonge* on our Right; where we immediately perceived the Enemy made a Stand, but with no other Design than to pass a Gutter that was behind them: Whereupon our Horse advanced towards them at full Gallop; but it proved impossible for ours to overtake them on this Side of the Defile of *Givete*; and having pass'd the Gutter, pursued them as far as the Village of *Quievrain*, where they had several Brigades of Foot, who obliged our Men to slacken their Pace, and to give them Time to pass the Rivulet *Baray*; nevertheless, till come within a Quarter of a League of the Rivulet, where the Squadrons which had fled before Eighteen Squadrons of ours, drew up on a Height, And thus, in short, after a long and sore Dispute, and sharp Encounter of many Assaults and Repulses, beat the Enemy from their triple Entrenchments through the Woods, and to the other Side of the Plain, before us, till the Right, Left and Center of the Enemies Army were dispers'd in three several different Bodies, and driven upwards of two Leagues beyond their Entrenchment, who continued their precipitate Retreat to the other Side of the Pass of *Maubeuge*, near unto *Valenciennes* and *Quesnoy*, where they made their first general Rendezvous after the said Battle: After which, that Night, our Army lay on and about the Field of Battle, at *Blaregnies*, two Leagues, full of Joy at this glorious and compleat Victory, the which cost us abundance of brave Mens Lives; and the next Morning the Duke and Prince *Eugene* fell our Army back a little, and repitch'd on somewhat fresher Ground at *Blaregnies*, near unto *Sant* and *Bleron*, one League; where both Losses were regulated, and computed thus as followeth, *viz.* first of the *French*, Marshal *Villars* was wounded in his Right Knee,

Campaign IX. *Anno* 1709.

Knee, Six General Perſons killed, and Ten wounded, and Twelve Hundred other Officers killed and wounded; of Centinels, &c. Seven Thouſand killed, and Ten Thouſand wounded: The Certainty of their Loſs were never known; however, it was judged, by an Officer's Account of theirs, that it could be no leſs than Twelve Thouſand. The Day after the Battle, the ſlain on both Sides appeared, to ſeveral Spectators, to amount to about Twenty Six Thouſand Men. The Allies took moſt of their Artillery and wounded Men, Twenty Six Standards, and Twenty Pair of Colours, Sixteen Cannon in one Place; few taken, but wounded, and of their wounded Three Hundred and One Officers, and One Thouſand and Sixty Eight Centinels. In another Account they had Fifty Four Officers of Note killed, and as many wounded; and in all, of all Ranks, Fifteen Thouſand Men killed and wounded: But which of the Accounts it be, it matters not. Doubtleſs, their Loſs was very great, and had been much greater in every Particular and Reſpect whatſoever, if they had not went off ſo ſoon as they did, with embracing that Opportunity before that our Army could well get through the Wood, and round it, and enter and form in the Plain for a clear and freſh grand Encounter of both our Horſe and Foot. The Enemy ſaid that they had but One Hundred and Twenty Battalions and Two Hundred and Sixty Squadrons, computed One Hundred Thouſand Men; and that the Allies had One Hundred and Sixty Two Battalions and Three Hundred Squadrons, with One Hundred and Twenty Cannon, and they had but Eighty, and Twenty thereof fired ſeveral Rounds at once into the Allies Center. They ſay they loſt but Eight Standards, and Two Pair of Colours. They farther reported, that they gathered up ſeveral of the Allies Colours and Standards. The Allies Loſs were

were computed, of killed and wounded, about Eighteen or Twenty Thousand Men, and others to Fifteen or Sixteen Thousand Men: But however that be, we, without doubt, gained a great Victory, and paid a great deal of Blood for it; and although the Enemy lost the Field, they recovered a Part of their former Reputation, by standing the Attack so boldly as they then did: But afterwards lying very quiet, and not attempting to relieve *Mons*, it makes it to appear that they lost in the said Battle many more than they pretended.

In the gaining of this glorious and honourable (but costly) Victory, the Allies had killed and wounded in all Nineteen Thousand Seven Hundred and Eighteen Men, including all Ranks and Stations, according to the Account as inserted in the following Table of each Corps's particular Loss.

(280)

Corps, Foot & Horse	Colons K./Wd.	Lt.Cols K./Wd.	Majors K./Wd.	Captains K./Wd.	Subalterns K./Wd.	Serjeants K./Wd.	Centinels K./Wd.	Total Killed / Wounded	Total K.&W.
Germans included	3 / 8	5 / 10	4 / 9	21 / 71	53 / 162	—	1873 / —	1959 / 3362	5321
Britains { 20 Battals of Foot	3 / 1	3 / 2	1 / 2	11 / 23	13 / 59	28 / 75	433 / 945	492 / 1107	1599
{ 6 Rts of Horse and Dragoons	— / 1	— / 2	— / 1	2 / 2	1 / 18	—	31 / 128	32 / 152	184
Their Sum	3 / 2	3 / 4	1 / 3	11 / 25	14 / 77	28 / 75	464 / 1073	524 / 1259	1783
Prussians { Foot	2 / 3	1 / 1	— / —	2 / 17	9 / 29	36 / 89	280 / 960	295 / 855	1150
{ Horse, &c.	1 / 2	2 / 5	1 / 5	6 / 7	5 / 11	—	133 / 380	146 / 398	544
Their Sum	2 / 3	3 / 1	1 / 5	8 / 24	14 / 40	36 / 89	413 / 1180	441 / 1253	1694
Hanovers { Foot	1 / 2	1 / 2	4 / 1	2 / 12	10 / 45	—	255 / 965	304 / 1115	1419
{ Horse, &c.	2 / 3	— / 5	— / 1	4 / 10	15 / 37	—	195 / 520	219 / 581	800
Their Sum	3 / 2	2 / 7	— / 5	6 / 22	25 / 82	36 / 89	454 / 1488	523 / 1696	2219
Hollanders { Foot	6 / 8	15 / 26	5 / 14	42 / 116	85 / 142	—	2190 / 5596	2343 / 5902	8245
{ Horse, &c.	2 / 2	1 / 1	— / 1	4 / 12	7 / 23	—	131 / 254	144 / 291	435
Their Sum	6 / 10	16 / 26	6 / 14	46 / 128	92 / 165	64 / 164	2321 / 5850	2487 / 6193	8680
Total { Foot,	14 / 19	25 / 41	11 / 34	78 / 239	170 / 437	—	5031 / 11415	5393 / 12340	17733
{ Horse and Dragoons	5 / —	4 / 7	1 / 2	14 / 31	28 / 89	—	494 / 1288	541 / 1422	1963
Total of both	14 / 24	29 / 48	12 / 36	92 / 270	198 / 526	64 / 164	5525 / 12693	5934 / 13762	19696
A far shorter Account given	6 / 6	5 / 11	5 / 14	42 / 116	85 / 242	83 / 252	4155 / 8440	4392 / 9096	13488

The Number and Names of the Allies Perfons of Note that were killed and wounded in the Battle, viz.

Campaign IX. *Anno* 1709.

Of Lieutenant-Generals killed Two, *viz.* Oxenftern and *Vackerbert*; wounded Six, *Harrick, Sparr, Wick, Banditz, Gore,* and *Webb:* Of Major-Generals killed Two, *viz. Tettaw* and *Waffaner*; wounded Four, *Kanitz, Keppel, Ells,* and *Hamilton:* Of Brigadiers killed Four, *viz. Hewcklin, Sparen, Lallo,* and Sir *Thomas Pendergaft*; wounded Five, *Crone, Stenfelt, Douglas, Bulin,* and *Landet.*

Prince *Eugene*'s Number in the Lines of Battle that Day were Sixty Six Battalions, and One Hundred and Eight Squadrons.

Sept. 2, The Duke and Prince *Eugene* decamp'd our Army from *Blaregnies*, and march'd Rearward to, and pitch'd Camp at *Bellin*, two Leagues; where the aforefaid Command lay with the Prince of *Heffe*, a blocking up of *Mons*; where, on the 4th in the Evening, they had a *Feu-de-joye* for the late Victory obtained.

7 and 8, All or moft of the Horfe and Dragoons of our Army were bufily employ'd in making and bringing of Fafcines within Cannon-fhot of *Mons*, in order to be ready to affift the expeditious carrying on of the Siege againft it.

9, The Duke detach'd and fet apart to the Siege thereof, with Prince *Eugene*, the Prince of *Orange*, and the Hereditary Prince of *Heffe*, Thirty One Battalions and Thirty One Squadrons, with Ordnance conform, who immediately invefted it round; in which there was a Garrifon, as aforefaid, with upwards of   Cannon and   Mortars mounted: And the fame Day the Duke decamp'd with our Army, and inclined from *Bellin*, a little Leftward to, and pitch'd Camp at *St. Dennis*'s, two Leagues, and fill'd up the Intervals of thofe Troops fet apart to the faid Siege, the better to cover the fame;

The Siege of Mons.

and

Campaign IX.
Anno 1709.

and at the same time sent off a General with Six Battalions to *St. Guillian-Pass*, the better to preserve the said Besiegers and our Grand Armies Communication with *Tournay, &c.* And the next Day the aforesaid Detachment that had been for some Time before blocking up of *Mons*, fell back into their respective Regiments; and the said Besiegers were then reinforced, and made up to consist of Fifty Eight Regiments of Foot and Horse, amongst whom there were Six entire Regiments of Dragoons: After which the Besiegers proceeded as regular as the marshy Ground and wet Weather would allow them, which made it somewhat the more tedious; but their Courage overcame all the Obstacles and Difficulties thereof, as they had often before.

Sept. 14, At Night, a competent Number of the Besiegers, with and without Arms, open'd their Trenches against *Mons* by two Attacks; the one on the South, and the other on the West-Side of the Town, and lost thereon about Four Hundred Men killed and wounded, being discover'd before they got into Cover; and the next Morning, a little after the rising of the Sun, a great Body of the Besieged boldly sallied out on the Besiegers Approaches, whom they at first somewhat surprized; but in a Trice after, the Cover of the Approaches sharply repulsed, and beat the Enemy in again to their former Lodgements, to their great Loss; and immediately after, a small Battery of Four Cannon of the Besiegers being ready, begun to play against one of the Enemies Flankers; the which they dismounted that Day before Night.

16, At Break of Day, another great Party of the Enemy also sallied, thinking to surprize the Approaches; but the Cover being timely aware thereof, boldly advanced out of their Approaches, and got between the Salliers and a little Sconce, and

and a fortified Water-Mill, on the South-East Side of the Town, and took both those Places, and instantly beat the Enemy in from thence to their former Lodgements, to their Loss of about Two Hundred Men killed, wounded, and taken.

Campaign IX. Anno 1709.

19, By Break of Day, two small Batteries more of the Besiegers being erected, and ready, each consisting of Nine Cannon, begun likewise to play smartly against the other two Flankers of the Enemies, and soon after dismounted them; the which, for some time before, did very much Prejudice to the Besiegers Approaches in their Proceedings therein: And that Day and Night following, the Besiegers dispatch'd and made ready their several Batteries on both Attacks, to the Number of Eighty Cannon, and Thirty Mortars and Howitzers.

20, About Sun-rising, all the aforesaid Batteries begun to play, with a great deal of Vigour and Fury, against, and for a Grand Breach on the main Counterscarp of the Town; the one Attack Batteries flanking the Impression of the other, the sooner to dispatch the Sieges: Both Attacks almost joined in Conjunction as in one, and acted accordingly; and that same Morning, after the Batteries begun to play, a competent Number or Detachment from our Grand Camp, for the Besiegers Assistance, and to hasten the same, vigorously attack'd two small Sconces; and after a small Brush, they took the same, and also drove out a Party of the Besieged out of the Out-Works or Fleches of and about the Town, on that Side by the aforesaid Mill, and took about One Hundred of the Enemy Prisoners of Discretion, and drove the rest into their former Lodgements, and that all with very little Loss, considering their Impostments.

21, A competent Number of the Besiegers attack'd, and took a little Horn-work; and that also with very little Loss.

Sept.

Campaign IX.
Anno 1709.

Sept. 23, Our Grand Army decamp'd, and clos'd and pitch'd a little more Leftward of *St. Dennis's*, one League, the better to cover and maintain the said Siege.

26, In the Night, a Party of the Besieged sallied out on a Part of the Besiegers Approaches; and by the Cover thereof they were soon sharply repulsed, and beat in again to their Lodgements to their great Loss.

27, About Nine in the Morning, in a heavy soaking Rain, a great Body of the Besiegers vigorously attack'd the aforesaid large high Counterscarp; and after about two Hours shot and sharp Dispute of Assaults and Repulses, they took it, and also the most of their Out-Works in the Front of their Approaches, with several of the Enemy Prisoners of Discretion; but with great Loss on both Sides.

29, At Break of Day, another Party of the Besiegers boldly attack'd, and took a small Redout, and some more of the Out-works on the West-Side of the Town; but with very little Loss on either Side.

October 5, At Break of Day, another competent Party of the Besiegers, vigorously attack'd, and took such another; with also very little Loss.

6, At Night, another sufficient Party of the Besiegers vigorously attack'd, and in a Trice took a small Ravelin, with also little Loss; whereon, in two Days after, they erected and compleated several fresh Batteries, ready and in good Order, against the main Wall of the Town, for a sudden Grand Breach and general Grand Storm thereon as soon as possible, to put an End to the Campaign.

9, At Break of Day, all the Batteries accordingly begun to play, and play'd with a great deal of Vigour and Fury, for the aforesaid Intent; both which so scared and terrified the Besieged, that
Monsieur

Monsieur *Grimaldy*, the same Day about Noon, beat a Parly, and capitulated on honourable Terms; whereupon, the next Morning, deliver'd to the Besiegers one of the Gates of the City; and on the 12th they march'd out thereof, with the usual Marks of Honour, to their nearest Garrison, *viz.* Eight Battalions and One Squadron to *Charleroy*, and Six Battalions and One Squadron to *Namure*; and at the same time the Besiegers took full Possession of *Mons*.

During the Siege of *Mons*, of six Weeks and three Days, begun with the Time that it was block'd up on the 26th of *August*, and ended with the Day that it capitulated, (*Oct.* 9.) the Besiegeds Loss was computed to about Three Hundred and Eighty Men killed, and Six Hundred wounded; Total killed and wounded, Officers included, Nine Hundred and Eighty: The Besiegers in general had Five Hundred and Fifty Five Men killed, and One Thousand Six Hundred and Forty Six wounded, Officers included; Total killed and wounded Two Thousand Two Hundred and One. It is here, as often happen'd, that I could not readily find the Particulars of each Corp's and Station's Loss; but commonly, by one Respect or other, found the Totals of the general Loss; but more especially, at some times when they might be found, I could not be exempt from my respective Duty to find them.

15, The Duke and Prince *Eugene* having settled the Affairs of *Mons*, and put a sufficient Garrison therein, decamp'd with our Army from *St. Denis* and *Mons*, and remarch'd Rearward over the small River *Trovile* to, and pitch'd Camp at *Tweeze*, two Leagues; from which, the next Day, several Garrisons of the *Dutch* Troops were dispers'd, and march'd off toward their respective Winter-Quarters.

Campaign IX.
Anno 1709.

Oct. 17, The Duke decamp'd and difpers'd the Remainder of our Grand Army from *Tweeze*, toward their refpective Garrifons or Winter-Quarters; and the Duke at the fame time went off to *Bruffels*, and from thence to the *Hague*, where he was highly entertain'd by the States-General; and fo from thence went off to *England:* And the faid Day General *Lumley*, with our *Britifh* Troops and Artillery, march'd off apart from *Tweeze* to, and pitch'd Camp at *Centurnal*, fix Leagues.

18, Decamp'd at, and march'd from *Centurnal* to, and pitch'd Camp at *Aux*, five Leagues.

19, Decamp'd at, and march'd from *Aux* to, and pitch'd Camp at *Oudingham*, five Leagues.

20, Decamp'd at, and march'd from *Oudingham* into their refpective Garrifon or Winter-Quarter of *Ghent*, four Leagues; and the reft of our Corps foon after alfo arrived at their refpective Garrifons or Winter-Quarters.

Here ended the Journal of our Ninth glorious Campaign in 1709, which was in Length Nineteen Weeks and Four Days, commenced the *6th* of *June*, and ended on the *20th* of *October*; of which our *Britifh* Corps march'd, with the Grand Army, and apart, in all Twenty Six Days, and therein Eighty Leagues, or Two Hundred and Forty Miles *Englifh*.

The End of the Ninth Campaign, A. D. 1709.

THE
Tenth CAMPAIGN,
Begun in the Year 1710.

ABOUT the 1st of *April*, the Duke of *Marlborough* arrived at the *Hague* from *England*; where he had several weighty Conferences with the States-General, &c. concerting Measures, or the Operations and Proceedings of the ensuing Campaign, and dispers'd his necessary Orders for all the Troops, that were to serve under his Command, to assemble forthwith near *Tournay*; toward which all were then expeditiously repairing, in order, as the Duke had before projected, to open his early Campaign with the Siege of *Douay*, or to draw the Enemy thereby again to Battle; and from the *Hague* the Duke went toward *Tournay*, near unto which he met and join'd the most of the Allies Army at a Village call'd *Ourney*, *April* 8; and in four Days after join'd Prince *Eugene*, with the *Germans*, on the other Side of *Douay*; of which more in its regular Course: But before I can proceed with my Journal, I must begin with the Time of our *British* Corps taking the Field, by the several Reasons before urged, *viz.*

April 3, General *Lumley*, with our *British* Troops and Artillery, set out of their Winter-Quarters or

Campaign X. *Anno* 1710. Garrisons of *Ghent*, and march'd from thence to, and pitch'd Camp at *Heurne* near *Oudenard*, four Leagues; and the rest of our Corps set out at the same time from their respective Garrisons, in order to join us at *Tournay*, as aforesaid, for an earlier Campaign than the Year before.

April 4, Decamp'd at *Heurne*, and march'd from thence to, and pitch'd Camp at *Bathem*, three Leagues.

5, Decamp'd at, and march'd from *Bathem* to, join'd, and pitch'd at *Daffney*, with the rest of our Corps, and some *Holland* Troops, three Leagues.

7, Decamp'd at, and march'd from *Doffney* to, and pitch'd Camp at *Phlange*, four Leagues.

8, Decamp'd at, and march'd from *Phlange* Leftward to, and pitch'd Camp at *Ovrey* Village near unto *Tournay*, three Leagues, and join'd with our Auxiliaries, and the most Part of our other Allies Troops, for the Duke of *Marlborough*'s Command; at which Place he then arrived, as aforesaid.

9, About Six at Night, the Duke decamp'd with the said Army from *Ovrey*, and march'd Frontward from thence, in order to invest *Douay*, as aforesaid, before the Enemies general Rendezvous thereat, toward which they were then a posting expeditiously, but came short thereof; for our Army continuing their March all Night thitherward, the next Day, by Noon, past the *French* Line at *Pont à Vendin*, and advanced over the little River *Juncket* at, and past *Lens*; and about Four in the Afternoon encamp'd on that Plain, on the South-Side of *Lens*; a great Round of about ten Leagues, without any Halt.

11, About Noon, the Duke decamp'd our Army from *Lens* Plain, and advanced Leftward, and about Sun-setting past that Part of the Scarp a little below *Vitri*; from which, at the first of our Armies Appearance approaching thitherward, a

French

French General, and Twenty Three Battalions, and some few Squadrons, that for some time before had been posted thereon, to prevent our Passage, and to secure that Ground for their general Rendezvous, withdrew therefrom, and quite abandon'd it, and retired to *Arras*, without giving any Opposition, leaving a great deal of their Baggage in their precipitate Retreat: After which our Army block'd up *Douay*, and kept marching with a slow Motion Leftward till about Twelve at Night, the better to cover the Town, and to bring up our long Rear, and for our several Corps to join and fall in, in their regular Post; and then the Duke caused our Army to form and pitch Camp with our Right near unto *Vitri*, and Left extended to *Gouage*, three Leagues; and so fully block'd up *Douay*.

12, The Duke decamp'd with the Army in his Command from *Gouage*, and inclined a little Leftward to, and pitch'd Camp at *Goulezin*, one League, the better to make Place for Prince *Eugene* with the Imperial Troops to fall in between our Right and *Lens*, being then just arrived from *Germany*; and then our Army being fully join'd, the Right Wing in Prince *Eugene*'s Command, consisted of Forty Five Battalions of Foot, and One Hundred and One Squadrons of Horse and Dragoons; and our Left in the Duke of *Marlborough*'s of One Hundred and Ten Battalions, and One Hundred and Sixty One Squadrons; both which made in all One Hundred and Fifty Five Battalions, and Two Hundred and Sixty Two Squadrons, with One Hundred and Two Cannon, Twenty Mortars and Howitzers, and Forty Pontons, with all other necessary Utensils of War conform, for the present Service. By this Time Marquis *Villars* had assembled, and rendezvous'd a puissant Army of the *French* between *Valenciennes* and *Cambray*, and was computed to consist of Two Hundred and Four Battalions of

Foot,

Campaign X.
Anno 1710.

Foot, and Three Hundred and Eight Squadrons of Horse and Dragoons, with Ninety Six Cannon, and Sixteen Mortars and Howitzers, and Thirty Six Pontons, with also all other necessary Utensils of War conform, all in Order for Battle, who soon after removed Leftward towards *Arras*; from whence they made several Attempts to battle our Army, and to relieve or reinforce *Douay*, after that our Army had laid close Siege thereto, but came far short of the Performance of either, by the judicious Care and good Conduct of our two heroical Generals, &c. and by the Alertness and Indefatigableness of our undaunted and couragious triumphant Armies, as in my following Descriptions doth plainly appear, notwithstanding the *French* vast Superiority in Number of Troops, but inferior much in Courage, otherwise they would never have stood gazing on, and seen their City taken.

April 13, The better to prevent the Enemies Surprizals after the Siege was form'd, and to maintain the same when form'd, and to make it the easier to the Besiegers when set apart thereto, the Duke immediately caused a Line of Circumvallation to be begun and carried on round the City, where most Need required, and was soon after accomplish'd.

The Siege of *Douay*.

17, The Duke fell back our Army a little, and pitch'd Camp within the said Line, one League; and at the same time he and Prince *Eugene* detach'd and set apart, for the carrying on the said Siege, Prince *Anhault* and the Prince of *Orange*, with Forty One Battalions and Thirty Two Squadrons, who immediately formed, laid close Siege to, and invested *Douay* round, with Ordnance conform; in which commanded Lieutenant-General *Albergoty*, &c. with Fourteen Battalions and Three Squadrons of Dragoons, computed Seven Thousand Seven Hundred Men, in City and Citadel, otherwise called

Fort

Fort *La Scarpe*, with, in all, Thirty Eight Cannon and Twelve Mortars and Howitzers mounted.

Campaign X.
Anno 1710.

18, All the Horse and Dragoons of our Army, and a competent Number of the Besiegers, were busily employ'd in the making and bringing of Fascines, &c. for the expeditious carrying on the said Siege now form'd against *Douay* and Fort *La Scarpe*.

22, At Break of Day, the Duke detach'd a Major-General and Six Thousand Men from our Grand Camp, with Six Cannon and Two Howitzers, to, and attack'd and took *Chateau-Loway*, a little to the North-Side of *Douay*, and took therein Two Hundred and Forty Men Prisoners at Discretion; and as they march'd out thereof, and the other in thereto, the Commanders of both, with several of their Men, were accidently blow'd up by some loose Powder, which lay carelessly on the Ground, upon which some Fire fell from some of their Pipes, to their own Ruin, and also blew up several Barrels of loose Powder.

23, At Night, Prince *Anhault* and the Prince of *Orange*, with a competent Number of the Besiegers, with and without Arms, open'd their Trenches by two Attacks against *Douay*, Prince *Anhault*'s on the North, and the Prince of *Orange*'s on the West-Side thereof, and that with little Loss, by getting into Cover before discover'd by the Besiegers.

25, In the Night, a great Body of the Besieged boldly sallied out on the Approaches on the Prince of *Orange*'s Attack, whom they at first somewhat surprized; but soon after, the Cover thereof sharply repulsed and beat in the Salliers to their former Lodgements, and that with great Loss on both Sides: The Salliers lost most.

27, At Break of Day, a small Battery of Eight Cannon and Four Mortars, being ready on Prince *Anhault*'s Attack, begun to play furiously against a

Campaign X.
Anno 1710.

little black Sconce, seated in the *Morass*, a little off from the South Corner of the Town, and soon after dismantled it; the which before much flank'd the Right of his Approaches: And that same Day, at Night, a small Party of the Besieged sallied on the said Attack; by the Cover of which they were soon sharply repulsed, and beat in again to their Lodgements, to their great Loss.

May 3, About Six in the Morning, the Besiegers Batteries on both Attacks being erected and compleated, consisting of Eighty eight Cannon and Thirty Two Mortars and Howitzers, begun to play very vigorously against the Counterscarp and Bastions of *Douay*, in the Front of their Approaches, in order for a sudden Grand Breach and general Storm thereon; but more especially Prince *Anhault*'s, which consisted of Forty Eight Cannon and Sixteen Mortars, which play'd with a great deal of Fury against the main Counterscarp and Walls of the Town, adjoining thereto on that Side and Attack where the Siege was the most regularly carried on: The other Side, on the Prince of *Orange*'s Attack, being boggy and muddy, they could not proceed altogether so regularly or advantageously; nevertheless their Valour and Loss was no ways inferior to the other, whom they did very much aid and assist.

6, At Break of Day, a great Party of the Besieged boldly sallied out on Part of Prince *Anhault*'s Approaches; by the Cover of which they were soon sharply repulsed and beat in again, to their great Loss of Men killed and wounded, besides One Hundred Men taken, by the said Cover, Prisoners at Discretion.

11, At Night, a competent Number of the said Attack couragiously attack'd and took a little Horn-work in the Front of their Approaches, with very little Loss.

12, About

12, About Noon, Monsieur *Villars*, with several others, and a great Body of their Horse, advanced a little in the Front of our Camp, reconnoitring the same, picqueering and gasconading how to attack the same, and relieve or reinforce *Douay*: Whereupon our Army being alarm'd, our Picquet was immediately turn'd out; and upon the same, the Enemy retired, and our Picquet fell back to their former Post.

<small>Campaign X.
Anno 1710.</small>

13, The Duke decamp'd with our Army from *Gouzelin*, and removed out of the said Line, and inclined the Army Leftward of *Vitri*, and pitch'd Camp with our Right extended near to the Abbey of *Flines*, two Leagues; where the Duke's Quarters were, for the most Part of the said Siege, ready, the better to prevent any sudden Surprizals of the *French* Grand Army on that Side; being, that in the Time of the Siege, they made many Attempts that Way, but all to no Effect. That same Morning, by Break of Day, a great Body of the Besiegers vigorously attack'd, and in a Trice took the aforesaid Grand Counterscarp, and begun their Bridges over the Grand Fossee to the Grand Breach of the main Wall of the Town; and at Night a great Party of the Besieged boldly sallied on the Besiegers Approaches, by the Cover of which they were soon sharply repulsed, and beat in again to their dismal Lodgements, to their great Loss.

14, Our Grand Army decamp'd, and inclined Leftward to, and pitch'd Camp at *Arlew-Pass*, on the *Sanset*, one League, with our Right Wing still extended near unto *Vitri*, the better to cover and maintain the said Siege; the Duke having Intelligence that the *French* Army was then in a grand Motion, to use some Means to keep their Honour somewhat alive, that it might not fall quite in Oblivion.

May

Campaign X.
Anno 1710.

May 15, At Break of Day, a competent Number of Prince *Anhault*'s Troops attack'd, and took a small Flanker of the Glacis of the Town, in the Front of their Approaches, with little Loss; and the same Day the *French* Grand Army removed Leftward from *Valenciennes* and *Cambray*, and advanced near to our Grand Army, and pitch'd their Camp opposite thereto, and ranged along on the South-East Side of the *Sanset*, with their Left extended near unto *Le Cluse*, within Cannon-shot of our Army, which lay all that Night on their Arms waiting the Enemies Motion, all ready and in very good Order to receive and repulse them, if assaulted or attack'd thereby, being they then (as we supposed) were fully bent to give Battle, relieve or reinforce *Douay*, as it stood them upon; for which they used several Stratagems and Means to the utmost of their Power, by gasconading, but wanting the real Courage to put their Attempts in Execution, all the rest proved in vain, as aforesaid, and in my following Prescriptions of their feint Attempts, and our couragious Defence, *viz.*

16, By Break of Day, they expeditiously march'd off Leftward from *Le Cluse*, with Design to slip in between our Right Wing and *Lens* and *Ponta Vendin*, thereby to cut off our Armies Communication with our Garrisons on that Side, or to fall on the Besiegers on that Side which lay the weakest; of all which they were suddenly frustrated by the good Conduct of our Generals, in immediately inclining our Army Rightward from *Arleu* by Break of Day, and by having the shorter March of the Enemy, got before them, and pitch'd Camp at *Crossange*, two Leagues, with our Right Wing in Prince *Eugene*'s Command extended near unto *Lens*; and thereby the better cover'd the Enemies Left from out winging us, and frustrated them of their Projects: And that Night likewise our Army lay on
their

their Arms very alert, waiting the Enemies Motion, and expecting Battle in the Morning, but they made no Motion thereto, nor that Day, but gasconaded at a considerable Distance.

17, Hereupon the Duke and Prince *Eugene* decamp'd with our Army, and inclined a little more Rightward, and form'd and pitch'd Camp on the Plains, and immediately decamp'd again, and inclined a little more Rightward, and raised somewhat of a Running Trench in our Front, where we lay also all that Night on our Arms very alert, waiting the Enemies Motion, expecting, by the Enemies gasconading, that they would in good Earnest give us Battle the next Morning; for which, that Night, all necessary Preparations were made, and every Thing put into very good Order. Our Running Trench was enlarged with several Batteries erected thereon, to the Number of One Hundred Pieces of Cannon, with Mortars and Howitzers, on an Height, the better to clear and cleanse the Plain of the Enemies advancing, if they should attempt to assault us; and to receive, battle, and beat them off from thence, if attack'd, or any ways assaulted thereby; as also for our better Security. The same Night the most of the Besiegers were order'd, and drawn off, to our Grand Camp, for a Reinforcement thereto, and to assist the same if Occasion should require, who immediately fell in the Lines in the Rear thereof for the same Intent; for the Enemy having a much superior Number than we, we could not, on such an Occasion, be too secure, especially being drawn up in a plain and level Country.

18, About Break of Day, Marshal *Villars* advanced a little with the *French* Army, in order for Battle, and to attack us, as we expected; but soon after having seen all the good Preparations of our Army more ready and better to receive and repulse them,

them, than they were to assault or attack us, it put them to a sudden Stand and strange Consternation, conjecturing what they had best to do, to preserve themselves and their Honour from being quite blasted, which lay then in a manner at Stake; for I do believe, that if they had attack'd that Day, that it would have proved as ill, if not worse to them, than *Hochstat, Ramillies, Oudenard,* or *Malplaquet*; but their fiery Courage being much cooled and abated, by the Destiny of what they saw before them, after they had paused a little thereon, and gasconaded the most Part of the Day, at a Distance in our Front, they fell back from thence (vanished away as a Cloud out of our Sight) and retired Rearwards in a huge Body to *Arras*, and there lay by and look'd on, with the Satisfaction of a Gasconade for their Pains, and were very quiet from making any more such bold Attempts during the Siege. The Enemy being gone, our Army repitch'd Camp on their old Ground, and the aforesaid Besiegers return'd to their former Posts; and the same Day, in the Besiegers Absence, a Body of about Six Hundred Men of the Besieged sallied out on the East-Side of the Town most open, near *Leeward*, with Design to take in, or away, all our Bread Waggons from thence, that were drawn up and posted there, till our Dispute, which was then in hand, should be decided; of which Attempt the Salliers were soon and suddenly frustrated by some of our reserve Squadrons, of which they were not aware, that immediately fell upon them, and killed and disabled above One Hundred and Fifty of them, and pursued the rest from thence a great Way toward *Cambray*, being not able to re-enter their Garrison of *Douay*.

May 22, In the Night, the Duke had Intelligence that the *French* Army was in a Motion Rightward; whereupon our Army being again somewhat alarm'd, alarm'd, our whole Picquet was turn'd out immediately Leftward, in order to sustain an Advance-Post of Two Captains, Four Subalterns, and One Hundred and Fifty Men, in a Morass-Pass at *Beash* Village; but by Six in the Morning, before our Picquet's Arrival thereat, nay, before they had left Camp, they were surprized and taken by a great Body from the Enemies Right Wing of about Ten Thousand Men, under the Duke of *Luxemberge*'s Command, with Six Cannon, after the firing five Rounds thereof, and immediately retired, with their small Prize, to their Grand Camp; after which our Picquet was recalled, and withdrew to Camp.

23, At Break of Day, a competent Number of Prince *Anhault*'s Attack couragiously attack'd, and took a Bastion in the Front of their Approaches at *Douay*; but it lying very open to both Sides, could not be maintained by either the one or the other.

June 6, At Night, the Duke having Intelligence that the *French* Army was in a Motion Rightward, with all the Grenadiers in the Van, designing to pass the *Sanset* near *Le Cluse* or *Arleu*, and to slip in between our Left Wing and *Douay*; whereupon our Army being alarm'd, the Duke first turn'd out our Picquet immediately Leftward, and by Break of Day he follow'd the same with our whole Army, and about Noon pitch'd Camp along the Morass Side by the *Sanset*, with the Left of our Left Wing extended near unto *Arleu-Pass*, with the Right of our Right Wing extended somewhat past *Crossange* Village; and thereby put a Stop to the Enemies Career, and baffled them in that Project, as of the rest to our Right before: After which they pitch'd on the other Side of the *Sanset* and Morass, as they had done the 15th of *May*, opposite to, and within Cannon-shot of each other, but lay both very quiet alert during the Remainder of the Siege; where, during the Time our Abode, there happen'd several

Campaign X. Anno 1710. ral Times Conferences between several of ours and the Enemies Soldiers, of what they pleased, on the Sides of the River which run about the Center of the Way between the Camps of the two Armies; and that Night a competent Number of Grenadiers and Fusileers of Prince *Anhault*'s Attack vigorously attack'd, and took a high Ravelin, with little Loss, which before did very much obstruct their expeditious Proceedings to their Grand Breach of the main Wall of the Town.

June 11, At Night, a competent Number of the Besiegers, assisted by a Detachment from our Grand Camp, open'd their Trenches against the Citadel of *Douay*, or Fort *Scarp*, (in which were Four Battalions of the aforesaid Number) and proceeded gradually therewith till the City surrender'd, and was then comprehended in the same Conditions therewith.

13, At Break of Day, a competent Number of Prince *Anhault*'s Attack likewise attack'd, and took another small Ravelin in the Front of their Approaches, and that also with little Loss; and at Night they laid and finish'd two Bridges of Fascines and Hurdles over the Grand Fossee, to the Grand Breach of the Walls, ready and in Order for a sudden general Grand Storm thereon: So that thereby, and the Fear and Dread thereof, and no Sign of Relief from their Grand Army, terrified the Governor and his Garrison, that he the next Day, about Four in the Afternoon, after several Conferences with his other Generals, &c. beat a Parly, *Douay surrender'd.* and capitulated for the City and Fort on honourable Terms; which being allow'd and approv'd of by the Duke and Prince *Eugene*, (who instantly intended a farther Progress in Conquests) the Besieged, on the 15th, about Four in the Afternoon, deliver'd up two of the Gates of the City to the Besiegers;

two

two Days being allow'd the Besieged to prepare to march out, &c.

18, General *Albergoty*, with his Garrison of Fourteen Battalions and Three Squadrons, with Eight Cannon, Two Mortars, and Fourteen Cover'd Waggons, march'd out of *Douay*, with all the usual Marks of Honour, and was conducted from thence by a Party of our Horse to *Cambray*; at which Time our Grand Army stood at Arms in two Lines, at the Head of our Encampment, till they were past, and then fell back to their Tents.

During this Siege against the City and Citadel of *Douay*, of nine Weeks and two Days, commenced the 11th Day of *April*, and ended on the 14th of *June*, the Besiegers Loss was computed to amount to in all Two Thousand Eight Hundred and Sixty Men killed and wounded, Officers included; and the Besiegers to Eight Thousand and Nine, all Stations included, as by the following Table of the several Particulars doth appear, *viz.*

(300)

Of the *Hollander*'s Artillery, One Lieutenant-Colonel killed, and Six wounded, and One Colonel wounded; other Officers, Two killed, and Seven wounded; and of their other Stations Eighty killed, and One Hundred and Forty wounded; Total of all Stations, Two Thousand One Hundred and Forty Two killed, and Five Thousand Eight Hundred and Sixty Seven wounded; killed and wounded in all Eight Thousand and Nine, as aforesaid.

Now the Siege of *Douay* being over, and our Army ready to draw together again, the *French* Army, who before in the Time thereof threaten'd to force us to Battle, fell back to, and under the Cover of *Arras*; of which more afterward in Course.

June 24, The Duke and Prince *Eugene* review'd all the Horse and Dragoons of our Army.

29, The Duke and Prince *Eugene* decamp'd with our Grand Army from between *Arleu* and *Crossange*, and the Besiegers from *Douay*; and both Armies march'd from their several Decampments Rightward to, join'd, and pitch'd Camp cross the Hill

at

Campaign X. Anno 1710.

The Two Attacks.	Batt s	Lt. Cols. Kd / Wd	Majors Kd / Wd	Captains Kd / Wd	Subalterns Kd / Wd	Serjeants Killed / Wound	Centinels Killed / Wound	Total Killed / Wound	Total Kd. Wd.
The First Prince *Ambault*'s	20	1	2 2	11 23	18 69	42 115	919 2635	993 2845	3838
The Second Prince of *Orange*	21	1 1	1	3 27	17 83	58 134	980 2634	1069 2882	3951
Total of both	41	2	3	50	35 152	100 249	1899 5269	2062 5727	7789

at *Vimy*, four Leagues, with *Arras* about half a League in our Front: To the South-side thereof the *French* Army removed, at the Front of our Armies Appearance approaching thitherward; where and thereabout they strongly entrench'd and abode the Remainder of the Campaign, after having detach'd and sent up a great Body of their Troops from thence into the *Milanese* and *Spain*; in which Time our Army was not idle on this Side, but very busy employ'd in besieging and taking of their Towns, whilst *Villars* look'd on.

July 1, Our whole Army decamp'd at, and march'd from *Vimy* Rightward to, and pitch'd Camp at *Villersbrutain*, four Leagues; where we abode during the Time and Covering of the Siege of *Bathun* till ended.

3 and 4, The Duke and Prince *Eugene* reviewed all the Foot of our Army, in two Parts, a little off the Right of our Encampment, and consulted on the Siege of *Bethune*.

Note, That the Night before we march'd to *Vimy*, our Quarter-Master-General was sent before, and pitch'd our Camp by the Arrival of our Army at *Vimy*.

4, After the aforesaid Review, the Duke and Prince *Eugene* detach'd to the said Siege the Generals *Fagel* and *Schulenberge*, with Thirty Battalions of Foot, and Twenty Squadrons of Horse and Dragoons, with Ordnance conform; who the next Day laid Siege to, and invested *Bethune* round, in which commanded Major-General *de Puys Vauban*, with a Garrison of eleven Battalions of *French*, with Twenty Four Cannon and Eight Mortars ready mounted: After which the Besiegers immediately begun making and bringing of Fascines, &c. for the expeditious carrying on of the Siege, and proceeded gradually.

Campaign X.
Anno 1710.

July 9, The Duke and Prince *Eugene* extended our Army a little Rightward, and pitch'd Camp, one League, and fill'd up the Intervals of those Troops that were gone off from thence to the said Siege.

13, As a Party of our Army was foraging a little off to the Right Wing of our Camp, a great Body of the *French* Horse and Foot, which had lain some time in Ambush, advanced from thence, with Design to cut off our Foragers from Camp; which doubtless they would have easily effected, had not Prince *Eugene*, by the Alertness of his Right Wing, instantly frustrated the same, by advancing out therewith, and attack'd the Enemy, whom he in a Trice beat back, and made retire with great Precipitation to their Grand Camp again near *Arras*, to the Loss of about Twelve Squadrons, either killed, disabled, taken, and deserted; but with very little Loss on Prince *Eugene*'s Side: After which our Foragers immediately retired to their several Corps, and the Prince fell back with his Troops to their respective Camp. And that same Night a competent Number of the Besiegers, with and without Arms, open'd their Trenches against *Bethune* by two Attacks; the one on the East-Side of the Town by General *Fagel*, and the other on its South-Side by General *Schulenberge*, but with considerable Loss.

Siege of Bethune.

20, The Duke and Prince *Eugene* decamp'd our Army, and removed a little more Leftward, and pitch'd Camp with the Left of our Left Wing extended to the Mount *St. De Locy Cloister*, within about one League of *Arras*, the better to cover the Enemies Right Wing, one League, and to prevent sudden Surprizals, and to cover and maintain the Siege against *Bethune*, that was then going briskly on.

22, About Eight in the Morning, the Besiegers several Batteries on both Attacks being fully erected and compleated, consisting of in all, and at most, Eighty

Eighty Nine Cannon and Thirty Three Mortars and Howitzers, begun to, and play'd very vigorous and furious againſt the Out-Skirts of the Town of *Bethune*, and afterward proceeded as expeditious and regular as the Ground would admit; and that ſame Day, about Noon, a great Body of the Beſieged boldly ſallied out toward the Approaches of General *Fagel*'s Attack, where our *Engliſh* Battalions were employ'd; to which the Cover thereof immediately advanced with undaunted Courage, and met the Enemy half Way, and in a Trice vigorouſly repulſed and beat the Enemy into their Works again, to their great Confuſion, but with very great Loſs on both Sides.

Auguſt 8, In the Duſk of the Evening, a great Party of the Beſiegers boldly attack'd, and took the moſt Part of the Enemies Out-Works in the Front of their Approaches, and that with very little Loſs.

12, About the ſame Time, they in like manner attack'd, and took the Remainder of the Out-Works in the Front of their Approaches; and that alſo with little Loſs.

17, In the Duſk of the Evening, our Grand Army had a *Feu-de-joye* for a Victory obtained by our Army in *Spain*; and the ſame Day the Beſiegers of *Bethune*, by their two Attacks, having near compleated two great Breaches in the main Walls of the Town, in order for a general Grand Storm thereon, the Fear and Dread thereof ſo terrified the Governor and the Beſieged, that he, the ſame Day, about Four in the Afternoon, beat a Parley, and capitulated on honourable Terms; and being granted by the Duke and Prince *Eugene*, they the next Day deliver'd up one of the Gates of the Town to the beſieging Army.

20, General *de Puys Vauban*, with his Garriſon of Eleven Battalions, march'd out of *Bethune* with

<small>Campaign X.
Anno 1710.</small> the ufual Marks of Honour, and was conducted by a Party of the Befiegers Horfe from thence to Arras.

During this Siege againſt *Bethune*, of fix Weeks and two Days, begun on the 5th of *July*, and ended on the 17th of *Auguſt*, the Befiegeds Lofs was computed to amount to in all One Thouſand Two Hundred Men killed and wounded, Officers included; and the Befiegers to Three Thouſand Three Hundred and Sixty Five, all Stations included, as by the following Table of the feveral Particulars thereof doth appear, *viz.*

(305)

The Two ATTACKS.	Batts	Colonels Kd.|W.		Lt Cols Kd.|W.		Majors Kd.|W.		Captains Kd.|W.		Subalts Kd.|W.		Serjeants K.|W.		Centinels Killed.|Wound.		Total Killed.|Wound.		Total K.&W.
First, General Fagel's	15				3	1	1	1	1	15	11	30	21	37	355	1076	389	1162	1551
Second, General Schulenberge's	15	2	2	1	2		1	2	5	9		4	34	18	42	429	1222	457	1313	1740
Total of both	30	2	2	1	5	1	1	3				624	15	64	39	79	784	2298	846	2475	3291

Campaign X.
Anno 1710.

Of the Artillery Two Engineers killed and Eleven wounded, One Lieutenant wounded; of their other Stations Eleven killed, and Twenty wounded; Total of all Stations killed Eight Hundred and Fifty Nine, and wounded Two Thousand Five Hundred and Six; in all killed and wounded Three Thousand Three Hundred and Sixty Five.

This Siege was no sooner over, than two others were taken in Hand at once, *viz.* that of *St. Venant* and *Aire*, both formed and closely laid at once, *St. Venant* the one Day, and *Aire* the other; of which in their Course.

Aug. 22, Our Grand Army, under the Duke and Prince *Eugene*, decamp'd at *Villersbrulain*, and the Besiegers from *Bethune*; and both march'd from their several Encampments Rightwards, and join'd and pitch'd Camp at *Delure* Village, four Leagues.

24, Decamp'd at, and march'd from *Delure* right, and a little Rearward to, and pitch'd Camp at *St. Andrew's Cloister*, three Leagues, on the South-Side, and within Cannon-shot of *Aire*; and thereby immediately it was block'd up,

Campaign X.
Anno 1710.

St. Venant invested.

up, and in two Days after both Sieges were laid as aforesaid, *viz.*

August 25, In the Morning, the Duke and Prince *Eugene* detach'd, and set apart to the said Siege, the Prince of *Orange*, with Twenty Battalions of Foot, and some few Squadrons, with Ordnance conform; to which he immediately march'd off, and that Afternoon invested it round; in which there was one Major-General *Silves*, with a Garrison of Seven Battalions of *French*, Six Cannon and Two Mortars mounted; and the next Day the Besiegers begun making and bringing of Fascines, &c. for the expeditious carrying on of the said Siege; after which they proceeded very regularly therewith.

Aire invested.

26, The Duke and Prince *Eugene* detach'd, and set apart to the said Siege, Prince *Anhault*, with Forty Battalions of Foot, and some few Squadrons, and Ordnance conform, who immediately invested it round; Lieutenant-General *Goesbriant* commanded in it, with a Garrison of Fourteen Battalions and Seven Squadrons, Thirty Eight Cannon and Ten Mortars mounted: And the next Day the Besiegers begun making and bringing of Fascines, &c. for the expeditious carrying on the Siege, and afterwards proceeded gradually.

28, The Duke and Prince *Eugene* decamp'd our Grand Army, and inclined it a little Rightward, pitch'd Camp, and filled up the most of the Intervals of those Troops gone off to the two aforesaid Sieges; and there lay firm during the Time thereof, the better to cover and maintain the same against all Assaults or Oppositions.

Sept. 1, At Night, a competent Number of the Besiegers of *Aire*, with and without Arms, open'd their Trenches against it by two Attacks, that of Prince *Anhault*'s on the South-Side of the Town, and the other on the West-Side of the Town, both

with

with little Loss, by getting somewhat into Cover before discover'd by the Enemy. Some time after a Morass parted the two Attacks; but at last, by draining away the Water, with much ado they were both join'd into one; the which the sooner dispatch'd the said Siege.

3, At Night, a competent Number of the Besiegers against *St. Venant*, with and without Arms, open'd their Trenches against it by one Attack, with little Loss, by getting first into Cover before fully discover'd by the Enemy.

8, As a small Convoy of Two Hundred Men was convoying of Sixty Boat Loads of Ammunition, &c. up the *Lys* from *Ghent*, towards *Courtray*, in order for the two aforesaid Sieges, they were sorely attack'd, and over-power'd at *Vine St. Eloy* Village, half Way between *Deinse* and *Courtray*, by General *Ravignan*, with a Body of about Four Thousand *French*, from the Garrison of *Ypres*, who killed, wounded, and took most of the aforesaid Convoy of Two Hundred Men, and blew up and sunk eleven of the said Boats, and immediately retired in great Haste to *Ypres* without any farther Booty, for fear of being attack'd by General *Ginkel*'s Command of Two Thousand Horse and Dragoons, who had been detach'd from our Grand Camp on the 5th instant, to meet and convoy up the said Ammunition from *Courtray* to the said Sieges; but by coming a Day too late, the Enemy got off as aforesaid: Nevertheless, the other Forty Nine Vessels being saved in the Front, and arrived at *Courtray*, he conducted and convoy'd them up safe from thence by *Menin* to *Aire*, leaving some of them behind him at, and for the Use of the Besiegers of *St. Venant*.

8, At Break of Day, the Besiegers several Batteries on both Attacks against *Aire*, being erected and compleated, to the Number of Fifty Eight Cannon

<small>Campaign X.
Anno 1710.</small> Cannon and Twenty Eight Mortars, begun about Nine in the Morning to play, and play'd very brisk and smartly against the Outer Counterscarps thereof.

Sept. 10, About Sun-rising, the Besiegers of *St. Venant*'s Batteries being also ready, of Eleven Cannon and Twelve Howitzers or little Mortars, begun and play'd very furious against the main Walls thereof, and into the Town; and that same Day, at Night, our Grand Army had another *Feu-de-joye*, for a farther Victory obtained by our Army over the *French* in *Spain*.

13, At Break of Day, a great Body of the said Besiegers boldly attack'd, with great Fury, the most of the Out-Works in the Front of their Approaches at *St. Venant*; and after several sore and sharp Assaults and Repulses, they beat the Enemy out thereof, and possess'd them, but with great Loss on both Sides.

<small>*St. Venant* surrender'd.</small> 17, The said Besiegers made and got all Things ready, and in very good Order, against the next Morning, for a general Grand Storm against *St. Venant*; but the Fear and Dread thereof so terrified the Governor and his Besieged, that he, to wave the same, the said Day, about Sun-setting, beat a Parley, capitulated and surrender'd the Town according to the Capitulations of *Bethune*; whereupon, the next Day, they deliver'd up one of the Gates of the Town to the Besiegers, and had two Days Time allow'd them to prepare to march out thereof.

21, Major-General *Silves*, with his Garrison of Seven Battalions, march'd out of *St. Venant* with the usual Marks of Honour, and was conducted by a Party of our Horse to *St. Omers*.

During this Siege against *St. Venant*, of three Weeks and three Days, begun on the 25th of *August*, and ended on the 17th of *September*, the Besiegeds

ſiegeds Loſs was computed to amount to Four Hundred Men killed and wounded, Officers included; and the Beſiegers to Nine Hundred and Seventy Three, all Stations included, as by the following Account of the ſeveral Particulars thereof doth appear, *viz.*

Campaign
X.
Anno 1710.

On the ATTACKS.	Killed.	Wounded.
Battalions	—	20
Captains	2	8
Subalterns	6	22
Serjeants	9	24
Centinels	211	678
Total —	228	732

Total kill'd and wounded — 960

Of the Artillery, Engineers and Officers, &c. Three killed, and Ten wounded; the which makes the Total of all Stations included to amount to Two Hundred and Thirty One Men killed, and Seven Hundred and Forty Two wounded; and in all killed and wounded Nine Hundred and Seventy Three.

The ſaid Beſiegers abode there, and repaired the Works of the Town, till the End of the Siege of *Aire*; to which I will next proceed more at large, it being of more Conſequence.

19, At Eight in the Morning, a competent Number of Prince *Anhault*'s Attack couragiouſly attack'd, and after a ſmart Bruſh, took a Flanker or Fleche near the Brick-Kiln in the Moraſs, on the Weſt-Side of the Cauſeway which leads out on the South-Side of *Aire*.

22, About Eight in the Morning, another competent Number of the ſaid Attack attack'd, and, after a ſharp Diſpute, took the Glacis, and all the

Out-

Out-Works thereabouts, next to the said Brick-Kiln on the Morass.

Sept. 24, At Break of Day, a competent Number of the said Attack boldly attack'd, and took a little Horn-work on the Middle of the aforesaid Causeway, adjoining near to the aforesaid Brick-Kiln; and at Night another sufficient Party thereof attack'd, and took a Cover'd Way adjoining to the aforesaid Glacis and Horn-work.

29, In the Dusk of the Evening, another competent Number of the said Attack vigorously attack'd, and took a small Counterscarp in the Front of their Approaches; and each of those four Attacks was with considerable Loss on both Sides: But in all this Time the Left Attack gain'd Ground but very slowly, it being much overflow'd with the Water of the Morass, for a considerable Time, in the Fore-Part of the Siege; nevertheless, by their Vigilance, they gained as much as possibly could be expected, considering their bad Situation, and very much aided the other, on which the greatest Burthen of the Siege lay, and closely hem'd up the Enemy, as well as on the other Side.

October 4, At Night, a competent Number of Prince *Anhault*'s Attack laid their necessary Bridges cross the Bogg, from the Corner of the aforesaid Horn-work to the Glacis, and immediately pass'd over the Bridge to the Palisadoes, and furiously attack'd the same; and in a Trice, after a smart Brush, beat the Enemy out, and possess'd themselves thereof: And on the 10*th*, at Night, they begun their Bridges from the said Palisadoes cross the Fossee, to the Grand Breach in the main Counterscarp, in the Front of their Approaches, against which their Batteries had been playing very smartly all along, compleating the said Breach for a Storm.

12, At Night, a great Body of the said Attack boldly attack'd the said Counterscarp, and that with

with unparallel'd Vigour and Fury; and after about half an Hour's sharp Dispute took it, and also an Half Moon, and the most of the other Out-Works in their Front, and instantly raised, erected, and compleated, at the Foot thereof, several fresh Batteries, as regular as the Ground would afford, in order for a Grand Breach on the main Walls of the Town.

18, At Night, another great Body of the said Attack couragiously attack'd, and took all the remaining Part of the Out-Works in the Front of their Approaches; and immediately begun their Bridges from thence crofs the Grand Fossee to their Grand Breach, and erected and compleated more fresh Batteries, in order to clear the said Breach. Now by this Time the Left Attack, which before had gained but little Ground, or advanced but a little Way, had with much ado drained off the Water, and made its Force abate; so that thereby the two Attacks had run a Trench of Fascines and Earth or Mud, quite through the aforesaid boggy Marsh or Morafs, from the Right of the Left Attack to the Left of the Right, and both fully join'd in a manner into one, ready and in Order, the better to assist and aid each other, as Occasion should or might require the same, in every Respect whatsoever: And then the Besiegers Batteries, as aforesaid, being renew'd and augmented, consisted of in all Eighty Five Cannon, and Thirty Seven Mortars and Howitzers, mounted ready, and was distributed thus in small Parcels, as the Ground would allow, viz. on the Right one Battery of Eighteen Cannon, one of Four, and another of Five, one of Eight Mortars, and two others, each of Six; on the Left one Battery of Thirty Cannon, one of Nine, one of Five, two each of Four, and two each of Three, one of Seven Mortars, one of Six, and one of Four; the most of which for some time

(312)

Campaign X. Anno 1710. time ceased from furious firing, and play'd but very slow, till the Arrival of the aforesaid Convoy of Ammunition from *Courtray* of a fresh Supply; the which soon after put an End to the Siege.

Aire surrender'd. *Oct.* 28, By Break of Day, all the aforesaid Batteries, being ready for present Service or Execution, begun a fresh to play, and play'd more vigorous and furiously than they had done at any Time before, and that against the main Walls of the Town, and continued the same without ceasing till about Sun-setting, for a general and sudden Grand Storm thereon; so that thereby, and the Fear and Dread thereof, so terrified the Governor and his Besieged, that without farther Delay he immediately beat a Parley, and capitulated to surrender the Town, on Condition to be admitted to march out thereof with the usual Marks of Honour to *St. Omers*, their nearest Garrison; to which the Duke and Prince *Eugene* consented, to put an End to the Campaign, Winter and very bad Weather being approach'd, and daily approaching apace: Whereupon, the next Day, the Besieged deliver'd up one of the Gates of the City to the Besiegers, who allotted them two Days Time to prepare to march out thereof, according to their Demands.

November 1, Lieutenant-General *Goesbriant*, with his Garrison of Fourteen Battalions and Seven Squadrons, march'd out of *Aire* with the usual Marks of Honour, and conducted from thence by a Party of our Horse to *St. Omers*; and at the same time a Party of the Besiegers took full Possession of *Aire*, where the next Day a sufficient Garrison was placed for its Defence, Count *Nassau Woudenburg* being made Governor.

During the Siege against *Aire*, of nine Weeks and three Days, commenced the 26*th* of *August*, and ended the 28*th* of *October*, the Besiegeds Loss was computed to amount to One Thousand Four Hundred

dred Men killed and wounded, Officers included; and the Besiegers to Six Thousand Seven Hundred and Eighty Five, all Stations included, as by the following Table of the Particulars thereof doth appear, *viz.*

Campaign X.
Anno 1710.

	Two Attacks	1st, Prince Anhault's	2d, The Left	Total of both
Batt.		19	21	40
Lt. Cols. Kd W.		3	—	3
Majors Kd W.		1 1	— 1	2 2
Capts. Kd W.		10 22	— 5	10 27
Subals. Kd W.		15 44	— 29	15 49·4794
Serjeants Kd Wd.		50 65	32 27	220 494
Centinels Killed Woun		78 741 995	41 1020 2502	119 1761 4497
Total Killed Woun K.W.		797 2143 2940	1127 2699 3826	1924 4842 6766

On both Attacks there were Nineteen Engineers killed and wounded, which makes the Total Six Thousand Seven Hundred and Eighty Five, besides the Artillery's Loss, which I could not find, yet judged about One Hundred and Nine.

4, The Duke and Prince *Eugene*, with our Grand Army, decamp'd from *St. Andre*, and Prince *Anhault* with the Besiegers from *Aire*, both march'd to, join'd, and pitch'd Camp at *Brool-Cloister* near *Bethune*, five Leagues; and was also join'd by the Besiegers from *St. Venant* at the same time.

5, Decamp'd at *Brool*, and march'd from thence past *Haine* to, and pitch'd Camp at *Ponta Vendin* (where he re-cross'd the Scarp) on its East-Side, four Leagues.

7, Decamp'd at, and march'd from *Ponta Vendin* past *Lisle*, and pitch'd Camp, somewhat dispers'd in Corps, on the Road-Side, half Way between *Menin* and *Lisle*, five Leagues.

8, All our Corps decamp'd at their several Encampments, and dispers'd from thence towards their respective Winter-Quarters; Prince *Eugene* with

Campaign X. Anno 1710. with the *German* Troops went off apart by themselves, and the *Hollanders* by themselves, and also the *Prussians*, &c. and General *Lumley*, with our *British* Troops and Artillery, march'd off apart by themselves, to, and pitch'd Camp on and about the Glacis of *Menin*, two Leagues; from whence the Duke of *Marlborough* went off to the *Hague*, and soon after from thence to *England*.

Nov. 9, Our Corps decamp'd at, and march'd from *Menin* past *Courtray*, and pitch'd Camp about half Way between it and *Oudenard*, four Leagues.

11, Decamp'd at, and march'd from thence to, and pitch'd Camp at *Astene* near to *Deinse*, three Leagues.

12, Decamp'd at, and march'd from *Astene*, where our *British* Troops dispers'd to their respective Garrisons or Winter-Quarters; those with General *Lumley*, with our Artillery, march'd into *Ghent*, three Leagues; and the rest in two Days after at most arrived at their respective Garrisons.

Here endeth the Journal of our Tenth and glorious Campaign in 1710, which was in Length Twenty Seven Weeks and Four Days, commenced the 3d of *April*, and ended on the 12th Day of *November*; of which our *British* Corps march'd, with the Grand Army, and apart, in all Thirty One Days, and therein Eighty Six Leagues, or Two Hundred and Fifty Eight Miles *English*.

The End of the Tenth Campaign, A. D. 1710.

THE
Eleventh CAMPAIGN,
Begun in the Year 1711.

ABOUT the Beginning of *April*, the Duke of *Marlborough* arrived at the *Hague* from *England*; and soon after some Conferences with the States-General, he repaired toward *Doway* to Head the Armies, which were then expeditiously assembling thitherward, for a general Rendezvous, in order for Service, as soon as Opportunity should serve: And from thence I pass, and proceed with my Journal from the Time of our *British* Troops first taking the Field, *viz*.

April 12, General *Lumley*, with the *British* Troops and Artillery, set out of *Ghent*, march'd from thence to, took Field, and pitch'd Camp at *Oudingham*, four Leagues; and at the same time the rest of our Corps set out of their respective Garrisons or Winter-Quarters, in order for Camp.

13, Decamp'd at, and march'd from *Oudingham* to, and pitch'd Camp at *Avelghem*, five Leagues.

14, Decamp'd at, and march'd from *Avelghem* to, join'd, and pitch'd Camp with all the rest of our Corps at *Pont d'Epiere*, two Leagues.

16, Decamp'd at, and march'd from *Pont d'Epiere* to, and pitch'd Camp at *Ourney* near *Tournay*, three Leagues.

Campaign XI.
Anno 1711.

April 19, Decamp'd at, and march'd from *Ourney* to, and pitch'd Camp at *Orchies*, four Leagues. 20, Decamp'd at *Orchies*, and march'd from thence over the Scarp at *Pont à Roche* at *Lalain*, join'd and pitch'd Camp with our Auxiliary Troops, the *Germans, Hollanders,* and the reft of our other Allies, under the Duke of *Marlborough*'s and Prince *Eugene*'s Command at *Levard* and *Vitri*, *Levard* half a League Southward of *Douay*, four Leagues; where the Duke was then juft arrived from the *Hague*; and then our Army was fully joined: The Right Wing at *Vitri*, in Prince *Eugene*'s Command, confifted of Sixty Five Battalions of Foot, and One Hundred and Twenty Squadrons of Horfe and Dragoons; our Left Wing at *Levard*, in Duke *Marlborough*'s Command, of *Britains* own and Auxiliary Troops, with the *Hollanders* and feveral others of the Allies, confifted of One Hundred and Nineteen Battalions of Foot, and Two Hundred and Twenty Six Squadrons of Horfe and Dragoons; both which included, made in all One Hundred and Eighty Four Battalions of Foot, and Three Hundred and Forty One Squadrons of Horfe and Dragoons, with One Hundred and Eleven Cannon, Eight Howitzers, and Forty Pontons, with all other neceffary Utenfils of War conform, in good Order for prefent Service, as Occafion might require: And at the fame time, the *French* Grand Army being join'd at and about *Arras*, under Marfhal *Villars*'s and the Duke of *Bavaria*'s Command, they were computed to confift of in all, *French* and *Bavarians*, One Hundred and Ninety Two Battalions, of Foot and Three Hundred and Forty Eight Squadrons of Horfe and Dragoons, with Ninety Cannon, and Twelve Howitzers or little Mortars, with alfo all other neceffary Utenfils of War conform; from whom we daily expected Battle, but they took all imaginable Care to avoid it, and both lay pretty

quiet

quiet for a considerable Time in their Encampments.

May 21, As a small Party of our Army was convoying up of some Vessels from *Tournay* to *Marchienne*, with Provisions for our Army, they were suddenly surprized a little below *Marchienne* by a great Party of the Enemy from *Valenciennes*, in a great Fog about Eight that Morning, who had been lurking in Ambush for the same the Night before; whereby they instantly, after the blowing up and sinking of Fifteen Vessels, retired in great Haste and Confusion back to *Valenciennes*, for fear of being suddenly attack'd by a Party of our Grand Camp, who knew nothing of the Matter till it was too late for rescuing the same.

28, The Duke and Prince *Eugene* review'd our whole Army at the Head of their Encampments.

June 3, The Duke and Prince *Eugene* decamp'd our Army from their several Encampments at *Levard* and *Vitri*, by Break of Day; the Duke with those in his Command of the aforesaid, with the Artillery entire, march'd off apart to, and pitch'd Camp on the Plains of *Lens*, six Leagues; and that Day, by the Heat thereof, several Men fainted and dropt down dead on the Road, one of which being not quite dead, and but slightly buried, revived and returned to his Camp at Night. Prince *Eugene* at the same time, with those under his Command, as aforesaid, being countermanded, march'd off by themselves apart from *Vitri* back towards *Germany*, in order to cover the Duke of *Bavaria*'s March thitherward, as aforesaid; each taking Ordnance conform with them from their respective Garrisons. And here I end with Prince *Eugene*'s farther Proceedings in this Campaign, being out of my Reach; and after their Departure, there remained two powerful Armies in the *Netherlands*, viz. that of the Allies, under the Duke of *Marlborough*'s

Campaign XI.
Anno 1711.

borough's Command at *Lens*, confisted, as aforesaid, of One Hundred and Nineteen Battalions, and Two Hundred and Twenty Six Squadrons, One Hundred and Eleven Cannon, Eight Howitzers, and Forty Pontons, *&c.* conform: That of the *French*, in Marquis *Villars*'s Command at *Arras*, confisted of One Hundred and Thirty Two Battalions, and Two Hundred and Four Squadrons, with Ninety Cannon, Twelve small Mortars, and Thirty Two Pontons, *&c.* conform. Yet, altho' superior in Number, they stood on the defensive Part that whole Campaign; and ours, although the inferior Number, the offensive, as described in my following Account thereof; otherwise they would never have done as at *Douay*, nay, rather worse; of which more in its regular Course, as it falls in our Journal.

June 7, In the Night, the whole Picquet of the *French* Grand Army advanced from *Arras* to *Vimi-Chateau*, designing to surprize or attack and take a small Advance-Guard of Four Hundred Men of ours, posted therein from our Grand Camp at *Lens*; but by our Parties Alertness, they suddenly discover'd the Enemy in their approaching, and briskly fired thereon, and put them to a sudden Stand with their Design; whereupon, our Army being alarmed, our whole Picquet was immediately turn'd out, in order to advance and assist our Party; but the Enemies fearing and dreading the same, instantly withdrew, and retired back to their Grand Camp at *Arras*; after which our Picquet also return'd to their Tents.

24, In the Night, the Duke turn'd out our Picquet, which immediately, by his Order, march'd Leftward from *Lens* to *Arleux* Pass, on the South-Side of the *Sanset*; and the next Morning after advanced thereto, took therein a Party of Four Hundred Men of the Enemy, which had been cutting off

off the Communication of a Part or Branch of the said River from *Douay*; after which our Picquet return'd back to our Grand Camp at *Lens*.

Campaign XI. Anno 1711.

27, The Duke detach'd, and sent back from our Grand Camp at *Lens* to *Douay*, General *Hompesch*, with Ten Battalions of Foot, and Twelve Squadrons of Horse, in order the better to prevent sudden Surprizals on that Side, and to preserve our Grand Camp's Communication therewith, and with the Scarp, &c. who accordingly after march'd back, and immediately pitch'd Camp close to, and by the Out-Works of the City of *Douay*; wherein, three Days after, they were somewhat strangely surprized, and suffer'd great Loss, viz.

July 1, By the very Break of Day, in a prodigious great Fog, a *French* General, with upwards of One Hundred Squadrons from the Enemies Grand Camp at *Arras*, which they had left in the Fore-Part of the Night, advanced to, and pass'd in among our People, by their own Watch-Word, in the Name of Friends, before fully discover'd; nevertheless, before they could fully accomplish their Design, or do great Execution, they were much sooner and sharplier repulsed by our People than they expected, by their instantly turning out of their Tents in their Shirts only, with their Cartouch Boxes and Ammunition, and seizing their Arms from their Bells, formed in a Trice, and that in much better Order, as their Ground would allow for Action, than possibly could be well expected, such a confused Hurry and short Time could afford: So that the Enemy finding them in that Posture, contrary to their Expectation, and themselves fully discover'd before they could effect their Design, Day-light approaching, and the Fog, their chief Mantle, over and gone, and no farther Advantage to be got in their Surprizal thereby, and lest our Grand Army should make one with them, and get between them and theirs, before they could have done duelling, if attack'd, besides being exposed to the Fury of the Walls of *Douay*, they instantly withdrew from thence, and retired in great Precipitation back to their Grand Camp at *Arras*, to avoid their own farther Danger. In this Hurly-Burly, or confused Attempt, there was great Loss sustained on both Sides, especially on our People's Side, by the cruel Barbarity of the Enemy in their Rear amongst their Sutlers, by some that had got round thither before discover'd, who grosly used and abused some thereof, and several others where they made their first Entrance, whom they cut and scarified in a most inhuman manner in their Tents, some asleep, and some awake; and some of whom they slaughter'd not, had cut their Tongues from out of their Mouths, &c. A very grievous and sad Spectacle for their Spectators to behold! too tedious for me to relate; of which I am sorry that I had so much to say. In the Enemies carrying on of this Attempt, as I had an Account, their Orders were, the one half of them to begin on our People's Right, and the other on the Left, and to seize all their Bells of Arms, and to sacrifice all the Troops from Right and Left to the Center, where they were to meet, and some few Squadrons of each Half to perform the little Massacre in the Rear; and that being done, and all met together again, to retire as soon as possible: But, Praise be to God, who favoured them not, but suddenly frustrated them in their cruel Design.

July 9, The Duke decamp'd and march'd our Grand Army from *Lens* to, and pitch'd Camp at the *Chartreuse* near unto *Bethune*, four Leagues.

10, Decamp'd at, and march'd from *Le Chartreuse* to, and pitch'd Camp at *Chateau de Cote* near *Aire*, three Leagues; the aforesaid Troops having join'd join'd the Army the Day before, after having reinforced *Douay*.

12, About Noon, the Duke having Intelligence that a great Body of about Four Thousand Men from the Enemies Right Wing, was march'd that Morning towards *Arleu* Pass, with Design to attack and take the same, and a small Command of Four Hundred Men from our Garrison of *Douay*; whereupon he immediately detach'd General *Cadogan*, with Thirty Squadrons, and all the Grenadiers of our Army, in order to sustain and re-inforce the said Command, or if taken before his Arrival thereat, to retake them if possible; and thereupon they immediately march'd Leftward, on great Expedition, toward *Arleu*, which that Morning, by Eight, after several sharp Repulses and Assaults, the Enemy had taken, and was return'd with the said Command Prisoners to their Grand Camp, and that long before General *Cadogan*'s, with his Command, Arrival at *Arleu*, with the Loss of One Hundred Men killed and wounded in the taking thereof: After which, the next Day, General *Cadogan*, with his Detachment, march'd back to our Grand Camp at *Chateau de Cote*.

15, The Duke detach'd General *Hompesch*, with other Ten Battalions, and Twelve Squadrons, who immediately march'd off to, and pitch'd his Camp at *La Bassee*, in order the better to preserve our Grand Army's Communication on that Side with *Lisle*, and to prevent sudden Surprizals, great Parties of the Enemy being then out, lying up and down in several Places, daily lurking on the Sides of the Roads, infesting them, for taking, stopping, and robbing the Convoys of our Provisions in coming from thence.

21, The Duke decamp'd and march'd our Grand Army from *Chateau de Cote* to, and pitch'd Camp at *Herbeval*, three Leagues; and the same time the aforesaid

Campaign XI.
Anno 1711.

aforesaid Troops from *La Bassee* fell into their respective Posts, as we enter'd the said Camp; but General *Hompesch*, Governor of *Douay*, went off thither.

July 23, The Duke decamp'd and advanced the Army exactly Frontward from *Herbeval* to, and pitch'd Camp at *Villersbrulain*, two Leagues, within about one League of the Left of the Enemies entrench'd Camp, whose Right extended near unto *Arras*, to found their Intention.

24, By Break of Day, the Duke, with Sixty Squadrons, and all the Grenadiers of our Army, advanced out a little in the Front of the Right of our Encampment, reconnoitring the *French* Grand Armies strongly entrench'd Encampment; a Feint as if design'd to attack the same; for which Fascines, Roads and Bridges were accordingly made: In which Time our whole Army was entirely drawn out, in order for Battle, a little in the Front of our Encampment, and lay on our Arms ready to assist the Duke, and for farther Action, if Occasion should require the same; and a little after, the Duke finding that the Enemy would not stir, but lay firm and close in their Entrenchments, about Noon he return'd with another fresh Project to our Army, which he immediately order'd to fall back to their Encampment; and that same Evening, a little after Taptoo, he decamp'd and march'd our Army from *Villersbrulain*, Leftward on great Expedition, far contrary to his Feint and the Enemies Expectation, in order and full Design to pass their Line or Pass of *Arleu* on the *Sanset*, and to force or draw the Enemy to Battle on that Side, or else slip in between them and *Bouchain*, and to lay Siege thereto; for which we expeditiously continued our March all that Night; but the Enemy dreading nothing thereof, lay firm at *Arras* till about Sun-rising, that the Rear of our Army was got quite past

past the same, and then they begun to bestir them-selves in great Haste Rightward towards *Cambray* and the said Pass, to which they came too late; for that Morning, *July* 25, at Three o' Clock, General *Hompesch* pass'd the same, and possess'd himself thereof, with Twenty Three Battalions, and some few Squadrons, from the Garrisons of *Lisle, Tournay,* and *Douay,* in order for the Passage of our whole Army, he having but three Leagues thither from *Douay,* and our Army a Round of upwards of twelve Leagues from *Villersbrulain,* and the Enemy not above eight from *Arras,* and pass'd it without any Opposition, and maintained the same till our Grand Army's Arrival thereat; where also that Morning, at Six, the Duke, with the aforesaid Sixty Squadrons, who in the Night went on thitherward with great Expedition before our Army, and pass'd at *Arleu,* and re-inforced the said General *Hompesch*'s Command till our Army's Arrival thereat; we arrived and pass'd entire about Four in the Afternoon, and form'd and pitch'd Camp regularly on the other Side thereof, on the Levels at *Verger-Abbey,* and balk'd the Enemy; a Round, as aforesaid, of twelve Leagues, without any Halt: Our Army striving on one Side to lay Siege to *Bouchain,* or force a Battle; the Enemy on the other Side to prevent and avoid both.

<small>Campaign XI. Anno 1711.</small>

26, The Duke decamp'd, march'd and inclined our whole Army from *Verger-Abbey,* about Ten in the Morning, Leftward, and about Noon pitch'd Camp on the Plain near and opposite to *Cambray,* two Leagues, where by that Time the *French* Army was fully arrived; and in about two Hours after, the Duke again decamp'd and march'd our Army Leftward from thence, with great Expedition, in order either to draw the Enemy immediately from *Cambray* to Battle, or else to pass the *Scheld,* and get between them and *Bouchain,* and then

<small>The Siege of *Bouchain.*</small>

Campaign XI.
Anno 1711.

then to inveſt it: The Enemy on the other hand to avoid Battle, march'd off expeditiouſly on the South-ſide of *Cambray*, deſigning to fruſtrate our Army's Intention of beſieging *Bouchain*, and paſſing the *Scheld*; both which, by our General's good Conduct, were accompliſhed; for about ten at Night, by our expeditious March, we paſſed the *Scheld* by *Eſtrun* Village, on our Bridges of Boats, on a Point a little above *Bouchain*, and that without any Oppoſition, leaving the *Sanſet* a little off to the left Hand of our March, where it a little below falls into and joins the *Scheld* three Leagues; near unto which, after having paſſed the ſame, our Army lay on their Arms the remaining Part of the Night, in a very heavy ſoaking Rain, as alert and in as good Order as could well be expected, to repulſe the Enemy if aſſaulted by them; but doubtleſs they were in no better, if not worſe Order than we. There our Picquet lay all Night alſo a little in our Front, and hereby *Bouchain* was in a Manner ſomewhat block'd up. And the ſame Night after our paſſing the *Scheld*, as aforeſaid, the Enemy fell backward nearer to *Cambray*, and alſo lay on their Arms.

July 27, About eight in the Morning, the Duke rouzed, and inclined our Army leftward from their Watry Beds, to, formed and pitch'd Camp regularly on the Plain at *Avene le Secq.* two Leagues, with the Right of our Right Wing extended within Cannon Shot of *Bouchain*, with *Valenciennes* and *Queſnoy*, Diſtance about two Leagues in our Rear; and at the ſame Time the *French* Army fell back a little cloſer to *Cambray*, and pitch'd and formed Camp on the South-weſt Side thereof, from which that Evening about ſix, their General advanced with the moſt of their Horſe and Dragoons to, and attempted to take off our Bridges of Boats from off the aforeſaid Point, there between the *Sanſet* and
Scheld

Scheld near *Hordain*, oppofite to our Right, where we had paffed, and left them the Night before; but by the fpeedy advancing of a great Body of our Right Wing thitherward, the Enemy was fuddenly fruftrated, and retired thence from a fharp and furious Repulfe of Cannon and fmall Shot, and in a Trice, in the Time of the Difpute, a Party of our Men quickly drew off the Tinn-Boats, and thus baulk'd the Enemy of that Project, who immediately retired back again to their Grand Camp without their fuppofed Booty, and ours fell back alfo to their refpective Encampment. That fame Evening the Duke fent down three intire Battalions to a little Village a little off to the Right of our Army, on the South-eaft Side of the Brink of the *Scheld* and Town of *Bouchain*, almoft adjoining near thereunto, in order to prevent Surprizals, and wait the Motion of the Enemy's Grand Camp; and there they abode that Night very alert, and the Day and Night following, 'till ordered off to the invefting of *Bouchain*; and at the fame Time *July* the 28th, the *French* Grand Army made a Motion, and *Cambray* being behind their Right Wing, with their Left bent and extending toward *Bouchain*, with the *Scheld* on their Front between them and our Army, and a Body of 15,000 of them, immediately intrench'd Crofs-ways a little to their Army's Left Wing Flank crofs the rifing Ground, between *Marquet* Village and the Morafs near thereunto, and to prevent our Armies invefting *Bouchain* on that fide; and indeed it was a great Let thereunto, and made it very difficult, from which, after that the Siege thereof was formed, during the fame, they both cannonaded and bombarded the Befiegers Approaches and Camp; which made it very tedious to them, and fomewhat the eafier to the befieged; altho' vigoroufly carried on and couragioufly maintained, both by

our

Campaign XI.
Anno 1711.

our Grand Army and the Besiegers, after closely and regularly formed, and that against a powerful Army lying within Cannon shot thereof, and of our Army, to which they were much superiour in Number.

July 29, About two in the Afternoon, the Duke detach'd and set apart for the carrying on this said Siege, from our Grand Camp at *Avene le Secq*, General *Fagell*, with 31 Battalions of Foot, and 40 Squadrons of Horse and Dragoons, with Ordnance conform. And in the Town there was Lieutenant-General Count *de Ravignan* with two Brigadiers, and a Garrison of eight Battalions of Foot, and one Regiment of dismounted Dragoons, and 600 detatch'd Foot of their Grand Camp, with Cannon, and Mortars mounted. The Besiegers were to approach thitherward on the North-west Side thereof. To which Lord *Orkney* at the same Time was set apart, with twenty Battalions for a Cover to that side, on the North-side of the Town and *Scheld*. And the Duke with the main Body of our Army to abide at *Avene le Secq*, on the South and East-side of the *Scheld*, to assist, cover, and maintain all thereof, against all Oppositions; within Cannon Shot of the *French* Grand Army under Mareschal, *Villars*'s Command, posted as aforesaid. And the said 29th at Night, the said Besiegers and Covers, begun their March to attempt the Siege; crossed the *Scheld* and Morass about half a League below *Bouchain*, and continued their March slowly all that Night in a great Fogg, with full Design to attack and remove the aforesaid Command of 15,000 Men, out of their Intrenchments, in the Morning following as soon as possible, the better thereby to make way for the investing of *Bouchain* closely; the which by most Spectators was thought incredible and difficult to be done, considering the Enemy's great Superiority in Number and also prodigious

gious strongly and advantageously posted for its Defence and Security with it, of it self strongly seated, besides in the very Bosom of their Army.

30, About seven in the Morning, the Fog being over, the said Besiegers and Cover, arrived within Cannon Shot of the aforesaid Intrenchment, and run down three Cannon near to *Marquette* Village, and discharged them on their Out-Guards, as they immediately returned from thence to their Intrenchments; the which was also a Signal to our Grand Army to be alert, and that the Attack was just about to begin. After which the Besiegers boldly advanced on thitherward, with undaunted Courage, till they came within Musket Shot of the Left of the said Intrenchment, led on by Lord *North* and *Gray* in the Van, with those of our British Foot, ready going on, and just to attack the same, and at the same Juncture, the Duke arrived there in Person, who was always ready to assist to the Utmost of his Power, with his good Conduct, graceful and awful Presence, when any Occasion required, and put a sudden Stop to the heedless Attack, having in a Trice penetrated into the Strength of the Place, and of the Readiness of their Army's larger Part, lying lurking in Ambush in the Bottom, just at the Foot of the Hill in their Rear, to assist them and come round in if attack'd, and to cut off our Communication from our Grand Army, which lay on the other Side of the *Scheld* and *Morass* two Leagues, too wide for our Assistance. So that thereby, and in Consideration of all thereof, the Duke neither seeing nor finding any Sign of visible Means, or Possibility for attacking the said Intrenchment, without great Loss, and no Victory to be obtained; he therefore ordered and caused the said Besiegers to immediately withdraw and march back to the other Side of the *Scheld* again, where they arrived that Evening. The Duke

Campaign XI. Anno 1711. Duke having projected an easier Method, for the investing and taking in of *Bouchain*, and that by Lines of Circumvallation and Contravallation, the which saved the Life of many a Man, that might have otherwise been carelesly thrown away without any Gain. That Morning the Enemy kept very close and quiet in their Intrenchment, till they found us begin to withdraw, and then they smartly cannonaded our Rear, but to no great Loss, having waited to give us all at once, for I do believe that if we had attack'd that Day it would have proved to the least Advantage on our side of any, during the whole War. Now at this Time before the Siege was formed, I must needs say, that we possess'd the *French* Side of the *Scheld*, and they ours. The which at first might have made a much greater Dispute on the *French* Side, if they had managed their Matters right, and frustrated us of *Bouchain*. But I will pass from these Digressions, to the better Proceedings of the Siege, and that as briefly as possible.

July 31. At Night, the aforesaid Besiegers and Cover again re-crossed the *Scheld* as aforesaid, and immediately after turned out Four Thousand Men thereof to work, and begun the Line of Circumvallation, at *Mastaigne* Village on the North Side of the Town, near to the Morass; and by break of Day, run the same Line cross the Hill near to the Morass, on the South West Side of the Town, below *Marquette* Village, opposite to the Enemy's Intrenchment, throwing the Town almost in their Rear. In which Time all the rest of the Besiegers and Cover, lay on their Arms very ready, and alert to repulse the Enemy if assaulted.

August 1, At break of Day, General *Cadogan* with a few Squadrons advanced out a little in the Front thereof, a reconnoitring whether the Enemy lay quiet in their Intrenchment or otherwise. At which

which Time he met with Mareſchal *Villars*, with a few Squadrons, who alſo had been a reconnoitring the Beſiegers Proceedings, both which ſharply attack'd each other, and had a very ſmart Bruſh, in which General *Cadogan* took ſeveral Perſons of Diſtinction, and others; and had alſo taken Mareſchall *Villars*, had not one of his Brigadeers inſtantly prevented it in the heat of the Diſpute; by which the Brigadier was mortally wounded. After which General *Cadogan* being returned, the Beſiegers and Cover inclined a little Rightward, and pitch'd Camp on the Inſide of the ſaid Line.

2, At Night the Beſiegers and Cover advanced again, and with the ſame Number of Workmen took in the moſt Part of the aforeſaid Hill to the Moraſs, a little below *Marquette* Village very quietly, before diſcovered by the Enemy.

3, At break of Day, after that the Enemy in the aforeſaid Intrenchments, found the Beſiegers regularly and expeditiouſly approaching to the ſaid Moraſs, thereby to cut off theirs, and their Armies Communication quite with the Town, they briſkly begun Cannonading the Beſiegers, and the Beſiegers them. The which continued very ſmart on both Sides, for ſome Time after during the Siege. So that it may be ſaid and that truly, That the Beſiegers beſieged, and were beſieged, and that by the Fury of the Enemy in, and without the Town.

At Night, the Beſiegers in like Manner, took in all the Remainder of the aforeſaid Hill, quite unto the Side of the Moraſs, ſo that the Enemy then had but one narrow Foot-path Road through a Part of the Bogg, from the Right of their Intrenchment to the Town, of the which ſoon after they were alſo deprived, and that by a very ſmall Number of Grenadiers, *viz.*

6, At Night, a ſmall Party of Four Hundred Grenadiers of the Beſiegers, waded through a little

Part

Part of the said Bogg, and boldly attack'd such a small Party of the Enemy in the aforesaid deep Road. And after a very small Dispute, beat them out, and possess'd themselves thereof, and thereby quite cut off the Enemy's grand Army's Communication with the Town, and then, and not before, the Town was quite invested round; after which the Besiegers and grand Army, made a Bridge of Hurdles and Fascines about one Mile long, quite through the Morass and Bogg, and over the *Scheld*, a little above the Town, and that from the Left of the Besiegers Line of Circumvallation, to the Right of our grand Army's Line; in Order for a Communication of our two Armies, the better to be ready to aid and assist, or sustain each other at any Time as Occasion should, or might require the same, during the said Siege. Which begun and appeared to prove, and proved very tedious.

August 8. About Noon, a great Party of the Besieged, sallied out, and attempted to take in a Captain's Guard of One Hundred Men of the Besiegers, that was then posted on a small Blind near to a little Chapel, a little to the North Side of the Town; by which the Enemy were soon sharply repulsed, and obliged to retire in again, with the Loss of several Men killed and wounded, and some doubtless deserted. And at Night another great Body sallied three several Times one after another, on the Left of the Besieger's Line of Circumvallation; and by the Cover thereof, they were each Time sharply repulsed, and beaten in to their great Loss.

10, The heavy Train from *Tournay*, arrived at the Besiegers Camp, for the Use of the Siege, the Convoy thereof was sorely attackt by the Way as they pass'd St. *Amand*, by a great Party from the Enemy from *Valenciennes*, who so sharply repulsed the Enemy, that after a smart Brush, they obliged

liged them to retire, and they came on from thence to the Siege.

11, At Night, all neceſſary Things being before made, prepared, and got ready for the Expeditious carrying on of the ſaid Siege, a competent Number of the Thirty one Batallions thereof, with and without Arms, opened their Trenches by two Attacks againſt the ſaid Town: The one on its North Weſt Side, by the Britiſh and their Auxiliary Troops; the other, or Left on its North Eaſt Side, by the *Hollanders*, &c. both under the Cover of two intire Battallions, and Four Thouſand detach'd Grenadiers: The Workmen of both were Fourteen Hundred, or to each Seven Hundred. And all the reſt of the Beſiegers, and alſo the Cover were at the ſame Time very alert, and ready to aſſiſt on the firſt Occaſion if aſſaulted; but the Enemy was very quiet, and we ſuſtained but little Loſs on this acting, by getting into Cover before diſcovered of them. But the

12, At Night, as the ſaid Cover and Workmen of both Attack, were about relieving, a great Body of the Beſieged, boldly ſallied out on the left Attack; by which they were ſuddenly and ſharply repulſed, and beat in again, by the Aſſiſtance of the right Attack, and that with but little Loſs on either Side, it being but a Spurt.

13, At Break of Day, another Party ſallied out on the Beſiegers Approaches, and by the Cover thereof, they were alſo ſoon ſharply repulſed and beat in again to their own Lodgements, and that to their great Loſs.

14*th*, The Beſiegers on the right Attack next to the Moraſs, ſapt in two little Fleches from the Enemy by their Zigzags, the which, for ſome Time before, did very much flank, gall, and prejudice their Approaches, theſe were gained with little Loſs. And at the ſame Time on the other Side, the grand Army

Campaign XI. Anno 1711. Army was not idle, for they carried on a third Attack with very little Difficulty, for the Besiegers Assistance, and much pent the Enemy, and was most supplied and covered by Ditches in their daily Approachings, and making up of their Batteries ready for Service.

August 18, In the Night all our several Batteries on the three Attacks being before erected, were fully compleated and finished, fit and ready for present Execution, consisting of in all of One Hundred and Twenty Cannon great and small, with 48 Mortars and Howitzers, all in very good Order. All which on the

19, At Eight in the Morning, begun and play'd with a great deal of Vigour and Fury, against *Bouchain*, so that thereby in two Days after, they dismounted all the Cannon thereof. That for the remaining Part of the Siege, the Besieged had but only two small Mortars, that they could play with against the three Attacks, which they preserved by their moving them to and fro from one Place to another, much under Cover, so that our Batteries could not bear thereon, or else they would probably have had their Fate with the rest.

20, In the Night, the Picquet and upwards of the *French* grand Army, attempted to pass the *Scheld* at *Hordain*, and to re-inforce *Bouchain* on the South Side thereof; but before they could accomplish the same, they were suddenly frustrated, after discovered by the four Battallions in the said Village next to the Pass. After which they immediately retired back over the *Scheld*, to their grand Camp; but in their Retreat, they somewhat surprized several small Guards in the Village next to the River, and took several thereof Prisoners with them, amongst whom there was one Major General *Burck*, and also several Persons of Note. And that same Night before they attempted to pass the *Scheld*,

there

there was three Pieces of Cannon fired in their Grand Camp, as a Signal for the carrying on of the same. The which soon after somewhat alarmed our Grand Camp, and also the Besiegers and their Cover; whereupon all the Cannon, Mortars and Howitzers from all the Batteries of the Approaches of the three Attacks, and also from our Circumvallation Line, immediately fired three smart Rounds into the Town, and upon the Enemy's Intrenchments and otherwise. The which Fury fully informed the Enemy, that all our Army was more ready to repulse them, than they were to assault us. After which *Aug.* 21, 22, 23, and 24, ours and the *French* Grand Armies stood at Arms, and briskly cannonaded each other from the one Side of the *Morass* and *Scheld* to the other: And also the aforesaid Cover of the said Siege, on their Side, and the Enemy in the aforesaid Intrenchments, in like manner cannonaded and bombarded each other; the which accordingly continued smartly on both Sides, during the Siege as aforesaid.

21, In the Evening in the Dusk, a competent Party of the Right Attack against *Bouchain*, attack'd and took a high Fleche in their Front, with little Loss.

22, Also in the Dusk of the Evening, a competent Party of the Left Attack, in like Manner attack'd and took such another new Fleche also with little Loss.

25, About Two in the Morning, a *French* General with a Detachment of about 10,000 Men, from their Grand Camp, made a bold Attack on *Douay*, having advanced thither in the Night, laid some Tin Boats over the Grand Fosse thereof, in Design to scale the Walls, and to enter the City; and as they were very busy thereabout, a Centinel from off an Out-Post of a Serjeant's Guard, heard and espyed them, and immediately challenged them

them who they were, who replyed that they were Fishermen a fishing for the Governour. And thereupon he suspected them aright to be what they were, the Enemy; and according to his Duty, discharged his Piece amongst the thickest Croud of them, and upon the same the rest of his Guard turned out and also fired upon the Enemy. Whereupon the whole Garrison was alarmed, and turned out for the Defence of the City. And so the Enemy being fully discovered in their Project, they immediately withdrew and retired with great Precipitation back to their Grand Camp; leaving one of their Tin Boats behind them in the Moat for fear of being cut off by our Army from their own. And soon after they made such another Attempt at *Menin*, but with the like Success, &c.

And about the same Time, a great Body of the Enemy's Horse and Dragoons, slipt down into the Borders of *Holland*'s *Brabant*, and raised some Contribution, and pillaged several Places, and took away a great many Horses out of the open Countrey, and instantly retired therewith to their Grand Camp.

Aug. 26, At Night, a great Party of the Right Attack against *Bouchain*, attack'd, and took in the most Part of the Pallisadoes, and other Out-works, in the Front of their Approaches, between the *Morass* and High *Ravelin*; and from thence begun a Sap and Way, long-ways of the Dyke, which led quite thorough the same between the said *Morass* and *Ravelin*, to the shallow Fosse just at the Foot of their Grand Breach, in the main of the Town or Fort, in order to be ready for a general grand Storm thereon.

28, Our Grand Army again stood to Arms all Day, alertly waiting the Motion of the *French* Grand Army, who were again in a moving Posture, a gasconading to relieve, or re-inforce the Town, but

but too late; and also in like manner kept in a hovering Posture to and fro, the two Days following, conjecturing what they had best to do, of something to suffice and satisfy the Clappers of their Court; but all their Labour was in vain, the Town was in our Clutches, and we must needs have it; it being out of their Power to rescue it.

Campaign XI. Anno 1711.

29, At Break of Day, a competent Number of our Grand Army, on their Attack on the Right of all, attack'd and took in a Ravelin, and also the most of the Out-works in the Front of their Approaches, on the South-side of the Low Town, so called, being the *Scheld* parts it from the other Part of the Town; which is most regularly fortified, and seated somewhat higher. And the same Day at Night, a competent Party of the Left Attack, begun their Bridges over the Fosse in the nearest Extent, in the Front of their Approaches, to the high Horn-work, on the Angle of their Grand Breach, also in Order and ready for a general Grand Storm.

Sept. 1, By Break of Day, the Right Attack having sap'd quite through the length Way of the aforesaid Dyke to the Grand Fosse, and erected and compleated some fresh Batteries, made and prepared all Things ready, and in order to lay their Bridges over the said Fosse to the Breach, for a sudden and general Grand Storm on the Town. Whereupon the Fear and Dread thereof so terrified the Besieged, that they about Noon beat a Parley, to surrender the Town, on conditions to be admitted to march out thereof with the usual Marks of Honour, to their Grand Camp, or elsewhere; but the Duke did not approve thereof, after so much Trouble, Loss and Prolongment of Time; so that after passing away the Day in Treaties, and to no Effect, he would grant them no other Conditions than the Prisoners of War. He ordered each

Bouchain surrendered.

side to withdraw to their several Posts under Cover. Whereupon, after the same, at eight at Night, ordering the Besiegers to proceed with all imaginable Vigour, all our Batteries begun again a-fresh, and played three Rounds very furiously into the Town, which put the Besieged into a greater Distraction than at any Time before, who in the Time thereof, several times beat and put up their Colours on the Breach, for another Parley, and cryed aloud to forbear; in which Time also a great many of them were kill'd and disabled, before that they were, could, or would be heard. And again after being heard and admitted to parley, there was Silence till about Midnight, and then again their other Demands being rejected as before, Differences arising thereabout, and the Besiegers secret incroaching on all Sides in the Time of the Parley, not willing to slip any Time or Opportunity in their Proceedings, Silence was again ordered, and all under Cover; and then all our Batteries begun again a-fresh, and played three or four Rounds more against the besieged and into the Town, and that with more Vigour and Fury than they had done at any Time before during the said Siege. In which Time, by the Enemy's own Computation, they had more Men killed and disabled, than in any Three Days before; because that during the said Time, they had stood more open and exposed than before, by standing on the Breach, putting up their Colours again and again several Times for another Parley, but were still beat down by the violent Fury of our Batteries: But at length penetrating Compassion being taken by our Men on them, by hearing them mournfully to call and cry out aloud, saying, Gentlemen, and good Soldiers, as we take and believe you to be, we pray you to cease and show us some Compassion in this out great Extremity, for ye may work on, and do do what ye will againſt us in this Place, we will in no wiſe fire any more from it againſt you. We being in a miſerable, diſmal and deplorable hem'd-up Condition, void of all Relief and Succour but yours, which we now wholly depend upon; and ſeveral ſuch more Words were heard to the ſame Effect. Whereupon, immediately after, our Batteries were ordered to ceaſe; and the Governour ſurrendered the Town, himſelf and Garriſon Priſoners of War, but the Duke out of a Complement allow'd their Officers to wear their Swords.

September 3. The Priſoners march'd out, *viz.* Lieutenant General *Count de Ravignan*, two Brigadiers, with the Remainder of eight Battallions, one Regiment of Dragoons, and the Six Hundred detach'd Foot, and was conducted by a Party of our Horſe to *Marchiennes*, and from thence to *Tournay*. And the next Day their ſick, wounded and maimed Soldiers, were ſent in our ſpare Bread and Artillery Waggons from our Garriſon of *Bouchain* to theirs of *Cambray*, for their Recovery.

(338)

	Batts	Lt Cols Kd. W.	Majors Kd. W.	Captains Kd. W.	Subalts Kd. W.	Serjeants Kd. W.	Centinels Killed / Wound.	Total Killed / Wound.	Total K.&W.
The Brittains, or Right,	15	1	—	5	6 17	1 28	247 839	264 890	1154
The Hollanders, or Left,	16	2	—	4 10	3 24	3 11	342 1662	352 1709	2061
The grand Armies by Detachments,	—	—	—	—	—	2 12	168 621	170 633	803
Total of the Three	31	3	—	4 15	9 41	51 16	757 3122	786 3232	4018

The Three Attacks. Campaign XI. Anno 1711.

DURING the Siege against *Bouchain* of five Weeks and four Days, commenced the 26th of *July*, and ended on the 2d Day of *September*, the Besiegers Loss was computed to amount to in all, Two Thousand Five Hundred and Fifty Men, Killed and Wounded, Officers included. So that they lost very near the half of what they consisted of, when the Town was first invested. And the Besiegers Loss on the three Attacks, amounted to Four Thousand and Eighty Men Killed and Wounded, all Stations included. As by this Table of the several Particulars thereof, doth appear, *viz.*

Major General *Sibourg*, and Brigadier *La-Roche*, were wounded on the right Attack; Engineers extraordinary, two Killed, and ten Wounded: Ordinary, five Killed, and three Wounded; of Artillery Officers, three Wounded. *French* Adjutants, one Wounded; two Serjeants Killed and three Wounded: Of Cannoneers, four Killed and nine Wounded; of Bombarders one Wounded, Battery-Mates three Killed; Miners, one Killed, and four Wounded; Helpers to the Train, two Killed

Killed and seven Wounded: The which made in all of the Artillery, nineteen Killed and forty one Wounded, or Killed and Wounded sixty: Total of the three Attacks Four Thousand and Eighty, Killed and Wounded.—There were several lost otherwise, in the maintaining of the Siege, whose Particulars having not found, I was obliged to wave. The Totals of the *Britains, Prusians, Hanovers, Hessians, Saxons, Danes* and *Hollanders* Corps, are all in one, as in several other Places before.

September 9, 10 and 14, each Night, our grand Army was somewhat alarmed, and stood to Arms, and each Time turned out their Picquet leftward a little, all ready, and in very good Order to repulse the Enemy, if assaulted thereby, they being then in a moving and hovering Posture, not knowing what to do to retrieve their blasted Honour, in lying by, and letting their Garrison be taken out of their very Bosom, by a much inferior Number, none of their Projects, Stratagems or Attempts taking any Effect, from their wanting true Valour and Courage, to execute, maintain and keep the same. They then in Field as aforesaid in Mareschal *Villars*'s Command, consisted of One Hundred and Thirty Two Batallions, and Two Hundred and Four Squadrons, with Ordnance conform. And the Allies in *Marlborough*'s Command, but One Hundred and Nineteen Battallions, and Two Hundred and Twenty Six Squadrons, with Ordnance conform; besides they were dispers'd in three different Bodies, for the carrying on, and maintaining the Siege of *Bouchain* as aforesaid. By this Time it plainly appear'd with what Difficuly this tedious Siege was begun, carried on, and ended, by the judicious Care of our General, and unparallel'd Valour of his Army.

September 15, The Duke sent off Nineteen of the weakest Batallions of the Besiegers, to the following

lowing Garrisons, *viz.* four to *Marchiennes*, eleven to St. *Amand*, and Four to *Tournay*. Into which, the last arrived the next Day; in Order the better to preserve his Communication with that Side, being willing to maintain the Field to the utmost Extent of the Campaign, and to wear out the Enemy thereof first, and to repair the Breaches of *Bouchain*, and to put it into a sufficient Posture of Defence, before he left it; which accordingly was done.

October 9, The Duke decamp'd and march'd our grand Army from *Avene le Secq*, (where his Quarters had been from the 29th of *July*) recrossed the *Scheld* a little below *Bouchain*, and pitch'd Camp cross the *Hill*, at St. *Dennis*, Three Leagues, and near unto *Marchioness*, and from thence he sent off several Troops towards their respective Garrisons, or Winter Quarters, the Besiegers Remainder having joined him. And by this Time Mareschal *Villars* having driven his Army closer to *Cambray*, begun also to disperse them from thence to their Winter Quarters.

14, The Duke decamp'd with our British Troops and Artillery, and the rest of the Allies from St. *Dennis*, recrossed the *Scarp* at *Marchiennes*, and march'd to and pitch'd Camp at *Orchies*, Three Leagues; having first repaired *Bouchain*, and settled a sufficient Garrison therein, Major General *Grovestein* being Governour.

October 20, The Duke decamp'd our Army from *Orchies*, and dispersed them to their respective Garrisons or Winter Quarters; and at the same Time the most of the *British* Troops and Artillery for the Garrison of *Ghent*, marched off with General *Lumley* apart by themselves, to and pitch'd Camp at *Templeuve*, Four Leagues; and the Duke of *Marleborough*, went off to the *Hague*, and from thence to *England*, and returned no more to our Army, which he had

glori-

gloriously headed, with Triumph and Fame, thro' **Campaign XI.** ten Victorious Campaigns, as is inserted herein, &c. *Anno* 1711.

21, General *Lumley* with the said Troops and Artillery, decampt at *Templeuve*, and march'd a little wide of *Tournay*, to and pitch'd Camp at *Pont-d'Epiere*, Four Leagues.

22, Decamp'd at, and march'd from *Pont d'Epiere*, to and pitch'd at *Pettehem*, near *Oudenard*, Four Leagues.

23, Decamp'd at, and march'd from *Pettehem*, to and pitch'd Camp at *Deynse*, Three Leagues.

24, Decamp'd at *Deynse*, and march'd from thence, into their respective Garisons and Winter-Quarters, of *Ghent*, Three Leagues; and the rest of our Corps, in two Days after at most, arrived also at their respective Garrisons.

Here endeth the Journal of our Eleventh Campaign, in *A. D.* 1711. Which was in Length twenty eight Weeks, begun on the 12th Day of *April*, and ended on the 24th of *October*. Of which our *British* Corps march'd with the grand Army and apart, in all twenty two Days, and therein eighty two Leagues, or two hundred and forty six Miles *English*.

An Account of some small noted Passages which happen'd in Flanders, *between the latter End of the Campaign in* 1711, *and the beginning of our* British 12*th or last Campaign therein in* 1712. *The Enemy striving to recover or regain somewhat of their former last Honour,* viz.

Campaign XI. *Anno* 1711.

ABOUT the latter End of *November*, a *French* General drew out their Garrison of *Arras*, and assembled thereat a great Body of most of the Troops of its adjacent frontier Garrisons; in order, and design to surprize, or take in *Bouchain*, by drawing a Line between it, *Douay* and *Marchiennes*, or otherwise. But the Governor of *Douay*, having timely Intelligence thereof, sent thither from this Garrison, a Re-inforcement of Three Thousand Men, and that the very Day before the Enemy set out from their Garrisons, and thereby frustrated their laying close Siege to *Bouchain*; and also for the better Security and Assistance thereof, Prince *Holsteinbeck* Governor of *Lisle*, march'd from thence on the 1st Day of *December*, with all the Horse and Dragoons, and a Detachment of Three Thousand Foot out of the twelve Battallions of this Garrison, in order to put a Stop to the Enemy's Proceedings, as aforesaid. And the same Day at Night, he pitch'd pitch'd Camp therewith at *Pont-a-Rache*; near unto which on the 3d Ditto, there assembled an equivalent Re-inforcement of Troops from all our frontier Garrisons of *Flanders*; being also then alarmed, *viz.*

Campaign XI.
Anno 1711.

From *Ghent, Bruges, Brussels, Oudenard, Tournay, Courtray, Menin, Celth, &c.* to join and assist Prince *Holsteinbeck, &c.* if Occasion should require it. But the Enemy finding that our Garrisons were then all alarm'd, ready and in very good Order, to defend and assist each other, they thereupon the same Day after our Troops arrival at *Pont-a-Rache*, expeditiously withdrew, and retired to *Arras*, and their other respective Garrisons, and had only a sore Fatigue for their Pains. But by the Advantage of being out two Days before our Troops, they broke down two of our Bridges; the one near *Pont-a-Vendin*, and the other near unto St. *Martin*, and likewise cut and let out the River *Scarp*, in a Spurt, in several Places between *Marchiennes* and *Quatre-Cloches*, the which for some considerable Time after, did very much prejudice the Communication of our Garrisons of *Bouchain* and *Douay* from *Tournay*. So that the Enemy being retired to their Garrisons as aforesaid, our Troops also withdrew from *Pont-a-Rache* on the 4th Inst. Those of *Lisle* and *Tournay* returned thither that Afternoon, and the other Detachments toward their aforesaid Garrisons respectively; into which in two Days after they all arrived, in order to be ready to turn out again on the first Alarm when called for. After which, on the 3d of *July* following, Prince *Holsteinbeck* sent from *Lisle* Garrison a Detachment of a Collonel and One Thousand Two Hundred Men to *Pont-a-Rache*, and from thence to *Avare* Village opposite to *Quater-Cloches*, in Order to cover the Workmen in the cleansing, and repairing the Banks of the *Scarpe*, and to prevent its further

Damage

Damage of the Enemy. The which Command was relieved by the like Number in every fourteen Days after; frequently also from *Douay* and *Tournay*, till fully repaired, till about the Spring Time that our Army took the Field; and then they were drawn off and fell into their respective Regiments. On the 26*th* of *January* at Night, the Governor of *Lisle*, having Inteligence from Lord *Albermarle*, Governor of *Tournay*, that the *French* Frontier Garrisons were again on Foot, out, and in a moving Posture, he immediately marched out with his whole Garrison toward *Tournay*, in order to join those of that Garrison. But Lord *Albermarle* having further Intelligence that the Enemy were only out a gasconading, to alarm and incommode our Garrisons, and no other real Intention could be found, he instantly sent a Courrier to the Governor of *Lisle*, whom he met with his Garrison on the Road, about half Way between *Lisle* and *Tournay*, and acquainted Prince *Holsteinbeck* therewith. Whereupon he immediately remarch'd his Troops back to their Garrison of *Lisle*, and at the same Time those of *Tournay* also, that were out, returned in thither. On the 7*th* of *February*, at Break of Day, Prince *Holsteinbeck* having Intelligence that the Governor of *Ypres* was out with his Garrison, on a Design to surprise or attack *Comine* and *Warneton*; whereupon he immediately march'd out of *Lisle* with his whole Garrison thitherward, and by ten that Morning, he arrived therewith on the West Side of the *Leys*, and immediately formed in Line of Battle, between *Warneton* and *Comine* ready, and in very good Order to receive and Repulse the Enemy, if assaulted thereby, who was just then arrived in Sight thereof: But the Governor of *Ypres* with his Troops, seeing what he expected not, and that very alert, more ready and better to repulse, than he was to assault, gasconaded a little at a great Distance

on

on the top of the Hill, and so retired the same Afternoon with his Troops to his Garrison of *Ypres*; and a little after the same, in the Dusk of the Evening, Prince *Holsteinbeck* with his Troops withdrew from *Warneton* and *Comine*, toward his Garrison of *Lisle*, at which he arrived about the middle of the Night.

The burning the *French* Magazines at *Arras*, being projected before by General *Cadogan*, Lord *Albermarle* and Prince *Holsteinbeck*, &c. was executed as follows.

Feb. 19, At Break of Day, Prince *Holsteinbeck*, marched out of *Lisle* thitherward, with all the Horse and a Dragoons, and a Detachment of 3600 Foot, who continued their March all that Day, and in the Dusk of the Night pass'd the *Scarp* at *Pont-a-Vendin*, where immediately after he was joined with an equivalent Number of each other's Garrison in *Flanders*, as aforesaid, under Lord *Albermarle*, General *Cadogan*, and *Holsteinbeck*'s Command, &c. then computed to amount to in all about 30,000 Men, in order to surprize and take, or else to burn *Arras*; all which also continued their March all that Night from *Pont-a-Vendin* over the Hills toward *Arras*. Where the next Morning about two, they arrived within a League thereof, and formed in Line of Battle, on the South-side of the said City and Citadel, and there halted till Break of Day for the Arrival of the Command from *Avare*, who brought necessary Utensils from *Douay*, for the speedy carrying on our Design, which the Fog much favoured. Before which they immediately advanced a little nearer to the City and Citadel; raised a running Trench, and erected two small Batteries thereon, of Cannon and Mortars; the which by nine o' Clock, what with Bombs and fiery Hot-Balls, set a great Part of the Enemy's Magazine of Hay on Fire, on the

Splanade

<small>Campaign XI. Anno 1711.</small> Splanade between the Citadel and City. After which some of the Clergy came out to Lord *Albermarle*, and having been told his Demand, they prevailed to save the City from being burned. Whereupon about ten in the Morning, he drew off his Cannon and remarch'd the Troops from thence to, and that Night lodged in and about *Vitrey*. And the next Day being the 21*st* of *February*, each Garrison's Detachments re-march'd from thence towards their respective Garrisons, and the same Day at Night, those of *Douay*, *Tournay*, and *Lisle*, re-enter'd them. And in two Days after, the several other Detachments re-entred their respective Garrisons, and brought off with them one Major General and the Governour of *Arras*'s Son. And about the same Time all our Garrisons on and about the *Maes*, marched out thereof, and in like manner served *Charleroy*, and afterwards returned. By these Particulars it appears, that this was a tedious and troublesome Winter, with those Troops in the Frontier Garrisons; especially *Lisle*, in which seven Regiments of our British Troops lay, *viz*. two of Dragoons, that of Lord *Hays* and *Ross*, Five of Foot, *Webb*'s, *Hearn*'s, *Sabin*'s, *Preston*'s and *Hamilton*'s.

THE
Twelfth CAMPAIGN,
Begun in the Year 1712.

In which all the Marches and Actions of the grand confederate High Allies Armies in Flanders, *were wholly under the good Conduct and Command of Prince* Eugene; *and some Time thereof in Concertion with the late Duke of* Ormond. *Against, and in Opposition to the proud and lofty* French *Armies, wholly in Marquis Villars's Command.*

THIS may well be termed an odd, separate, and somewhat unfortunate Campaign to the Allies in *Flanders*, but much fortunate to the *French*, mostly occasioned by our odd Peace; whereby the Allies were dispirited, and the *French* elated, and again freshly revived, and advanced to Honour; which for the ten Campaigns before, had been fully trampled under; their many conniving Projects having now taken somewhat of Effect.

Of

Campaign XI. Anno 1711. Of great Secrecy hidden and unknown to me to relate herein. From which I will pass to that which best becomes me, of what I do know in my Journal, of our Proceedings to, and in the Field with our other Allies, and of our Departure from, and what after happened to the Allies. All which, altho' prov'd tedious, I have collected and compiled together according to the best of my Knowledge and Genius, in very brief, for Brevity and Curiosity sake; and to put a Period or End to, and make a Revolution of what I first proposed in my Introduction to the whole: And I will gloss it over without giving any Occasion to blush, frown, or smile, if my Words are not taken as moulded amiss.

But before that I could begin my Journal of our British Corps and Artillery, intire taking the Field in the beginning of this Campaign, I could not properly omit speaking somewhat of those of our Allies that took Field first, some Days before our Corps; especially because that those of our Corps which had wintered in *Lisle* had taken the Field first therewith, in Lord *Albermarle*'s Command, &c. viz. On the 31*st* Day of *March*, Prince *Holsteinbeck*, and Brigadier *Preston*, with all the Horse and Dragoons, and eight Battallions of Foot, of which four were British, set out of their Garrison of *Lisle*, and march'd from thence to, and pitch'd camp at *Abbey-de-Flange*, near unto *Pont-a-Rache*, were joined with the Garrisons of *Douay*, *Tournay*, *Oudenard*, *Clith*, *Mons* and *Lovain*, and several others in Lord *Albermarle*'s Command. All which amounted to Fifty Battalions and Sixty Squadrons, with some *Holland*'s Artillery.

April 1, They decamp'd at *Abbey-de-Flange*, crossed the *Scarpe* a little below *Douay*, and joined the Forces, as aforesaid, and advanced from thence gradually toward the Pass of *Arleu*, which the

French

French had before secured, in order to attack and beat that Part thereof there-from, and to pass the Scarp and Sanset thereat, and to take Possession of the South-side thereof for a general Rendezvous of our whole Army thereat: For which each Corps was then on their expeditious March thitherward. But the said Day before Lord *Albermarle* with his Troops could arrive at the said Pass, all the Forces of the Enemy's frontier Garrisons, being out three Days before, had possess'd themselves thereof; whereupon Lord *Albermarle* not finding, or seeing any visible Possibility to attack or remove the Enemy from thence without great Loss, and no sign of any Victory to be obtained thereby, he withdrew his Troops backward to lee-ward, near *Douay*, where some pitch'd Camp, and some lay on their Arms all Night. And the next Day, being the 2d of *April*, there formed and pitch'd Camp regularly; where, soon after being joined with some more Troops, the said Army in Lord *Albermarle's* Command consisted of seventy Battalions of Foot, and an hundred thirty Squadrons of Horse and Dragoons, with Ordnance conform.

April 3, General *Lumley* with our British Troops and Artillery set out of their Garrison of *Ghent*, march'd to, and pitch'd Camp near *Gavre*, Four Leagues.

4, Decamp'd at and march'd from *Gavre* to, and pitch'd Camp on the North-side of *Helchin*, Four Leagues.

7, Decamp'd at and march'd from *Helchin*, to, and pitch'd Camp on the South-side of *Pont-a-Piere*, Three Leagues.

8, Decamp'd at *Pont-a-Piere*, and march'd to, and pitch'd Camp near unto *Tournay*, Two Leagues; where on the 28*th Ditto*, the late Duke of *Ormond* arrived, Captain General to our British and auxiliary Troops; and there abode till For-

Campaign XII. Anno 1712. rage was up; neither could our Armies joyn so soon in one as they would, Forrage being then very scarce on that side, by reason of the two powerful Armies that had made it very scarce and bare about *Bouchain* in the Time of the Siege thereof, in the latter End of the Campaign the Year before.

21, Lord *Albemarle* detach'd from lee-ward Forty Battalions of Foot, and six Squadrons of Horse, under General *Fagel*'s Command, betimes in a foggy Morning, in order to pass the *Scheld* at *Bouchain*, and to secure that side, and the pass, for a general Passage of our whole Army to the South-side thereof, for a general Rendezvous of all our Troops thereon. Having then a full Design to open our Campaign on that side, and that with the Siege of *Quesnoy* as soon as possible.

And that same Day General *Fagel*, with the said Troops marched off accordingly from lee-ward, and crossed the *Scheld* a little below *Bouchain*, and pitch'd his Camp at *Branlesehim* Village, ranging all along the South-side of the said River and Morass, with them and the Town just in his Rear. And in that Night they raised and threw up an Intrenchment in their Front near unto *Hordain* Village, in order thereby the better to secure the same, and to prevent sudden Surprizes of the Enemy. At the same Time, their Troops begun assembling about *Cambray* for a general Rendezvous thereat; with a Body thereof at *Hordain*, on a Point between the *Scheld* and *Sanset* opposite to *Fagel*'s Right, where our British Brigade lay with Brigadier *Preston*. The which the next Morning they greeted with one Round of Three Cannon, and immediately ceased, after they understood that our Brigade from *Lisle* lay on the Right of all next to them. Being at that Time as we understood thereby, that our Queen of *Great-Britain*, and the King of *France* was

was on, or about a Ceſſation of Arms, or Entrance of Peace. If not, we needed not to have expected any Favour from them, more than the reſt of our former Co-Partners.

May 8, The late Duke of *Ormond* decamp'd with our Britiſh Troops and Artillery at *Tournay*, and march'd from thence to, join'd and pitch'd Camp with ſome imperial Troops at *Orchies*, Four Leagues.

May 9. All decamp'd at, and march'd from, *Orchies*, two Leagues, to, and pitch'd Camp at *Marchienneſs*.

10, All decamp'd at *Marchienneſs*, croſſed the Scarp, march'd to, and pitch'd Camp on the top of the Hill at St. *Dennis*, near unto *Bouchain*, three Leagues, where they were joined by ſome of our Auxiliary Troops.

All which the Duke the next Morning reviewed. And the ſaid 10*th* about Noon, General *Fagel*'s Camp was ſomewhat alarmed, and their Picquet turned out by falſe Information, that the *French* Army as joined, were about paſſing the *Scheld*, a little below *Cambray*; in Deſign to attack his Camp, before that the reſt of our Army could join him. They then lying a great Way void in ſeveral ſeparate Bodies, for Conveniency of Forrage, as aforeſaid, ſome at *Douay*, ſome at *Marchienneſs*, and ſome at St. *Dennis*, &c. But General *Fagel* finding it only a falſe Feint, returned in his Picquet again to their former Poſt.

15, All the aforeſaid ſeveral Bodies decamp'd at, and march'd from ther ſeveral Encampments, over the *Scheld*, to, join'd and pitch'd Camp at *Sollein*, ſix Leagues. Our right Wing in Prince *Eugene*'s Command, on the North Eaſt Side of *Sollein*, conſiſted of Seventy Five Battalions, and One Hundred Sixty Nine Squadrons, with Eleven thereof Huzaers. Our left Wing in the late Duke of *Ormond*'s

Campaign XII. *Ormond*'s Command, on the South West Side of
Anno 1612. *Sollein*, confisted of Sixty Nine Batallions, and One Hundred and Thirty Six Squadrons, amongst which some few Huzaers. The which made in all, One Hundred and Forty Four Battallions of Foot, and Three Hundred and Five Squadrons of Horse and Dragoons, with One Hundred and Twenty Cannon, Sixteen Howitzers, and Forty Pontoons, with also a flying Hospital, and all other necessary Utensils of War conform. And about the same Time the *French* grand Army in Marquis *Villar*'s Command rendezvouzed about *Cambray*; where they were computed to consist of in all, One Hundred and Fifty Battalions of Foot, and Three Hundred Squadrons of Horse and Dragoons, with Ninety Two Cannon, Sixteen small Mortars, and Thirty Two Pontoons, with also all other necessary Utensils of War conform.

17, At Break of Day, our General under Cover of Sixty Squadrons, advanced from our left Wing leftward, a reconnoitring the Country about *Cambresis*, to see for a fresh Encampment, after which they returned at Night to our Camp at *Sollein*.

19, At Break of Day, the Prince, and the Duke detach'd and sent back from *Sollein*, rightward to between St. *Dennis*, or *Denain* and *Souches*, thirteen Batallions, and thirty Squadrons, in order the better to preserve our Communication with *Bouchain* and *Marchiennnes*, and all our Garrisons on the other Side the *Scheld* and *Scarp*. Two Sieges being then soon intended, *viz.* That of *Quesnoy* and *Landrecies*. There went back to the said Place, from our left Wing, Brigadier *Preston* with six Batallions, and fourteen Squadrons. And from our right Lord *Albemarle*, with seven Batallions, and sixteen Squadrons, with also some Field Artillery conform, for the Defence of the said Place.

20, The

20, The late Duke reviewed a Part of the afore- *Campaign*
said two Regiments of Dragoons, and five Battal- *XII.*
lions of Foot, that had wintred in *Lisle* with Briga- *Anno 1612.*
dier *Preston*.

27, Our whole Army decamp'd from *Sollein*, our left Wing inclined a little leftward to, and pitch'd Camp at *Cambresis*, both Lines facing outward, Front and Rear Back to Back. Our right Wing inclined also leftward, and pitch'd Camp on our old Ground at *Sollein*, in order the better to cover the Siege against *Quesnoy*, which was then first intended to be laid. Against which, none of our *British* Corps were employ'd, being then under a Cessation of Arms, as aforesaid; altho' not publickly known to us, or doubtless we had given our Quota thereto, as we had formerly done to each other before, in Conjunction with our other Allies; nevertheless, we bore a Share in the Cover thereof, and therefore I could not avoid nor omit inserting somewhat of the Proceedings thereof as regular as possibly I could collect the same, for the better com- *Quesnoy be-*
pleating of my general Journal of the War. *sieged.*

May 28, Prince *Eugene* and Lord *Albemarle*, detach'd and sent off to the said Siege from *Sollein* Camp, General *Fagel* with twenty six Batallions of Foot, and twenty five Squadrons of Horse and Dragoons, with Ordnance conform; of *Germans* and *Hollander's* Troops. Who the same Day in the Afternoon, invested it round. In which there was one Lieutenant General *Daranchie*, and Major General *Labadee*, with a Garrison of ten Batallions, and one *French* Company, and two Squadrons of Dragoons, with forty Cannon and eight Mortars mounted. After which the Besiegers immediately begun making and bringing of Fascines, &c. for the expeditious carrying on the Siege, and afterwards they proceeded regularly and gradually.

Campaign XII.
Anno 1712.

June 10, At Night, a Competent Number of the said Besiegers with, and without Arms, opened their Trenches by one Attack against *Quesnoy*, on the South Side thereof, and immediately erected two small Batteries, the one of Eleven, and the other of four Cannon, against two Flankers of the Town, against which the next Day about four in the Afternoon, they begun, play'd smartly. So that thereby they soon after dismounted them.

At Break of Day, a great Body of the Besieged, boldly sallied out a little towards the Besiegeds Approaches, from which by the Cover thereof, they were soon sharply repulsed and beat in again to their Lodgments to their great Loss.

15, About three in the Morning, the Siegers grand Batteries being erected and compleated against *Quesnoy*, consisting of upwards of one hundred Pieces of Cannon, with forty Mortars and Howitzars, *Quesnoy furrendered,* begun to play, and play'd very smartly against the Out-works, and main Walls thereof, for a sudden grand Breach, and a general grand Storm thereon.

19, In the Dusk of the Evening, a competent Number of the Siegers, couragiously attack'd, and took all the Out-works of the Town in the Front of their Approaches, and that with very little Loss, considering the Enemy's strong Situation.

22, About Noon, as the Besiegers Batteries were all playing very furiously, the Besieged fear'd thereby, that a Storm would soon ensue: Whereupon the Governor immediately beat a Parrley, and offered to surrender the Town, on Conditions to be admitted to march out thereof with the usual Marks of Honour, the which Prince *Eugene* rejected, and would allow them no other Terms, than Prisoners of War. And thereupon at Night, Parley broke, and all the Siegers Batteries begun afresh, and play'd three or four Rounds more into the Town upon the Enemy, and that with a great deal of more Vigour,

and

and terrifying Fury than at any Time before, for a sudden grand Breach, and a general grand Storm on the Town. So that thereby, and the Fear and Dread thereof, so terrified the Besieged, that the Governor in the next Morning, at Break of Day, again beat a second Parley, and surrendred the Town, and the Garrison Prisoners of War, as Prince *Eugene* before had offered them.

26, General *Duranchie*, and *Labadee*, with the Remainder of their ten Batallions, one Company, and two Squadrons, marched out of *Quesnoy* Prisoners of War, as aforesaid, and were conducted by a Party of the Besieger's Horse to *Tournay*, &c.

During this Siege against *Quesnoy* of three Weeks and six Days, begun on the 28th of *May*, and ended on the 23d of *June*, the Besiegeds Loss was computed to amount to upwards of Six Hundred Men Killed and Wounded, Officers included ; the Besiegers Loss against *Quesnoy*, was computed to amount to upwards of One Thousand Two Hundred Men, Killed and Wounded, Officers included ; whose Particulars I must wave, having not found them.

July 4, A sufficient Garrison being settled at *Quesnoy*, by Prince *Eugene*'s Order, General *Fagel* marched from thence with all his Horse and Dragoons, and the like Number from their grand Camp, to, and block'd up *Landacies*, in Order for another Seige, the which they soon after laid. But they were very soon after, obliged to abandon it, and to withdraw far contrary, and that with very great Loss, the which I am heartily sorry to have Occasion to relate ; yea, most fomented by the withdrawing of our Troops, and the Loss of our illustrious Heroe ; of which somewhat more afterwards as it falls in Course.

July 4, The late Duke of *Ormond* made known to Prince *Eugene* and the other Generals, her Majesty

Campaign XII. Anno 1712.

jesty the Queen of *Great-Britain*'s Order for the withdrawing off her Troops; the which made a great Muttering, and somewhat of a silent Distraction in the whole Army, so that the Guards of our Artillery were reinforced double; being dubious of being detained and stop'd by the Allies Army.

5, Whereupon the next Day, Prince *Eugene* and Lord *Albemarle*, with the *Germans*, other Allies and *Holland*'s Armies and Artillery, decamp'd at *Sollein*, and fell back apart from our British Troops and Artillery to, and pitched Camp on the Plains near unto *Quesnoy*, it being in their Rear; and also that same Afternoon, all the other Allies, with all our auxiliary Troops of our aforesaid Left Wing, fell back from our Corps to, and joined the Imperialist and *Holland* Army. And then our Corps were left quite alone at *Cambresis* to shift for our selves.

And as they marched off that Day, both Sides look'd very dejectfully on each other, neither being admitted to speak to the other, to prevent Reflections that might thereby arise, being there was then made a strange Revolution between us, and the Allies, by our Cessation of Arms, or Entrance of an odd Peace with *France* apart.

6, The late Duke, with our *British* Corps then consisting of in all Five Regiments of Horse, Five of Dragoons, and Twenty Four Battalions of Foot, including two Regiments of Dragoons and one Batallion of Foot, of Prince *Holsteinbeck*'s, sixty-six Pieces of Cannon, Ten Howitzars, and Eighteen Pontoons, decamp'd from *Cambresis*, and marched rightward past *Sollein*, toward *Ghent*, where we were to make our Abode till further Orders, and pitch'd Camp at *Branllesefscheim* Four Leagues, near *Bouchain*, where at the same Time as we enter'd our Camp, and each Regiment of Horse, Foot, and Dragoons, and also our Artillery, drawn up

at

at the Head of our Encampments before difmiffed to their Tents, they had publifhed at the Head of each thereof the Ceffation of Arms, between the Queen of *Great-Britain*, and the King of *France*. fome of the *French* Officers came over at the fame Time from *Cambray* to fee our Camp, and bought fome of our fpare Horfes.

July 7, Our Corps decamp'd at, and marched from *Brazllefecheim*, croffed the *Scheld* below *Bouchain*, and the *Scarpe* at *Pont-Arache* to, and pitched Camp at *Abbey-de-Phlange* Five Leagues.

8, Decamp'd at, and marched from *Abbey-dePhlange* to, and pitched Camp at *Orchies*, Two Leagues.

9, Decamp'd at, and marched from *Orchies* paft *Tournay*, to, and pitched Camp at *Ramil* Cloifter near *Pont-Peer*, Four Leagues, where halted One Day.

11, Decamp'd at , and march'd from *Ramell* to, and pitched Camp at *Petteghem* near *Oudenard*, Four Leagues.

12, Decamp'd at, and marched from *Petteghem* to, and pitch'd Camp at *Nazrith*, near *Deynfe*, Four Leagues.

13, Decamp'd at, and marched from *Nazrith*, croffed the *Lys* at *Deynfe* to, and pitched Camp between *Dronghen* Cloifter, and *Mary-Kerke*, a little weftward of *Ghent*, Four Leagues. And on the Third Day after, the Duke fettled a Garrifon of Four Battalions in *Ghent*.

23, He review'd all our Britifh Troops by his own Quarters at *Dronghen* Camp.

24, He detach'd and fent off Brigadier *Sutton* with Four Battalions, Six Cannon, and two Mortars, to *Bruges*, in order to keep Garrifon there, where they arrived the next Day. And alfo Lord *Orkney* with Six Battalions, Twenty Cannon, and Four Mortars, to *Dunkirk*, where they arrived the Second Day after. Of which General *Hill* with Six Battalions from *England*, had taken Possession some Time before, in Pledge of our odd Peace, which was then in hand, but not fully concluded, till our Grand Alliance came to a general Conclusion of Peace. And at *Dronghen* the Duke kept Field with the Remainder of our Troops, till near the End of that Campaign, that Prince *Eugene* broke up Camp with the Allies Army, and dispers'd them to Winter-Quarters.

On all our March from *Cambresis* to *Ghent*, no Man was admitted to cut down any Corn, nor scarce to tread on it; nor to do any Damage to the Countrey; nor to meddle with any Thing on any Pretence, in any respect whatsoever, without paying the full Value for it; neither suffered to go into any of the *Holland*'s Garrisons, for any Provisions, or any thing else. But at some Places with much to do, they handed over their Walls to us some Things which our Men most wanted, taking our Money first, especially at *Bouchain*, *Douay*, and *Tournay:* This was a very great Alteration indeed, to be debarred Entrance for Necessaries, where we had shed a Torrent of our Blood; and in a Manner to see our Bosom Friends turn'd our hateful Enemies, &c. But here I must wave, curb, and put a little Stop to the Carrier of my Mind, Hand and Pen, and but touch a little at the Allies Misfortune after our Departure therefrom, to which they imputed most thereof: That whereas they daily gained Ground, victorious for the ten Campaigns, before they then begun to lose it, and that very much faster and easier than ever it was gain'd. With which I will be as brief as possible, to make a Revolution, and to put an End to the said War, and for a compleating of my Journal thereof, viz. the Day after our Departure from *Cambresis*, Prince *Eugene* with the Grand Allies Army

Armies of a Hundred forty Eight Battalions of Foot, and Two Hundred Ninety Two Squadrons of Horse and Dragoons, being reinforced by some more Troops from their Garrisons, with upwards of a Hundred and Twenty Pieces of Cannon, and Sixty Mortars and Howitzars, with Thirty Two Pontoons, and all other Necessaries of War conform, for maintaining the Field, and forming a Siege, decamp'd from near *Quesnoy*, and marched directly to *Alte* near *Landrecies*. The which Prince *Anhault*, with Thirty Four Battalions of Foot, and Thirty Four Squadrons of Horse and Dragoons, and of the said Artillery conform invested, which General *Fagel* had block'd up with some Horse and Dragoons, some few Days before, as aforesaid, where was a strong Garrison.

On the other Hand Mareschal *Villars*, with a powerful Army also, of *French*, consisting of as aforesaid, of One Hundred and Fifty Battallions, and Three Hundred Squadrons, &c, with necessary Utensils of War conform, decamp'd from *Cambray*, and marched to, and took up our old Ground at *Cambresis* that Night, after that we had left it; in Order to use all Stratagems or Means to raise the Siege by the Allies, from *Landrecies*; and thereupon *July* the 9th, they advanced from *Cambresis* toward the Allies Army at *Landrecies*, and on the 12th, they gasconaded all Day, and made a Feint, as if they designed to attack, and battel the Allies grand Army, but in the Night they slipt off very quietly, leftward, contrary to the Allies Expectation. Whose Army was too much scattered in several small Bodies all the Way from *Landrecies* to *Tournay*. Which was a great Fault, and Occasion of the most of their following Misfortunes. In short, the *French* Army continued their March all Night with great Expedition, so that the next Morning by Ten, they arrived at the *Scheld*, a little below

Campaign XII.
Anno 1612.

low *Bouchain*, oppofite to where Lord *Albemarle* lay at *Denain-Pafs*, with thirteen Battallions of Foot, intrench'd, with alfo twenty eight Squadrons, which Prince *Eugene* took off with him at that Juncture, he having been there viewing the faid *Pafs*, as the Enemy appeared, in full Defign to attack the fame, and left the Foot behind for loft, and retired to his Camp. After which, about Noon, the *French* Army paffed the *Scheld*, with little Oppofition; and attack'd the faid Troops in their Intrenchments; and in a Trice, after fome fharp Affaults, and Repulfes, they beat them from their Intrenchments, and quite broke and defeated, and took Lord *Albemarle* Prifoner, two Lieutenant Generals, three Major Generals, and Two Hundred and Ninety Four other Officers, and One Thoufand Five Hundred private Men. And in another Account, Two Thoufand Two Hundred: twelve Brafs Cannon, and a confiderable Quantity of Ammunition. One Thoufand killed on the Spot, One Thoufand Five Hundred drowned; amongft whom was Count *Dhona*, and Count *Naffau-Woudenburg* Lieutenant General, and feveral other Officers of Diftinction. And as for the *French*, they loft not above Four Hundred Men, killed and difabled. And from thence they immediately marched to *Marchiennefs*, where the Allies grand Magazines lay for the Siege of *Landrecies*, and for the Ufe of their whole Army. Where there was One Hundred and Forty Seven Veffels juft arrived, loaded with Ammunition, Money, and all Sorts of Provifions and Neceffaries for the Army; and invefted it; in which there was a Garrifon of fix Battallions of Foot, and One Regiment of Dragoons, computed Four Thoufand Men, effective; befides Eight Hundred of the Wounded of *Quefnoy*, commanded by   all which in about feven or eight Days after, the *French* made to furrender

der Prisoners of War. And took therein One Hundred Pieces of Cannon; Fifty Two thereof Twenty Four Pounders, and Forty Eight serviceable, Three Hundred Waggons with their Harnesses, and their Army's Hospital; One Hundred By-landers, in which and the Store-houses, they took a prodigious Number and Quantity of Powder, Bombs, Granadoes, Bullets, Musket-Balls, and Flints; Hatchets, Bills, Planks, Matches and Ladders, Corn, Meal, Hambs of Bacon, Butter, Cheese, Beer, Wine and Brandy; and other Merchandize, without describing how much; and in short, great Plenty of all Stores, sufficient for the making of Two Sieges. And Besides, at *St. Amand* found Five By-landers loaded with Three Hundred Thousand Weight of Powder, which had been sunk in the Scarpe before the Siege: And they also took in and about *St. Amand*, between Five and Six Thousand Men, of Detachments under General *Fagel*, from the Allies Grand Army, of Horse, Foot, and Dragoons, who had been covering that Road to *Tournay*, for the better Communication of their Army therewith. And next after the taking of the said Places, *Villars* removed his Army to, and invested *Douay*, and that on the 3d of *August*, O. S. in which there was General *Hompesch* with a Garrison of *Hollanders*. The great Misfortune of the losing of those Passes, Stores, and a great Number of Men, immediately occasion'd Prince *Eugene* to abandon *Landrecies*, and to withdraw the Allies Army from thence other ways for fresh Supplies of Ammunition and Provisions, and to see to put a Stop to the *French* Career in the Siege against *Douay*, which was not then begun. Whereupon, after Days Siege against *Landrecies*, Prince *Eugene* remarch'd the Allies Army with great Expedition by the Way of *Quesnoy*. And for the more Dispatch left his battering

Campaign XII.
Anno 1712.

Campaign XII.
Anno 1712.

tering Train of an Hundred Pieces of Cannon, and Sixty Mortars, and continued his March from thence round *Mons*, and leaving *Clith* on their Right, they pass'd through *Tournay*, and pitch'd about two Leagues westward thereof, and from thence advanced to mount *Faux-vivier* near to *Pont-a-Rache*, all this while without any Day's Halt. And there halted Three Days in design to raise the *French* Siege from *Douay*, which by this Time was closely formed unmoveable. And thereupon *Eugene* remarch'd his Army from thence to *Tournay*; sending a strong Reinforcement into *Lisle*; and from *Tournay*, where he made no Halt, march'd back to, and pitched Camp near unto *Mons* in order to remove their heavy Train from *Quesnoy*: But in the Time of their remarching, and countermarching, the *French* cut them also out thereof; having the same Day that they laid Siege to *Douay*, block'd up *Quesnoy*, and also hem'd up *Bouchain*. Which made the Allies Army to spend the Remainder of their Campaign about *Mons*, and to look on whilst it run away on the *French* Side in a Current of Conquests: For after that the Allies Army had withdrawn to *Mons*, the *French* Army proceeded very briskly with the Siege against *Douay*, and brought it to surrender on the 28*th* of *August*. And that same Day a great Body of the *French* Troops, laid close Siege to *Quesnoy*, in which there was General *Puoy*, and Sir *James Wood*, with a Garrison of six Battalions, whom they brought to surrender on the 23*d* of *September* Prisoners of War, after a very smart Siege, and took the aforesaid Train therein, and several other Stores. And on the 21*st* of *September* they closely invested *Bouchain*, in which there was Major-General *Van-Grovestein*, with three entire Battalions, and the Number of one of the Detachments, whom the *French* also brought to surrender Prisoners

soners of War, on the 6*th* of *October*. All whose punctual Particulars I must wave, being no Eye-Witness of neither thereof.

Sept. 25, At Break of Day, a Partizan Party of the *Hollanders*, of about Fifty Men, in *French* Livery, surpriz'd and enter'd *Knock-Fort* in *Flanders* and took it, and a Company of *French* Invalids from *Ypres*. And in the next Spring, the *French* by their Conditions of Peace received back from the Allies, *Lisle*, *Aire*, *Bethune*, and *St. Vepante*. And in lieu thereof delivered up to the Allies, *Ypres*, *Namure* and *Charleroy*. All the said Towns they got very easy, which some Time before had cost the Allies an immense Flood of Blood, and other great and vast Expences; beyond my shallow Reach to relate. From which I will pass, and in short bring both this Campaign, and also my Journal of the long and tedious War, to a full Conclusion.

September 28, The late Duke of *Ormond*, sent off from *Dronghen* Camp, our five Regiments of Dragoons to *Bruges* Garrison for their Winter Quarters. And on the 1st Day of *October*, he decamp'd at, and removed the Remainder of our *British* Corps from *Dronghen* into *Ghent* for their Winter-Quarters, viz. Five Regiments of Horse, Fourteen Batallions of Foot, Forty Pieces of Cannon, Six Howitzars, or little Mortars, and Eighteen Pontoons; and soon after he went off to *England*, and General *Lumley* in Chief, commanded the Garrison and Troops therein, and elsewhere in *Flanders*.

And about the latter End of *October*, Prince *Eugene* broke up Camp at *Mons*, and disperst the *Germans* and *Hollanders* Troops or Army, from thence to their respective Winter-Quarters. And in the Spring following, our Peace, and also the grand Allies in general with *France*, was concluded at *Utrecht*.

Campaign XII.
Anno 1712.

On the 31*st* of *March*, 1713. And on the 2*d* of *June*, our *Brittish* Troops were reduced in *Flanders*, and afterward by Degrees, all were difperft from thence to *England*. Only the royal Regiment of *Ireland*, in Lieutenant Colonel *Moses Leathe*'s Command, kept Poffeffion of *Ghent*, till the 25th of *February*, 1715-6. and then delivered it up to the *German* Troops, and returned alfo to *England*. And thus and here, I have brought my general Journal of twelve Campaigns of the late War, to a Conclufion, begun on the 15th Day of *September*, in *A. D.* 1701. and ended on the 1*st* Day of *October*, in 1712. The collecting and compiling thereof together, took me a great deal of Time, and coft me a great deal of Trouble, in Labour, Pains and Expence both Day and Night, before fully compleated and brought to an End.

Note, That I have computed the Beginning, Ending and Length of each Campaign of the faid War, Number of Days and Leagues by our Corps, with the grand Army and Apart, from the Time of our Train of Artillery's marching out of Winter Quarters, to the Time of its Return thither again. It being the Metropolitan Enfign of an Army in Time of War.

F I N I S.

A GENERAL LIST of our BRITISH CORPS, with their Strength, as marched off with the late Duke of Ormond, from our other Allies Army, on the 6th of July, 1712.

CAPTAIN-GENERALS *Lumley* and *Orkney*.

LIEUTENANT-GENERALS, Lord *North*, Lord *Stair*, *Cadogan*, *Withers* and *Wood*.

MAJOR-GENERALS, *Primrose*, *Kellum*, *Sibourgh*, *Sabine* and *Evans*.

BRIGADIERS, *Panton*, *Napper*, *Preston*, *Sutton*, *Dural*, *Russel* and *Corbet*.

The Names of the Regiments, Number of Squadrons and Battalions, with their Strength.

			No. of Men	
5 Regiments of Horse 11 Squadrons	3	General *Lumley*'s.		
	2	Lieutenant-General *Cadogan*'s.		
	2	Lord *Harwitche*'s.	1824	And of Pontoons, 18. Howitzars or little Mortars, 10. Pieces of Cannon, 66. More of our Artillery apart, all Ranks included, 682.
	2	Major-General *Palme*'s.		
	2	Lieutenant-General *Wood*'s.		
24 Battalions of Foot.	1st	Battalion of Guards.	664	
	2d	Of Guards.	658	
	1st	Of Royal Britains.	604	
	2d	Of ditto.	590	
	1	Battalion, Colonel *Selwin*.	619	
	1	Lieutenant-General *Webb*'s.	641	
	1	Lord *North*'s, a Lieutenant-General.	623	
	1	Earl *Hartford*, a Brigadier.	652	
	1	Brigadier *Dural*.	681	
	1	Brigadier *Stearn*.	658	
	1	Brigadier *Sutton*.	652	
	1	Major-General *Sabine*.	670	
	1	Lord *Orrerey* a Major-General.	521	
	1	Major-General *Primrose*.	646	
	1	Brigadier *Preston*.	540	
	1	Colonel *Hans Hamilton*.	574	
	1	Lieutenant-General *Sibourgh*.	562	
	1	Colonel *Newton*.	664	
	1	Major-General *Evans*.	663	
	1	Colonel *Lee*.	450	
	1	Brigadier *Windress*.	620	
	1	Major-General *Wynn*.	488	
	1	Colonel *Pocock*.	482	
	1	Of *Holstein*'s *Berner*'s.	500	
5 Regiments of Dragoons 14 Squadrons	3	Lord *Staire*'s, a Lieutenant-General.		
	2	Colonel *Kerre*'s.		
	3	General *Ross*, a Lieutenant-General.	2412	
	3	Of Prince *Holstein*'s.		
	3	Of *Walef*'s.		

Total, 5 Regiments of Horse, 24 Battalions of Foot, and 5 Regiments of Dragoons 18664

Total, all Stations included. Then march'd off upwards of, 22,000 Men.
But the *French* thereby computed the Allies Army 30,000 Men less in Number.
But further, if each Regiment and Battalion had been compleated, we could not have made above 28294.

THE
Names of the Subscribers.

A

HIS Grace the Duke of Argyle 2 Books
Lord Afhburnham, Earl of Albemarle
Lord Abergavenny
Col. Armſtrong
Col. Anſtruther
Capt. Sheffield Auſten
———— Arabin
———— Aſtell
———— Arundel
———— Adair
Captain S. Adlercron
Robert Arnott
John Arnott
Jonathan Andrews
Dr. James Auchmuty
Capt. A' Court

B

Ducheſs of Bedford. 2 Books
Duke of Bedford. 2 Books
Duke of Bolton. 2 Books
Earl of Burlington
Marquis of Bowmont

Lord Viſcount Bateman
Lord Boyne
Lord Vere Beauclair
Lord George Beauclair
Sir John Buckworth
Brigadier General Barrell
Major General Biſſett
Col. Bland
———— Blaithwaite
———— Blakeney
———— Bragg
———— Burton
———— Bellendine
John Brown 2 Books
———— Berkeley
Capt. Beak
———— Bellendine
Newton Barton
William Bland
Charles Bowles
William Berkeley
Francis Baillie
———— Bright
———— Bodvil
———— Bateman
———— Burton
———— Baſil
———— Bru-

Subscribers Names.

———— Brudenel
———— Bludworth
———— Bladen
———— Bowling
Art. Barnadiston *Esq*;
Serjeant Baynes
Capt. Bessiere   2 Books
———— Borrett   2 Books
Fred. Bruce
Capt. William Baird
William Brodie
Henry Barrett
H. Boisragon
John Blair
Robert Barton
James Biggar
George Broun
Edward Booth
Edward Butler
Richard Burchett
Rupert Batt
George Burston
Anthony Bligh

C

Lady Cardigan
The Right Honourable Lord
  Cadogan
———— Carpenter
———— Clinton
———— Crawford
———— Cowper
———— Carmichael
———— Cardigan   2 Books
———— Carteret
———— Carnarvon
Admiral Cavendish

Sir Clement Cotterell
Col. Chudleigh
Col. Chomsley
Brigadier Churchill
Col. Peter Campbell
Major Compton
William Corbet *Esq*;
Col. Cope
— Clutterbuck
Capt. Lockran
———— Clayton
———— Chenowix
Thomas Charleton
Thomas Crofton
R. Coke
— Conolly
Dr. Alexander Cornwall
Col. Cutumbine
Capt. William Cropp
John Corbett
P. Carew
James Clutterbuck
John Cuningham
David Cuningham
George Crofts
James Clarke
John Congreve Chillcot
Arch. Cuningham
George Chalmers
William Clenahan
Edward Comeille
Cla. Colvill
Dr. James Cuningham
Capt. Robert Cotten
Col. Colston
Col. William Cosby 2 Books
Brigadier-General Clayton

D.

Subscribers Names.

D.
Duke of Devonshire 2 Books
Lord Dunmore
Lord Dyzarl
Lord Duffy
Sir Fran. Dashwood
General Dalzeel
Sir Conyers Darcy
Col. Charles Douglas
Col. Duncombe
Col. ——— Douglass
Major Duroure
——— Dabzac
Capt. John Dobbin
James Durand
——— Dickson
———Dambon
Richard Dickinson 2 Books
Peter Dumas 2 Books
Michael Doyne
— Dalrymple
——— Digby
Col. Deviesher 2 Books
Capt. James Dalrymple
M. Delabene
Wington Dell
Thomas Dunbar
John Dalbos
Ar. Debize
J. L. Duponcett
Alexander Dury 34 Books

E.
The Rt. H. Earl of Effingham
Major Cuthbert Ellison
Lt. Gen. Wm. Evans 2 Books
Capt. Elliot
Thomas Erle
James Edgar
Mr. George Evans
Mr. Edgcombe
Capt. Richard Ellis
Meridyth Everard
William Elwes
Augustine Erle, *Esq*;

F
Lord Forbes
Lord Falkland
Col. Fane
——— Ferrers
——— Frampton
——— Fuller
Sir Andrew Fountain
Thomas Fredrick, *Esq*;
Henry Finch, *Esq*;
Martin Folkes, *Esq*; 2 Books
Everard ⎫
William ⎬ Falkener *Esqrs.*
Edward ⎨
Henry ⎭
Major Folliot
Capt. Furnace
— Fane
Henry Fox
— Fisher
Col. James Fleming 3 Books
Col. Ferguson
Capt. Ferguson
Capt. George Forbes
John Fleming
Col. Thomas Fowks
Capt. Tho. Forth 29 Books

Subscribers Names.

G.
Duke of Grafton
Lord Gilford
Lord Glenorchy
Sir Samuel Garret
Lord Gage
Major General Gore
Major Thomas Gery
——— Grove
Col. St. George
Richard Greenville, *Esq*;
B. Goldsworthy, *Esq*;
Capt. Gumley
— Gumley
Rowley Godfrey
——— Guyon
George Gray
Mr. Thomas Garnier
Mr. Anthony Garmansway
Mr. Maynard Guerin
Col. Graham 3 Books
Capt. Steph Graham 4 Books
Capt. Andrew Gimpson
Thomas Griffith
Lovelace Gylby
John Gilchrift
Mr. Peter Guerin 30 Books

H.
The Rt. H. the E. of Hallifax
Lord Harrington
Lord Hobart
William Hamilton
Charles Hay
Sir Thomas Hobby
Sir Charles Hotham 5 Books
Col. Roger Handasyd
William Handasyd

Thomas Howard
——— Hatton
——— Hanmer
——— Huske
Thomas Herbert
Charles Howard
——— Hawley
Gil. Hill
Capt. Herbert
——— Hervey
Charles Handasyd
William Harler
——— Herring
Capt. Richard Harwood
Richard Honywood, *Esq*;
— Hudegger
Basil Hamilton
Charles Holzendorf, *Esq*;
Mr. Herbert
Henry Herbert
Capt. James Hamilton
Robert Holburn
David Home
Richard Harris
Charles Hutchinson 2 Books
Edward Higgins
Dr. Johnathan Hilder
Francis Hearne, *Esq*;
Capt. Richard Hartshorne

I.
The Rt. Hon. the Lord Jersey
Col. Irwin
——— Jeffrys
Capt. Fairfax Jenkins
George Johnson
John Irwine
— Jeneson

Mr.

Subscribers Names.

―― Jansen
Henry Johnson
Capt. Charles Jackson
―― James
Jasper Johnston
Col. Ingoldesby
Major Robert Johnson

K.
The Rt. Hon. the Ld. Viscount
    Killmorey
Lord Mark Kerr
Brigadier General Kerr
―― Kirk
Governor Rd. Kane 10 Books
―― King
―― Kelsal
Major Kennedy Two Books
Capt. James Kerr
Charles James Kirke
William Kerr
William Kinneer

L.
Rt. Hon. Lord Lifford
Lord Lovel Two Books
Lord Lymington
Col. Lumley
Peregrine Lascelles
―― Lowther
―― Ligonier
Major La Meloniere
Lancelot Charles Lake, *Esq*;
Capt. John Lee
―― Lemon
John Legg
Dym. Lisber
Gilfred Lawson

James Latour
―― Lambert
David Linsey
Mr. Anthony Lowther
―― Lowndes
Dr. La Motte

M.
Duke of Montagu
Duke of Manchester
Duchess ditto   2 Books
Lord Morpeth
―― Marchmont
―― Malpas
―― Mordaunt
―― Middleton
William Manners
Sir Humph. Monoux
Sir Roger Mostyn
Governor Matthews
Col. Merrick
Thomas Murray
―― Mordaunt
―― Morton
John Montague 4 Books
Thomas Mostyn, *Esq*;
Capt. James Madan
George Martin   2 Books
William Merrick
Henry Macneede
Capt. John Maitland
Robert Makenzie
Alexander Mitchelson
M. Marshal
James Montresor
―― Maxwell
Charles St Maurice
Whitney Mackane

N

Subscribers Names.

N.
Count Henry Naſſau
William Nepeu, *Esq*; 2 Books
Peter Nepeu, *Esq*; 2 Books
Thomas Noel, *Esq*;
Capt. A. Neſbitt
James Nicholls
———— Newcomen
William Netherſole
———— Needham
———— Nelthrop

O.
Right Honourable Lord Orkney
Sir Adolphus Oughton
Sir Daniel A' Carroll
Col. Charles Otway
Richard Offarell   3 Books
———— Onſlow
———— Ormſby
Henry Ormſby
Capt. Stephen Otway
———— Orfeur

P.
Right Honourable Lord Pembroke
———— Portmore
———— Primroſe
Naſſau Pawlett
Sir Thomas Pendergraſs
Col. Pagett
———— Pierſon
———— Ponſonby
———— Pyot
———— Peirs
———— Poulteney
———— Pawlett
———— Price
———— Parſons
Major Anthony Pujolas   4 Books
Henry Popple *Esq*;
Thomas Page *Esq*;
Richard Powis *Esq*;
Capt. Auguſt Pynyol
Charles Perry
Charles Parker
Abraham Pinchinat
Capt. Robert Pearſon
William Potts
John Preſton
———— Peppys
— Page
William Patten *Esq*;

Q.
— St. Quintin

R.
Duke of Rutland
The Right Honourable Lord Rothes
Sir Robert Rich *Baronet*
Major-General Ruſſell
Col. Read
Charles Chamberlane Rebow *Esq*;
Thomas Revell *Esq*;
Capt. Ransford
Charles Ruſſell
———— Rivett
Benjamin Rudyerd
Thomas Ramſor
                William

Subscribers Names.

William Remington
James Rietfield
Nich. Romain
Richard Ruffell
— Rolt
Capt. Reedyard

S.
Right Honourable the Earl of
    Scarborough   2 Books
Earl of Stairs
Lord ——S——well
Sir William Stanhope
Sir Hans Sloane
Major-General Sutton
Col. Skelton
————Sinclair
————Scott
————Selwin
————Suckling
Major Sclair
Charles Stanhope *Senior Esq*;
Charles Stanhope *Junior Esq*;
Thomas Spence *Esq*;
Capt. William Sharman
                    2 Books
William Stevens
Benjamin Sladden
Hugh Scott
Capt. James Stuart
————Stevenson
Marcus Smith
Charles Sharkie
————Skinson
————Sanderson
————Shugburgh
Mr. Sambrooke
Mr. Stanley

Mr. Sloper *Junior*

T.
Right Hon. Ld. Torrington
——— Tankerville
——— Thomond
——— Tyrconnel
Col. Townsend
Brigadier General Tyrrell
Henry Talbot, *Esq*;
Capt. Charles Talbot
James Turnbult
——— Taffels

V.
Capt. Wm. Upton 2 Books
Capt. Gilbert Vane
Dr. Edward Vernon

W.
Rt. Hon. Lord Wallingford
Rt. Hon. Sir Charles Wager
General Wade
General Whetham
Col. Wentworth
——— Williamson
——— Wingfield
Major Warbarton
——— Wardour
Gilbert West, *Esq*;
Peter Wyck, *Esq*;
Capt. William Wentworth
Thomas Weldon
John Waite
Major Wright
Capt John Wynn
——— Wilson
William Whitmore
                    William

Subscribers Names.

William Wightman
Edward Windus
David Watson
Thomas Wilson
William Wyvile
Dr. Giles Wakeman
— Windham
— Whitmore

Y.

Edward Young, *Esq;*
John Paul Yoounett, *Esq;*
Capt. —— Yough
Capt. Joseph Young.

www.ingramcontent.com/pod-product-compliance
Lightning Source LLC
Chambersburg PA
CBHW031249230426
43670CB00005B/97